The Procurement Revolution

IBM Endowment for
The Business
of Government

THE IBM ENDOWMENT SERIES ON
THE BUSINESS OF GOVERNMENT

Series Editors: Mark A. Abramson and Paul R. Lawrence

The IBM Endowment Series on The Business of Government explores new approaches to improving the effectiveness of government at the federal, state, and local levels. The Series is aimed at providing cutting-edge knowledge to government leaders, academics, and students about the management of government in the 21st century.

Publications in the series include:

E-Government 2003, *edited by Mark A. Abramson and Therese L. Morin*
E-Government 2001, *edited by Mark A. Abramson and Grady E. Means*
Human Capital 2002, *edited by Mark A. Abramson and Nicole Willenz Gardner*
Innovation, *edited by Mark A. Abramson and Ian D. Littman*
Leaders, *edited by Mark A. Abramson and Kevin M. Bacon*
Managing for Results 2002, *edited by Mark A. Abramson and John M. Kamensky*
Memos to the President: Management Advice from the Nation's Top Public Administrators, *edited by Mark A. Abramson*
Transforming Organizations, *edited by Mark A. Abramson and Paul R. Lawrence*

The Procurement Revolution

EDITED BY

MARK A. ABRAMSON
IBM ENDOWMENT FOR
THE BUSINESS OF GOVERNMENT
and
ROLAND S. HARRIS III
IBM BUSINESS CONSULTING SERVICES

ROWMAN & LITTLEFIELD PUBLISHERS, INC.
Lanham • Boulder • New York • Oxford

1004091651

ROWMAN & LITTLEFIELD PUBLISHERS, INC.

Published in the United States of America
by Rowman & Littlefield Publishers, Inc.
A Member of the Rowman & Littlefield Publishing Group
4501 Forbes Boulevard, Suite 200, Lanham, Maryland 20706
www.rowmanlittlefield.com

PO Box 317
Oxford
OX2 9RU, UK

British Library Cataloguing in Publication Information Available

Library of Congress Cataloging-in-Publication Data Available

0-7425-3272-0 (alk. paper)
0-7425-3273-9 (pbk.: alk. paper)

Printed in the United States of America

♾™ The paper used in this publication meets the minimum requirements of
American National Standard for Information Sciences—Permanence of Paper
for Printed Library Materials, ANSI/NISO Z39.48-1992.

TABLE OF CONTENTS

PART I

Toward a New Vision
of Government
Procurement

CHAPTER ONE

The Transformation
of Government Procurement

Mark A. Abramson
Executive Director
IBM Endowment for The Business of Government

Roland S. Harris III
Managing Partner, Americas and Global Public Sector
IBM Business Consulting Services

Introduction

During our travels over the past 20 years, we have had many conversations with individuals knowledgeable about and interested in government. It is appropriate to recall one of those conversations at the opening of this chapter. During a long discussion about the strengths and weaknesses of government, a former government executive reflected, "You know, government spends a lot of time performing two sets of activities: hiring people and buying things. And it doesn't seem to be able to do either one very well."

In the years since that remark, government has made progress in both arenas. Government is still working hard to improve its ability to hire, yet progress has been made. In *Human Capital 2002,* a recent publication in the IBM Endowment Series on The Business of Government, the challenge of improving government recruiting and hiring is discussed (Abramson and Gardner). In this book, we examine the state of government procurement as we enter the 21st century.

Government procurement is now being transformed across the nation—at the federal, state, and local levels. What used to be a rather mundane, dull subject, populated by rule-following civil servants, is becoming an exciting, challenging area of endeavor. In recent years, the procurement field has begun to attract a new breed of public servant—individuals eager to experiment and develop creative new ways of doing the business of government. While it may be an overstatement to imply that these entrepreneurial and creative civil servants now make up the majority of procurement specialists in government, their number is clearly rising.

At the same time this new breed of procurement specialist is assuming increasing levels of responsibility throughout government, the job of government itself is changing. The transformation of government procurement is a reflection of the changing nature of government and the increased reliance on the private sector. In the "old days," government directly operated many activities and purchased many commodities, also known as the proverbial "widgets." Those days are long past. Today, both the activities of government and the nature of government procurements have gotten much more complex.

This book describes the three major transformations now taking place in the world of government procurement:

- *Transformation One:* Moving from buying goods to buying services
- *Transformation Two:* Moving from a "command and control" relationship between government and contractors to a partnership relationship
- *Transformation Three:* Moving from a paper-based procurement system to electronic procurement

Transformations one and two are clearly related. The "buying" of services (transformation one) will require a new partnership relationship (trans-

The Transformation of Government Procurement

	From:	To:
Transformation One	Buying Goods	Buying Services
Transformation Two	A "Command and Control" Relationship	A Partnership Relationship
Transformation Three	Paper-Based Procurement	Electronic Procurement

formation two). Transformation three reflects technology as an enabler to provide faster, more cost-effective services, as well as the movement to e-government across the nation as governments at all levels attempt to provide more services to citizens and businesses online (Abramson and Morin).

Transformation One: Moving from Buying Goods to Buying Services

While government will continue to buy goods (although it may do so differently, such as purchasing goods via an electronic catalogue), the driving force behind the procurement revolution has been government's increasing need to buy services. When buying services, it is not easy to specify the height or weight of the desired product or deliverable. In chapter two, Jacques S. Gansler, former Under Secretary of Defense for Acquisition, Technology, and Logistics in the Department of Defense, writes that the procurement transformation reflects "the recognition that the role of government is changing—from the *provider of goods* to the *manager of the providers of goods and services....*" This change, reflects Gansler, is going to dramatically change the skills needed for the 21st century government acquisition workforce. Gansler emphasizes that it also is important to realize that the overall U.S. economy is shifting from the buying of goods to the buying of services. This shift, states Gansler, has not yet been fully recognized by the government:

> Clearly the buying of services and the specifying of what the desired service should result in is very different (and often more difficult) than the buying of a piece of equipment; yet almost all of the government's rules, regulations, and practices are based upon the more traditional equipment buying. Similarly, all of the education and training programs are focused in the

traditional direction. Thus, a *major transformation in the overall process* (including the education of the workforce) *must be toward an ability to acquire sophisticated services* as more and more of government's acquisitions will be done in this way in the future.

In chapter three, Kathryn Denhardt also emphasizes the importance of transformation one. She writes, "In the past, the government procurement process started with specifying exactly—and in excruciating detail—what the contractor was to do. Writing the specifications usually took months and gave rise to a request for proposals (RFP).... The vendor who was awarded the contract was responsible for delivering what was *specified,* whether or not it turned out to be what was *needed.*" Fewer and fewer of this type of contract, writes Denhardt, are being used. Today, describes Denhardt, a procurement is more likely to start with specifying objectives that need to be achieved or the work that needs to be done. "The 'new' RFP is likely to describe the destination, not the route or the means of the transportation," writes Denhardt.

One cannot underestimate the impact of this shift from buying goods to buying services. Government, writes Denhardt, is now contracting for solutions and knowledge, not for specific goods or standardized services. In describing this new type of contract, Denhardt explains:

> The new contracts are nonroutine, start with many more unknowns, and take unexpected turns as a project unfolds. These efforts require thinking through complex issues, putting together information from disparate sources, and trying out new ideas or innovative solutions for which results are uncertain. Many times the efforts require bringing together capabilities from across organizational boundaries in government and across the public, private, and nonprofit sectors.

In chapter four, Lawrence L. Martin describes the operational implications of the change from buying goods to buying services. Martin writes, "The transition to service contracting constitutes a fundamental paradigm shift for federal procurement. Federal procurement must find new ways of conducting the federal government's business including the development of new policies, procedures, concepts, and tools to deal with a new service reality."

When buying goods, government specified inputs in great detail—the famous "milspecs" used by the Department of Defense to buy everything from cookies to nails to military hardware. When buying services, however, the job of government is to specify outcomes or performance. Thus, the rise of performance-based contracts (PBC). Martin writes, "PBC requires the use of performance specifications. The essence of PBC is telling the contractor *what* is expected and letting it decide on the *how.*" Martin argues that state and local governments are ahead of the federal government in developing and experimenting with performance-based contracts. He emphasizes that the goal of PBCs is "changing the behavior of contractors to focus more on performance."

The transformation from buying goods to buying services is also seen clearly in the area of information technology. In chapter five, Yu-Che Chen and James Perry describe the trend—occurring in both the public and private sectors—to outsource information technology services. Chen and Perry write that moving to information technology outsourcing requires a shift in perspective, the same change in perspective advocated by Gansler, Denhardt, and Martin in their chapters. Chen and Perry write:

> Traditionally, an IT outsourcing arrangement has been treated as a procurement deal. With this [traditional] approach, it is the equipment or software that a client organization is getting.... However, to fully realize the potential of an IT outsourcing arrangement requires a different perspective. It is no longer the IT equipment but the service that is the center of management. As a result, the new direction should be on a relationship management that secures the quality and level of services provided by the vendor.

In the use of performance-based contracts and information technology outsourcing, we clearly see government operating very differently from the past. Based on the increasing recognition that buying service is different from buying goods, government is now changing the way it buys services. The major question now facing government is how quickly it will continue to change both the way it operates and its relationship with contractors.

Transformation Two:
Moving from a "Command and Control"
Relationship to a Partnership Relationship

Transformation two is based on the premise that buying services is a more complex and uncertain activity than buying goods. While buying goods can indeed be complex, there are many more unknowns when buying services. The concepts of complexity and uncertainty are used by Wendell Lawther in chapter six as guiding principles for government to use in determining the type of relationship and interactions required in managing large contracts in the 21st century. Lawther writes, "The complexity of the service/ product and the uncertainty about how to best deliver that service/product are two factors that are closely related. They are causally related, as the greater the complexity of the service, the greater the uncertainty about how to deliver it. The reverse statement is true as well, as uncertainty about means of delivery contributes to complexity."

Lawther concludes that the old ways of operating will no longer be effective for highly complex activities and that a new style of operating is clearly required. Lawther writes, "If the service is highly complex, and understanding of the service delivery means not clear, then the agency and the contractor should enter into a true public-private partnership.... to be fully effective, the roles of both agency and contractor personnel must change from the traditional contractor-agency relationship that characterizes the low and mid complexity services. All participants must interact as equals."

The concept of operating as "equals" is indeed revolutionary for government. It was not part of the traditional procurement model. Lawther uses the definition of public-private partnerships (PPPs) set forth by the National Highway Institute, which states, "An arrangement of roles and relationships in which two or more public and private entities coordinate/combine complementary resources to achieve their separate objectives through joint pursuit of one or more common objectives." Lawther also notes that nonprofits firms may also become part of a PPP.

A key element in a true partnership is that both partners have discretion to identify ways and means for achieving goals. Lawther sees many positive attributes to such partnerships. "There is greater opportunity for innovation and creativity as a result," he writes. This new relationship, argues Lawther, must be based on trust, on commitment to problem or conflict resolution, and "on the recognition that flexibility is necessary and that the relationship will evolve and change over time."

The concept of public-private partnerships is not a new one. Such partnerships have long been used effectively in the building of highways and other large infrastructure projects. In chapter seven, Trefor Williams describes the various types of public-private partnership models used around the world. Williams argues the use of such partnerships will not only be driven by the shift from buying goods to buying services, but also by government's need to develop innovative funding approaches. Williams writes:

> In the decade ahead, a major challenge for government at all levels—federal, state, and local—will be to find and develop new ways to finance and implement large-scale projects. In the future, large-scale projects will not be limited to just highways and infrastructure as they will increasingly include large-scale technology projects. The use of public-private partnerships will offer an increasingly attractive alternative to traditional approaches to the financing and procurement of large projects.

Transformation Three:
Moving from a Paper-Based Procurement System to Electronic Procurement

The third procurement transformation is just as profound and significant as the first two. This transformation will also significantly alter the way procurement officials operate. While the first two transformations centered on the impact of the shift from buying goods to buying services, the impact of electronic procurement will likely have the greatest impact on government's ability to buy goods more quickly, efficiently, and at a reduced cost. In chapter eight, M. Jae Moon presents results from three surveys of state government procurement officials to ascertain the impact to date of e-procurement initiatives. Such initiatives include the adoption of digital signatures, posting solicitations and bids and contract-award information online, Internet-based bidding and reverse auctions, electronic ordering, automated procurement systems, and purchasing cards. Moon reports that e-procurement "both enhances the overall quality of procurement management through savings in cost and time and leads to a more accountable procurement system." E-procurement also has the potential, writes Moon, "to be an innovative alternative that leads to better, more efficient, and more effective procurement management by overcoming many traditional paper-based procurement problems."

But e-procurement, concludes Moon, is still in its relatively early stage of acceptance across the United States. He writes: "E-procurement remains in

---

Definitions

e-government: e-government is the inventive application of all forms of new information and communication technologies to improve the functioning of government itself, with the ultimate aim being to improve the delivery of governmental services to the citizen-customer served by the public sector.

e-procurement: e-procurement is the use of electronic means to improve sourcing of goods and services, both in the private and public sectors. E-procurement seeks to improve the workings of the acquisition process and the communications along the supply chain, while simultaneously reducing the costs of the purchasing operation. E-procurement encompasses a wide variety of tools, including purchase cards, online catalogs, electronic payments, and reverse auctions.

Source: Wyld, Chapter Nine.

the experimental stage, however, and most state governments have not reached the mature point of realizing benefits from their e-procurement practices. A promising alternative rather than an instant panacea, e-procurement leaves state governments facing many technical, financial, legal, and managerial challenges."

In chapter nine, David Wyld presents three transformational tools that now can be used in the world of procurement. Wyld examines three types of dynamic pricing that can be used in government procurement: reverse auctions, demand aggregation, and forward auctions. The use of auctions is revolutionary for the world of procurement. Wyld writes, "Public procurement has operated for decades with the presumption that, in order to ensure the integrity of the process, sealed bids work best." In contrast, both reverse and forward auctions are characterized by bid prices being immediately known to all. Reverse auctions have the potential to provide financial savings, improve efficiency, and enhance the transparency of the process. Wyld describes the three P's of reverse auctions: price benefits, process benefits, and precision benefits. In describing the potential impact of the use of auctions and demand aggregation, Wyld writes: "... there is a great deal of interest and activity in reinventing the whole area of the government supply chain. What had formerly been a sleepy area of activity is now looked upon as an area of opportunity. For those inside government, officials are now seeking to find ways to yield more revenue from what was formerly seen as a problem area."

Moving Toward the Future

There can be little doubt that the world of government procurement will look far different in the year 2010 from what it does today. The speed of the three transformations described here is likely to accelerate in the coming years, not slow down. Thus, this book attempts to provide a glimpse into the future of procurement in government. The future is fast approaching. Government executives should clearly begin preparing for doing business far differently in the years ahead from how they have done it in the past.

Bibliography

Abramson, Mark A. and Nicole Willenz Gardner, *Human Capital 2002* (Lanham, Md.: Rowman and Littlefield, 2002).

Abramson, Mark A. and Therese L. Morin, *E-Government 2003* (Lanham, Md.: Rowman and Littlefield, 2002).

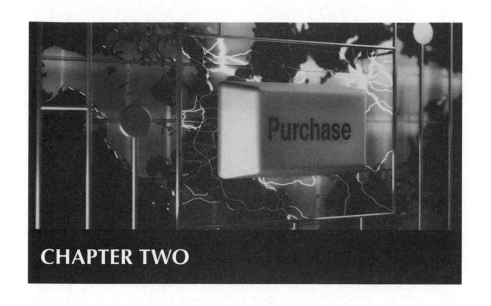

CHAPTER TWO

A Vision of the Government as a World-Class Buyer: Major Procurement Issues for the Coming Decade

Jacques S. Gansler
Professor and Roger C. Lipitz Chair
Director, Center for Public Policy and Private Enterprise
School of Public Affairs
University of Maryland

This report was originally published in January 2002.

13

Overview

This chapter examines the federal government's procurement system, whose practices have been questioned since the country's founding in the 18th century. In equipping the troops at Valley Forge, George Washington had to deal with considerable "waste, fraud, and abuse," and over the years this has been a recurring issue.

In the mid-1980s, however, the problem reached headline proportions. There were a series of revelations of "grossly overpriced" common commercial items (coffeepots, hammers, and toilet seats), exposing the federal government's poor procurement acumen. As a result of these headline scandals, there was a loss of public confidence and trust in government procurement. People thought it was probably too much to pay a billion dollars each for a new bomber, but they didn't know exactly what one should cost. By contrast, they knew they could buy a hammer at the store for a few dollars and that when the government was paying $400 for one, something was wrong.

Government clearly was not keeping up with world-class purchasing practices. Its processes were way out of date, but even worse, its result was unacceptable. Unfortunately, public outrage resulted in a highly regulated and legislated process, unique to government procurement, but one that failed to achieve the desired objectives of efficiency and effectiveness.

Since then, great progress has been made in the way in which government does its business. Nonetheless, major problems still remain within the acquisition process, and there are many opportunities for not only assuring that those reforms are continued during the 21st century, but also that others are introduced to maintain the momentum and increase the benefits significantly. There is still an enormous opportunity for improvement.

Traditionally when considering government procurement, people tended to focus almost entirely on the question: *How does government buy?* However, to achieve the desired long-term effectiveness and efficiency, a total transformation is required in many areas. Specifically, the four areas covered in this report—*Who does the buying? What do they buy? How do they buy? From whom do they buy?*—all require numerous changes. All four areas of acquisition must be addressed together in order to enact significant government changes that will transform the U.S. government into a world-class buyer.

The overall objective is to gain public confidence in the government and its ability to effectively and efficiently perform its mission. Key elements in this required transformation are the recognition that the role of the government is changing—from the *provider of goods* to the *manager of the providers of the goods and services*—and the impact that this has on the acquisition workforce. Simultaneously, dramatic changes in procurement technology and market forces require that the government implement reforms in order to take advantage of the increased effectiveness and efficiency of modern technologies and competitive forces. Finally, this study finds that there are several areas that require significant changes in legislation and regulations.

The following five procurement challenges are discussed in this chapter:
- Challenge One: Recruiting and developing the acquisition workforce
- Challenge Two: Changing the "requirements" and budget processes
- Challenge Three: Reforming the acquisitions process
- Challenge Four: Implementing competitive sourcing
- Challenge Five: Strengthening the supplier base

Recommendations for resolving these challenges and making dramatic improvements in the government's procurement process follow from this discussion and are provided to help government realize its vision as a world-class buyer.

Major recommendations include:
- Transforming the acquisition workforce
- Changing the "requirements" and budget process
- Using commercialization and market forces to reform the acquisition processes
- Shifting to electronic supply chain management
- Integrating commercial/government suppliers

Understanding the Procurement Challenge

Introduction

Lack of public confidence and trust in the government's ability to effectively and efficiently procure its goods and services has been a continuing "headline" issue. Each time a new example of "waste, fraud, and abuse" has occurred, new legislation and/or regulations have been implemented to address the particular problem. As a result, over the years, a specialized way of doing the government's business has built up based on volumes and volumes of legislation, regulation, case history, and practice. The resulting *unique* government procurement system has—unfortunately—*not* achieved the desired objectives of effectiveness or efficiency.

There is general agreement about the need to "fix" the system, and major steps have been taken over the last few years in the right direction (as will be discussed herein). Yet a major transformation is still required in the near term if the government is to become a "world class" buyer of needed goods and services.

Such a transformation requires looking, in depth, at all four of the critical questions associated with how the government does its business:

1. *Who* does the buying?
2. *What* do they buy?
3. *How* do they buy?
4. *From whom* do they buy?

Traditionally, when considering government procurement, people tend to focus almost entirely on the third of these questions. However, it is actions, and resulting changes, in all four areas—taken together—that will result in a world-class buying process for the U.S. government.

The magnitude of this transformation is large; therefore, it will take significant time and effort for its achievement. *Consistency* of message is essential. The process has begun and is well under way. Now the challenge is to maintain the momentum and accelerate it so that, in fact, the government is able to achieve the following vision: *A highly skilled and innovative government acquisition workforce, buying high-quality, low-cost goods and services in an efficient and effective fashion from high-quality, low-cost innovative suppliers, with a process that has total public confidence and trust.*

Who Does the Buying?

Taking the first of these issues—*Who does the buying?*—it is essential to recognize that in the 21st century the role of the government will shift from its more historic mission of being primarily the "provider" of goods and services to the role of being the "manager of the providers" of the goods and services. This means, essentially, that the government changes from hiring people who are more of the "doers" to hiring people with the skills to manage and oversee the "doers"—and the latter will largely come from the competitive private sector (which includes both for-profit and not-for-profit organizations).

Thus, the *skill requirements* for the government acquisition workforce in the 21st century will be significantly different than they have historically been. And this change is increasingly being accentuated as the government both procures modern technology and utilizes modern technology far more extensively (for example, in electronic commerce). Therefore, a different set of skills—more management oriented and more technologically capable—will be required. Yet this need is taking place in an environment in which these same skills are increasingly being required in the private sector (which is also "contracting out" much more of its work and moving rapidly to apply advancing technologies to remain competitive). Thus, the recruiting, retention, continuous training and education, compensation levels, career opportunities, and—particularly—job challenges associated with government employment will all have to be competitive with opportunities in the private sector to attract the required talent. This means dramatic changes in the personnel systems associated with the government's acquisition workforce.

Importantly, this is happening at a time when the government's acquisition workforce has been experiencing two major impacts. First, over the last decade there has been a *dramatic reduction* in the size of the workforce—partly as a result of executive branch efficiency moves; partly as a result of the end of the Cold War, significant reductions in defense expenditures, and the corresponding cuts in the federal government's largest workforce; and partly as a result of legislative mandates (for example, annual laws requiring the Department of Defense to reduce the workforce by over 20,000 each year). The result has been not only an approximately 50 percent reduction, but also a cessation of recruiting and hiring, with very few younger people (many of whom would have been educated and trained on modern technology) entering the government's acquisition workforce. And second, since many of the government workers were hired during the build-ups of the Kennedy/Johnson era, in just a few years (by 2004) *over 50 percent of the government's acquisition workforce will be eligible for retirement.* Clearly, this combination of events represents both a challenge and an opportunity. But it's an issue that must be addressed immediately if the government is to have the "right" workforce fully in place within a very short time.

This will require working closely with the Office of Personnel Management (regarding new personnel policies), the Office of Management and Budget (regarding adequate funding), and the Congress (regarding the criticality of this effort and full support for it). Bringing in new people with the right skills and experiences, and training those already on board, will be very challenging, but it is critical to the successful transition to a world-class government acquisition organization. A major portion of this effort has to be in terms of the creation of an environment (in the government's acquisition workforce) of "continuous learning." Some of this will come through greater job rotation opportunities, including between industry and government (in both directions), while a major share of it will come through increased civilian workforce career planning and computer-based education. With new-product technology cycles of 18 months being typical, there is no way that a person in the government's acquisition workforce can maintain currency without continuous education. And, because the way in which the government does its business will have to change equally rapidly—to keep up with the technological and mission changes happening in the world—it also requires those who are managing this business to be continuously upgraded in the new tools, techniques, and practices of world-class buyers.

Finally, it is essential to recognize that it is not only the people in the government who have the official title of "acquisition personnel" that are involved in the government's acquisition process. Rather, the *users* of the goods and services (who specify the "requirements" for new goods and services) are just as much involved in how this process works and how successful (or unsuccessful) it is. Similarly, those who establish the *budgets* (and thus determine whether programs are adequately funded), those who do the *test and evaluation*, those who do the *logistic support* of the equipment, and those who perform the *oversight* for the government (from Congress through the General Accounting Office and the inspectors general) are all intimately involved in the government's acquisition process. Thus, they all need to have the same vision of where it is heading, and the same understanding of how to achieve that vision and of the role they must play in its successful implementation. Over all, the government's acquisition workforce is composed of hundreds of thousands of people who must truly transform this process if the public is to have the confidence and trust that this process is achieving effectiveness and efficiency in supplying the goods and services required to achieve the government's various missions.

Therefore, the first and most essential step is to assure that the government, in the future, has the highest quality and best-trained people possible to run its acquisition processes.

What Do They Buy?

While having the right people is clearly the first and most essential step, it is equally true that there is no point in "perfectly buying the wrong things." While this may seem self-evident, the government has a very long history of frequently buying things—goods or services—that are better matched to a prior mission need than to a future one. The easiest justification for buying something new is because the old one has worn out or become obsolete, and sometimes that is a sufficient justification. However, in many cases a new technology, a new process, or a new service has come along in the meantime that promises to result in a far more effective and, simultaneously, far more efficient way of achieving the mission. This is most obviously seen through such areas as the evolution of information technology from generation to generation, where the performance enhancements have gone up dramatically while the costs have gone down equally dramatically. However, shifting from paper-based to computer-based processes can be done either by simply automating the old process or by dramatically revising the whole process.

These new products or processes—so-called "disruptive technologies"—are usually counter-cultural (requiring major changes in how things are done and by whom), so they tend to be strongly resisted by the existing institutions (which are the ones likely to be impacted). Thus, the drafting of new "requirements" for goods and services will often result in being strongly endorsed if they support the traditional approach, and strongly resisted (and rejected) if they move in a new direction, even if this new direction is far more effective and efficient.

An example of this is seen today in the "transformation" that the Defense Department is going through, in what is known as the "revolution in military affairs." Here, the requirement for new equipment to match the new concepts of warfare is heavily dependent upon communications equipment, sensors, smart weapons, rapid mobility, etc., while the traditional acquisition process is geared around military platforms (ships, planes, and tanks). In essence, for government agencies to take advantage of the potential (in mission effectiveness improvements and greater efficiencies) offered by advancing technologies, there needs to be a clear recognition that the old myth associated with the acquisition process—i.e., that "a user writes requirements, and then throws them over the transom to the acquisition people, who then deliver on those requirements"—is no longer applicable. Rather, there needs to be *a close working relationship and a continuous process of trade-offs* between those who will use the goods and services and those who are responsible for providing the goods and services—i.e., between the specifiers of needs and the suppliers of goods and services to satisfy those needs.

The most obvious place in which this set of trade-offs occurs is between the desired performance of the goods and services to be acquired and their cost. One of the major changes made over the last few years in the defense acquisition process was the joint directive, signed in July of 1999 by the vice chairman of the Joint Chiefs of Staff (as the user) and the under secretary of defense for acquisition, technology and logistics (as the supplier), which stated that one of the very few firm "requirements" for all future weapon systems would be the costs to produce and support them. Since all agencies operate within constrained budgets, the dollars available for buying a given good or service clearly determines the quantity and/or quality (usually a combination of these) that can be afforded, and thus establishes a threshold of affordability for procuring, operating, and maintaining the equipment or service. This "affordability requirement" is common in the commercial world. (We don't specify just what kind of a car we want to buy, we also specify how much we can afford to pay—otherwise, we would all drive Ferraris.)

Of course, equally essential to an affordability approach is having an adequate budget to cover the likely cost of the needed goods or services. Too often, an agency will estimate the likely cost (which is an essential step in any well-performed acquisition process) and then budget significantly below this level—"hoping" that the bid prices will come in to match this budget. And sometimes they do, but it is often simply because the bidders "bought in," fully expecting that subsequent contract "clarifications" and/or changes will allow them to raise their prices to "get well." Here, the empirical data are overwhelming; when programs are inadequately budgeted they always run into problems, with quality negatively impacted and costs rising well above the originally estimated level. Over all, the concept of introducing "cost as a requirement" for the purchase of government goods and services, and adequately budgeting to cover the likely cost, clearly transforms the way in which the government has traditionally done its business. It will also greatly influence what equipment and services are procured in the future, since they will be the result of trade-offs between performance "desires" and "budget realism."

Another major change in the government's requirements process is the recognition of the short product life cycles in the current commercial world; for example, 18 months or less for modern information technology. In the past, the government could sit down and write a requirement for what it might like to have in 15 or 20 years; then proceed to develop that product to satisfy the request; and plan on keeping it for an additional 20 or 30 years. However, that process is no longer applicable; in fact, it has resulted in the government having old, obsolete, and worn-out equipment, which costs far more to operate and maintain than its modern equivalent. And it has the government in a "death spiral," wherein it is spending more and more of its acquisition dollars to operate and maintain old equipment and, thus, less and less is available for satisfying its modernization needs. The government clearly must get out of this spiral, or face a total breakdown.

The alternative acquisition model—as used by the commercial world today—is known as an evolutionary, or "spiral," approach. Here, rather than having the acquirer write what capability (or, even worse, what design) they would like to have in 15 or 20 years, they instead evaluate what current state-of-the-art technology and processes will allow. And, if this turns out to be significantly better than what it now has, the government would acquire that as the "block 1" version toward its desired future needs. Then, as technology evolves, and as the equipment is tested in the field by the users (with feedback for future enhancements), the system is evolved to a "block 2" version; and subsequently, a "block 3" and "block 4," etc. This, of course, changes the overall logistics support requirements for this equipment to more of a commercial model, where contractor support becomes the dominant factor. The contractors provide warranties for the reliability of the equipment and for its ability to be continuously upgraded (for example, through the use of software and hardware "open architectures"). The net effect of this "spiral" acquisition process is low-risk, proven technology, rapidly acquired with minimum costs, and updated frequently (as advanced technology is developed and proven).

Finally, in terms of what the government will be buying in the coming decades, it is important to recognize that the overall U.S. economy is shifting from the buying of goods to the buying of services, and that this is also happening with the government's acquisition process.

Unfortunately, neither has this shift been recognized, nor has the government's acquisition process been adjusted accordingly. For example, in the past when the Defense Department wanted to buy a communications satellite, it purchased a launch rocket, it purchased launch services, and it purchased a satellite. In the future it will simply purchase the *services* associated with a certain number of channels and bandwidth from a communications satellite (in many cases a commercial satellite, but in other cases a service of "communication" from a contractor-supplied and launched, government-unique satellite). In the same way, the government has been moving toward buying (from the private sector or, in some cases, even from the public sector) the *service* of operating a base, or the *service* of providing privatized housing, or the *service* of paying for the use of a jet aircraft engine by the hour (rather than buying the engine).

Clearly, the buying of services and the specifying of what the desired service should result in is very different (and often more difficult) than the buying of a piece of equipment; yet almost all of the government's rules, regulations, and practices are based upon the more traditional equipment buying. Similarly, all of the education and training programs are focused in this traditional direction. Thus, a *major transformation in the overall process* (including the education of the workforce) *must be toward an ability to acquire sophisticated services* as more and more of the government's acquisitions will be done in this way in the future.

How Do They Buy?

The acquisition process itself is, of course, the traditional area of "acquisition reform." Over the last decade, both the executive and legislative branches have been active in addressing this issue. For example, with the Federal Acquisition Streamlining Act of 1994 (FASA) and the Federal Acquisition Reform Act of 1995 (FARA), Congress moved toward simplifying procurement procedures to allow (and encourage) the government to buy commercial and "modified commercial" items. Similarly, in the Information Technology and Management Reform Act of 1996 (known as the Clinger-Cohen Act) the Congress recognized the importance of information technology in the government's business activities.

On the executive branch side, federal agencies were attempting to *take greater advantage of the capabilities of the commercial world.* Examples include the initiative of then-Defense Secretary William Perry in moving the

Defense Department from military specifications to commercial specifications for its equipment, and the government's move to more widely utilize
"electronic procurements" (e.g., via the General Services Administration's
Internet "schedules"). In general, these steps were a recognition of the fact
that no longer was the government driving many of the requirements for
advanced, technology-based goods and services—the government had
become a small user relative to the commercial sector—and that the government needed to be able to take greater advantage of the rapid advances
taking place in the commercial sector.

As noted in the prior section, the government had to change its way of
doing business, from specifying what it would like to have as a small user
of specialized equipment and services to looking at what the commercial
market had to offer, in terms of capabilities, and to using free-market forces
to achieve (through competitive innovation and competitive pricing) the
best possible performance at the lowest reasonable cost.

Because many of the desired services in the past had been provided—
sole source—by the government itself and were now available from the
competitive marketplace (in the private sector), in recent years the government has been switching to *greater use of "competitive sourcing,"* in which
competition is created between the public sector and the private sector.
And, it was found, after thousands of such competitions, that no matter
whether the public or the private sector was declared the winner, the real
winner was the taxpayer and the government agency because performance
tended to go up while cost went down—on average, by over 30 percent.
More recent studies have shown that these performance improvements and
cost savings continued into the out-years.[1]

Such "competitive sourcing" is, of course, totally consistent with the
above-noted "changes in the role of the government," with the reevaluation
of the various governance roles of the government, the private sector, and
the third sector (nonprofits, think tanks, universities, non-governmental
agencies, etc.). As part of this reevaluation, one of the requirements of the
Congress (the Federal Activities Inventory Reform Act of 1998, known as the
FAIR Act) was to identify those positions that could be competitively
sourced in each government agency; and, as would be expected, major
portions of these have to do with the (broadly defined) acquisition workforce. This has also caused an important reevaluation of the potential associated with various "public-private partnerships," where benefits can be
realized from the best that the government has to offer and that the private
sector has to offer. For example, when major aircraft and engine maintenance work was competed by the Air Force, it was found that the public
sector was able to win the competitions, but only by subcontracting out 60
or 70 percent of the work to the private sector. Such public-private partnerships are becoming more and more the norm.

To more efficiently and effectively run such competitive sourcings in the future, the procedures associated with them (whether it be for maintenance-type competitions or for the broader application of the Office of Management and Budget Directive A-76) will have to be significantly streamlined. One particular aspect that has to be emphasized is the importance of the government buying the "best value"—rather than simply buying from the lowest bidder. "Best value" means making the important trade-offs between getting a high-quality product at a reasonable cost versus simply getting a cheap, but only minimally acceptable, product. An important aspect of assuring that the government is getting the best value is clearly the *past performance* of the supplier, which (while not eliminating new suppliers) certainly must be a significant consideration in the selection of the supplier of a new product or service. Unfortunately, it is much more difficult to make a "best value" selection than simply opening the envelopes and comparing the prices bid (on a detailed design specification). However, it is clearly the right way for the government to buy, and is consistent with the need for a highly skilled workforce (in making the product and supplier selections).

Also, consistent with "best value" awards is the need for the government to focus its acquisitions on the desired results—that it needs to achieve and that it can measure—so as to determine when they are achieved. This *focus on output measures,* i.e., performance results, is a major shift in the government's acquisition process from a detailed design requirement to which all bidders must respond, but for which no one has the exact product already available, to an emphasis upon what is really needed and what existing technology can provide at a reasonable cost. In the latter case, obviously, there will be significant differences between different products and different services, and (similarly) significant differences in their prices. This is the challenge for the government source-selection personnel (since they are now looking at dissimilar products, or services, at different prices), but it is the way the commercial world works every day, and it is the direction to which the government must move. Thus, instead of the government specifying the exact item or service it wants and then giving detailed specifications for how it is to be achieved, the government will simply state, "This is the *need* that I have," and all bidders will propose their solution to solving that need. It goes without saying that as the government shifts in this direction (which it has begun doing in its "performance-based contracting"), the whole acquisition process from requirements, through source selection, budgeting, testing, and oversight will have to be revised accordingly.

Additionally, instead of using regulations for controls, the government's acquisition process will work far better by a shift to *incentives* for motivating contractors to achieve the desired results (i.e., higher performance at lower costs). Such incentives may be in the form of awarding additional business and/or higher profits as a result of outstanding performance; or it could be in terms of such specific contractual items as warranties, wherein the contractor makes much more money if the quality of their products and services are much higher.

As noted above, in order to have the government always purchasing state-of-the-art capability at low cost, the *concept of an evolutionary, or "spiral," development process must be fully integrated into the new acquisition model.* Recently, the Defense Department has officially introduced this concept both in its new requirements process and in its new acquisition directives. In this common commercial model (utilized on software, as well as on hardware), the first "block" of a system utilizes proven technology and gets it quickly into the hands of the users for their evaluation. The users then recommend additional things they would like to see and things they don't need. These recommendations are combined with the potential of next-generation technologies (which frequently come along in 18-month cycles) and are combined into the "next block." Of course, for this concept to be implemented requires that user training on each of the "blocks" accompanies the new system. And, in the approach being taken in the commercial world, the training is actually "built-in" to the products themselves—a highly efficient and effective method of both training and utilization of new products that is also a very low risk approach.

The Shift to E-Business

A major potential for improving the third of the key issues—*how the government buys*—is the shift to electronic business (e-business). If properly implemented, it will have a dramatic impact, and therefore is worthy of a separate focus. The key point here is that one should *not* perceive that the government's moving to e-business is simply digitizing the current acquisition process. Rather, it is necessary (and desirable) to *transform the acquisition process to take full advantage of the potential offered by electronic commerce.* In fact, early attempts at implementing e-business within the government have been greatly hampered by existing regulations and practices—so much so that commercial world-class tools and practices (as have been rapidly evolving in the commercial world) could not be effectively utilized by the government. In essence, to take full advantage of the potential offered by electronic commerce, the government's acquisition process must completely change. When this is done, it has been found that the power in the government/contractor relationship shifts dramatically from the supplier to the buyer.

The existence of a web-based system, with all suppliers providing their information and the government having instant access to that information, provides far greater options to the government buyer, as well as providing higher visibility and fairness to the process. In fact, it has even been found that these shifts yield a larger share of the business going to the smaller, innovative firms (as discussed later). Additionally, the move to the web-based acquisition process dramatically reduces not only the time periods involved (for the whole process, from requirements to payments), but it also dramatically reduces transaction costs (in most cases by more than an order of magnitude). Thus, the implementation of e-commerce throughout the full supply chain, especially in the logistics area, provides dramatic improvements in timeliness, responsiveness, performance, fairness, visibility, and cost reductions.

Of course, this will require some "up-front" investments on the government's part, as well as assurance of legacy systems' interoperability and continuous performance during the transition period. It will also require strong leadership on the government side to overcome the institutional resistance (that is already being felt) in achieving the full implementation of these *integrated-supply-chain, e-commerce systems.*

It is critically important to realize that for the government to implement a web-based, e-commerce supply chain, the first and most important aspect is that associated with the *privacy and security of the system.* While it is recognized that establishing the overall system architecture—based first and foremost on privacy and security—is less efficient, it is absolutely essential that this be the focus of the government's e-commerce system in order to maintain public trust and confidence in the acquisition system. This point cannot be overemphasized; and in the explanations and training associated with the government's implementation of its e-commerce supply chain, it should be the focus of all discussions. Even early demonstration systems must explicitly address the areas of privacy and security to build up the public's trust. Also, it will be necessary to establish confidence in the "keeper of the keys" for the security system as an essential element in the system. This could be the government itself or a certified third party, but it must be very clear that such an organization is fully certified and has no potential for any conflict of interest whatsoever.

It must be emphasized here that the benefits from this shift to a modern, web-based electronic-commerce supply chain are not simply a theoretical estimate of what the government can gain, but are based on actual and dramatic results being achieved today in commercial activities. The benefits have been proven, and the government must move rapidly in this direction to take advantage of them.

From Whom Do They Buy?

Moving to the last of the four key acquisition issues, namely, that associated with the supply-side of the equation—*From whom does the government buy its goods and services?*—the answer here seems obvious: "the best." However, to do so means that the government has to significantly change its acquisition process, because right now it has significant barriers to doing just that. For example, Hewlett-Packard is clearly a world-class research and development electronics firm, and yet they refuse to do development work with the Department of Defense because of its unique government cost accounting and auditing practices. Such barriers (including not only cost accounting and auditing, but also intellectual property rights, criminal prosecution for administrative errors, delays in payments, etc.) will have to be explicitly addressed and removed if the desire is for the government to be a world-class buyer, from world- class suppliers, in a world-class fashion.

In today's world, where high-quality, advanced-technology-based goods and services are produced for the commercial world, the government must be capable of taking full advantage of these goods and services that have met the market test of high performance at low cost. Clearly, the government, like most buyers, will have requirements that are unique; but supplying such differentiated products is the direction that the commercial world is moving as well. For example, in the automobile industry, people will soon be able to order a car to be built with exactly the color, parts, design, etc., that they desire. These "unique" requirements will simply be sent into the information system that drives the flexible manufacturing operation to achieve a one-of-a-kind automobile at high efficiency— because it has been integrated into a large-volume production operation. However, for the government to fit into this model, it must do its business in a commercial fashion.

The challenge here for the government is to recognize that its objectives are, in fact, efficiency and effectiveness, not regulatory control for its own sake. Naturally, transparency and fairness will be required in all government actions, but the detailed, specialized nature of current government acquisition processes and practices will have to be removed. And, we should expect that there will be an occasional abuse, as there is in society at large (that's why nations need jails). However, the prior practice of writing another new law to address that one, single (infrequent) violation, and then having it applied to all other cases, has resulted in the current situation of incredibly detailed regulations and rigid practices that essentially isolate the government's procurement system from the normal competitive, efficient, and effective commercial marketplace. The changes that have been legislated in recent years so the government can buy off-the-shelf commercial items are an important first step. But they do not address the essential issue of how the government can buy the unique goods and services that it requires from commercial operations in a commercial fashion.

The Vision

The direction in which the government must be prepared to move in the future is one in which commercial suppliers will be providing government-unique goods and services as part of their normal commercial operations. For example, if the military needs some unique electronic cards, these can be built on a high-quality, high-volume commercial assembly line as long as there are no government-unique process requirements (such as specialized cost accounting) placed on that purchase. Such an experiment was run for electronic cards to be used in the F-22 fighter plane and in the Comanche helicopter program, where these cards were built on the same industrial production line with the high-volume parts that are used in automobile-safety electronic systems. The result was very high reliability and high quality, yet at over 50 percent cost savings for the government-unique items. But it did require the removal of all government-unique regulations and practices.

It is important to recognize that this is not the same as simply buying commercial items; rather, *it is satisfying the government's unique requirements for goods and services from a commercial plant or a commercial service operation.* In this way, the government gains the huge benefit associated with the high-volume commercial business' absorbing the low-volume government business into its overhead, and allows the efficient and effective processes developed for the competitive commercial markets to be applied to government needs. At the same time, removal of the unique government process requirements will allow traditional government suppliers to diversify into commercial businesses without the high-cost burdens of current government practices.

The way to approach solving this problem is to clearly identify each government-unique barrier, and then remove them one by one. For example, when Secretary Perry said that the Department of Defense will shift from using military specifications (unless commercial ones could be justified) to using commercial specifications (unless military ones could be justified, at a very senior level), a major barrier was removed. In exactly this same way, the remaining barriers must be addressed, item by item. This will require the full cooperation of the Congress. It will, of course, be met with fierce resistance from those specialized government contractors who are not competitive in the world-class marketplace and who need to be "protected and subsidized" through the barriers created by specialized government acquisition practices. Nonetheless, until these barriers are removed, the government cannot achieve the required efficiency and effectiveness that it must have to satisfy taxpayers' needs.

Recent Progress

Overview

Since the country's founding in the 18th century, government procurement practices have been questioned. In equipping the troops at Valley Forge, George Washington had to deal with considerable "waste, fraud, and abuse," and, over the years, this has been a recurring problem. Numerous congressional commissions, such as the Hoover Commission and the Truman Commission, have focused on the issue, and "procurement reform" has been an elusive target.

In the mid-1980s the problem reached headline proportions. There were a series of revelations of "grossly overpriced" common commercial items (coffee pots, hammers, and toilet seats) in defense procurements, as well as excessively high prices for common aircraft spare parts. And, to top it off, there was an actual illegal bribery scandal, known as "Ill Wind," involving totally improper actions by a few senior Defense officials. These culminated in the congressional establishment of the so-called Packard Commission, named after its chairman, David Packard, the co-founder of the world-class electronics firm Hewlett-Packard.

As a result of these headline scandals, there was a total loss of public confidence and trust in government procurement. People somehow thought it was probably too much to pay a billion dollars each for a new bomber, but they didn't know exactly what one should cost. By contrast, they *knew* they could buy a hammer at the store for a few dollars and that when the government was paying $400 for a hammer something was clearly wrong. Importantly, as the Packard Commission showed, the commercial world by the mid-1980s had not only caught up with but actually surpassed the Department of Defense (DoD) in terms of state-of-the-art technology in both higher performance and lower costs. Similarly, the average person knew he or she could utilize Federal Express to have packages delivered within 24 hours anywhere in the United States and 48 hours anywhere in the world, with 99.9 percent confidence and at relatively low cost. By contrast, the DoD at that time was taking, on average, 36 days to deliver items that were already in their inventory ("on the shelf") for its logistics support, and with very low customer confidence (in fact, sometimes it would take up to two years). Clearly, the government was not keeping up with world-class performance, and its processes were way out of date.

This was not only the case for services, it also was found in high-technology products. For example, in a new car bought by the average citizen, there was a semiconductor (a small computer) directly mounted on the engine block that controlled many of the car's functions. As the Packard Commission showed, that commercial semiconductor could meet or exceed all military specifications (such as vibration, shock, and temperature—it actually had a 10-degree greater temperature range), and its performance would meet or exceed that required for most military applications. Yet its cost was an order-of-magnitude cheaper and its reliability an order-of-magnitude greater than the "special military semiconductors" that the DoD was buying at the same time. Therefore, based on the headline scandals and the comparisons of government results with comparable commercial results, the public (understandably) had a widespread image of great "waste, fraud, and abuse" in government procurement.

Unfortunately, the press—and, therefore, the public's perception—combined "waste, fraud, and abuse" into a single category. The reality, as demonstrated by numerous sources,[2] is that there is very little actual fraud or other illegal actions, but there is enormous waste in government procurements. In analyzing this further, it was found that *the problem is not the people, it is the processes being used.* And these processes are not solely those of the procurement act itself, but extend from the writing of the "requirements" for the product or service being bought (so-called "gold plating") to inadequate budgeting for the products and services (so that more of them could be inserted into the initial budgets and "paid for later when the overruns appeared"). Most importantly, the Packard Commission showed that there was great potential for improvement in the government's overall acquisition process simply by emulating what was being done by world-class private-sector firms. For perhaps the first time in the long history of "procurement reform," no longer were the arguments based on theoretical potentials for improvements; rather, there was now a clear "demonstration" of what could be done if government practices were significantly changed.

But these changes could not be marginal adjustments to the current systems. Instead, there was a need for a *total transformation*—essentially a "cultural change" that would take years to achieve and certainly could not be done simply by putting out government directives. Fortunately, both the Congress and the executive branch during the 1990s responded with significant actions to get the process started.

It might be noted that while the Packard Commission was specifically focused on DoD actions, their findings were applicable across the board since they addressed a broad range of issues in the acquisition process, with an emphasis on commerciality and the supplier base. It also must be emphasized that the defense procurement process tends to dominate the government's overall acquisition process because of its size. In fact, when one looks at the overall federal budget (for example, for fiscal year 2001) the largest category is retirement income ($689 billion), then health and medical ($391 billion), and then Defense ($305 billion). The sum total of Commerce, Housing, "General Government," Science, Space, International

Affairs, Agriculture, Natural Resources, Environment, Justice, Transportation, Education, Training, Employment Services, etc. (for *all* other departments besides Defense) is $293 billion; and the interest on the debt is $208 billion. Thus, Defense clearly dominates the overall discretionary portions of the federal budget—and, correspondingly, of the acquisition budgets and personnel. So, if improvements can be made in Defense, they are most likely to be reflected in the other agencies' practices.

Congressional Actions in the 1990s

In immediate reaction to the headline horror stories in the Defense arena, in 1986 the Congress passed the Goldwater-Nickels bill, which established the position of the under secretary of defense for all acquisition, technology, and logistics work (defined as the "Acquisition Czar") and increased that position's authority significantly to get control over the acquisition process. This bill also established the position of the vice chairman of the Joint Chiefs of Staff and gave that individual specific authority over the military's "requirements process." Both of these important actions were necessary steps, but they were not sufficient. There was still much imbedded legislation and regulation, as well as many practices that had to change. Thus, during the 1990s Congress issued a series of wide-ranging reforms addressing not only the narrower area of defense acquisition, but also the related areas of the budget process and the financial management controls necessary. Additionally, they addressed the broader question of getting effective *output* measures of government management—i.e., of relating performance results to resources expended by all of the various government agencies. Specifically, some of the bills of importance during this period were:

- Federal Acquisition Streamlining Act of 1994—made it far easier for the federal government to purchase commercial items.
- Federal Acquisition Reform Act of 1995—went further and encouraged not only the purchase of commercial items but also of commercial-like items ("modified commercial items").
- Government Performance and Results Act of 1993—was a major effort to get the various government agencies to relate their actions and resource plans to the desired strategic objective of their agencies, and to identify the measures of effectiveness they would use to evaluate their achievements. In many cases, this was the first time that agencies had attempted such a correlation, and it forced them to do much more "strategic planning."
- Information Technology and Management Reform Act of 1996 (known as the Clinger-Cohen Act)—recognized the importance of information technology in the government's business activities.

- Government Paperwork Elimination Act of 1998—encouraged online electronic government activities, including enabling the use of electronic signatures.
- Federal Activities Inventory Reform Act of 1998 (FAIR Act)—required the identification of those government positions that could be competitively sourced in each government agency (i.e., those positions which were not "inherently governmental" and could, therefore, benefit from public/private competition).
- Chief Financial Officers Act of 1990, Budget Enforcement Act of 1990, Government Management Reform Act of 1994, and Federal Financial Improvement Act of 1996—all emphasized the importance of the government reforming its budget process, specifically, in attempting to link the budget process to *financial management.* Such a linkage had been missing and had been a major cause of poor government financial performance—i.e., having a budget process geared to simply accounting for the expenditure of all dollars as contrasted to a financial system that provides visibility for managers to be able to actually reduce their total costs through effective financial management.

The fact that Congress was willing to step up to some of these difficult decisions and implement some of the required legislation is a sign that the public clearly was demanding change and that it was up to Congress to at least *remove the barriers* that had been created to such change. Nonetheless, the day-to-day leadership for the changes still was the responsibility of the executive branch.

Executive Branch Initiatives

Because many of the required changes were "counter-cultural," making them more than just changes in appearance required strong leadership. In the early '90s this was supplied by William Perry in the Defense Department (first as deputy secretary, then as secretary) and by Dan Goldin as the director of the National Aeronautics and Space Administration (NASA)— with the full support of Vice President Gore and the Office of Management and Budget. Secretary Perry had been on the Packard Commission, and from his first day in office he made "acquisition reform" one of his major personal activities. He saw (from the example of semiconductors provided earlier) that the government was paying much more for its products and getting much lower performance because of its unique *military* specifications and standards. Thus, one of his early steps was to change the government's practice from a requirement to "always use unique military specifications and standards unless commercial items could be justified by a decision approved at two levels above the program office," to a new set of requirements that said "*commercial* specifications and standards will always be utilized unless a unique military specification or standard could be justified and approved at two levels above the program office."

Needless to say, this "cultural change" was strongly resisted and has taken a number of years to be fully implemented, but it is typical of exactly the type of changes required. Additionally, Secretary Perry set up a high-level organization within his office to initiate additional "acquisition reforms" and to monitor their implementation (with his personal attention being strongly supportive of each of their initiatives). Thus, it became clear to everyone at the Department of Defense that they were to pay close attention to acquisition reform and that creative initiatives taken by individual program offices would be rewarded rather than punished.

Similarly, at NASA, Dan Goldin started his "better, faster, cheaper" cultural change. His message was that things with higher performance—i.e., "better"—could be achieved much more rapidly and at much lower cost through dramatic changes in practices and procedures within the organization. Again, this top-level attention by the leader of the organization was absolutely essential to achieve a change from the historic acquisition model of the agency.

Over time, such initiatives within Defense and NASA spread to other government agencies. For example, the General Services Administration began using the Internet to advertise its procurements. Reviews by outsiders, even including the press, affirmed that things were beginning to change.

Recent Assessments

Overcoming institutional resistance is extremely difficult, and requires constant attention and leadership if it is to have any chance of succeeding. Nonetheless, by the end of the 1990s it was clear that change was being institutionalized. An early but clear sign of this recognition from the external world was a *Fortune* article in December of 1998 titled "The Pentagon Finally Learns to Shop."[3] Subsequently, university researchers and independent agencies began to have sufficient data over an extended time period to make quantitative comparisons and to see that things, in fact, were changing. Kimberly A. Harokopus, a Visiting Scholar at Boston College, in analyzing the reforms of the 1990s, wrote:

"Remarkably, the time-honored but previously ill-fated defense reform effort has finally met with success. In large measure, a cadre of top leaders is responsible for that success. Their feats are remarkable, in part, for the sheer scope of the reform. The changes involve almost every aspect of defense procurement:
- Replacement of overly prescriptive military specifications and standards with commercial or performance specifications;

- Widespread applications of process-speeding information technologies and the introduction of electronic commerce;
- Loosening of the restrictions on communications between government personnel and industry;
- Increased use of corporate past performance as a factor in subsequent contract awards;
- Greater use of commercial products; and
- Use of functionally-integrated government acquisition teams, also called Integrated Product Teams (IPT)."[4]

In summary she stated: "At bottom, the reforms seek to introduce market-centered approaches to public procurement. It is an effort to replace unique and onerous military acquisition processes with industrial practices and commercial managerial techniques. It loosens the restrictions of bureaucratic rules set forth in the Federal Acquisition Regulations, invoking greater use of subjective, case-specific, and participator decision making. It trades a rule-bound system for devolution of power to front-line bureaucrats with the ability to use personal discretion and best judgment."

Other independent assessments focused on different aspects of the acquisition reform initiatives, but reached a similar conclusion. For example, a May 2001 report by Acquisition Solutions, Inc., an organization that independently tracks the overall acquisition reform activities, stated: "The 1990s saw remarkable changes in the way federal procurement can be conducted. We say, 'can be' rather than 'is' because in some instances—performance-based service contracting, for example—reform has barely caught on. But many other reforms have. Use of past performance as a selection criterion, greater use and delegation of purchase card authority, increased use of governmentwide contracts, and the greatly expanded use of federal supply schedules are just a few examples of the reforms that have swept through the acquisition communication recently. Over all, these reforms have been good for customers and good for business."[5]

The report summarized: "In the face of challenges to become more like their commercial counterparts, the federal acquisition community has proved itself up to the task."

Because of the importance of small business to innovation and competitiveness, one of the considerable concerns about the acquisition reform initiatives of the 1990s was what would be their effect on small business awards. At the request of Congress, the General Accounting Office (GAO) recently evaluated what has been the impact of the earlier legislation on small business awards.[6] Specifically, they looked at the effects of the Federal Acquisition Streamlining Act of 1994 and the Clinger-Cohen Act of 1996 on small business opportunities. What they found was that, in fact, the small business share of awards using these procurement reform "streamlining vehicles" had a *significant increase*. For example, using the multiple award contracts from FASA, the percent of the business and the dollar value of small business shares from 1994 to 1999 went up from 8 percent to 16 percent and from $0.5 billion to $2.0 billion respectively.

Similarly, using the GSA schedules, the changes for small business shares from 1994 to 1999 went from 26 percent to 36 percent and $0.5 billion to $3.0 billion respectively. As might be expected, when the Internet is used to access potential sources, and the information and costs about their products and services are made visible to government buyers, it makes it a lot easier for small firms to compete against larger firms—and the growth in small business awards confirms this.

Thus, *the acquisition reform results seem to be demonstrating that not only does the government get better products and services at lower prices, but that the supplier community is better off and more competitive.* Nevertheless, in spite of the initial success of the acquisition reform efforts during the 1990s, it is very clear that major problems still remain within the acquisition process, and that there are many opportunities for not only assuring that those reforms are continued during the 21st century, but that others are introduced to maintain the momentum and increase the benefits significantly.

Addressing the Procurement Challenge

Clearly, great progress has been made over the last decade in the way in which the government does its business. Nonetheless, there is an enormous opportunity for further improvement. In some areas, such as Human Resources, the nation is facing a "crisis" in its government workforce; in other areas, if one were to simply fully implement the new regulations and laws, taking full advantage of the flexibility they *allow* (but perhaps do not require), very considerable progress can be made. Finally, in a few other areas there is still a requirement for significant changes in legislation and regulations. At a very top level, the trends are positive, but without significant additional effort and much greater forward progress, the *potential* for dramatic improvement in the effectiveness and efficiency of government business cannot be realized. The five key areas for near-term *action* are discussed below.

Challenge One: Recruiting and Developing the Acquisition Workforce

During the 1990s the federal workforce was reduced by around a half million people, led by the Defense Department's reductions in the post-Cold War era. Naturally, with this large a reduction, there was very little recruitment being done, and the accessions of the younger portion of the workforce declined dramatically. Unfortunately, the vast majority of the more than 2 million federal workers were all hired during the government buildups of the past (e.g., during the Lyndon Johnson era) and are thus nearing their retirement age. In fact, the Office of Management and Budget estimates that 71 percent of federal employees will be eligible for retirement by 2010.[7] In some areas this occurs even sooner. For example, in the Defense acquisition workforce, approximately 50 percent of the workforce will be eligible to retire by the year 2004.

What is particularly critical—in fact, some call it a management or leadership "crisis"—is that approximately half of the Senior Executive Service (SES) and GM-15 employees will be eligible for retirement over the next five years.[8] These are the people who currently run the essential programs and government organizations. As they leave, they will be taking with them their intellectual capital—their detailed knowledge of the laws, the procedures, and the programs. And because no younger people have been brought along in the last decade to replace them, there will be a critical gap building up rapidly, one that will be difficult to fill, especially when there is a dramatic change taking place in the whole role of the government and the required skills for its workforce. Specifically, as the government is less a provider of services than it is a manager of the providers of services, leadership and management skills come into greater demand. Additionally, decision making becomes much more important, and the analytic tools for doing it become essential in terms of operations research, as well as understanding technology (particularly information technology) and what technology change can offer in terms of new processes and organizations.

Naturally, these are the same skills that are increasingly being required in industry, and it is becoming recognized that the government's salary structure, along with its personnel policies and regulations, make it uncompetitive in terms of either recruitment or retention of top people.

The civil service system was set up many years ago and has proven extremely effective in professionalizing the government's workforce and in keeping it out of the political abuses to which it had been subjected many years ago. However, these same rules and regulations have resulted in a system which today lacks the *flexibility* required for the government to compete with the private sector for the top-notch candidates it requires. In fact, this lack of flexibility works in both directions—i.e., top candidates cannot move along rapidly enough and, therefore, tend to leave, while poor performers cannot be easily removed in spite of their lack of performance. These barriers, combined with inadequate training in modern processes, tools, and management techniques, are areas that clearly will have to change over the next few years.

A necessary step in this process, and one that President George W. Bush has recognized as one of his top priorities for management in the new administration, is that of *strategic management of government's human capital*.[9] Essentially this means the creation of a long-range human resource plan that details the skill levels and numbers of people required, over time, in the various categories of the civilian workforce. Adopting such a strategic perspective and converting it into specific actions in terms of career planning can result in great progress toward satisfying the government's human capital needs in recruitment, training, personnel development, and civil service flexibility.

However, none of this will be achievable unless the government increases its budgets for salaries, training, tools, and other human resource needs. Obviously, this is a difficult choice, because resources are also required elsewhere in every agency. Nonetheless, it must be recognized that "people are the number one priority," and the budgets must be adequate to match this priority.

Challenge Two: Changing the "Requirements" and Budget Processes

While not normally included in the acquisition process, requirements and budgets are the two areas that most directly result in the poor performance of the traditional acquisition process. In fact, it is likely that the lack of recognition of this direct coupling between these two "external" areas and the acquisition process itself may well be the major cause of much of the ineffectiveness and inefficiencies associated with the process. At the surface level this should be obvious: If you ask for the wrong thing, you'll get it, and if you inadequately budget for it, you clearly will have problems. But at the more subtle level there are major changes that could be made in both the requirements and budget processes that could result in the government's doing its business in a much more commercial-like fashion and thus achieving far greater efficiency and effectiveness. For example, in the requirements process, if one can learn to think about using technology that previously has been demonstrated and instead of specifying a "requirement" for what one "would like to have," simply look at how to use what is available in the best possible fashion, then much of the technology development costs, and time, are greatly reduced, and one can obtain the required goods and services much faster and cheaper.

This, of course, requires much more "market analysis" to be done as part of the requirements process than is typical of the government. However, when one recognizes that the technology cycles of new products often come in 18- to 36-month periods, the government's old way of doing business (for example, having to wait 15 or more years to get a new system) simply has to change. Instead, the government should have a new rule (let's call it a "five-year rule") that says that no development should be undertaken without the assurance that it can be done within a five-year period. This requires that the technology has been previously proven and that all that's left to do is systems integration and testing prior to entering production. Consistent with this five-year rule is the recognition that systems being acquired will be updated very frequently—the so-called evolutionary or "spiral" development process. What is particularly important about this development process is that it recognizes the importance of getting the "users," or customers, into the acquisition process because they are the true "requirers." In essence, *the government's acquisition process must be much more geared to the customer's perspective.* A clear example of this is that as the government moves toward e-government, or e-business, it should not think in terms of how to simply take the current processes and put them onto the Internet. Rather, it must think of how to make the result not only more "user-friendly" but much more user-effective, which means changing the government's processes and having the customer (not the bureaucracy) drive the requirements.

Additionally, the government must be much more sensitive to the external changes that are taking place. For example, as the government becomes more and more dependent on information technology, its "requirements" must focus on the *security and privacy* aspects of these information systems since this is critical in today's environment. Similarly, the government must recognize that in many areas where they used to buy goods, they now buy large, sophisticated services (as part of the shift from the government as the "doer" to the government as the "manager of the doers"). This means writing "requirements" much more in terms of what needs to be done rather than how to do it.

For example, if the government's objective is more communication channels from satellites, it should state that and not specify the design of the satellite. Thus, it is purchasing a communications service rather than a satellite. A recent example of such service purchases is that of the United Kingdom's Ministry of Defence recognizing that when they go to war, they will need significantly more transportation aircraft than they need in peacetime. So they are leasing C-17 transport aircraft on an as-required basis. The rest of the time these large aircraft can be used for other purposes by the commercial company that rents them to the Ministry of Defence. Such "creative requirements" then lead directly into "creative contracting," wherein one is buying a service *when* they require it, and not being forced to buy equipment or facilities when their use is not needed on a full-time basis.

In the same way that the requirements process has to change to accommodate efficient and effective acquisitions, so does the budget process. Clearly a process that takes over three years to get an item into a budget is incompatible with the rapid 18-month changes in technology that occur today. Thus, a far greater flexibility is required in the budget process. This, in turn, requires a much closer working relationship and even more "trust" between the executive and legislative branches. But it is a necessity if the government is going to be able to move rapidly when opportunities are presented. Similarly, the budget process needs to be adjusted to match the "spiral development" concepts described above. In this development concept, engineering is a *continuous* process, as is procurement and even replacement. So the traditional (linear) budget process assumption of first doing research and development, then doing procurement, and then doing support is no longer valid. Again, the budget process needs to be changed.

Finally, perhaps the greatest area of budgeting abuse today is that associated with underfunding of programs—somehow "hoping" they will come in for less money than had been expected. The empirical data are overwhelming here. Rarely, if ever, does the government under-run on a program that has been under-budgeted; and, in fact, the best that is normally the case is that it comes in for the expected price. Therefore, the very least that should be budgeted is the price that was determined by a government independent cost analysis—and, in most cases, there should be some additional money put in to cover the "likely" cost increase in the program, based on history. If programs were budgeted to cover the "likely" increase, then from those programs that came in at the independently estimated level, there would be adequate dollars available for those that overrun. This would minimize the effects of under-budgeting and having huge costs growths on programs.

While this may all seem self-evident, it is certainly not the case today. In fact, the result of continuous under-budgeting (and thus trying to fit in 10 programs when there is only enough money available for eight) results in not even being able to do the eight, because of cost growths in all 10 programs. Such "Alice in Wonderland budgeting" simply has to be stopped. This, again, is only a question of leadership; everyone knows that under-budgeting is wrong, and yet many continue to practice it.

Challenge Three: Reforming the Acquisition Process

In spite of the significant gains made during the last few years, it is still a fact that government purchases of goods and services *take too long, cost too much, and often don't result in the highest quality.* Clearly, there is a lot of room for additional improvements. Several areas require particular attention. First is the ability to better manage contractors supplying goods and services to the government. It may sound simplistic, but the government's objective should be "to get the maximum performance at the lowest cost." This is very different from an objective of "achieving minimum acceptable performance while accounting for all dollars spent." Unfortunately, much of the traditional procurement practices are geared around the latter approach.

For example, the concept of accepting the lowest bid for a specified minimum performance when a slightly higher bid could result in a dramatic improvement in performance is not the way that commercial markets work. They buy based on "best value," where the ability to make trade-offs between the marginal gain from an improved performance is balanced against the marginal cost increase. Similarly, the government's cost accounting system focuses on trying to fully account for every dollar while the commercial market has as its objective the reduction of the total cost to the buyer. And, in this commercial model, the focus is not on how much profit the supplier makes, but on how much it costs the buyer for the good or service being acquired. Thus, it is in the buyer's interest to get a lower cost item, even if the supplier makes a higher profit on it. Again, this is counter to the government's normal way of thinking about profit.

The government must learn to use *incentives* rather than regulations as the way to create higher performance at lower costs. Obviously, if contractors are rewarded for improving their performance and lowering their costs, they will make every effort to do that. Such incentives can be either added business or added profit. The government should think in terms of "sharing the benefits" with the supplier to give the supplier an incentive for improving its performance and lowering its cost—and, of course, penalizing the supplier when this doesn't happen. And if the supplier repeatedly doesn't meet its performance or costs measures, then it should simply not be given additional business. Again, in the commercial world "past performance" weighs heavily in source selections, and this should be the case in government procurements as well.

The second area of significant improvement required in the government's way of doing business is to recognize the significant shift from buying goods to buying sophisticated services. Here, the procurements must be "performance based"—i.e., telling the supplier what is needed versus simply thinking of it as buying labor hours at the lowest possible rate, which is the historic basis for time-and-materials contracts). If the government wants a service to be done with high quality, that's what they should ask for, and let the suppliers decide (in their bids) how many people that takes and what quality people it takes to do the job. Then the government has to learn how to manage and oversee such contractors. Giving a job to the private sector does not remove the responsibility from the government to manage and oversee that supplier. The government workforce will require considerable additional training in how to buy and manage sophisticated services and how to create proper incentives for these suppliers such that they are encouraged to continuously improve the quality of their service while lowering their costs.

The third area of focus in the acquisition process is that of the government learning how to properly buy and manage commercial and commercial-like equipment, software, and services. While the passage of FASA and FARA were both intended to encourage the government to buy commercial items or commercial-like items, one clear additional need is to have these amended to include commercial services as well. However, there are still two remaining "barriers" to the purchase of commercial goods or services, namely, the government's practices with regard to intellectual property and specialized cost accounting and auditing. In both cases, there is a need for a change in the government's practices and regulations, but even more importantly for a change in the "culture" with which these two areas are viewed.

In the case of intellectual property, the government has always taken the position that it needs to have drawings and any proprietary information in the event the contractor goes out of business, or suddenly decides to raise its prices unrealistically, or begins to supply poor goods or services. Obviously, the government needs to be given some degree of confidence that none of these things will happen, or that if they do, the government has some recourse. Nonetheless, those provisions can be written into the contract, and the contractor can be assured of retaining its intellectual property as long as those conditions are met. It is a reasonable way of approaching the issue of intellectual property and is the one normally practiced in the private sector. Using standard intellectual property provisions from the private sector, the government can then work closely with commercial suppliers and take full advantage of their higher-quality and lower-cost goods and services.

It's not a legal question; it's a question of mind-set. The government doesn't have to place total trust in the contractor; it simply needs to carefully monitor the results being supplied, and as long as the performance is good and the costs are low, the government has no need to do anything about the intellectual property provided by the contractor. For the government to move in this direction will require significant training of the government workforce and, undoubtedly, some regulatory and legislative reform. Importantly, there is considerable flexibility available in the current regulations, but they need to be rewritten in a clearer form. It should not be necessary for a commercial supplier to have to hire government-contract lawyers to be able to understand the provisions of a contract written by the government. Rather, the government needs to make an effort to attract these commercial suppliers by doing business in their fashion, which was, of course, the intent of the FASA and FARA laws.

Another major area in which a cultural change is required is that associated with the government's *unique* cost accounting and auditing practices. Here the issue is that the very specialized accounting and auditing rules associated with government contracting actually discourage commercial firms from doing business with the government. In fact, a study[10] comparing the costs of building essentially the same items in a factory controlled by government cost accounting and one using normal commercial accounting practices showed about an 18 percent difference in costs. Even more critical—and far more costly to the government—is the fact that most firms aren't willing to pay that extra 18 percent for their commercial work, and therefore simply separate the commercial and government operations. This dramatically increases the government's costs (perhaps by 50 percent or more),[11] because they now supply government items out of a much smaller volume facility, and thus have a much higher overhead cost for the government items. It is this *separation* of commercial and government work, which is both more expensive for the government and results in lower quality work, that is the major barrier that needs to be removed.

It must be repeated here that the reason for the difference in the two accounting systems is primarily that the government wants to account for every dollar spent on every item. The commercial world, however, is interested in reducing the costs of every item supplied, and in many cases is willing to allocate their overhead in different ways to get greater management visibility into their costs and thus reduce their costs still further.

In 1999, a study was done by various government agencies (co-chaired by the General Accounting Office) that made two major recommendations with regard to this problem.[12] First, they recommended that a large number of firms (approximately 40 percent) that were currently required to do business under specialized government accounting practices could, because of their smaller size, be allowed to use "generally accepted accounting principles." This was a significant step forward for the smaller firms. But the actual implementation of this rule has been slow in spreading, because very frequently these smaller firms are subcontractors to the large prime contractors, who, in turn, frequently impose the same requirements on their subcontractors that they have placed on themselves. Nonetheless, the fact that a waiver is allowable is a matter of training both government procurement people and contractor procurement people to apply it.

The second recommendation of the task force was to greatly simplify the government's accounting requirements and, wherever possible, to shift the government's system to utilizing generally accepted accounting practices. Responsibility for making this change rests with the Office of Federal Procurement Policy, and is a necessary step that must be taken to allow and encourage the government to take far greater advantage of commercial suppliers, who otherwise will simply refuse to do government contracting. For example, Hewlett-Packard refuses to take research and development contracts from the Department of Defense because of the specialized accounting and auditing requirements. This is clearly not in the government's interest, but is understandable from Hewlett-Packard's position. Thus, it is the government that must change its practices to encourage such world-class commercial firms to do research and development work with the government.

The last of the major changes that needs to be made in terms of the government's overall acquisition practices is a shift toward *e-business* in its overall supply chain. This requires a total transformation of the processes, not simply a digitizing of the current processes. Clearly, removing paper from the process and putting it all on a computer will improve the accuracy and speed of the current processes, but a far greater gain can be made by taking full advantage of e-business opportunities to *transform* the government's total supply chain management—from the purchasing and finance areas all the way through the inventory, transportation, and logistics support areas. Here the government has ample "demonstration cases" in world-class commercial firms. There is no reason why Wal-Mart, Caterpillar, Federal Express, etc., can efficiently and effectively perform all of the supply chain functions much more accurately and much more rapidly—and at lower cost—than the government can.

The government must take full advantage of commercial software and commercial practices. It will, of course, require the government to change its regulations and practices, and its organizational behavior, to make this change; but there is no question about the benefits that will result or of the need for the government to rapidly move in this direction. Obviously, it will require "up-front" resources, since current processes will have to be continued until the new ones can be brought online. When commercial firms make a transformation of this sort, they do it incrementally, with systems brought online within six-month periods—and usually they pay back the up-front costs within a relatively short time period. This is an area receiving much attention in the new administration, and it should be strongly supported.

Challenge Four: Implementing Competitive Sourcing

Since the mid-1950s it has been federal government policy to rely on the private sector to provide commercial products and services as long as those products or services can be obtained more economically. To implement this policy, and to address the fact that during the long history of the evolution of the federal government many functions that could be done in the private sector were being done in the public sector, a directive coming out of the Office of Management and Budget (known as OMB Circular A-76) has been utilized to perform competitions between the public and private sectors for work that is not considered "inherently governmental." Because, as noted earlier, there has been so much empirical evidence gathered of the improved performance and lower costs that come from such competitions, the Congress required (in the FAIR Act inventories supplied by each of the government agencies), that all those current positions that could be performed by the private sector be clearly identified. In the year 2000 inventory, this came out to be 850,000 federal positions. Therefore, since almost half of the total federal workforce is defined by the agencies themselves as amenable to public/private competitions (and since many believe the number could be even higher), there has been much discussion about improving the process for these public/private competitions. Currently, they tend to take up to two years to run and utilize very considerable government resources in implementing the competition itself, therefore discouraging government agencies from performing the competitions (even though they promise savings in the range of 30 percent, on average).

As currently structured, the A-76 competition compares a number of bids from the public sector with a number of bids from the private sector. While private sector bids are done in the normal competitive environment, the public sector bids are based not upon their current projected costs but upon what they believe they could do with the "most efficient organization." Naturally, cynics ask why they aren't using the most efficient organization already; but when the government's bids come in for the most efficient organization at dramatically lower cost than current costs, it is clear that competition works and that the potential benefits should be utilized.

As expected, there have been difficulties in identifying the "ground rules" for public sector overhead costs, since most public sector operations do not carefully account for all their costs. In fact, one of the great benefits of running the public/private competitions is that when the public sector wins, the government usually requires as part of the win that the public sector implement some form of much greater cost visibility (for example, using activities-based costing or a similar technique), thus providing the necessary cost visibility for improved management within the public sector in the future.

Besides reforming the A-76 competition process so it can be done faster and for less cost, it is also critically important to assure that selection is being done on the basis of "best value"—i.e., a combination of cost and performance—not simply "minimally acceptable performance and lowest possible costs." Clearly, all of the discussion with regard to the enhanced ability of the government to buy sophisticated services applies in the case of the A-76 competition. Also, the government needs to work out ways to make it easier for there to be public/private partnerships in the bidding process wherein a public sector bidder can take full advantage of some of the benefits that the private sector could offer, and vice versa. Finally, when the private sector wins these competitions, they will need added labor force to perform the work, so there needs to be a way to make it easier for the private sector to utilize the public sector workforce. Over all, the objective of these competitions is to gain the full benefit of the innovation and cost savings that come from the process of competition itself, not whether the work is done in the public or private sector.

Challenge Five: Strengthening the Supplier Base

Under ideal conditions, the government would not just be buying commercial items and services, since in many cases the government truly has unique requirements. Instead, it should be buying its unique requirements from an *integrated,* i.e., commercial and government, industrial base for both goods and services. Today there are firms that do work in both sectors, but they tend to do it in separate factories or with separate service organizations, because of the government's unique way of doing business. Thus, the small volume of government business has to carry a much larger share of overhead than it would in an operation that was integrated—not at the corporate accounting level but at the "factory floor" and at the service worker level. The benefits to the government of such an integrated operation are numerous. They include:

- Far lower costs to the government
- More rapid application of state-of-the-art technology to the government's applications
- Higher quality of goods and services (because of the application of best practices to the higher-volume commercial work)
- Broadening of the supplier base for the government (rather than being limited solely to the government-unique suppliers or divisions of large corporations)
- Greater "surge" potential in periods of crisis (either natural or man-made)
- Greatly enhanced support services (because of the worldwide operations and large support staffs associated with the commercial activities)

To be able to realize these benefits, the government must change many of its practices—from unique procurement and design requirements to specialized cost accounting practices—and must utilize equipment and services that come from normal commercial operations, with commercial parts, subsystems, and commercial support systems. For example, even though the end items may well be government-unique, they still have to be capable of being built on commercial production lines.

This concept is particularly applicable today, because of the dramatic changes that have taken place in commercial production operations—with the shift to "flexible manufacturing." In this process, as different assemblies come down the production line, the computer knows which one is coming next, and it instructs the flexible machine tools to insert the right parts at the right spot for whatever that unique item is. Thus, as long as the *process* is similar, the items can be different. This lends itself to government-unique items being built on commercial production lines. In fact, it goes so far that not only would the concept cover different electronics subassemblies, but you could even use a large rotary forge, for example, to make both cannons and railroad-car wheel axles.

Since this integrated operation is clearly the direction the commercial world is moving to achieve efficiency and effectiveness for differentiated products, one needs to look carefully at the current *barriers to integration* created by government business practices and how these can be removed. Fortunately, in recent years the government has started to address many of these barriers, but there is still a long way to go. Specifically, the five principal barriers are:

- *"Requirements" differences.* The fact that the commercial world uses the evolutionary, or spiral, development process means the government's "requirements" will have to change correspondingly. Similarly, since the commercial world uses *cost,* along with performance, as principal design considerations means that the government will need to place more emphasis on cost as a "requirement."
- *Unique cost accounting and auditing practices.* As noted earlier, this is a great concern to commercial operations, but it can be eliminated through changes in government practices and policies, including the commercial concerns about "criminalization" due to unintentional, improper administrative charges.
- *Specialized standards or specifications.* The government should not tell the supplier how to do things, but simply define what is desired in terms of performance and let the supplier use the best commercial practices to achieve it.
- *Unique government procurement laws and regulations.* Examples include unique provisions that require any item purchased off-shore to have bought its "specialty metals" within the United States, or other such special provisions in law that apply only to government procurements (as contrasted to commercial procurements).
- *Unique government support requirements.* One example is requiring the use of government maintenance operations instead of the normal commercial warranty provisions.

Each of these barriers needs to be addressed one by one and removed if the government is to successfully achieve the quality, timeliness, and lower costs of commercial products in future procurements.

Recommendations for Realizing the Vision

Recommendations: Transforming the Acquisition Workforce

Changing the government's acquisition workforce is not a quick or easy thing to do. Yet it is necessary to begin immediately to do so because of the looming "human capital crisis."[13] Of course, recognition of this *crisis* is the first step in aggressively attacking the problem.

1. Create a strategic human resource plan.

A critical step for each agency is the identification of its future strategic human resource needs and the development of a detailed plan to acquire the capabilities needed over the coming years.[14] This strategic plan would naturally recognize the fact that many of the skills required in the future are not the same as those which the organization needed in the past. Partly, this is a reflection of the changing nature of government (for example, from the "manager of supplies" to "the manager of suppliers") and, partly, there is a recognition of the new or strengthened skills that the workforce must have in areas such as management and leadership, operations research, information technology, etc.

2. Implement a set of specific human resource transformation actions.

With these future needs identified, and with the recognition of the large turnover expected as a result of retirements over the next few years, a specific set of actions are required:

- Aggressive recruiting—focused on challenging job content, personal responsibilities, the value of public service, and the career opportunities being offered
- Streamlined hiring—to compete with the private sector, which can make offers in a short period of time versus the government's lengthy process
- "Over hiring" (i.e., temporarily exceeding allowable headcounts) as long as it is within budget—to address the fact that government positions are frequently understaffed, because the selection process doesn't begin until someone leaves, often resulting in a six-month dead time
- Career planning—to greatly encourage retention of high-quality people (for example, through job enrichment, education rotation, and promotion)
- Greatly increased training—especially in the skills required to keep up with technology and allow career advancement
- Job rotations and cross-discipline training—for broadening of career advancement opportunities and better teamwork within the organization
- Enhanced quality-of-life changes for the workforce—such as allowing family visits on extended remote stays
- Far greater salary flexibility—especially for critical skills (such as information technology)
- And, most important, the provision of resources within agencies' budgets to cover each of these activities

3. Carry out a set of human resource innovation demonstrations.

To achieve all of these changes in a short time will require a great deal of leadership and innovation. Fortunately, because of the growing recognition of the need, there have been some recent "experiments" approved. For example, Congress has encouraged the Department of Defense to experiment with alternative personnel management concepts for its acquisition workforce. Under the Office of Personnel Policy purview, a five-year project has been initiated that has as its objectives:

- Gaining greater managerial control/authority over personnel processes down to the lowest levels
- Linking employee pay to employee contributions
- Achieving a flexible/responsive personnel system
- Attracting, motivating, and retaining a high-quality acquisition workforce

In this experimental system, managers are allowed to make reassignments that do not require formal personnel actions. Managers can also set pay based upon their assessment of the employee's contribution. Thus, employees who make significant contributions can move ahead rapidly and receive larger pay increases, while those who don't and/or are already overpaid for their relative contribution would get significantly less increases (and, in some cases, zero if they are already overpaid). Thus, the total compensation budget doesn't change, but simply moves dollars away from low contributors and gives it to high contributors. The experimental process does allow for some increases in the total pool as a result of the bonus process. In general, it gives managers much more responsibility over job descriptions, as well as compensation for new and current employees, relating all to the employee's contributions.

For this experimental program (or "demonstration" program), Congress actually allowed it to be applied to 95,000 people. However, participation was voluntary, and initially only 5,083 participants signed up. (It was opposed by the government unions.) After the first round of evaluations, the experiment achieved the desired objectives—namely, there was a differentiation between the high contributors and the low contributors (in contrast to the historic system that tended to simply increase everyone for having lived another year). Also, as expected, those who didn't get any significant increase protested that they were "unfairly" treated. Obviously, the system will take a while to get used to, but it appears to not only be demonstrating the desired objectives but gaining far broader acceptance. One clear action will be to work more closely with the unions in the future. In general, demonstrations of this sort should be greatly expanded not only within the Department of Defense but within other government agencies as well.

Another "demonstration" of a direction in which the government needs to move is the initiation of an innovative *internship* program to bring new talent into the federal acquisition workforce by an inter-agency procurement executives council, in conjunction with the Department of the Interior University. The first class of 12 interns was inducted into the Government-Wide Acquisition Management Intern program in July 2000. A year later, these interns were interviewed[15] and were found to be extremely stimulated by the challenges and rewards of their jobs. In fact, one of the interns was quoted as saying: "This is the most rewarding job I have held. The federal government has proven to be employee-friendly and proactive." Again, programs of this sort need to be greatly expanded if they are to truly have an impact on the overall federal workforce.

Other innovations which should be considered include a public/private interchange program, wherein employees from the private and public sectors would exchange jobs for a two-year period, with employees keeping their salaries and benefits. This would form an excellent educational program for both parties. Or consider creating new entry points into the government for career employees who enter at a mid-career point from the private sector (either for-profit or nonprofit firms). Still another area for exploration would be that of hiring employees for a pre-determined term period—for example, three years. That way, people could come into the government and apply their knowledge from industry for a few years—eliminating any direct conflict-of-interest issues—and then return to industry after their government service. A program of this sort did exist in the 1960s and 1970s to bring scientists and engineers into the government for three-year periods (under something known as PL-313).

One way to expand the current short-term employee program is to use the one that now exists for bringing in people from the nonprofit and university sector (known as the Intergovernmental Personnel Act) and expand that to allow people to come from the private sector. All of these are simply examples of innovations that should, and must, be considered with the changing nature of America's workforce and the government's need for a new and diverse group of skills.

4. Create an overall "learning culture."

Finally, the most critical step is to create a "learning culture" wherein it is recognized that the technology and the nature of the work is continuously changing, and that it is necessary for government workers to have some form of *continuing education* to be current with the latest best practices. The Department of Defense has specified that all those in its acquisition workforce shall have a total of 80 hours of continuing education within every two-year period. For this to occur, of course, means that tuition reimbursement funds must be available. Another way to create a significant "learning culture" is through a "phased retirement" program. Rather than retire, government workers would agree to work part-time and new employees (at much lower salaries) would be hired on a full-time basis, so that the total cost for both matches the current level. In this way, new workers can be trained by those with experience, allowing a transfer of knowledge and much more rapid learning by the young. With computer-based learning today, it is possible, as long as the software programs are available, for a great deal more continuous learning by the entire workforce without having to send people off to school for extended periods.

Over all, there is no more valuable investment that the federal government can make than to put aside adequate resources for its workforce of the future. Clearly, the recommendations offered will have some initial costs, but they will be more than paid back in the coming years.

Recommendations: Changing the "Requirements" and Budget Process

In this area, most of the institutional changes that are required are nominally in place. The big problem is the cultural changes that are needed so that the people specifying what the government should buy and those budgeting for it can learn to think in a commercial fashion and in terms of commercial cycle times.

1. Implement a commercial-like requirement process.

In the requirements process, not only does the government need to consider cost as a major part of the requirement (along with performance) but they need to do much more market analysis to determine what technologies have been proven and then apply them as they come along—in an evolutionary (or spiral) fashion. This allows much more rapid deployment of state-of-the-art techniques and technologies, lower total costs, and lower risks for new items and new types of services.

2. Take a "customer's" perspective.

Similarly, the government needs to think of these new services and products from a *customer's* perspective, not only in terms of the supplier's or the government's perspective. Thus, for example, when specifying the new e-government systems, it is absolutely essential that government procurers put themselves in the position of the consumer, or the user, rather than of the government people who are supplying these goods and services.

3. Emphasize short products realization cycles.

Then, to be responsive to the short product-realization cycles from the commercial world (for example, in terms of 18-month technology cycles), the government needs to be able to plan and budget for changes much more rapidly. This requires far greater flexibility in the budgeting process. For example, one might budget for a likely future change in a system or a service without knowing precisely, three years in advance, what that change will be, but with total confidence that a future change will be required because the technology in that area or the mission need in that area will be evolving very rapidly.

4. Budget only for "likely" costs.

Lastly, it is absolutely essential that the government place greater emphasis on the importance of *cost realism* in its budgeting process, because the cost to the government of under-budgeting is incredibly high. Under-budgeting impacts not just the single under-budgeted program, but all of the others from which it then has to steal money.

Clearly, for the transformation of the government's overall acquisition process, it is necessary to develop a very close working relationship in each agency between the requirements process, the budget process, and the acquisition process. This interrelationship is absolutely critical for success in the government's realization of its acquisition vision for the 21st century.

Recommendations: Using Commercialization and Market Forces to Reform the Acquisition Processes

1. Fully utilize commercial best practices.

The emphasis on "commercialization" and use of market forces is not exclusively intended to focus on greater private sector activities for government functions; rather, it is intended for all activities—public and private— to be geared much more to commercial best practices. This includes such things as "benchmarking," use of proven technology, and, most importantly, extensive use of *competition* to gain the benefits of innovation for higher performance while at the same time reducing costs. All activities, again public or private, should be geared toward enhancing performance with greater efficiency. And the measure of successful performance is that associated with the customer's (or user's) satisfaction.

2. Maximize competitive sourcing for all non-inherently governmental work.

In the case of current public sector work, it is desirable to emphasize the importance of all work that is not inherently governmental being done in a competitive fashion. In some cases, this may be competition between multiple public sector activities, and in many cases it will be between different private sector activities. But there will certainly be a number of examples of public/private competitions for much of the work that is now being done (sole source) by the government, but could be done in a competitive fashion (either in competitions involving teams partnering with the private sector or in direct competition with the private sector).

3. Emphasize "continuous improvement."

The key to overall reform of the acquisition process within the government is the concept of *continuous improvement*. This is a mind-set in which "good enough" is not good enough. It also recognizes that the old paradigm of assuming that to get higher performance you had to pay more is no longer valid. As the commercial world has demonstrated, it is possible to get higher performance at lower cost through innovation and process changes. Recognition of this paradigm shift and striving to continuously improve the government's acquisition process (whether it be in the public or private portion) must be the objective of a transformed acquisition process.

Recommendations: Shifting to Electronic Supply Chain Management

1. Focus on process change.

The use of e-business by the government *can* represent a dramatic change in the way the government does its business, but to have a significant impact requires a transformation of the government's processes rather than simply a digitization of the current systems. By the year 2005 it is estimated that e-government spending for the federal government alone will reach $2.3 billion.[16] Obviously, when one considers that the total government purchases of goods and services will exceed hundreds of billions of dollars, the impact of e-business can be dramatic. For example, the purchasing department of the Australian Department of Natural Resources and Environment reported a 70 percent efficiency improvement after deploying an e-business system.[17] In 1998 the Government Paperwork Elimination Act was passed, requiring governmental agencies to provide the ability for those dealing with them to complete electronic transactions, and to use electronic signatures by October 21, 2003. This provides a "forcing function" for the federal government to accelerate its use of e-commerce in all of its future transactions.

2. Provide for privacy and security.

As would be expected, the most critical aspect of this shift to e-commerce for the government is the need for *privacy and security* in all of its systems. Since the Internet was initially designed to be an open and free system, the subsequent introduction of privacy and security concerns has been somewhat of an afterthought. It has only recently become a major consideration in the design of the architectures that the commercial world has been introducing, and, subsequently (with a significant lag in time), that the government has been introducing. Thus, it is important, as the government now is accelerating its use of e-commerce, that it pays particular attention to privacy and security. Needless to say, this will add some complexity and cost to the system, but in view of the dramatic savings and improved performance that will be realized, the small increase in cost and complexity are more than warranted.

3. Provide leadership and resources.

As with other areas associated with transforming the government's way of doing business, it will be necessary to overcome the very significant resistance that is likely to be seen when introducing e-commerce into the government acquisition processes. And it will be absolutely necessary to provide adequate resources, up front, to pay for the initial investments (including training) that these changes require—with the obvious intent that they be paid back in a very short period of time as a result of the enormous improvements in service and reductions in cost that will come about from their introduction. Over all, the introduction of e-commerce in the government's acquisition processes will clearly shift the power of buying activities from the suppliers to the buyers, and the government's benefit to this leverage will be enormous.

Recommendations: Integrating Commercial/Government Suppliers

One of the largest quality and cost gains that could be made in the acquisition process is the government's ability to draw on a far broader industrial base of suppliers for goods and services, particularly if it can draw on an *integrated* industrial base of corporations that supply—*from the same operation*—both the high-volume commercial world and the government's needs, which are usually of much smaller volume. As noted earlier, the benefit of this integrated operation is that the government gains the overhead absorption from the high-volume commercial business and also gains the state-of-the-art technology and high quality associated with commercial firms, which have to compete on a worldwide basis. Initial demonstrations of what an integrated operation can do tended to yield savings in the 30 to 50 percent range with high-quality, state-of-the-art products and services. Ten actions are specifically required to transform the supplier base of the government into an integrated one:

1. Create incentives for the government (program managers and acquisition executives) to utilize commercial firms rather than government-unique firms.

The best mechanisms for creating these incentives include allowing waivers of unique government requirements; requiring competition on all goods and services; making unit costs and support costs firm requirements; making integrated operations a key selection criterion; utilizing warranties for reliability and maintenance; and utilizing "price-based" versus cost-based developments.

2.   Create incentives for the prime contractor to integrate its operations and to utilize commercial suppliers.

The federal government should directly address legislative, regulatory, and other unique government barriers that currently exist. For example, specialized cost accounting standards waivers should be greatly expanded to include common fabrication as being "commercial in nature." Issues to be addressed include the current intellectual property practices of the government, the practices on civil false claims such that the criminalization threat is removed unless obviously warranted, and the issue of commercial parts obsolescence by assuring that suppliers develop interchangeable next-generation parts. Finally, for those few items that simply have to be done on a cost-based contracting arrangement, the implementation of greatly streamlined accounting standards consistent with generally accepted accounting practices and written in a language that the commercial supplier can understand would help to partially remove this barrier.

3.   Create incentives for commercial suppliers themselves to be interested in making the effort to do business with the government rather than being discouraged, as they are now.

Utilize the common commercial practice of fixed-price, incremental development contracts (i.e., based on "best efforts") rather than the current government practice of cost-based development contracts, which require the contractor to establish unique government accounting systems. But also recognize that some of these developments may be long term and, therefore, utilize milestone billings as a way to minimize the cost of borrowing to fund these developments. It is particularly important that the focus of the government be on the *price* it pays for the service or goods acquired, rather than on the profit that the contractor makes on the delivery. This is an incentive for the contractors to continuously lower their prices to the government, since if they can lower the total price, then the government should not be really interested in what share of it goes to their profits—and the presence of continuous competition will assure that the profits are not exorbitant.

4.   Encourage the prime contractors to shift from a "make" decision for their subsystems to a "buy," but allow them to have a "management fee" for assuming this responsibility.

In this way the prime contractor becomes primarily a "systems integrator" of subsystems that can come from integrated factories. Additionally, reward the prime contractors on a multi-year basis if they achieve plant consolidations of their commercial and government work. Finally, since there is a general shift of government purchases from products to services, if these are broadly defined, then the prime contractors can make, as a part of their business, the full provision of the services that they provide—from development through deployment, support, and updating.

5. Attract commercial suppliers.

Since their markets are based on the combination of performance and costs, it is essential that the government do its buying on the basis of "best value" and that one of the major "requirements" for any goods and services explicitly addresses not only the desired performance but also the desired cost. If these requirements specifically are geared to mission (versus product) requirements, then the suppliers will be able to figure out the best way to satisfy that need rather than being forced to use a government-specified solution. Thus, changing the requirements process is critical to achieving an effective and efficient solution to the government's mission needs.

6. Shift to modern support processes.

For most goods and services that the government procures, the major share of the costs is not in the initial acquisition but rather in the maintenance and support of the equipment. Thus, the government needs to transform its logistics operations utilizing world-class processes. A commercial firm that is competitive will be using these processes. Thus, if the government's acquisition focuses on it (for example, with warranties), then it will attract not only the world-class suppliers but it will achieve the desired world-class performance at far lower costs for their logistics and support requirements.

7. Move all processes to e-business.

World-class commercial suppliers are moving heavily to e-business for their full supply chain. If the government moves to a similar system, then it will have the market visibility into all commercial items and suppliers, thus providing it with a far broader set of suppliers and greater competition for high performance at low cost. Additionally, if the e-commerce systems utilized are linked to the corporation's internal systems on an interoperable basis, then the government would have access to such information as existing inventories, lead times for deliveries, etc.—again, things that the commercial world is now utilizing. This action would clearly encourage corporations to integrate their commercial and government business, but it would require changes in the government's practices, as well as, in some cases, changes in regulations and laws.

8. Emphasize, and fund, education and training.

A key element of the cultural shift in the government toward utilizing an integrated industrial supply base is a focus on education and training of the workforce—both in the government and industry. This would include a demonstration of the benefits and opportunities, as well as the techniques required to overcome the barriers to integration. It would also include education on commercial practices from design, through integrated production, through support.

9. Demonstrate the benefits of integration.

A critical element of the education and training process is the analytic basis for demonstrating that the integrated operations provide enormous benefits to the government. Thus, full-cost comparisons are required on a case-by-case basis to see the potential benefits of an integrated (versus a separate) supplier base. Since what is required is basically a "cultural change," it will be necessary to *demonstrate* the benefits that can be achieved and how to go about achieving them.

10. Gain widespread high-level support.

It will be necessary to educate the Congress as well as the senior career members and political appointees of the administration on the benefits and required actions associated with achieving an integrated (commercial and government) supplier base. Here again, case-by-case examples will prove invaluable. But, as with any cultural change of this magnitude, significant resistance should be expected—and it is likely to come from those firms that have been doing government business in the past, but cannot compete on a "world-class" basis.

Conclusion

Perhaps, disappointingly, there is no "silver bullet" to achieving the required change in the way the government does its business to achieve the desired long-term effectiveness and efficiency. Rather, a *total transformation* is required in many areas. Specifically, each of the four areas covered in the report—*Who does the buying? What do they buy? How do they buy? From whom do they buy?*—all require numerous changes. And it is the sum of these, and particularly their interrelationship, that will result in the broad cultural change that is necessary.

The hardest part will be recognition that there are bound to be some (hopefully rare) cases of waste, fraud, or abuse. These must be treated as "special cases," since they will be statistically rare—i.e., outside of the "Six Sigma" coverage of a high-quality process. And, thus, they must be dealt with as special cases, rather than the traditional practice of writing more regulations and more encompassing rules to bog down the overall acquisition process. If there are examples of waste or abuse, then the system needs to explicitly address them with process correction, so that they won't recur. And if there are examples of fraud, the culprits should be jailed and/or blacklisted and fined. The key issue is not to end up with a full set of specialized rules and regulations for government work that would isolate the government from *best practices* in the commercial world. The government needs to be a "world-class" buyer of common and/or specialized goods and services—but *not* an inefficient or ineffective differentiated buyer of needed goods and services.

To make such a broad change requires strong *leadership* from the acquisition community and a very real sense of *urgency*. The steps for such a transformation are unambiguous. First, set a clear vision. Then, align and motivate the full workforce, so they understand the benefits and understand the actions they, individually, must take to achieve this vision. Then, reward the risk takers and publicize the success stories. There must be a continuous and aggressive repetition of the message. Everyone must understand it, and they must become active participants in the transformation. Finally, it will require close working relationships with the Congress and the press, so that the actions being taken and the positive results being achieved are clearly understood by all—and strongly supported by the legislative branch as well as the executive branch.

The overall objective is to gain public confidence in the government and its ability to effectively and efficiently perform its missions. Key elements in this are the recognition of the changing role of the government in the governance process and the impact that this has on the acquisition workforce. It also means a shift in resource expenditures, and a shift in focus from internal infrastructure activities to external mission and customer focus. Clearly, as part of this shift the government must take advantage of modern technologies—such as e-commerce—in order to change the processes, to open up the processes, and to more effectively serve the "customers." Finally, it is necessary for the government to define its true needs and utilize *performance* contracting—with adequate *incentives* for suppliers to achieve the required mission need rather than being told "how to do it."

The magnitude of this transformation is large; therefore, it will take significant time and effort for its achievement. *Consistency* of message is essential. The process has begun and is well under way. Now the challenge is to maintain the momentum and accelerate it so that, in fact, the government is able to achieve the following vision: *A highly skilled and innovative government acquisition workforce, buying high-quality, low-cost goods and services in an efficient and effective fashion from high-quality, low-cost innovative suppliers, with a process that has total public confidence and trust.*

Endnotes

1. "Long-Run Costs and Performance Effects of Competitive Sourcing" (Alexandria, Va.: Center for Naval Analysis, Fall 2001).

2. For example, see Jacques S. Gansler, *Affording Defense* (Cambridge, Mass.: MIT Press, 1989), pp. 195-207.

3. "The Pentagon Finally Learns to Shop," *Fortune,* December 1998.

4. Kimberly A. Harokopus, "Transforming Government: Creating the New Defense Procurement System" (Arlington, Va.: The PricewaterhouseCoopers Endowment for The Business of Government, April 2000).

5. "Update," Acquisitions Solutions, Inc., May 2001.

6. "Small Business Trends in Federal Procurement in the 1990s," GAO-01-119 (Washington, D.C.: General Accounting Office, 2001).

7. Steven Barr, "Federal Diary," *Washington Post,* September 5, 2001.

8. Thomas Dungan III, in *Memos to the President* edited by Mark A. Abramson (Rowman & Littlefield Publishers, Inc., 2001), p. 49.

9. "The President's Management Agenda" for fiscal year 2002 (Washington, D.C.: Office of Management and Budget, 2001).

10. "The DoD Regulatory Cost Premium: A Quantitative Assessment" (Coopers & Lybrand/The Analytic Sciences Corp. [TASC], December 1994). The study looked at a comparison of costs of government contract work with commercial work in the same factories.

11. This is based on an Air Force experiment in which identical electronic assemblies were built in two different operations, and the costs decreased by 50-70 percent for the commercially integrated line.

12. "Future Role of the Cost Accounting Standards Board." Prepared for Congress by the Cost Accounting Standards Board Review Panel (Washington, D.C., April 2, 1999).

13. Paul C. Light, "The New Public Service" (Washington, D.C.: Brookings Institute Press, 1999).

14. A number of the ideas contained in this discussion come from "The Acquisition Work Force 2005 Task Force Final Report: Shaping the Civilian Acquisition Work Force of the Future," Under Secretary of Defense (Acquisition, Technology and Logistics), and the Under Secretary of Defense (Personnel and Readiness) (October 2000).

15. *Federal Times,* July 30, 2001.

16. Janine S. Hiller and France Bélanger, "Private Strategies for Electronic Government" (Arlington, Va.: The PricewaterhouseCoopers Endowment for The Business of Government, January 2001).

17. M. Symonds, "Government and the Internet: No Gain Without Pain," *The Economist,* June 24, 2000, pp. 9-14.

CHAPTER THREE

The Procurement Partnership Model: Moving to a Team-Based Approach

Kathryn G. Denhardt
School of Urban Affairs and Public Policy
and Institute for Public Administration
University of Delaware

This report was originally published in February 2003.

Understanding the New Reality of Procurement

In the past, the government procurement process started with specifying exactly—and in excruciating detail—what the contractor was to do. Writing the specifications usually took months and gave rise to a request for proposals (RFP) that only a mother could love. The vendor who was awarded the contract was responsible for delivering what was *specified,* whether or not it turned out to be what was *needed.*

Today, procurement is more likely to start with specifying objectives that need to be achieved or work that needs to be done. The "new" RFP is likely to describe the destination, not the route or the means of transportation. The government project manager no longer waits at the destination for the vendor to deliver. Instead, the project manager and the vendor make the journey together. The journey can be rough, with both the vendor and the project manager arriving at the destination bloodied and angry, having resolved never to travel together again. But, increasingly, government administrators and vendors are finding ways to work together that resemble a collaborative partnership, not a battle. When they get to the destination, they celebrate the achievement together, laughing about the arguments and rough spots they had along the way. They might even look forward to making another trip together.

This chapter focuses on those success stories. It is based on dozens of confidential interviews with project managers, procurement professionals, and contractors who found ways to work together effectively to get where they needed to go. (Throughout this chapter, quotes from these interviews are indented and not attributed to specific individuals.) In addition to the interviews, findings are based on a wide range of materials related to the issue of government contracting, including *Government Executive* magazine's 2000, 2001, and 2002 winners of the Business Solutions in the Public Interest Award competition,[1] the final report of the Commercial Activities Panel entitled *Improving the Sourcing Decisions of the Government* (April 2002),[2] recent contracting-related reports published by the IBM Endowment for The Business of Government,[3] and reports of the General Accounting Office (GAO).[4] What they learned along the way suggests a new partnership procurement model that works. Understanding this model, and the lessons learned as it was emerging, can help future contracting relationships be more successful and productive.

Government, no less than the private sector, is eager to put available knowledge to work in solving problems, making decisions, and taking action. New ways of doing things need to be discovered. Public management reform efforts of the past decade have demanded that government achieve outcomes more efficiently and effectively and that it do so with fewer public employees. Thus, the government is increasingly eager to capitalize on the knowledge, resources, and experience of those outside government. In fiscal year 2001, the federal government acquired $109 billion in vendor services related to information technology (IT) and professional, administrative, and management support services. But according to William T. Woods, GAO's director of acquisition and sourcing management, it was money that was "not always well spent."[5] Ensuring that the money is well spent in the future is the challenge before all those involved in the contracting process.

Contracting became increasingly complex as government began to contract for solutions and knowledge, not for specific material goods or standardized services.[6] The new contracts are nonroutine, start with many more unknowns, and take unexpected turns as a project unfolds. These efforts require thinking through complex issues, putting together information from disparate sources, and trying out new ideas or innovative solutions for which results are uncertain. Many times the efforts require bringing together capabilities from across organizational boundaries in government and across the public, private, and nonprofit sectors. Achieving one objective, such as the U.S. Census Bureau conducting the 2000 census, might require dozens of contracts with multiple vendors.

> [F]or the 2000 census, 25-year bureau veteran Michael Longini decided the bureau could not do all the work on its own and do it well, particularly on the technology side of operations.... The census comes hard, comes fast, and comes once, says Longini, chief of the bureau's Decennial Systems and Contracts Management Office. The decennial census is the federal government's largest peacetime effort, requiring the establishment of more than 500 temporary offices and the hiring of 800,000 temporary employees.... Along with the Census Promotions Office, which was handling an advertising contract, the Decennial Systems Office was preparing to do $1 billion in business.[7]

This effort demanded a procurement process that would accommodate uncertainties and a project management approach that would encourage collaborative partnerships between the government and vendors. In addition, the process had to be one that allowed for the speed and flexibility necessary to get everything done in a timely manner, since the Constitution does not allow for delays in meeting the deadlines: April 1 for completing the census and December 31 of the same year for reporting the results.

The Census Bureau accomplished this by developing a contracting culture based on the assumption that "close relationships with contractors could reduce the risk of failure."[8] There was daily communication between the bureau and vendors, where both progress and problems were discussed freely and solutions were developed in partnership. "The bureau's contracting specialists and program managers worked side by side, rather than in different offices."[9]

This team approach—between contract specialists and program managers within the bureau, and within the complex working relationships of the bureau and its various vendors— served the bureau well. Both the bureau and the vendors recognized and appreciated the difference made by this team approach. Everyone was focused on the same mission. A program manager for the census data capture reflected on the relationships this way: "Everyone had shared problems, the same timelines, the same goals."[10] The experience differed noticeably from that of a decade earlier when the Census Bureau "so distrusted contractors that they rarely outsourced any work.... In the rare instances when Census did outsource, Bureau officials and contractors regularly faced off in bid protests and in finger-pointing over who was responsible for frequent contract failures."[11] The Census Bureau made this dramatic shift by changing the culture of contracting within the bureau, as well as the structural and interpersonal relationships with vendors. Much can be learned from its experience, as well as the successes other federal agencies have achieved by making similar changes.

Procurement Reforms

The Census Bureau's experience during the 2000 census is representative of the large-scale changes that have been occurring in federal procurement. In response to the problems and failures of past contracting practices, the federal government initiated significant contracting and procurement reforms in recent years. Steven Kelman, former head of the Office of Federal Procurement Policy (OFPP) and now at Harvard's Kennedy School of Government, recently summarized the most important reforms in this way:

- *Streamlining*—purchasing cards, simplified vehicles such as government-wide acquisition contracts (GWACs) and blanket purchase agreements, page limitations on supplier proposals, and reducing the number of evaluation criteria in a solicitation
- *Best value*—government's current use of past performance of a supplier in making source selection decisions (rather than selecting the lowest bid); introduction of innovations such as share-in-savings contracts and award term contracts that reward outstanding performance of suppliers by extending the contract's duration
- *Commercial items*—the move by the Department of Defense (DoD) toward purchasing commercially available food items instead of using "MilSpecs" that demand unique products for military purchase; FASA's [Federal Acquisition Streamlining Act of 1994] elimination of many onerous oversight requirements for subcontractors

- *Government-industry cooperation*—the changes in the Federal Acquisition Regulation (FAR) Part 15 in order to permit one-on-one meetings between government and potential bidders during the early stages of the procurement process, and to encourage a relationship with suppliers built on trust and a shared mission rather than on distrust and severely limited communication[12]

In addition to those reforms, *performance-based contracting* became increasingly important at all levels of government,[13] and federal procurement policy strongly encourages using this approach to contracting. FAR 2.101 states that performance-based contracting means "structuring all aspects of an acquisition around the purpose of the work to be performed with the contract requirements set forth in clear, specific, objective terms with measurable outcomes as opposed to either the manner by which the work is to be performed or broad and imprecise statements of work."

Though performance-based contracting has been a policy of the federal government for nearly two decades, implementation of it had been exceedingly slow. In January 2002, an interagency-industry partnership published *Seven Steps to Performance-Based Services Acquisition* in order to "make the subject of PBSC [performance-based service contracting] accessible for all and shift the paradigm from traditional 'acquisition think' into one of collaborative performance-oriented teamwork with a focus on program performance and improvement, not simply contract compliance."[14] The "virtual guide" to performance-based contracting lays out the following seven steps:

- Establish an integrated solutions team
- Describe the problem that needs solving
- Examine private-sector and public-sector solutions
- Develop a performance work statement (PWS) or statement of objectives (SOO)
- Decide how to measure and manage performance
- Select the right contractor
- Manage performance

The importance of focusing on performance and outcomes was certainly a theme that ran through the interviews conducted for this study. Government needs to contract for help in *finding solutions,* not for a vendor to deliver solutions previously specified in the contract. This shift in focus means significant changes in the nature of contracts, necessitating a greater variety of contracting vehicles oriented to the nature of the project.

Needing to contract for expertise to help integrate and simplify its tangled mass of IT systems, the federal government's Office of Federal Student Aid (FSA) needed to work in partnership with the contractor if there was to be any hope of achieving success. The partnership FSA formed with a contractor in March 2000 was based on an innovative share-in-savings contract. The contractor assumes most of the up-front costs of modernizing FSA's loan-servicing computer systems; then each year it receives a declining percentage of the resulting savings in operating costs.[15]

In fiscal year 1999, FSA's operating costs for servicing 1.8 million direct student loans was $20.3 million. By working with the contractor to get rid of duplicative functions and by streamlining the central data system, FSA expects to bring operating costs down to $9.1 million by 2005. FSA will use its share of the savings to speed up its agency-wide computer systems modernization, so it too had a major incentive to work as a team with the contractor to achieve the goals of the project. Together, FSA and the contractor finished the project in eight months. One judge who helped select this procurement as one of the 2001 Business Solutions in the Public Interest awards said, "It took courage for FSA to tune out critics and move forward to tackle a contracting project using a concept that did not have a proven track record in the government."[16]

The Partnership Approach

Procurement reforms and new contracting vehicles have provided a variety of new options and tools. But according to those interviewed for this project, it is the partnership among the people working on the contract that makes a contract successful or unsuccessful, not the contracting vehicle. Many government managers and the consultants they work with are still struggling to build collaborative partnerships. The culture of procurement in many agencies has not moved away from the environment of distrust and rigid rules. Here are a few observations from those interviewed that might cast some light on why change has been slow.

> The rules have changed but the "legends" persist. I can't tell you how many times I've heard procurement officers and even agency counsels say that multi-year contracts aren't possible, when clearly the rules do permit such arrangements. Obviously we need a lot more training.

> I left the procurement ranks because my peers didn't want to change. They were too comfortable with the old way of doing things.

> We still find program offices resistant to truly competitive and performance-based contracts. It is difficult to change the culture.

Candid insights such as these were offered in confidential interviews with highly regarded professionals in government procurement and program offices, as well as contractors with track records of success in complex government contracts. Their views were corroborated by analyzing award-winning acquisitions and by the findings of such disparate sources as the General Accounting Office (which provides independent research-based critiques from within the federal government) and the Professional Services Council (which advocates for the consulting industry doing business with government). The perspectives from these sources were different, but the conclusions were amazingly similar:

- The contract vehicles now available for federal government procurement provide adequate flexibility to meet the needs of the changing contracting environment. The secret to success, however, is in implementing them with a spirit of partnership and trust.

- The right people need to be in leadership positions. For both the government and the contractor, this means having a single executive leader with the power and authority to make crucial decisions on the project, and they need to be individuals who are willing to stake their career and reputation on making the project successful.

- Procurement officers and program managers need to work together as a team from the beginning of a project. Once the contractor(s) have been selected, a team-based approach needs to be continued throughout the project in order to achieve the desired outcomes.

- Knowledge of contracting options and best practices in procurement and project management are not sufficiently well known throughout the federal workforce and among contractors. This problem can be alleviated only through an investment in training.

- While excellent examples of successful contracting are available, the culture of procurement cannot yet be described as having embraced the values and methods represented in those successes. Cultural change will take more time and effort.

Details of these findings and examples of successes are described in greater depth in the remainder of this chapter. It is in the interest of all the relevant communities—procurement professionals, program managers, and contractors—to work together to bring about these changes. Most certainly, it is in the interest of taxpayers and the general public that these changes happen so that we can all work more effectively and efficiently in addressing the most challenging problems of society. We rely on government to serve these public interests, but we cannot ask government to engage these problems alone. This chapter outlines ways in which we can improve the ability of government to provide innovative, high-quality, cost-effective, and timely services or solutions to problems.

New Contracting Vehicles

The variety of contracting vehicles available to government has expanded during this recent procurement reform era. With the right people involved, all these vehicles can incorporate both a performance-based management orientation and a partnership approach. But each contracting vehicle has characteristics that make it more or less appropriate for a given situation.

Share-in-savings contracts (such as the FSA contract described previously) can be used when contracting for the reengineering of a business process that will substantially reduce costs for the government over time. In some cases, the vendor makes the up-front capital investment and realizes return on investment over a one- to three-year period following the reengineering. The agency pays the vendor through savings from what the agency would have spent under the old system and keeps a share of the savings itself.

Commercial item purchase or service contracts are used for the purchase of items or services available on the commercial market rather than specially developed for the government. Such contracts are appropriate in order to reap the price benefits of competition among multiple providers and to allow immediate purchase of widely accessible products and services. Purchasing commercial items avoids the problematic issue of intellectual property rights that arises when vendors develop solutions for government that also have a commercial value to the vendor. These intellectual property issues present a significant barrier to successful partnerships between government and the vendor, and may be avoided by using commercial items and services. Purchasing commercial items usually results in more timely delivery as well.

Government-wide acquisition contracts (GWAC), contracts intended for multi-agency use, are also known as *IDIQ (indefinite delivery/indefinite quantity)* task order contracts. A program manager might utilize a GWAC to access services without going through a new procurement process. Program managers who do not have successful relationships with their own agency's procurement office have been known to utilize GWAC or IDIQ vehicles from another agency.

Fixed-price contracts are appropriate for services that can be objectively defined in the RFP and for which there is a track record of what such services cost. With fixed-price contracts the vendor maximizes profit by providing the service in the quickest possible fashion, so it is essential to have good performance and quality measures in the contract, or it will be difficult for the project manager to hold the contractor accountable for quality and outcomes.

Cost-reimbursement contracts are sometimes necessary when it is impossible to clearly define in advance what will be required of the vendor. In those cases government might enter into cost-reimbursement contracts in which vendors are reimbursed for the actual costs of performing the service. The incentive for the contractor is to have the project take longer in order to maximize profit. Thus, services that have been previously acquired under cost-reimbursement contracts should utilize that previous experience to convert to a fixed-price contract.

Fixed base price plus performance incentive contracts are appropriate when periodic measures of performance such as target completion dates or levels of quality can be determined and rewarded (or sanctioned) based on actual performance during the contract period.

Time-and-material contracts should be avoided whenever possible because the incentive is for the vendor to take longer to complete the work in order to maximize profit, much like cost-reimbursement contracts. However, utilizing good performance-based contracting methodologies can help hold the vendor accountable when time-and-material contracts must be used.

Characteristics of the Procurement Partnership Model

Successful contracting requires arrangements and relationships that have been adapted to a results-driven, resource-constrained government. The word "successful" is used here to indicate contracting efforts that are entered into in a timely manner and then achieve desired results on time, within budget, and without violating any laws or ethical standards. Reaching these desired outcomes requires a synergy between the best ideas and contributions of both the government and the contractor, and necessitates a spirit of partnership that past contracting practices often discouraged rather than encouraged. Experiences throughout the federal government—both successes and failures—suggest that achieving this synergy requires certain characteristics that were not found in the traditional model of procurement. Table 3.1 outlines those characteristics, which are then discussed in detail.

Table 3.1: Procurement Partnership Model Characteristics

Traditional Procurement Model	Partnership Procurement Model
Low Trust	High Trust
Diffusion of Leadership	Executive Leadership
Stovepipe Organization	Team-Based Approaches
Accountability to Rules and Audits	Accountability for Results

High Trust

A true spirit of partnership and trust among all parties is one of the key adaptations found in the successful contracting of complex projects.

> It can't be a "performance at all costs" culture because that extremist mentality doesn't work. A culture of success requires people on both sides whose personalities click and who trust one another. If those dynamics aren't working, we need to be able to bring in people who can work together as partners without there being a stigma attached to that.

> The key ingredients to successful partnerships are 1) honesty (because trust is fundamental), 2) flexibility, and 3) executive commitment.

By their very nature, complex contracts will encounter unexpected problems. Solving those problems will almost always depend on a close partnership between the government and the contractor in order to share information, brainstorm ideas, and find mutually agreeable ways to move forward. The resulting synergy stimulates creativity, overcomes barriers, and brings together the knowledge and energy of both government and contractor in order to create solutions. The partnership allows government and the contractor to build on one another's strengths and compensate for one another's weaknesses.

The expertise and personalities of the individuals involved in a contracting arrangement are the most important factors in achieving a spirit of partnership.

> If we get the right people together, we can make any contract work. If we have the wrong people involved, we can't do anything.

The "right people" on the contractor's side have the necessary knowledge or technical expertise, communicate effectively, and are willing to be completely honest with the government project manager even when reporting something the government does not want to hear. They understand the legal requirements of government contracting and adhere to those requirements. They resist the temptation to alter their findings or recommendations under implicit or explicit pressure from government officials, even though this could mean reducing the likelihood of future contracts with that agency. They build their business on the basis of their expertise, competence, and reputation for professional excellence, not on the basis of pandering to particular biases of those who approve the contracts.

The "right people" on the government's side have a thorough understanding of what can be done in the procurement process, including all the flexibilities that have been instituted in recent years. They have the knowledge and expertise to clearly define either the SOW or SOO,[17] a willingness to be open to new ideas or ways of doing things, and the capacity to balance reasonable levels of risk with opportunities for innovation. Government project managers must also have the capacity to walk the narrow path of functioning as part of a team with the contractor while providing effective oversight of that contract.

The renovation of the Pentagon reflects the transition from the traditional model of federal contracting to the successful partnerships more evident today. Begun in 1993, the plan was to "gut and then rebuild each of the Pentagon's five 1-million-square-foot 'wedges,' one at a time," with the Army Corps of Engineers managing the projects and "supervising hundreds of contractors through a stovepiped management structure common in construction projects."[18]

> The results weren't pretty. Renovation teams missed most of their deadlines, and Congress placed tight spending caps on the project ... because of cost overruns. In 1997, the Corps was poised to award a low-bid contract to renovate Wedge 1 when Defense officials brought in a new project manager, former NASA and Air Force contracting chief Lee Evey. He promptly suspended the award and restructured the contract so it was based on performance, not just cost.[19]

Neither DoD nor the construction industry was entirely comfortable with the idea of developing performance standards for a building rather than providing the contractor with step-by-step specifications for every inch of the building. Nor were contractors entirely comfortable with the idea that the contract was structured so that their profit was based on quarterly performance ratings that would be determined by the government. But this did not deter Evey and his deputy, Michael Sullivan. The construction requirements for Wedge 1 had been more than 3,500 pages. Under a new performance-based approach, the requirements for Wedges 2 through 5 were just 16 pages long.[20]

One of the key changes that helped make this an award-winning procurement process was a shift from a design-bid-build approach to a design-build approach that "helps create a strong partnership between the contractor and the government.... Since one firm is in charge of both design and construction, the builder has little reason to make costly changes to the design once construction has begun."[21] Project managers in government have long known that contractors routinely bid a construction project at cost, knowing that they will make their profits in "change orders" for every variance from the original plans on which they bid. The design-build approach all but eliminated that dysfunctional incentive structure, as well as shaved months off the time it took to start construction. It also built in a partnership approach with trust as a key foundation. The government worked right alongside contractors every day to address problems and questions as they arose.

Government's reliance on contracting—and the need for a trusting partnership approach to cope with complexity—increased faster than the capacity of the procurement and contract management environments to adopt the changes in culture and human resource competencies necessary to manage in that highly interdependent world. But successful, replicable strategies have been developed along the way.

> Some contract officers have written partnership agreements with contractors in which they specifically articulate commitments to one another such as a commitment to being completely honest, to communicating effectively, and to being willing to work together to resolve differences.

> We were operating with a multi-year firm fixed price contract that was far from perfect. But we made it work for both of us. We went out of our way to be open and honest in our relationship. As the contract went along, we each developed a "wish list" of the things we would love to change in the contract if we had it to do over again. Then we traded items from each of our "wish lists" dollar for dollar, which made the contract work better for both of us without violating any laws.

But more than trust and the right contracting vehicles are needed to ensure a successful partnership. Excellent leadership and a compelling impetus are also needed to overcome the powerful inertia that encourages continuing to do things the way they have always been done.

Executive Leadership

Those interviewed for this chapter suggested that structural arrangements could play a significant role in the success or failure of a contracting initiative, particularly how executive leadership is structured. Each side of the contracting partnership needs a single executive leader who is fully committed to making the project successful and who has sufficient authority to make necessary decisions along the way. Contractors typically identify a single executive leader responsible for the project from start to finish. However, on the government side, where a project is likely to impact multiple organizational units, it is not unusual for a project to be led by a committee of representatives from the affected units.

> "Leadership by committee"" is one of the best predictors of a failed project because it creates a situation in which no one has responsibility for ensuring the success of the project, and no one has the authority to make quick and/or difficult decisions when those are needed.

Who the single executive leader should be depends on the particular situation. The leader should be sufficiently high in the organization to be able to assess and influence the external environment, as well as have the legal authority to make decisions. Because many of today's contracts are nonroutine and high-stakes, not uncommonly the contracts are subject to intense scrutiny by political, media, or advocacy groups. So executive leaders for both government and the contractor need to have the capacity to serve as a "champion" for the project before such groups as the Inspector General (IG), Congress, the Office of the President, watchdog organizations, and the press. In fact, the experience of government and consultant executive leaders working together to champion a project under fire has cemented some of the most effective contracting partnerships reported in the interviews.

> Before the contract even got under way, Congress convened hearings to consider pulling the plug on the project. We had to come together to testify in those hearings and be persuasive in championing the project. That wouldn't have been possible if the government's project leader didn't have the status and authority necessary to make the case.

Top-level government leadership will change as administrations change, as political appointees come and go, and as priorities of government change. This makes it tempting to keep a project below the radar screen of top-level agency leadership, hoping to move the project forward without calling attention to it. The experiences of highly successful partnerships, however, indicate that it is better to engage those who have leadership authority in the early stages of the process to enhance the likelihood that they will be champions of the project even as changes in the environment occur. The government's single executive leader must have decision-making authority and assume a sense of responsibility for the outcome of the project. The executive leader usually delegates management of day-to-day operations of the project to others but remains a crucial actor in the overall performance of the project.

> Senior leadership buy-in is essential. They need to be [in]vested in the outcome, but they don't need to be involved in the day-to-day management of the contractor.

> The executive leader needs to have authority to make the hard decisions, but more importantly needs to be committed enough to making this project successful that he is willing to stake his career on it.

> With these high-profile projects, the leader has to be able to successfully control the flow of information. Everyone can't be disseminating information, or the message gets confused. But at the same time, the leader has to be making information readily available to the right people by briefing the IG, GAO, and others.

> The leader needs to be a "champion" who can brief the president and Congress. This is not all about economics. It is political as well.

The single executive leader needs to claim the project and feel pride in it. Otherwise the project will face abandonment every time a problem is encountered. Since problems are inevitable, it is essential to have leaders who are willing to work through those problems and who have sufficient authority to make necessary changes along the way.

Leaders need to be able to make a compelling business case for the contracting arrangements they are championing. An examination of the projects that won Best Solutions in the Public Interest awards between 2000 and 2002 suggest one compelling impetus for successful partnerships that leaders draw on: The government simply cannot get the job done any other way.

When the Air Force "inherited" the dilapidated Hunley Park military family housing project in 1996, Congress earmarked $7.4 million to help with the renovations. "Congress allocated the funding for the project in November of 1997 and wanted the money spent by March 31, 1998."[22] The Air Force knew there was asbestos in the houses but had no idea what other problems it would encounter behind the walls or in the underground utilities. With only a five-month window in which to spend the money, the Air

Force had no choice but to be innovative in the way it approached contracting for the project. Normally it would have taken that long just to complete the design for the project. The resulting contract was a very innovative partnership with the contractor that involved prototyping three model unit renovations and then seeking input from enlisted families who would ultimately live in the renovated housing units. With this input and the experience of having renovated three units, the design and contract were finalized. The Air Force was very satisfied with the outcome but probably would not have approached the project in this innovative fashion had it not been forced to by the circumstances.

"Necessity" as the impetus for developing good partnerships with contractors is evident in many other awards as well. The staff of the Defense Department's Supply Center in Philadelphia (DSCP) had been reduced from 7,000 in 1993 to 2,700 in 2000. With far fewer people to supply military personnel, DSCP looked for new ways to distribute products and came up with the highly successful and innovative National Mail Order Pharmacy.[23] Without the impetus of huge staff reductions, there would have been less necessity to find alternative ways to distribute supplies.

Necessity provides a wonderful impetus for innovative partnerships with nongovernmental service providers. Leaders who want to encourage innovation would be wise to see every crisis or challenge as an opportunity to innovate. It may be a tough idea to sell at the outset, but the results are something everyone can take pride in.

Team-Based Approaches

Though a single executive leader is necessary, the track record of successful project management suggests that a team-based approach to contracting is also needed. The multiple stakeholders within government will do far more negotiating with one another than any of them will do with the outside contractor. The Interagency-Industry Partnership led by the Department of Commerce developed a virtual guide called the *Seven Steps to Performance-Based Services Acquisition*.[24] It begins with "Step 1: Establish an Integrated Solutions Team," in which you tap multidisciplinary expertise from within government that may include staff from contracting, programming, financial, user, IT, and legal offices. The single executive leader needs to have jurisdiction over this team but does not necessarily need to function as a member of the team on a day-to-day basis.

The purpose of government agencies taking a team-based approach to contracting for knowledge is to get all the necessary expertise together and to facilitate "buy-in" of all essential stakeholders. At a minimum, the government's team will consist of a procurement officer with contracting expertise and authority, and a program officer with the technical expertise needed to define the SOO and manage the work once the contract is in place. However, many projects will require more stakeholders to be at the table, perhaps because multiple units are affected or because the project is likely to have political or legal ramifications that necessitate broader involvement. GAO testimony before Congress suggests that agencies can do a better job of acquiring services that meet their needs by "ensuring that acquisition teams consisting of all key stakeholders—which can include the customer or end user, the contracting officer, representatives from the budget or finance offices, and legal counsel, among others—devote sufficient time early in the acquisition process to clearly define their requirements and consider alternative solutions."[25]

In 2000, *Government Executive* magazine along with the Council for Excellence in Government and OFPP joined together to present Business Solutions in the Public Interest awards to people and programs leading the federal government's transformation in the way it acquires business solutions. They described fundamental changes in the role of acquisitions experts in this way: "[A]cquisition experts now must become business advisers developing strategies for driving effective deals in commercial markets, partnering with top-notch providers, and acquiring the best overall solutions for government programs."[26]

It is not always easy to shift from fulfilling a stovepipe specialist role to functioning as a member of an integrated solutions team. In fact, cultural resistance on the part of the federal workforce (both acquisitions and program specialists) is one of the most significant barriers to successful contracting arrangements. In the *Seven Steps to Performance-Based Services Acquisition*, a contracting officer described the impact of a team approach in this way: "The team approach takes some getting used to. Before, I worked more independently and it seemed I had more control. Now I'm one of 12. It took me a while to realize that operating as part of a team makes for a better acquisition. By having a close association with the program people, I can make sure the acquisition is constructed in a way that makes it more likely the contract will meet their needs."[27]

Teams are utilized and structured in a variety of ways. One interesting model for addressing problems that arise in government contracting arrangements is the Program Assist Visit (PAV) project developed by the Navy's Acquisition Reform Office. When a procurement team (including procurement managers, project managers, and contractors) finds itself "going in the wrong direction or bogged down in cost overruns and delays …program managers have the option of calling in a strike team … of outside experts to … help design—or redesign—the strategy."[28]

Requesting help from a PAV is strictly voluntary and is kept confidential. Such an approach provides advice, expertise, and assistance for all parties in a contracting arrangement at the time a problem arises. The model can provide technical advice and expertise, but it can also help a procurement team work out difficulties in their relationships and promote teamwork. The PAV strike team is made up of experienced consultants as well as government procurement and project management professionals. Christine Stelloh-Garner, head of the Navy's Acquisition Reform Office, has only five people on her staff, but she is able to draw on a pool of nearly 50 Navy personnel and contractors to assemble a strike team. People who have been down the path of a troubled procurement are willing to give their time to help others find a better way to manage their procurement.

The team-based approach requires a significant change in the culture of services acquisition and project management in the federal government. Procurement officials can no longer limit themselves to ensuring that the right process has been followed. Instead they must become more knowledgeable about the technical aspects of their organization in order to be fully functioning members of the solutions team. The technical experts who will manage the project find that they must become more willing to work with acquisitions experts to define the project in ways that enhance the likelihood of attracting competitive vendors to bid on the project. The shift in culture is often difficult, but the success of projects utilizing the team approach demonstrates the value of engaging the difficult task of changing organizational culture.

DoD offered a different team-based model when it created the Change Management Center[29] to enhance the change efforts in defense acquisitions. They recognized that "change" was the real challenge that had to be managed, and they take a team-based approach to bringing about change, working across traditional organizational "stovepipes" in order to achieve results. On their website under the heading of "How do you manage change?" you will find the following strategy:

1. The first thing you do is jump in. You can't do anything about it from the outside.
2. A clear sense of mission or purpose is essential.
3. Build a team. "Lone wolves" have their uses, but managing change isn't one of them. On the other hand, the right kind of lone wolf makes an excellent temporary team leader.
4. Maintain a flat organizational team structure, and rely on minimal and informal reporting requirements.
5. Pick people with relevant skills and high energy levels. You'll need both.
6. Toss out the rule book. Change, by definition, calls for a configured response, not adherence to prefigured routines.
7. Shift to an action-feedback model. Plan and act in short intervals. Do your analysis on the fly. No lengthy up-front studies. Remember the hare and the tortoise.

8. Set flexible priorities. You must have the ability to drop what you're
    doing and tend to something more important.[30]

The success of the team-based approach is based on trust and excellent
communication as well as having the right people with the right knowledge
on the team. Most who utilize this process describe the development of routine, informal communication strategies.

> Every morning the program manager and the contract manager sat down
> and chatted. The relationship fouls if there is no trust here.

> We [the contractors] never had meetings where the government's project
> manager wasn't included. We couldn't have secrets from one another if we
> were on the same team.

But it is not easy to get everyone on board with a team-based approach.
Expert observers of the field comment that while senior-level federal procurement officers have embraced this new team-based role for acquisitions,
they still find significant resistance to the change among staff. When the
acquisitions department urges this kind of approach, it often finds resistance
from program offices. When acquisitions and program offices are ready to
go down this path, they often hear from the IG or the department's legal
counsel that it cannot be done that way. Perhaps the greatest challenge
remaining in procurement reform is to influence the culture of government
in a way that embraces partnerships with vendors and values teamwork
across organizational stovepipes. Many times the resistance is based on a
lack of knowledge about what practices are legal and which ones have
worked for other agencies. Above all, achieving buy-in among all those
stakeholders requires assurances that accountability of the contractor will
not be sacrificed in the team-based approach.

Accountability for Results

Ensuring that procurement processes are fair and that contractors are held
accountable are as important in today's environment as ever before. The principles of fairness, transparency, and accountability have driven much of the
culture and practice of government procurement—and for good reason.
Government procurement is structured to ensure open competition for lucra-
tive government contracts, fend off corruption, and ensure that taxpayer
resources are spent prudently. In the past, this led to procurement rules that
strictly limited communication between the government and contractors, and
gave rise to a culture of distrust and antagonism. Unfortunately, such limited
communication often magnified the risks and costs of contracting and con-

tributed to failures to achieve desired results. When innovative partnership-based approaches were proposed, there were plenty of critics who said they would lead to abuses and a loss of accountability.

If partnership-based approaches to procurement are to be accepted, proponents need to be able to articulate both why a partnership approach is valuable and how accountability and oversight will be maintained.

> One person's synergy is another person's cronyism. It is counterproductive to force project managers to artificially establish barriers in order to maintain an arm's-length relationship with contractors. However, project managers must be trained to maintain effective oversight as well as work as a team with the contractor, or we won't be able to ensure that the system will remain honest, fair, and competitive.

Government contracting for services is a $110 billion a year industry in the federal government, representing about one-third of the federal budget. Therefore, it is essential that contracting be approached in ways that ensure adherence to the principles of fairness, transparency, accountability, and good stewardship of taxpayer resources. Those values remain guiding principles in today's procurement environment, but much has changed about how those principles are interpreted and implemented in federal contracting. For example, at one time it was perceived that awarding a contract to the lowest bidder was the best way to be a good steward of taxpayer resources. Today, good stewardship is understood to mean selecting the "best value" bid, taking into consideration cost, quality, and past performance of the vendor.

Another dimension of accountability emphasized by those interviewed for this chapter is the importance of training project managers in balancing the dual roles of "partner" and "oversight" in a contracting relationship. Psychologically, it is a difficult balance to maintain. Yet it is one of the key elements for assuring all stakeholders that government contractors are being held accountable.

> Project managers need training to help them psychologically walk the line between oversight and being a team player. They aren't getting that kind of help right now.

> How do we manage the partnership to ensure neutrality and accountability? We lay out our objectives and guidelines for the relationship. We avoid the breakfast and the ballgame.

Both contractors and government employees need training to understand the essential values and laws that govern contracting. Many contractors

who are new to contracting with government lack familiarity with a governmental environment that places high value on fair and open competition and
accountability for performance. While contractors may flock to the new
opportunities to sell their services to government, they are not all prepared
for the differing demands of that market. Professional associations and others need to provide guidance and training for those contractors so that they
have the specific knowledge and skills necessary to function in the government contracting environment. For example, the Professional Services
Council (PSC), formed in 1972 to serve the interests of member firms who
provide professional and technical services to the federal government, "has
as its objective ensuring that its Member Firms render professional services
to the federal government of a high quality at a reasonable price. Quality
must include a strong commitment to ethical business practices consistent
with laws and regulations related to government acquisition."[31] PSC
requires member firms to implement ethics programs that are consistent
with federal ethics and procurement laws, and PSC provides member firms
with assistance and training in developing such programs. All federal contractors need to be aware of federal ethics and procurement laws that affect
every aspect of the contracting relation, but not all contractors are.

    This section focused on the essential characteristics of the procurement
partnership model: high trust, executive leadership, team-based approaches,
and accountability for results. Lessons derived from the interviews and
analysis of award-winning procurements suggest some helpful implementation strategies as well. These are addressed in the final section.

Implementing the Procurement
Partnership Model

Developing the Contract

    The interviews were rich in recommendations on how to approach pro-
curement and develop contracts in ways that encourage a spirit of partnership and trust between government and the contractor.

Do not rush to award a contract, but spend that up-front time wisely.

    Federal agencies are now much less likely to spend months writing
detailed SOWs and wait additional months for all the necessary approvals
to be gathered before an RFP is distributed. Performance-based contracting
is more likely to rely on a brief SOO, asking each bidder to propose an
SOW to meet those objectives. While this approach allows the government

to get an RFP out sooner, vendors will need more time and access to information in order to develop well-grounded proposals that will meet the needs of the program. This additional time and access to information must be built into the process, but it is well worth the time. Questions and observations of vendors prior to proposals being submitted could lead to important clarifications in the SOO and could greatly enhance the likelihood of a successful contract. By sharing more information and having more interaction between the government and potential vendors up front, the proposals are likely to be better and a foundation of trust can be established.

Invest more time in due diligence before awarding a contract.
Steven Kelman describes due diligence this way: "The idea behind due diligence is to allow a number of vendors to kick the tires of the operation about which they're bidding—to spend as much as several weeks being able to observe, ask questions, and generally poke around. The idea is to reduce the risk to vendors to the point where they are willing to sign up to requirements they otherwise might have been unwilling to bid on."[32] The government needs to conduct its own due diligence as well by learning what it can about the experience and qualifications of those submitting proposals, their past performance on other government contracts, and their ability to deliver on what they promise. A due diligence period that is too brief results in neither party knowing the reality of the situation when the contract is signed. That leads to surprises, contract modifications, cost overruns, and disputes. Due diligence takes time, but it is time well spent.

Procurements with extremely limited scope and duration do not attract competitive bids.
It is essential to design procurements so that they attract a reasonable number of competitive bids. This is much more likely to happen if the procurement is for a broader scope of work and a longer duration, since the bidding process itself requires a substantial commitment of resources on the part of each vendor who participates. To address this problem, bundle projects together or include multiple phases of a project in one contract. Recognize, though, that while bundled contracts may attract proposals from more large contractors, smaller businesses may be less likely to submit a proposal. Multi-year awards are more attractive to all potential vendors, but it is important to build in "exit ramps" along the way so that either party may choose to end the arrangement at agreed upon times if it is not working out.

Contracts should clearly define the roles and responsibilities of each party, and regular reporting and progress evaluation meetings should be scheduled.
Working in a true spirit of partnership requires ongoing communication and a sense of shared responsibility for the outcomes. The contract should

reflect that type of relationship. Clear roles and lines of communication will support and enhance a spirit of partnership, as well as encourage open and honest communication at all times.

Both the contractor and government need executive leaders who are willing to stake their reputations on the success of the contract.

Select people for leadership roles who embody both the art and the science of successful contracting and who are willing to be innovative even in the face of criticism. In addition to a strong commitment to the outcomes of the project, leaders need to exhibit a commitment to ethical integrity, creativity, and good interpersonal problem-solving skills. Other members of the team can supply the technical know-how.

Contracts should contain specific mechanisms for resolving disputes related to the contract.

Using mediation, arbitration, or an ombudsman to resolve disputes could save considerable time and money if the "partnership" falters because of a dispute the parties cannot resolve. These alternative dispute resolution options tend to reach resolution faster and with less expense than lawsuits. Some types of mediation are designed to work on improving the relationship between the parties as well as working out a resolution to the problem at hand.

Avoid contract award challenges by conducting fair and open competitions with broad communication up front.

Too many projects are sidelined or set aside by award challenges from unsuccessful vendors. This tends to happen when the project manager enters into the contracting process with a bias toward a particular vendor (perhaps because that vendor has significant knowledge based on prior work with the agency) but fails to communicate this in the procurement process. If other vendors know in advance that an incumbent vendor has a high likelihood of getting the award in a procurement, they can make informed decisions about whether to invest their time and resources into submitting a bid. It is when the procurement *appears to be* a completely open competition—when in reality one vendor has a significant advantage—that award challenges are most likely to occur. Because vendors invested scarce resources in preparing proposals, they are more likely to challenge an award they believe they would have won in an open competition not impacted by one vendor's prior experience with the agency. It is more honest and appropriate to state up front what factors might give a vendor a significant advantage.

Investing in Training

When the right people get together, contracting for services can and does deliver on the promise of blending the best thinking of both the public and the private sectors to solve problems. When those interviewed for this chapter were asked why these successful contracting practices were not more widely practiced, their responses suggested a widespread lack of understanding of the available tools and processes. That lack of understanding is perceived to exist among government procurement and project managers, government's IG and legal staff, and the consultants with whom they contract.

Why is such knowledge and understanding in short supply? In part it is due to the rapidity in which government has moved toward contracting rather than relying only on the knowledge of its own employees. It takes time and resources to familiarize government professionals with the types of contracting vehicles and methodologies that work best. Because this training has not been in place, some in Congress proposed the Truthfulness, Responsibility and Accountability in Contracting (TRAC) Act in 2002 in order to freeze the trend toward contracting out work and to return to greater reliance on government employees. Stan Z. Soloway, president of PSC, testified against the contracting freeze included in the TRAC Act but agreed that training of government contract managers does need to be improved:

> No one doubts that the government has challenges in the contract management arena, that training of the acquisition workforce has lagged, or that shifting the government's thinking into the contemporary era of value- and performance-based business relationships is difficult. That is why the Professional Services Council has been a strong and consistent advocate of more training and developmental opportunities for the acquisition workforce.[33]

Downsizing of the federal workforce has also contributed to a situation in which it is unclear whether the acquisition workforce will be adequate in coming years. This problem has been recognized by the federal government and is beginning to be addressed, as indicated in this testimony of GAO's director of acquisition and sourcing management before a Congressional subcommittee debating the proposed Services Acquisition Reform Act (SARA) in March 2002:

> We believe it is essential for agencies to define the future capabilities needed by the [acquisition] workforce and to contrast these needs with where the workforce is today.... In our current work for this and other

committees, we are examining ... 1) the adequacy of agency training requirements for the acquisition workforce and agency practices for determining the level of funding needed for training, 2) selected federal agencies' strategic planning efforts to manage and improve the capacity of the acquisition workforce, and 3) strategies being used to ensure that the acquisition workforce is prepared to meet the new challenges for acquiring services.[34]

There seems to be agreement that more training is necessary, so perhaps this is an indication that significant resources will be committed to providing such training. If that training is well designed and readily available, the improved performance should provide a very positive return on investment.

If training is to be helpful, what should the content of the training convey to the participants?

- Innovative, performance-based approaches to contracting that emphasize partnership, team-based approaches, accountability for results, and familiarity with the variety of contracting vehicles available for use
- Competencies in developing strategic objectives and writing clear SOOs at the outset of the contracting process, so that the focus is on outcomes or results, rather than inputs
- Lessons learned from the experience of others who have utilized these approaches, including skills and strategies necessary for working effectively in procurement and project teams within government, as well as in partnership with service providers outside government
- A thorough understanding of how federal ethics and procurement laws impact partnership-based approaches to projects so that all parties will be able to walk the tightrope of balancing teamwork and oversight

Training can be used to help all stakeholders learn about the variety of tools available to them, the approaches that have been successful for others, and the legal and ethical framework within which they must operate. But such knowledge is only useful if the culture in which it is to be implemented is one amenable to these ideas and approaches.

Transforming the Culture

Cultural change takes time, leadership, and a persuasive case that it is necessary. When new tools and practices are introduced in any organization, they will meet resistance if they challenge in any way the assumptions about how things are done or should be done in the organization. Being able to articulate how and why the innovations are consistent with the organization's philosophy, values, and purposes will be essential to overcoming resistance. Even when a strong case can be made for the innovations or changes, we have to expect that it will take three to five years to see real change in the organizational culture.

Proponents of the new partnership procurement model need to prepare themselves for several years of resistance from the culture in which they are operating. They will need to find support and encouragement from like-minded professionals outside their agency until such time that the organizational culture embraces the new approaches.

When the organizational culture puts up roadblocks to change and innovation, it helps bring the focus back to the mission that must be achieved rather than on how we are going about it. A sense of urgency and a willingness to find creative ways to solve problems come when the needed outcome is in the forefront of the conversation.

> My own procurement and program officers were giving me every reason in the book why we couldn't do it this way or that. Finally, in exasperation, I said, "We're arguing about techniques here while our troops are running out of food in the field!" Then the conversation shifted to getting food to the troops, and we started finding ways to solve the problems.

We also need to be concerned about the public-private organizational culture that is created when government and contractors attempt to work in partnership. It is helpful to remember that both the government and the contractors have a shared interest in achieving the intended results of the contract. The product or outcome of a project is perhaps the one place where government and the "business partner" have a relatively equal stake. In many other ways, their individual organizational cultures diverge.

Government places high value on the integrity of the contracting process, while the contractor places high value on making enough money to stay in business. Government does have an interest in business partners staying in business (if only to ensure steady supply and a competitive bidding environment), but the government certainly does not value this as much as the consultant. The consultant has an interest in the integrity of the contracting process (if only because it ensures that they can participate in fair and open competition for contracts), but that value is not highest on the business' list of concerns.

But both parties value and have a vested interest in achieving the outcomes sought by the contract. Government's procurement and project management professionals are likely to define their job success and satisfaction by whether they were able to facilitate delivery of important outcomes in an effective, high-quality, and timely manner. Vendors also have a vested interest in the outcomes of the contract. It is a matter of professional pride to point to a successful project—not to mention a marketing tool when making a pitch for the next contract. So "results" becomes the fulcrum of the government-contractor relationship—the point where the two parties can meet and around which they can build an effective organizational culture. It is the purpose that will provide all stakeholders with the sense of motivation and urgency to resolve problems.

In large organizations, however, it is easy to lose sight of outcomes in the day-to-day focus on process and procedure. When making efforts to change the procurement culture, it is helpful to keep reminding everyone that we share a commitment to achieving certain outcomes and adhering to important values necessary to ensure fairness in the procurement system. Cultural change becomes more likely when the innovations that are meeting resistance can demonstrate adherence to the fundamental values and an ability to deliver outcomes better than the old practices.

Contracting in a spirit of partnership is an enormous cultural shift. If change is to be successfully institutionalized, structures, systems, and culture will need to be aligned to support partnership approaches to contracting. This will take strong commitment by leaders and innovators, as well as an investment in training. But where our current system is failing to achieve the outcomes we need, such change is as necessary as it is difficult. It will take several years to see fundamental change in the culture of contracting. But if we can then see a federal contracting environment that is characterized by a "spirit of partnership" as well as fairness, then the painful process of change will have been worthwhile.

Endnotes

1. Award information can be found at http://www.govexec.com/top200/ 2000top/00tops1.htm, http://www.govexec.com/top200/01top/mag.htm, and http://www.govexec.com/ top200/02top/mag.htm.

2. This report can be found at http://www.gao.gov/a76panel/dcap0201.pdf.

3. These reports can be found online at http://www.businessofgovernment.org/ publications_grantreports.asp.

4. When a specific acquisition is discussed in this chapter, the information comes from one of these published accounts and not from any of the interviews conducted. In order to protect the anonymity of those interviewed, statements from the interviews do not name a specific acquisition or identify the source.

5. *Contract Management: Taking a Strategic Approach to Improving Service Acquisitions* GAO-02-499T March 7, 2002.

6. For a discussion of how complexity impacts contracting, see Wendell C. Lawther, "Contracting for the 21st Century: A Partnership Model," at http://www.businessofgovernment.org/ pdfs/LawtherReport.pdf.

7. Brian Friel, "Relationships Count," *Government Executive,* August 1, 2001, found at http://207.27.3.29/top200/01top/census.htm.

8. Ibid.

9. Ibid.

10. Ibid.

11. Ibid.

12. Steven Kelman, "Remaking Federal Procurement," *Public Contract Law Journal* 31:4 (Summer 2002).

13. See, for example, Lawrence L. Martin, "Making Performance-Based Contracting Perform: What Federal Departments and Agencies Can Learn From State and Local Governments" at http://businessofgovernment.org/ pdfs/Martin2Report.pdf.

14. See http://oamweb.osec.doc.gov/pbsc/introduction.html.

15. Tanya Ballard, "Share in Savings, Share in Glory," *Government Executive,* August 1, 2001, found at http://www.govexec.com/top200/ 01top/osfa.htm.

16. Ibid.

17. An SOO communicates the top-level objectives of a solicitation, leaving those who submit bids on the solicitation the freedom to structure and define an SOW that will meet those objectives. SOOs are being used increasingly often because they are thought to encourage greater creativity and innovation on the part of those submitting bids.

18. Jason Peckenpaugh, "Building Innovation," *Government Executive,* August 15, 2002, found at http://govexec.com/top200/02top/dod.htm.

19. Ibid.

20. Ibid.

21. Ibid.

22. See "Family Housing Renovation, Air Force" at http://www.govexec.com/top200/ 2000top/00tops1s4.htm.

23. See "National Mail Order Pharmacy, DOD" at http://www.govexec.com/top200/ 2000top/00tops1s6.htm.

24. See http://oamweb.osec.doc.gov/pbsc/index.html.

25. *Contract Management: Service Contracting Trends and Challenges,* GAO-01- 1074R August 22, 2001.

26. See "Award-Winning Acquisition" at http://www.govexec.com/top200/2000top/ 00tops1.htm.

86   Kathryn G. Denhardt

27. See http://oamweb.osec.doc.gov/pbsc/step1f.html.

28. Described by Matthew Weinstock in "Buying Teams," *Government Executive*, August 15, 2002.

29. See the Change Management website at http://www.dodchanges.org/kc/cmc_portal/login.asp.

30. See http://www.dodchanges.org/kc/cmc_portal/ manage2.asp.

31. See the PSC Code of Professional Conduct at http://www.pscouncil.org/2day/codeconduct.htm.

32. Steven Kelman, "Due Diligence at Cutting Edge of Contracting," *Federal Computer Week* (June 22, 1998) available at http://www.itduediligence.com/articles/cutting.html.

33. Soloway's March 6, 2002, testimony can be found at http://www.pscouncil.org/alerts_news/testimonies/testimonies.htm.

34. *Contract Management: Taking a Strategic Approach to Improving Service Acquisitions* GAO-02-499T March 7, 2002.

CHAPTER FOUR

Making Performance-Based Contracting Perform: What the Federal Government Can Learn from State and Local Governments

Lawrence L. Martin
Associate Professor
School of Social Work
Columbia University

This report was originally published in June 2002, revised January 2003.

Key Characteristics of the
Federal Procurement Environment

Federal procurement is undergoing a major transformation. It has ceased to function simply as a support activity. Instead, federal procurement has evolved into a primary management and administrative function that is playing an increasingly critical role in enabling federal departments and agencies to discharge their primary missions.

In assessing the changing environment of federal procurement today, five key characteristics stand out: (1) the general acceptance of privatization and contracting out, (2) the increasing importance of service contracting, (3) the human capital crisis in federal procurement, (4) the Government Performance and Results Act, and (5) federal performance-based contracting initiatives.

General Acceptance of Privatization and Contracting Out

The 1980s and 1990s involved considerable ideological warfare over the appropriate role of privatization and contracting out within the federal government. A 1989 report issued by the National Academy of Public Administration entitled *Privatization: The Challenge to Public Management* captures the tension of the times (Salamon et. al, 1989). Today, one can argue that the war is over, although many battles may yet be fought. Rather than being viewed as a challenge *to* public administration, privatization and contracting out today are seen more as challenges *for* public administration. Having decided as a society that privatization and contracting out are legitimate forms of government service delivery, the issue for federal departments and agencies has become one of determining how best to utilize these alternative service delivery tools (Salamon, 2002).

The general acceptance of privatization and contracting out creates a major challenge for federal procurement. The ability of federal departments and agencies to deliver services and discharge their primary missions is directly related to the quality of federal procurement.

Increasing Importance of Service Contracting

Just as the economy of the United States is transitioning from being goods based to being services based, so is federal procurement. Federal procurement increasingly involves contracting for services. Between 1990 and 2000, federal procurement of equipment and supplies declined by $25 billion, while procurement of services increased by $17 billion. Today, contracting for services represents the single largest category of federal procurement, representing some $88 billion, or about 43 percent of total federal contract dollars (GAO, 2001a:4; 2001b:203). The growth in contracting for services is attributed to two primary areas: information technology services and professional, administrative, and management support services (GAO, 2001a, 2001b). Service contracting presents different problems for federal procurement. Services are not generally procured in the same manner and with the same techniques commonly employed in the acquisition of equipment, supplies, and material.

The transition to service contracting constitutes a fundamental paradigm shift for federal procurement. Federal procurement must find new ways of conducting the federal government's business including the development of new policies, procedures, concepts, and tools to deal with a new service reality.

Human Capital Crisis in Federal Procurement

During the 1990s, the federal workforce was significantly downsized. In many instances, this downsizing was driven not by an orderly plan that assessed future federal workforce needs, but rather by retirements, voluntary separations, "buy-outs," and other quick-fix approaches. The knowledge, skills, and expertise of the current federal workforce do not necessarily match the knowledge, skills, and expertise that will be needed by the federal workforce of the future. The result is a "skill imbalance" in the federal workforce.

This skill imbalance is further exacerbated by the approaching retirement of the baby-boom generation. Those employees born in the years immediately following World War II and who entered federal service during the 1970s are now approaching retirement age. As these federal employees walk out the door, the institutional skills, knowledge, and expertise of many federal departments and agencies will be accompanying them. This situation is particularly critical for the federal procurement workforce. One estimate puts the proportion of the federal procurement workforce eligible to retire between 2000 and 2005 at 22 percent, with the figure steadily increasing after 2005 (Commercial Activities Panel, 2001:7). Another estimate suggests the proportion will be closer to 50 percent by 2005 (Gansler, 2002:7).

The federal procurement workforce of the future will be smaller and less experienced. New and creative ways must be found for the federal procurement function and the federal procurement workforce to operate more efficiently and more effectively.

Government Performance and Results Act

The Government Performance and Results Act (GPRA) (Public Law 103-62) requires federal departments and agencies to report annually to the U.S. Congress on the performance of all programs and activities. In section 1115(a), GPRA states that each agency "shall be required to prepare an annual performance plan covering each program activity set forth in the budget of the agency." Further on in Section 1115(a)(4), GPRA comments that the annual plan shall "establish performance indicators to be used in measuring or assessing the relevant *outputs,* service levels, and *outcomes* of each program activity." Still further on in Section 1115(f) (2) and (3), GPRA provides the following clarification: an "*outcome* measure means an assessment of the results of a program activity compared to its intended purposes," while "an *output* measure means the tabulation, calculation, or recording of activity or effort." Finally, in Section 1115(f)(5), GPRA states that a "'performance indicator' means a particular value or characteristic used to measure *output* or *outcome.*" (emphasis added).

GPRA explicitly acknowledges that performance has at least two dimensions (output and outcome). A third dimension (quality) is acknowledged implicitly in that GPRA consistently refers to "qualitative" measures. The fundamental theoretical underpinning of GPRA (performance accountability) as well as its language (output, quality, and outcome) have yet to permeate all aspects of federal management and administration. Federal procurement is a case in point. Guidance provided by the Office of Federal Procurement Policy (OFPP, 1997, 1998a) on performance-based contracting (PBC) does not make full or consistent use of the GPRA performance accountability framework and language.

If PBC is going to become a primary tool of federal procurement, then it must become more compliant with GPRA. As David Walker, the comptroller general of the United States, has observed, GPRA "must provide the foundation and framework for how the federal government does business every day" (Walker, 2001:20).

Federal Performance-Based Contracting Initiatives

Performance-based contracting is one of the hottest topics in government procurement today (Gordon, 2002). The interest and attention is understandable considering the success the Office of Federal Procurement Policy (OFPP, 1998b) had with its initial experiment with PBC. The OFPP experiment produced some remarkable results including significant decreases in costs, significant increases in customer satisfaction, and the reduction of financial audits to nearly zero. The OFPP experiment validated

---

Office of Federal Procurement Policy Experiment with Performance-Based Contracting

Results of the evaluation of 26 performance-based contracts issued involving 15 federal departments and agencies with a value of $585 million:
- Costs Decreased 15%
- Customer Satisfaction Increased 18%
- Financial Audits Decreased 93%

Source: OFPP (1998b:3-4)

two basic assumptions of PBC: first, that the structure of contracts can influence the behavior of contractors to focus more on performance; and second, that monitoring costs (in this instance auditing costs) can be reduced through the use of PBC.

In light of the success of the OFPP experiment with PBC, the Office of Management and Budget (OMB) has established a goal of making 20 percent of all eligible federal service contract dollars over $25,000 performance based during fiscal year 2002, and the Procurement Executives Council has established a goal of making 50 percent of all service contract dollars performance based by fiscal year 2005 (GAO, 2001a; OMB, 2001).

Federal PBC initiatives can be viewed as both a challenge for federal procurement as well as a potential response to the general acceptance of privatization and contracting out, the increase in service contracting, the human capital crisis in federal procurement, and GPRA. PBC involves new policies, procedures, concepts, and tools designed specifically to meet the needs of service contracting. Thus, PBC holds at least the promise of providing federal procurement and the federal procurement workforce with the wherewithal to function more efficiently and more effectively in a new service environment.

Performance-Based Contracting: The Federal Perspective

Performance-based contracting is one of those phenomena that arise in government from time to time where practice has outpaced theory. Consequently, PBC has come to mean different things to different people (GAO, 2002). Variations in approaches to PBC exist at the federal, state, and local government levels. However, the basic objective of PBC is quite simple: *to change the behavior of contractors to focus more on performance.* Beyond this basic objective, considerable ambiguity exists as to exactly what constitutes PBC.

Definitions of Performance-Based Contracting

In an attempt to bring some clarity to the concept, the Office of Federal Procurement Policy (OFPP), the Department of Defense (DoD), and the Federal Acquisition Regulation have all developed operational definitions of PBC. The results, however, have created as much confusion as clarification.

The Office of Federal Procurement Policy provides the following definition of performance-based contracting: an approach where the statement of work is based on "objective, measurable performance standards *outputs*" (OFPP, 1998:5). In a related policy memorandum, the OFPP further states that a performance-based contract contains "performance standards (i.e., *quality,* quantity, timeliness)" (OFPP, 1997:2). The Department of Defense, which contracts for more services than any other federal department or agency, defines a performance-based contract as one that "describes the requirements in terms of measurable *outcomes* rather than by means of prescriptive methods" (DoD, 2000:1). The Federal Acquisition Regulation (FAR) Part 2.101 states that "performance-based contracting means structuring all aspects of an acquisition around the purpose of the work to be performed with contract requirements set forth, in clear, specific, and measurable *outcomes* as opposed to either the manner by which the work is to be performed or broad and imprecise statements of work." In a different section, the Federal Acquisition Regulation Part 37.601 further states: "Performance-based contracting methods are intended to ensure that required performance *quality* levels are achieved and that total payment is related to the degree that services performed meet contract standards" (emphasis added).

Elements of Performance-Based Contracting

	Output	Quality	Outcomes
Office of Federal Procurement Policy	YES	YES	NO
Department of Defense	NO	NO	YES
Federal Acquisition Regulation (FAR)	NO	YES	YES

Essential Elements of Performance-Based Contracting

The Office of Federal Procurement Policy (OFPP, 1997:2-5) has also enumerated what it considers to be the minimum essential elements that a performance-based contract must contain: (1) performance requirements, (2) performance standards or acceptable quality levels (AQLs), (3) a quality assurance or monitoring plan, and (4) positive and negative incentives if the contract is mission critical or involves a relatively large expenditure of federal funds.

Problems with the Federal Perspective on Performance-Based Contracting

The federal perspective on performance-based contracting suffers from several problems: (1) definitional confusion, (2) the failure to link performance-

---

Office of Federal Procurement Policy Minimum Requirements for Performance-Based Contracting

1. **Performance Requirements** that define in measurable terms the work to be accomplished or the service to be provided. Also called "performance measures" and "performance indicators."

2. **Performance Standards** that define the allowable deviation, if any, from the performance requirements. Also called the "acceptable quality level" or AQL.

3. **Quality Assurance Plan** that specifies the means by which contractor performance will be determined and documented. Also called a "QA plan," a "surveillance plan" and a "monitoring plan." Acceptable approaches to quality assurance plans include:

   A. 100% Inspection
   B. Random Sampling
   C. Periodic Inspection
   D. Customer Input

4. **Positive and Negative Incentives** tied to the quality assurance plan. Also called "incentives" and "penalties."

Source: OFPP (1997:2-5; 1998a:16).

based contracting more closely with GPRA, (3) a "one size fits all" approach, and (4) a preference for design considerations over performance considerations.

Definitional Confusion

How should one interpret the various federal definitions of performance-based contracting? The Office of Federal Procurement Policy views PBC as contracting for *outputs* and *quality*. The Department of Defense views PBC as contracting for *outcomes*. And the Federal Acquisition Regulation views PBC as contracting for *outcomes* and *quality*. Two alternative interpretations can be taken from this definitional confusion. Either the definitions are saying different things or they are saying the same thing differently. Under the first interpretation, the argument can be made that the definitions are saying different things and thus real confusion exists on the part of federal departments and agencies as to what exactly constitutes PBC. Under the second interpretation, the argument can be made that the various definitions are simply saying the same thing differently in that they recognize the multidimensional nature of performance, but choose to focus on different dimensions (outputs, quality, and outcomes).

Regardless of which of the two interpretations is correct, the Office of Federal Procurement Policy needs to promulgate clarifying guidance. If the first interpretation is correct and considerable confusion does in fact exist over what is meant by PBC, then OFPP needs to provide a clarifying definition. If the second interpretation is correct, then OFPP needs to issue clarifying guidance, recognizing that performance in PBC has three dimensions (outputs, quality, and outcomes).

Failure to Link Performance-Based Contracting More Closely with GPRA

At least part of the explanation for the federal definitional confusion over PBC can be attributed to its failure to be linked more closely to GPRA. The question needs to be asked and answered as to why PBC is not fully

---

Author's Discussion with a High-Ranking Procurement Official of the Department of Defense

Question: "Will your agency have any difficulty meeting the goal of having 50 percent of its service contracts performance based by 2005?"

Response: "Not al all! All we have to do is slap a QA [quality assurance] plan on our existing contracts and we're done."

compliant with GPRA's performance accountability framework and language. If federal departments and agencies are going to be held accountable for performance as defined by GPRA, why shouldn't contractors? Additionally, in a federal service environment characterized by increased privatization and contracting out, the only way many federal departments and agencies will be able to meet the reporting requirements of GPRA is to pass along those requirements to their contractors. Thus, there must be at least some consistency in the performance accountability framework and language used internally by federal departments and agencies and their approaches to PBC.

"One Size Fits All" Approach

By identifying what it considers to be the essential elements of a performance-based contract, the Office of Federal Procurement Policy has *de facto* decreed a "one size fits all" PBC policy. In fairness to OFPP, it is attempting to get federal departments and agencies and the federal procurement workforce to break out of the traditional ways of doing business and to think "outside the box." Unfortunately, the end result may be the replacement of an old box with a new box. By adopting a "one size fits all" approach, OFPP is retarding experimentation with PBC. At the present time, no reason exists to assume that OFPP has discovered the one best way to implement PBC. Other ways may exist that can produce equal or better results in terms of changing the behavior of contractors to focus more on performance.

Preference for Design Considerations over Performance Considerations

By choosing to emphasize the essential elements of PBC, while simultaneously failing to provide definitional clarity, the federal perspective represents a triumph of design considerations over performance considerations. Public procurement theory makes a distinction between the use of design specifications and performance specifications in government contracts. The National Association of State Purchasing Officials (NASPO, 1997:147 and 153) defines a design specification as "a type or manner of writing a purchase description characterized by detail as to how the product is to be manufactured or the work performed" and a performance specification as "a purchase description accenting performance over design." When design specifications are used, the government tells the contractor *how* to provide the service. When performance specifications are used, the government tells the contractor *what* is expected and leaves it free to determine how best to accomplish the desired end result.

PBC requires the use of performance specifications. The essence of PBC is telling the contractor *what* is expected and letting it decide on the *how*. But the OFPP (OFPP, 1998a) guidance on PBC represents a design specifications approach. If a contract is designed so as to meet the OFPP essential elements, it constitutes PBC regardless of the extent to which it ultimately succeeds in changing the behavior of the contractor to focus more on performance. In other words: *The federal perspective on PBC is not performance based.* If the federal perspective is to simply view PBC as a set of design specifications that must be included in a contract, rather than as an attempt to change the behavior of contractors to focus more on performance, then the potential usefulness of PBC will be greatly diminished.

Performance-Based Contracting: The State and Local Government Perspective

The state and local government perspective on performance-based contracting differs considerably from the federal perspective (Martin and Miller, 2003). Two reasons account for this difference. The first is the performance accountability framework provided by the Service Efforts and Accomplishments (SEA) reporting initiative of the Governmental Accounting Standards Board (GASB). The second is the greater freedom that state and local governments have to experiment and innovate with PBC.

Influence of the Service Efforts and Accomplishments Reporting Initiative of the Governmental Accounting Standards Board

The Governmental Accounting Standards Board is the organization that establishes "generally accepted accounting principles" for state and local governments. The Service Efforts and Accomplishments (SEA) reporting initiative of GASB (1994) represents an attempt to do for state and local governments what GPRA has done for the federal government: create a system of performance accountability.

From the outset, SEA reporting has viewed "performance" as a multidimensional concept consisting of outputs, quality, and outcomes. SEA reporting defines an output as the "quantity of service provided"; quality as the "quantity of service provided that meets a quality requirement"; and outcome as the "accomplishments or results that occur (at least partially) because of services provided" (GASB, 1994:22). SEA reporting does not take the position that any one dimension of performance is more important than another, but rather suggests that all three dimensions are important. This tripartite conceptualization of performance creates what can be called an "expanded systems model" (see Figure 4.1).

Figure 4.1: Performance Accountability and the Expanded Systems Model

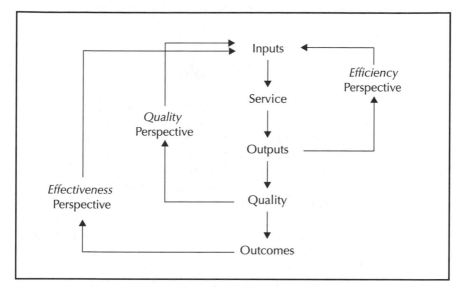

As Figure 4.1 demonstrates, performance feedback on the production of outputs compared to the consumption of inputs provides a measure of program *efficiency.* Performance feedback on quality in relationship to the consumption of inputs provides a measure of program *quality.* And feedback on the production of outcomes in relationship to the consumption of inputs provides a measure of program *effectiveness.* All three perspectives are considered important in the evaluation of government programs (Martin & Kettner, 1996).

SEA reporting has also had a major impact on the design of state and local government performance measurement and performance budgeting systems (Melkers & Willoughby, 1998; Martin, 1997). These performance measurement and budgeting systems have, in turn, influenced the perspectives state and local governments have taken with respect to PBC (Martin 2002a, 2002b).

Greater Freedom to Experiment and Innovate with Performance-Based Contracting

Unlike federal departments and agencies, state and local governments have fewer policies, procedures, and guidelines on how to construct performance-based contracts. Consequently, state and local governments have greater freedom to experiment with approaches to PBC that differ from the federal perspective.

The next section reviews some of the more interesting case examples of state and local government use of performance-based contracting.

Case Examples

This section reviews the use of performance-based contracting by nine state and local governments and the Province of Ontario, Canada. These cases were selected because of their novel approaches to various aspects of PBC as well as their potential to serve as exemplars for federal departments and agencies. Figure 4.2 describes each of the 10 case examples.

The case examples were identified and selected through a combination of approaches. The author contacted state and local governments known to be actively experimenting with PBC. The National Institute of Governmental Purchasing also solicited its U.S. and Canadian members and encouraged them to provide the author with information about their PBC practices. Finally, the author participated in a series of best practices conferences on PBC conducted in the United States by The Performance Institute and in Canada by The Canadian Institute.

Case Example 1—Metropolitan Government of Nashville & Davidson County: PBC for Share-in-Savings with Partnering

Background
Federal departments and agencies contract for a variety of consulting type services (e.g., evaluation, management consulting, policy analysis, auditing, etc.) in which the *output* is a report, but the hoped for *outcome* is sound recommendations that will lead to service improvements, greater customer satisfaction, and reduced costs. The Metropolitan Government of Nashville and Davidson County, Tennessee (Metro) is using performance-based contracting for "change management" services (a form of management consulting) designed to improve the operating efficiency of Metro Water Services (MWS). In considering its contracting options, Metro wanted to ensure to the greatest extent possible that the contractor's recommendations would be implemented by MWS staff and that the recommendations would result in actual cost savings. Metro decided to use a share-in-savings approach to PBC with a partnering provision that included MWS employees.

Share-in-savings approaches to PBC have been used by some federal departments and agencies. The most common applications, however, are in the areas of recovery auditing, building energy savings, and the leasing and

Figure 4.2: Description of Case Examples

Case Example	Description
1. Metropolitan Government of Nashville & Davidson County, Tennessee: PBC for Share-in-Savings with Partnering	PBC for change management services using share-in-savings and partnering whereby the contractor and public employees share in the cost savings
2. Washington State Lottery: PBC for Revenue Enhancement	PBC for advertising services with the contractor's fee tied to lottery sales
3. Arizona Department of Economic Security: PBC with Indefinite Performance	PBC for job training and placement services with indefinite performance where the contractor's compensation and performance standards are tied to the performance benchmarks of another provider
4. DeKalb County, Georgia: PBC with Independent Third Party Performance Requirements and Monitoring	PBC for correctional health services using one quality/outcome performance requirement: The contractor must seek and secure accreditation
5. City Of Charlotte, North Carolina: PBC with Step-Up/Step-Down Incentives and Penalties	PBC for help desk and desk side support services with incentives and penalties that step-up/step-down from the performance standards or acceptable quality levels (AQLs)
6. Oklahoma Department of Rehabilitative Services: PBC for Individual Client Milestones	PBC for employment services using a milestone approach where each person served is treated as an individual project with a start point, end point, and major milestones
7. Pinellas County, Florida: PBC with Penalties for Incomplete Service Data	PBC for ambulance services with penalties for data integrity problems
8. Metro (Portland, Oregon) Exposition-Recreation Commission: PBC for Goals	PBC for convention marketing services using goals and an incremental/developmental approach
9. Illinois Department of Children & Families: PBC by Manipulating Contractor Workload	PBC for child permanency placements (family reunification, adoptions, and subsidized guardianship) using workload manipulation to increase contractor performance
10. Ontario (Canada) Realty Corporation: PBC with "Floating" Incentives and Penalties	PBC for multi-year property management services using "floating" incentives and penalties tied to 112 performance requirements

utilization of government buildings and properties (Beaulieu, 2000). Under a typical share-in-savings arrangement, incentives (increased contractor compensation) are used to encourage contractors to reduce service delivery costs. Metro's approach to share-in-savings PBC is unusual in that it involves management consulting services.

Implementation

Metro's performance-based contract requires the contractor (Brown & Caldwell, an environmental engineering and consulting firm) to reduce the MWS's operating and maintenance budget from a base of $74 million in fiscal year 1999 to a level of $64 million in fiscal year 2002 and to a level of $60 million in fiscal year 2004. This $10-million dollar reduction is a contractual obligation. As an incentive, 10 percent of the contractor's monthly compensation is being held in escrow by Metro until MWS's operating and maintenance budget is reduced to the $60 million level. As an additional incentive to both the contractor and the MWS staff, the contract also includes a share-in savings provision as well as a partnering provision:

*   For the first $4 million in additional savings (when the MWS's operating and maintenance budget is between $64 and $60 million per year), the contractor and the MWS staff are to share in 15 percent of the annual cost savings over the term of the contract.
*   For savings in excess of the $4 million (when the MWS's operating and maintenance budget is less than $60 million per year), the contractor and the MWS staff are to share in 20 percent of the annual cost savings over the term of the contract. (Metropolitan Nashville & Davidson County, 1999:1-4).

Under the terms of the contract's partnering provision, any share-in-savings is to be divided among the contractor, the MWS, and the employees of the MWS as follows: 15 percent to the contractor, 15 percent to the MWS employees on payroll at the time the partnering provisions become activated, and 70 percent to be carried over and available for use by the MWS. Current trended projections indicate that the MWS's operating and maintenance budget for fiscal year 2002 will be $66.2 million (Metro Water Services, 2002). This $66.2 million figure represents an overall reduction of $7.8 million, but is still $2.2 million above the level at which the share-in-savings and partnering become activated. The share-in-savings and partnering provisions can still be activated during fiscal years 2003 and 2004 (Metro Water Services, 2002).

Assessment

This case example makes two major points that should be of interest to federal departments and agencies. First, PBC using a share-in-savings approach can be applied to consultative type services. Second, allowing federal employees to share in cost savings through a partnering provision may increase the likelihood of a consultant's recommendations being implemented.

Case Example 2—Washington State Lottery: PBC for Revenue Enhancement

Background

Performance-based contracting for revenue enhancement is the flip side of share-in-savings. Under PBC for revenue enhancement, incentives (increased contractor compensation) are tied to the amount of additional revenue generated as a result of the contractor's work. Increased revenue becomes the performance *outcome* of the contract.

The Washington State Lottery was spending some $6.5 million annually for advertising services. The previous contract type had been "level of effort," where the contractor was paid for performing certain tasks including advertising services, production activities, printing, and television and radio media buys. The contractor's compensation was set as a percentage (15 percent) of the contract price. From a performance perspective, the contract suffered from a major structural fault: The contractor was not accountable for any results, either in terms of the success of the advertising campaign(s) or in terms of increased lottery sales. In the view of the Washington Office of State Procurement, the purpose of the advertising contract was to generate lottery sales through effective advertising, yet there was no financial risk to the contractor, only the state, if the efforts were unsuccessful (Joplin & Bunker, 1998).

Implementation

The Washington Office of State Procurement (OSP) provided consulting and technical assistance services to the Washington State Lottery (Lottery) to make the advertising services contract more performance based. Because advertising services is a complex activity, the OSP and the Lottery met several times with industry representatives to brainstorm issues before the release of a request for proposals (RFP). The RFP led to a totally new approach to contracting for advertising services. Under the terms of the performance-based contract, the contractor (Publicis in the West, a division of Publicis SA, a French multinational advertising company) is being compensated on the basis of a fixed-fee tied to Lottery sales with a range between 90 percent and 115 percent (Joplin & Bunker, 1998). Thus, the contractor's compensation can be as low as 90 percent of its fee if lottery sales are below the specified benchmark amount or as high as 115 percent of its fee if lottery sales are greater than the specified benchmark. The actual fee to be paid the contractor is computed using the formula in Figure 4.3.

Figure 4.3: Washington State Lottery Computation of Contract Fee for Advertising Services

---

Step 1:   Actual Sales/Projected Sales = S% (rounded down to 3 decimal places)

Step 2:   S% X Annual Fee Bid = Actual Annual Fee Payment (The actual annual fee to have a floor of 90% and a ceiling of 115%)

Source: Adapted from Joplin & Bunker (1998).

Assessment

Federal departments and agencies spend over $500 million annually on media and advertising (GAO, 2000:3). To what end? While federal departments and agencies may not be concerned with revenue enhancement, they are concerned with increasing the effectiveness of their media and advertising expenditures. Tying contractor compensation to the effectiveness of media advertising through PBC is a creative and attractive approach to accomplishing this objective.

Case Example 3—Arizona Department of Economic Security: PBC with Indefinite Performance

Background

A major challenge in implementing performance-based contracting is the need to specify up front in the contract the performance standards, or acceptable quality levels, by which contractor performance will be assessed. An associated problem is that historical performance data may not be readily available. Also, changes in economic conditions during the term of a contract can affect contractor performance. The performance of a contractor may be higher when the economy is expanding and may be lower when the economy is constricting. How can federal departments and agencies account for the lack of historical performance data and changes in economic conditions when developing performance standards? The Arizona Department of Economic Security (Arizona DES) is experimenting with an interesting potential solution to these problems.

The Arizona DES used PBC to implement a welfare-to-work program called "Arizona Works" (State of Arizona, 2001). Like other welfare-to-work programs across the country, the purpose of Arizona Works was to transition people from various kinds of public assistance and support to jobs and independent living status—the performance *outcome*. The Arizona DES approach to PBC did not include specific performance standards or AQLs.

Performance Requirements for Arizona Works Performance-Based Contract

1. Number of individuals placed in jobs
2. Number of individuals placed in the highest and most appropriate jobs
3. Reduction in welfare caseload
4. Reduction in the length of stay on public assistance
5. Number of individuals placed in jobs who continue in those jobs for at least 90 days

Source: Adapted from Arizona DES (2001, 45-48).

Instead, the contract calls for indefinite performance using the Arizona DES's own performance as a benchmark.

Implementation

The Arizona DES approach to PBC called for the contractor to operate the Arizona Works program in one portion of Maricopa County (Phoenix), Arizona. The contractor, MAXIMUS, Inc., is a large multistate provider of welfare-to-work services to state and local governments. In the remaining portions of Maricopa County, the Arizona DES continues to provide the same services as the contractor. The situation is analogous to the classic control group/experimental group research design. The Arizona DES functioned as the control group; the contractor represented the experimental group. The contract contained five performance requirements, but without any specific performance standards or AQLs. Instead, the contract simply stated that the contractor *had to* exceed the performance of the Arizona DES by a minimum of 30 percent on each of the five performance requirements. Incentives and penalties included in the contract for performance that exceeded or fell short of the performance benchmarks achieved by the Arizona DES.

The Arizona DES was subjected to criticism for using the 30 percent figure, which is considered by some to be too high (Phillips & Franciosi, 2001). Why not 25 percent or even some lesser figure? Nevertheless, the contractor agreed to the 30 percent figure. During the initial contract term, the contractor did succeed in outperforming the Arizona DES by 30 percent on four of the five performance measures. The Arizona Works program was repealed during the 2002 Arizona legislative session. However, in January 2003 the Arizona DES released a request for proposals (RFP) to contract out employment services statewide using the performance standards pilot test in the Arizona Works program.

Assessment

Using PBC for indefinite performance by tying performance standards or acceptable quality levels to the performance benchmarks of another service provider (either a contractor or an in-house department) is a creative approach that federal departments and agencies may find useful. Specific performance standards were established at the outset of the contract. Contractor performance expectations are automatically adjusted for changes in economic conditions. And federal departments and agencies, as well as other stakeholders, are provided with a research-based approach (control group/experimental group) to assess the success and relative merits of various alternative service delivery approaches.

Case Example 4—DeKalb County, Georgia: PBC with Independent Third Party Performance Requirements and Monitoring

Background

One of many insights into service contracting provided by principal/agent theory (OECD, 1999) is the realization that governments (principals) have little economic incentive to monitor their contractors (agents). A major reason that governments use service contracting is to reduce service delivery costs; contract monitoring represents an additional cost. Consequently, principal/agent theory suggests that governments should design low-cost but reliable approaches to contract monitoring. The Office of Federal Procurement Policy (OFPP, 1998, 16) guide to best practices for performance-based contracting identifies four acceptable methods for structuring the quality assurance or monitoring plan: (1) 100 percent inspection, (2) random sampling, (3) periodic inspection, and (4) customer input. One hundred percent inspection is highly reliable, but is also quite costly. Conversely, customer input is low cost, but can be highly unreliable. Random sampling and periodic inspection are mid-range approaches in terms of reliability and cost. DeKalb County, Georgia, is experimenting with another method, third party certification, that is both low cost and highly reliable.

DeKalb County, Georgia, was sued, *Adams v. DeKalb,* over allegations of inadequate medical services provided to prisoners of the DeKalb County Jail. As part of the settlement agreement reached in the case, the county agreed to ensure that in the future correctional health services would be provided in accordance with the Standards for Health Care in Jails established by the National Commission on Correctional Health Care.

Implementation

As part of a plan to upgrade correctional health services at the county jail, DeKalb County decided to contract for services. The county chose to use performance-based contracting. The contract was awarded in April 2001 to Correctional Medical Services, Inc. The contract contains a large number of design specifications dealing with such input and process issues as staffing levels, staff qualifications, hours of operation, etc. Rather than attempting to develop output, quality, and outcome performance specifications for such a highly specialized service as correctional health, DeKalb County chose instead to include just one *quality/outcome* performance requirement and associated performance standard or acceptable quality level. The contractor must become accredited by the National Commission on Correctional Health Care by February 2003 from the effective date of the contract (DeKalb County, 2001).

Assessment

Attempting to monitor a contract for a professional service such as correctional medical requires a level of in-house expertise that many federal departments and agencies may not have. Even those federal departments and agencies that do possess the required in-house expertise may have other equally or even more pressing uses for that expertise. A solution in both situations is to use third party certification to perform the quality assurance or contract monitoring function. For services where licensure, certification, or accreditation organizations exist, their use represents a low-cost and highly reliable alternative, or augmentation, to direct quality assurance or monitoring. Licensure, certification, and accreditation usually involve meeting multiple performance requirements, including *quality* and *outcome*. Third party certification can also be made a requirement for doing business with a federal department or agency. For example, human service contractors must seek and secure accreditation as a condition of doing business with the states of Florida and North Carolina.

Case Study 5—City of Charlotte, North Carolina: PBC with Step-Up/ Step-Down Incentives and Penalties

Background

The Office of Federal Procurement Policy (OFPP, 1997:2) suggests that performance-based contracting should include incentives and penalties when the service is either mission critical or involves relatively large expenditures of public funds. Many state and local government performance-based contracts include incentives and penalties regardless of mission criticality or dollar value. Incentives and penalties usually take the form of additional compensation contractors can earn for performance that exceeds the performance standards or acceptable quality levels, or compensation that is denied contractors for performance that is below the performance standards or AQLs. The appropriate mix of incentives/penalties can, and does, vary from contract to contract depending upon the type of service, the preferences of individual governments, what contractors are willing to agree to, and other factors. State and local governments frequently structure their performance-based contracts so that incentives and penalties step up and step down from the performance standards or AQLs.

Implementation

The City of Charlotte, North Carolina, is using PBC for help desk and desk side support services. The contractor is the UNISYS Corporation. The contract contains three performance requirements and associated performance standards or AQLs, plus a quality assurance/monitoring plan. The contract also contains incentives and penalties that increase and decrease from the performance standards in a step-up/step-down fashion. One of the performance requirements calls for the contractor to "repair broken personal computers including hardware, operating system problems (desktop and laptop) and supported software..." (City of Charlotte, 2001:34). The associated performance standard is that 85 percent of personal computers will be restored to operations (the performance *outcome*) within two hours. The maximum total incentive payment that the contractor can earn for exceeding the contract's three performance requirements and associated performance standards or AQLs is 2 percent of a monthly billing. Conversely, the maximum total penalties that the contractor can incur for failure to meet the three contract performance requirements and associated performance standards is 4 percent of a monthly billing.

Figure 4.4 illustrates how the incentives and penalties step up/step down from the performance standard or AQL. For superior performance above the performance standard or AQL of 85 percent, the contractor can earn an incentive payment of up to 2 percent of a monthly billing. Because of the importance the City of Charlotte places on this particular performance standard, the contractor can also have penalties imposed of up to 4 percent of a monthly billing. If the contractor's performance is between 88 percent and 89 percent for a given month, it earns an incentive payment equal to 1 percent of the monthly billing, stepping up to 1.5 percent of the monthly billing for performance between 90 percent and 91 percent and stepping up again to 2 percent of the monthly billing for performance at or above 92 percent.

Conversely, if the contractor's performance falls below the performance standard of 85 percent, the contractor's compensation is reduced in a step-wise fashion: 1 percent for a performance level of 84 percent, 2 percent for a performance level of 83 percent, 3 percent for a performance level of 82 percent, and a maximum of 4 percent for a performance level of 81 percent and below.

Figure 4.4: Incentives and Penalties for Help Desk & Desk Side Support Services

Contractor Premium	Baseline Performance Metric Percentage	
2.0% Max	92% and above	
1.5%	90%–91%	
1.0%	88%–89%	
0.0%	86%–87%	
	85% Baseline	
	84%	1.0%
	83%	2.0%
	82%	3.0%
	81% and below	4.0% **City of Charlotte Credit**

Source: City of Charlotte, North Carolina (2001, 34).

Assessment

The concept of using step-up/step-down incentives and penalties in PBC may be an attractive approach for federal departments and agencies to consider. Step-up/step-down incentives and penalties highlight, and tend to keep contractors focused on, the performance standards. Additionally, contractors also have both positive and negative motivations to achieve the performance standards. The implications of superior and inferior performance are made quite clear to contractors. When the incentives and penalties step up/step down in similar fashion and in similar quantities, an appeal is also made to fairness. However, at least some research exists suggesting that the use of penalties can be quite effective (perhaps even more effective than incentives) in changing the behavior of contractors to focus more on performance (e.g., Shetterly, 2002, 2000; Martin, 2002).

Case Example 6—Oklahoma Department of Rehabilitative Services: PBC for Individual Client Milestones

Background

Federal departments and agencies have long used project management to administer contracts for construction and non-recurring services. The Oklahoma Department of Rehabilitation Services (Oklahoma DRS)

has taken the concept of project management one step further by applying
it to performance-based contracting for a recurring service: supportive
employment. The Oklahoma DRS calls its approach "milestone" PBC
(Frumkin, 2002).

Implementation

The Oklahoma DRS is using PBC for supportive employment (job training and placement services for persons with physical and mental disabilities).
Under the Oklahoma DRS approach to milestone PBC, each person served
under a contract is treated as an individual project. As Figure 4.5 demonstrates, each person served has a definable start point (entrance into service), end point (exit from service), and identifiable major milestones (e.g.,
job placement) to be accomplished in between. The payment mechanism
used by the Oklahoma DRS equates to a fixed-fee contract with progress
payments. A fixed fee per person is established, and contractors (nonprofit
community rehabilitation agencies) earn a portion of that fee (the progress
payment) every time a person achieves one of the milestones. Since contractors are only paid for accomplishing the milestones and receive no
other compensation, incentives and penalties are automatically built into
the contract.

**Figure 4.5: Oklahoma Department of Rehabilitation Services Performance-Based
Milestone Contracting for Supportive Employment**

Milestone	Type of Milestone	% of Fee
1. Determination of Need	Process	10
2. Vocational Preparation	Process	10
3. Job Placement	Output	10
4. Job Training	Process	10
5. Job Retention	Process	15
6. Job Stabilization	Quality/Outcome	20
7. Case Closed	Outcome	25

Sources: Adapted from Oklahoma DRS (n.d.):1-2; Novak, Mank, Revell & O'Brien (n.d.):29.

Assessment

In addition to being a creative application of project management, three aspects of the Oklahoma DRS approach are worthy of highlighting because they challenge the federal perspective on PBC (OFPP, 1998). First, all three dimensions of performance (output, quality, and outcome) are included in the Oklahoma DRS milestone approach. Second, the Oklahoma DRS's milestone approach does not view PBC as an "all or nothing" proposition. While 55 percent of contractors' fees are tied to output, quality, and outcome *performance specifications* (i.e., performance standards), the remaining 45 percent is tied to input and process *design specifications*. Third, different contractors can have different mixes of design and performance specifications (performance standards) and different associated payment schedules. Thus, milestone PBC can be used in a developmental approach whereby contractor focus is shifted over time away from design specifications to performance specifications (performance standards).

The Oklahoma DRS is not the only state human service agency experimenting with milestone PBC. Kansas, North Carolina, and Pennsylvania have also used milestone PBC. In all instances, the results in terms of changing the behavior of contractors to focus more on performance have been impressive (Martin, 2002a; 2002b). The milestone approach to PBC should be of interest to those federal departments and agencies that contract for professional, health, or human services provided to federal employees or where the federal government is a third party payer.

Case Example 7—Pinellas County, Florida: PBC with Penalties for Incomplete Service Data

Background

A long-standing problem associated with attempts to implement performance-based contracting is data integrity. Both the Office of the Texas State Auditor (2000) and the Florida Office of Program Performance and Accountability to the People (1998) have documented problems with the validity and reliability of performance measurement data. In PBC the issue of data integrity is particularly important. When contractor compensation, either partially or in toto, is tied to performance, the performance itself becomes auditable. If the performance data cannot be documented, verified, and replicated, audit exceptions and questioned costs can arise. In the Office of Federal Procurement Policy's (OFPP, 1998) initial experiment with PBC (see p. 9), the number of financial audits was reduced by an astounding 93 percent. The implications of this finding have not been lost on auditors and the auditing profession; they are presently gearing up to conduct more performance audits.

When Pinellas County, Florida, decided to use PBC for ambulance services, one of the many issues it had to confront was data integrity (a *quality* performance standard). Third party payers (e.g., insurance companies, managed health care programs, Medicare, Medicaid, and others) generally will not pay for services rendered unless complete and accurate data are provided documenting the need for the service, the type of service provided, and the name and relevant personal information of the person receiving the service.

Implementation
In order to ensure that it would be able to properly invoice third party payers, Pinellas County built stringent data integrity penalties into its ambulance services contract:

> Pinellas County "shall automatically deduct from the Additional Service Amount equal to the Wholesale Rate for one transport for every Patient served by Contractor for whom all the information required to be supplied by Contractor (i.e., dispatch record, Billable Run Report, and any required forms) is incomplete, illegible, inaccurate, altered, or lacking evidence of medical necessity, where such medical necessity exists, as to result in (Pinellas County's) claim for payment being denied by responsible payors, or to otherwise prevent (Pinellas County) from effectively utilizing its data processing, billing and collection procedures" (Pinellas County, 1999:58). (parentheses added)

This well-defined penalty clause has apparently had the desired effect. Pinellas County reports that data integrity problems are minimal.

Assessment
As federal departments and agencies adopt PBC for more and more services, the issue of data integrity will become increasingly important. Including stringent data integrity requirements in contracts, and disallowing payments for services when complete and accurate data are missing, may be an approach that federal departments and agencies can use to "audit proof" their performance-based contracts.

Case Example 8—Metro (Portland, Oregon) Exposition-Recreation Commission: PBC for Goals

Background
When is a contract "performance based" and when is it not? Must a contract contain all the essential elements as enumerated by the Office of Federal Procurement Policy (OFPP, 1997) to be considered a performance-

based contract? These are questions that confront not only federal departments and agencies, but other governments as well. When it comes to state and local governments, performance-based contracting is conceptualized less as a "yes or no issue" (the contract is or is not performance based) and more as an "issue of degrees," ranging from non-PBC to full or complete PBC.

In September 2000, the Metro (Portland, Oregon) auditor conducted a review of the marketing services contract between the Metro Exposition-Recreation Commission (MERC Commission) and the Portland Oregon Visitors Association (POVA), a private nonprofit organization that promotes tourism and conventions in the metro Portland area. As part of the audit report, the Metro auditor recommended that the contract be made more performance based (Metro Auditor, 2000). The question to be resolved was: to what extent?

Implementation

POVA developed six goals (performance requirements) that were included in the contract by amendment dated October 2001. The goals include *output* and *outcome* performance requirements as well as process requirements. The goals, or performance requirements, also include ratings that are analogous to performance standards or acceptable quality levels. Goal 1 (a performance *outcome*) and its associated rating (AQL) is shown in Figure 4.6. As Figure 4.6 illustrates, the overall goal for the two-year contract is to book 12 new convention groups. Since conventions are

Figure 4.6: Marketing Services Goals

Goal #1—Book 6 New Convention Groups
To book 6 new groups per fiscal year who meet the following preferred Oregon Convention Center (OCC) booking guidelines:

Years Out	Gross Sq. Ft. Exhibit Space	Peak Night Rooms
5+	120,000	800
3–5	90,000	600
1.5–3	60,000	500

Ratings:
Exceeds Standard = more than 6 new groups per fiscal year booked
Meets Standard = 5–6 new groups per fiscal year booked
Needs Improvement = less than 5 new groups per fiscal year booked

---

Source: Adapted from MERC Commission (2001):1

frequently booked many years in advance, sub-goals are included that cover one and a half to three years out, three to five years out, and five-plus years out. The performance standard or AQL is to book a minimum of five new groups per year over the two-year period.

From a federal perspective (OFPP, 1998), two major criticisms can be leveled against the MERC Commission performance-based contract: (1) it does not contain a quality assurance or monitoring plan, and (2) incentives and penalties are not included even though the contract is mission critical and involves the expenditure of substantial government funds. Nevertheless, a contract that previously had no performance requirements and no performance standards or acceptable quality levels now contains them. And both a government and a contractor that had little previous experience with PBC are now gaining experience. The MERC Commission and the contractor have jointly made a substantial move along the continuum from non-PBC to full-PBC. At the expiration of the current contract term, both the MERC Commission and the contractor will be poised and prepared to take the next steps in a developmental approach to PBC.

Assessment

Treating PBC as an incremental and developmental process would appear to have obvious benefits for federal departments and agencies. Not all services and not all contractors may be capable of transitioning from non-PBC to full or complete PBC at one time. Such a transition can create difficulties for contractors as well as disrupt service delivery and affect mission-critical activities. Federal departments and agencies might be better served by conceptualizing PBC as an incremental and developmental process for some services and for some contractors.

Case Example 9—Illinois Department of Children & Families: PBC by Manipulating Contractor Workload

Background

During the 1990s, the Illinois Department of Children & Families (Illinois DCF) had one of the highest child welfare caseloads in the nation. The Illinois DCF decided something had to be done to change the behavior of its contractors (private nonprofit organizations) to focus more on *outcome* performance: finding suitable permanent placements (reunification, adoption, or subsidized guardianship) for children in care. The Illinois DCF decided to adopt performance-based contracting.

What is most interesting about the Illinois DCF approach is that it violates nearly every aspect of the federal perspective on PBC. Based on the essential elements as enumerated by the Office of Federal Procurement

Policy (OFPP, 1998), the Illinois DCF approach does not remotely qualify as PBC. While use is made of performance requirements, the Illinois DCF approach does not include: performance standards or acceptable quality levels (AQLs), incentives, or penalties, and no quality assurance or monitoring plan. Despite these "shortcomings," what the Illinois DCF approach has achieved is impressive contractor performance.

Implementation

The Illinois DCF suspected that its traditional cost reimbursement approach to contracting might be creating perverse incentives. Contractors might be keeping children in care longer than necessary because no incentives or penalties existed in the contract tied to the length of time children were in care. In thinking about its contracting options, the Illinois DCF could have opted to tie contractor payment to performance as is done in the milestone approach used by the Oklahoma Department of Rehabilitative Services (see case example 6). Milestone contracting, however, would put their nonprofit contractors at financial risk for failure to perform. The Illinois DCF decided against adopting a milestone approach, choosing instead to develop its own unique approach to PBC.

The premise of the Illinois DCF approach to PBC is to increase contractor outcome performance (measured in terms of child permanency placements) while holding inputs (measured in terms of dollars) constant (Illinois DCF, 2000; n.d). The Illinois DCF approach accomplishes this objective through the manipulation of contractor workload. Contractors are still compensated using cost reimbursement contracts at a level of 25 cases per caseworker. However, caseworkers are now expected to find permanent placements for at least five children each fiscal quarter. At the beginning of every fiscal quarter, each contractor caseworker is assigned five new cases by the Illinois DCF (see Figure 4.7). No additional compensation is provided to the contractors or the caseworkers.

Figure 4.7: Illinois Department of Children & Families Contractor Caseworker Caseloads

	Caseworker 1	Caseworker 2	Caseworker 3
Old Caseload	25	25	25
Cases Closed	(5)	(0)	(10)
New Cases	5	5	5
New Caseload	25	30	20

If a contractor caseworker places five children during the preceding fiscal quarter, his/her caseload remains constant at 25. If fewer children are placed, the caseworker's caseload goes up; and if more than five children are placed, the caseworker's caseload goes down. The Illinois DCF's approach to PBC has demonstrated impressive results. Contractor performance in terms of the number of child permanency placements has increased over 200 percent since the transition to PBC (Illinois DCF, 2000:3).

Assessment

The Illinois DCF's approach to PBC does not include the minimum OFPP essential elements. Consequently, the Illinois DCF approach is not considered to constitute PBC according to the federal perspective. What the Illinois DCF lacks in terms of federal purity, however, is more than made up for in terms of changing the behavior of contractors to focus more on performance. Again, the issue is raised as to when should a contract be considered performance based and when should it not. Should the decision depend upon the process that is used or the performance achieved? PBC is supposed to change the way federal departments and agencies contract for services—to get federal employees to think "outside the box." It would be unfortunate if the OFPP essential elements for PBC simply result in an existing box being replaced by a new box.

Case Example 10—Ontario (Canada) Realty Corporation: PBC with "Floating" Incentives and Penalties

Background

When and how to include incentives and penalties is yet another challenge facing federal departments and agencies in implementing performance-based contracting. Not every performance requirement and associated performance standard or acceptable quality level merits, or would necessarily benefit from, having an incentive or penalty attached. Conversely, situations can arise in which numerous performance requirements are included in a performance-based contract and any particular one might be more or less important depending upon what happens during the contract term. The second situation represents a particular challenge in using PBC. Contracts can always be amended to meet unforeseen circumstances, but formally amending a contract requires the agreement of the contractor.

This last case example comes not from a state or local government, but from the Provincial Government of Ontario, Canada. The Ontario Realty Corporation has devised a novel solution to the challenge of dealing with multiple important performance requirements and associated performance standards, or AQLs, contained in a long-term performance-based contract.

Implementation

The Ontario Realty Corporation (ORC) is a public corporation of the Ontario, Canada, Provincial Government. The ORC is currently using PBC for land management services. The performance-based contract covers 65,000 acres; 3,500 properties; 1,500 leases; and 1.6 million square feet of commercial and industrial space. The contractor, Del Management Solutions, Inc., is one of Canada's largest real estate and facility management compa-

Ontario Realty Corporation Performance Objectives	
Management	(15%)
Financial	(20%)
Asset Integrity	(20%)
Customer Service	(20%)
Rent Collection	(20%)

Source: Adapted from Kessel (2001).

nies. In addition to its massive scale, what is perhaps even more interesting about ORC's approach to PBC is the complexity of the contract. The contract contains five output, quality, and outcome performance objectives weighted for relative importance. Associated with these five performance objectives are 13 broad measures, 30 performance measures and *112 performance requirements*. The contract includes two types of incentives/penalties: (1) a 10 percent quarterly management fee hold back, and (2) an annual share-in-savings arrangement (Kessel, 2001).

An issue ORC had to resolve in developing its approach to PBC was: Which of the 112 performance requirements should have associated incentives and penalties? Given the size and complexity of the contract, ORC believed that all the 112 performance requirements were important. But ORC also realized that it would be difficult to administer a contract with incentives and penalties tied to 112 performance requirements and associated performance standards or AQLs. The solution devised by ORC was to create a system of "floating" incentives and penalties. At any one time, the contract incentives and penalties are tied to only about a dozen performance requirements. But ORC reserves the right to change the mix with 30 days' notice to the contractor (Kessel, 2001).

Because the contractor can't be sure which set of performance requirements may have associated incentives and penalties at any one time, ORC believes that the contractor will necessarily have to pay attention to all 112. For example, if the contractor's performance falls below the performance standard or AQL on any one of the 112 performance requirements, ORC can simply change the mix of incentives and penalties to include that specific performance requirement.

Assessment

Federal performance-based contracts can often be complex and contain numerous performance requirements. The use of "floating" incentives and penalties that can be changed during the term of a contract should have numerous potential PBC applications for federal departments and agencies.

Lessons Learned

In summarizing the experiences of state and local governments, drawing conclusions, and identifying lessons learned, the discussion returns to, and is guided by, the basic objective of PBC: *changing the behavior of contractors to focus more on performance.*

Lesson 1. PBC at the state and local government levels differs considerably from what is generally recognized as PBC under federal guidelines.

The federal approach to PBC represents a design specifications approach. To be considered performance based, a service contract must contain certain essential elements: performance requirements, performance standards or acceptable quality levels, a quality assurance or monitoring plan, and, in certain circumstances, positive and negative incentives.

Not being bound by federal guidelines as to what does and does not constitute PBC, state and local governments are free to think "outside the box" and to experiment with various performance-based policies, practices, techniques, approaches, and tools. Instead of being overly concerned with the elements of PBC, state and local governments have adopted more of a performance-specifications approach. State and local governments classify as PBC any service contract that attempts to change the behavior of contractors to focus more on performance, regardless of the approach or the contractual elements involved.

Lesson 2. PBC at the state and local government levels defines "performance" as consisting of outputs, quality, outcomes, or any combinations thereof.

While some confusion appears to exist at the federal level in terms of what constitutes "performance" in PBC, no such confusion exists at the state and local government levels. "Performance" in state and local government PBC is taken to mean outputs, quality, outcomes, and various combinations. This tripartite conceptualization of performance: (1) provides greater clarity as to the purpose of PBC, (2) gives state and local governments more options in structuring performance-based contracts, and (3) aligns more closely the concept of performance in PBC with the concept of performance contained in the service efforts and accomplishments reporting initiative of the Governmental Accounting Standards Board.

Lesson 3. PBC at the state and local government levels involves varying degrees of being performance based.

A goal of PBC is to make *less use* of design specifications (input and process) and *more use* of performance specifications (outputs, quality, and outcomes). The experiences of state and local governments demonstrate that service contract specifications can be conceptualized on a continuum (inputs → process → outputs → quality → outcomes) from "non-PBC" to "full-PBC." At the non-PBC end of the continuum are service contracts that make exclusive use of design specifications; at the full-PBC end of the continuum are service contracts that make exclusive use of outcome performance specifications. In between fall varying degrees of being performance based. Conceptualizing PBC on a continuum allows for an incremental and developmental approach to be taken with certain services and with certain contractors.

Lesson 4. PBC at the state and local government levels challenges the notion that there is one best way to do performance-based contracting.

The state of the art in PBC today is insufficiently well developed to make any claims about how best to implement this new form of service contracting. What can be said is that state and local governments utilize a variety of different approaches in implementing PBC. The common denominator in these various approaches is the conscious attempt on the part of state and local governments to change the behavior of contractors to focus more on performance.

Lesson 5. PBC at the state and local government levels includes share-in-savings contracting, revenue enhancement contracting, and milestone contracting.

The experience of state and local governments clearly demonstrates that share-in-savings contracting, revenue enhancement contracting, and milestone contracting can affect the behavior of contractors to focus more on performance. Thus, these approaches warrant being called PBC. In the case of both share-in-savings contracting and revenue enhancement contracting, contractor behavior is changed to focus on the accomplishment of certain processes and outputs that lead in turn to the accomplishment of certain desired outcomes (reduced service delivery costs and increased revenues). In the case of milestone contracting, contractor behavior is changed to focus more on performance because output, quality, and outcome performance requirements, as well as incentives and penalties, are automatically built into the contract.

Lesson 6. PBC at the state and local government levels makes frequent use of incentives and penalties regardless of mission criticality or the dollar value of the contract.

The federal approach to PBC suggests that positive and negative incentives should be included in a performance-based contract when the contract is mission critical or when the contract involves the expenditure of a large amount of public funds. State and local governments routinely make use of incentives and penalties in PBC regardless of mission criticality or the dollar value of the contracts. The inclusion of incentives and penalties is a major motivational factor in changing the behavior of contractors to focus more on performance.

Lesson 7. The manipulation of workload can change the behavior of contractors to focus more on performance, exclusive of other PBC considerations.

As the case example of the Illinois Department of Children & Families demonstrates, the manipulation of workload can change the behavior of contractors to focus more on performance without the contract containing all of the essential elements identified in the federal approach to PBC. While use is made of performance requirements, the Illinois DCF approach does not include performance standards or acceptable quality levels, incentives, or penalties—even though the contracts are mission critical—and has no quality assurance or monitoring plan. Despite these "shortcomings," the Illinois DCF approach to PBC has achieved impressive results in terms of changing contractor behavior to focus more on performance.

Lesson 8. The adoption of "floating" incentives and penalties is a useful approach when a performance-based contract contains numerous important performance requirements.

Conventional wisdom suggests that PBC should involve a small number of incentives and penalties tied to an equally small number of performance requirements and associated performance standards or acceptable quality levels. The Ontario (Canada) Realty Corporation case example demonstrates how this rule can be applied to a complex contract with multiple (112) important performance requirements. By tying incentives and penalties to a small number (12) of performance requirements and AQLs, but maintaining the unilateral right to change the mix with 30 days' notice, the contractor is forced to concern itself with all 112 performance requirements. Because the contractor can never be sure which mix of performance requirements will have associated incentives and penalties, it must ensure that none diverge too far from their performance standards or AQLs.

Lesson 9. Third party certification is a low-cost and highly reliable approach to quality assurance and monitoring.

The DeKalb County, Georgia, case example demonstrates how the quality assurance or monitoring function can be delegated to an independent third party when licensure, certification, or accreditation requirements exist. Third party certification is low cost as well as highly reliable in that licensure, certification, and accreditation usually require meeting multiple performance requirements, including *quality* and *outcome*. Third party certification can be used to either augment or replace other approaches to quality assurance or monitoring. The use of third party certification for quality assurance or monitoring is a good example of "working smarter, not harder."

Lesson 10. The step-up/step-down method is a useful approach to structuring incentives and penalties.

Structuring incentives and penalties to step up and step down from the performance standard or acceptable quality level makes clear to contractors the implications of acceptable performance and unacceptable performance. As detailed in the City of Charlotte case example, step-up/step-down incentives and penalties tend to keep the contractor focused on the performance standards. Additionally, the contractor also has positive and negative motivations to achieve the performance standards. When incentives and penalties step up/step down in similar fashion, and in similar quantities, an appeal is also made to fairness.

Lesson 11. Contracting for non-specific performance is a creative approach to structuring PBC that may be useful in at least some situations.

The idea of contracting for non-specific performance tied to the benchmark of another service provider (a contractor or an in-house department) represents an interesting approach to PBC that may be useful to some federal departments and agencies in at least some situations. As the Arizona Department of Economic Security case example demonstrates, contracting for non-specific performance represents a way of automatically adjusting for changes in economic conditions and other factors that may affect contractor performance during the term of the contract. This approach has the added advantage of simulating a classic experimental research design, with the benchmark provider representing the control group and the performance-based contractor representing the experimental group.

Recommendations

The Office of Federal Procurement Policy formed an interagency working group in April 2002 to address performance-based contracting. The working group, comprised of procurement and program analysts from a number of federal departments and agencies, is examining the basic tenets of PBC including the essential elements and goals. The working group will make recommendations to the administrator of the OFPP concerning possible changes to existing guidance and regulations. The following recommendations are addressed to the working group and to the OFPP.

The OFPP should consider revising the guidance it provides federal departments and agencies on performance-based contracting to:

Recommendation 1. Make federal PBC more compatible with the performance accountability framework and language of the Government Performance and Results Act and the Service Efforts and Accomplishments (SEA) reporting initiative of the Governmental Accounting Standards Board.

This action will make PBC more compliant with what is rapidly becoming a common language of government performance accountability. Also, if PBC is to become a primary tool of federal procurement, then it must become more compliant with the primary performance accountability frameworks of the federal government and state and local governments.

Recommendation 2. Operationally define "performance" as including outputs, quality, outcomes, or any combination thereof.

This action will resolve the current conflicting and contradictory operational definitions of PBC provided by:
- the OFPP, which views PBC as contracting for outputs and quality
- the Department of Defense, which views PBC as contracting for outcomes
- the Federal Acquisition Regulation, which views PBC as contracting for outcomes and quality

This tripartite conceptualization (outputs, quality, outcomes) will also ensure that federal PBC takes a comprehensive view of performance to include considerations of efficiency (outputs), quality, and effectiveness (outcomes).

Recommendation 3. Recognize that varying degrees of being performance based can exist.

This action will recognize PBC as existing on a continuum from "non-PBC" to "full-PBC" and will allow for an incremental and developmental approach to be taken with some services and with some contractors. The

federal perspective is that a service contract is either performance based or not depending upon the presence or absence of four essential elements:
- performance requirements
- performance standards or acceptable quality levels
- a quality assurance or monitoring plan
- positive and negative incentives if the service is mission critical or involves a large expenditure of public funds

The "all or nothing" federal perspective may result in federal departments and agencies choosing not to attempt PBC with some services and with some contractors.

Recommendation 4. Include share-in-savings, revenue enhancement, and milestone contracting as recognized optional forms of PBC.

This action will recognize the validity of existing practices. Share-in-savings, revenue enhancement, and milestone contracting all seek to change the behavior of contractors to focus more on performance (outputs, quality, and outcomes). As such, they constitute optional forms of PBC and should be so recognized. This action will also begin the process of identifying and classifying various approaches to PBC.

Recommendation 5. Adopt third party certification as an acceptable optional approach to quality assurance and monitoring.

This action will add a low-cost and highly reliable form of quality assurance and monitoring to the list of recognized and acceptable approaches. Currently, the federal approach to PBC recognizes only: (1) 100 percent inspection, (2) random sampling, (3) periodic inspection, and (4) customer input. Third party certification (licensure, certification, or accreditation) usually requires meeting multiple performance requirements, including *quality* and *outcome*. Third party certification should be allowable to either augment or replace other approaches to quality assurance or monitoring.

Recommendation 6. Promote the use of the step-up/step-down method for structuring incentives and penalties in PBC.

This action will provide federal departments and agencies with a simple and easy-to-use strategy for structuring incentives and penalties in PBC. Structuring incentives and penalties to step up/step down from the performance standards or acceptable quality levels will make clear to contractors the implications of acceptable performance and unacceptable performance. When incentives and penalties step up/step down in similar fashion, and in similar quantities, an appeal is also made to fairness.

Bibliography

Arizona Department of Economic Security (2001). Arizona Works Contract with Amendments 1–6. Phoenix: Author.

Beaulieu, M. (2000). *Share in Savings: Summary of Interviews and Comparison to Federal Agencies' Missions.* Washington, D.C.: The Council for Excellence in Government.

City of Charlotte, North Carolina (2001). Help Desk and Desk Side Support Services Statement of Work. Charlotte: Author.

Commercial Activities Panel (2001c). "Current Condition of Federal Contracting." PowerPoint presentation to members of the Commercial Activities Panel. http://www.gao.gov/a76panel/meeting.html (11/01/01).

DeKalb County, Georgia (2001). "Request for Proposals (RFP) No. 01-05 to Provide Inmate Health Care at the DeKalb County Jail." Decatur, Ga.: Author.

Department of Defense (2001). *Guidebook for Performance-Based Services Acquisition (PBSA) in the Department of Defense.* Washington, D.C.: Author.

Frumkin, P. (2001). "Managing for Outcomes: Milestone Contracting in Oklahoma." In Abramson, M., and J. Kamensky (Eds.) *Managing for Results 2002.* Lanham, Md.: Rowman & Littlefield Publishers, 145-169.

Gansler, J. (2002). *A Vision of the Government as a World-Class Buyer: Major Procurement Issues for the Coming Decade.* Arlington, Va.: The PricewaterhouseCoopers Endowment for The Business of Government.

General Accounting Office (GAO) (2001a). "Contract Management: Trends & Challenges in Acquiring Services." PowerPoint presentation to members of the Commercial Activities Panel. http://www.gao.gov/a76panel/meeting.html (11/01/01).

General Accounting Office (GAO) (2002). *Contract Management: Guidance Needed for Using Performance-Based Service Contracting.* Washington, D.C.: Author GAO-02-1049.

General Accounting Office (GAO) (2001b). *Contract Management: Trends & Challenges in Acquiring Services.* Washington, D.C.: Author. GAO-01-T53.

General Accounting Office (GAO) (2000). *Federal Advertising Contracts: Agencies Have Discretion in Setting Work Scope & Requirements.* Washington, D.C.: Author. GAO-GGD-00-203.

Gordon, S. (2001). *Performance-Based Contracting.* Washington, D.C.: International City/County Management Association. IQ Report, Vol. 33, No. 6.

Governmental Accounting Standards Board (GASB) (1994). Concepts Statement No. 2 of the Governmental Accounting Standards Board on Concepts Related to Service Efforts and Accomplishment Reporting. Norwalk: GASB.

Illinois Department of Children & Families (Illinois DCF, 2000). Harvard University "Innovations in American Government" Application.

Illinois Department of Children & Families (Illinois DCF, n.d.) Cook County Private Agency Performance Contract Program Plan.

Joplin, B., and R. Bunker. (1998). *Performance-Based Contracting for the Washington State Lottery.* Olympia: State of Washington, Department of General Administration, Office of State Procurement.

Kessel, C. (2001). Performance-Based Contracts Case Study: Ontario Realty Corporation Land Management Contract with Del Management Solutions, Inc. Presentation at the Conference "Performance-Based Contracting in the Public Sector," Ottawa, Ontario, Canada, November 5 & 6, 2001. Sponsored by The Canadian Institute.

Martin, L. L. (2002a). "Performance-Based Contracting for Human Services: A Proposed Model." *Public Administration Quarterly* (in press).

Martin, L. L. (2002b). "Performance-Based Contracting for Human Services: Lessons for Public Procurement?" *Journal of Public Procurement* 2(1):55-71.

Martin, L. L. (1997). "Outcome Budgeting: A New Entrepreneurial Approach to Budgeting." *Journal of Public Budgeting, Accounting & Financial Management* 9 (1):108-126.

Martin, L. L. & J. Miller. (2003). *Contracting for Public Services.* Herndon, VA: National Institute of Governmental Purchasing.

Martin, L. L., and P. Kettner. (1996). *Measuring the Performance of Human Service Programs.* Thousand Oaks: Sage Publications.

Melkers, J., and K. Willoughby. (1998). "The State of the States: Performance Budgeting Requirements in 47 out of 50." *Public Administration Review* 58 (1):66-71.

Metro (Portland, Oregon) Auditor (2000). Metropolitan Exposition-Recreation Commission—Portland, Oregon, Visitors Association Contract. Portland: Author.

Metro (Portland, Oregon) Exposition-Recreation Commission (MERC Commission) (2001). Addendum to Market Services Agreement (the "Agreement") Between the Portland, Oregon, Visitors Association ("POVA") and the Metropolitan Exposition-Recreation Commission ("MERC" or "Merc Commission). Portland, OR: Authors.

Metro Water Services (2002). *Performance Measurement and Analysis Update.* PowerPoint presentation. Nashville: Author.

Metropolitan Government of Nashville & Davidson County (1999).
    Contract Between Metropolitan Government of Nashville and Davidson
    County and Brown and Caldwell for Purchase of Services. Nashville,
    Tenn.: Author.

Novak, J., D. Mank, G. Revell, and D. O'Brien (n.d.). *Paying for
    Performance: Results Based Approaches to Funding Supported
    Employment.* Oklahoma City: Oklahoma Department of Rehabilitative
    Services. http://www.onenet.net/~home/milestone (11/10/01).

Office of Economic Cooperation & Development (OECD). (1999).
    *Performance Contracting: Lessons from Performance Contracting Case
    Studies, A Framework for Public Sector Performance Contracting.* Paris:
    Author.

Office of Federal Procurement Policy (OFPP). (1998a). *A Guide to Best
    Practices for Performance-Based Service Contracting.* Washington,
    D.C.: Author. http://www.arnet.gov/Library/OFPP/ PolicyDocs (5/06/02).

Office of Federal Procurement Policy (OFPP). (1998b). *A Report on the
    Performance-Based Service Contracting Pilot Project.* Washington,
    D.C.: Author. http://www.arnet.gov/Library/OFPP/PolicyDocs (5/06/02).

Office of Federal Procurement Policy (OFPP). (1997). "Memorandum for:
    Agency Senior Procurement Executives, the Deputy Under Secretary of
    Defense (Acquisition Reform) Performance-Based Service Contracting
    (PBSC) Points of Contact. Subject: PBSC Checklists" August 8, 1997,
    Washington D.C.: Author. http://www.arnet/gov/Library/OFPP/PolicyDocs
    (5/06/02).

Office of Management and Budget (OMB) (2001). "Memorandum dated
    March 9, 2001 for Heads & Acting Heads of Departments and
    Agencies, Subject: Performance Goals and Management Initiatives for
    the FY 2002 Budget." Washington, D.C. Author.

Office of Program Policy Analysis and Government Accountability
    (1998). PB2 Performance Report for the State's Library, Archives
    and Information Program, Report No. 98-72 March 1999.
    http://www.oppaga.state.fl.us/reports.html (2/26/02).

Office of the Texas State Auditor (2000). An Audit Report on Performance
    Measures at 11 State Agencies—Phase 13 of the Performance Measures
    Reviews. Austin: Author.

Office of the Texas State Auditor (1997). An Audit Report on Performance
    Measures at 26 State Agencies—Phase 11 of the Performance Measures
    Reviews. Austin: Author.

Oklahoma Department of Rehabilitative Services (Oklahoma DRS)
    (n.d.). Milestone Payment System. Oklahoma City: Author.
    http://www.onenet.net/~home/milestone (11/10/01).

Phillips, K., and R. Franciosi. (2001). *Does Arizona Works Work? Welfare Reform in Arizona*. Arizona Issue Analysis 163. Phoenix: The Goldwater Institute. http://www.goldwaterinstitute.org/publications/azia.htm (9/27/01).

Pinellas County, Florida (1999). Ambulance Service Agreement. Largo, Fla.: Author.

Salamon, L. (2002). *The Tools of Government: A Guide to the New Governance*. New York: Oxford University Press.

Salamon, L., A. Campbell, L. Korb, J. Lordan, G. Miller, R. Moe, B. O'Connell, H. Seidman, and D. Waldo (19890). *Privatization: The Challenge to Public Management*. Washington, D.C.: National Academy of Public Administration.

Shetterly, D. (2002). "Contracting for Public Bus Transit: Do Techniques Employed Make a Difference in Service Outcomes." *Journal of Public Procurement* 2(1):73-92.

Shetterly, D. (2000). "The Influence of Contract Design on Contractor Performance." *Public Performance & Management Review* 24(1):53-68.

State of Arizona (2001). Arizona Works Pilot Project. Phoenix: Author.

Walker, D. (2001). "Managing By Results to Benefit Our Citizens." *The Public Manager* 30 (3):19-23.

CHAPTER FIVE

IT Outsourcing:
A Primer for Public Managers

Yu-Che Chen
Visiting Assistant Professor
School of Public and Environmental Affairs
Indiana University–Bloomington

James L. Perry
Associate Dean and Chancellor's Professor
School of Public and Environmental Affairs
Indiana University–Indianapolis

This report was originally published in February 2003.

IT Outsourcing: Opportunities and Challenges

Background

IT outsourcing has recently emerged as a popular means to meet the demand for e-government services. Government IT outsourcing is expected to be the fastest-growing segment of the overall federal IT market. The growth rate is estimated to be about 16 percent per year between fiscal year 2001 and 2006, reaching $13.2 billion.[1] One of the most recent visible IT outsourcing projects was the recent Navy-Marine Corps Intranet (NMCI) contract. The $6.9 billion NMCI contract, awarded in October 2000, was the biggest technology outsourcing contract ever.[2] Other large outsourcing opportunities are also on the horizon. The $4 billion HUD Information Technology Services program and the $2 billion communication infrastructure for the state of Georgia are two examples (Wait, 2002).

The continued push for federal IT spending is the result of the confluence of several factors. First, the Bush administration has continued and expanded the emphasis on e-government projects. In a 2001 count, there were 1,371 unique federal e-government initiatives (GAO, July 2001). The e-government initiatives are expected to grow due to legislative mandates for the reduction of paperwork and regular reviews of information and security practices.[3] Second, the use of information technology is regarded as a critical element in protecting homeland security. Due to the war on terrorism, our nation's cyber critical infrastructure is at greater risk. As a response, the federal government has taken some initial actions to improve federal information system security. However, more needs to be done to deal with the growing threat of computer-based attacks according to the General Accounting Office (GAO, July 2002). Therefore, information assurance—the protection of sensitive information systems and networks—is likely to be at the top of the administration's agenda for the Department of Homeland Security.

The aforementioned two factors coupled with the need for quick deployment and a shortage of IT workers in government make IT outsourcing an attractive option. Quick deployment is critical in dealing with security

---

IT Outsourcing

IT outsourcing is the utilization of external organizations for production/provision of information technology services. Network, desktop, application, and web hosting are examples of commonly outsourced IT services.

threats. The recent upgrade of information technology at the Federal Bureau of Investigation illustrates the importance of quick deployment to address security threats. Technology companies are generally better equipped to deploy technology solutions more quickly because of their IT capabilities. The shortage of in-house IT talent to handle the complexities of government IT projects forces government to embrace IT outsourcing. To counter this shortage, the government has made various efforts to keep IT talent in government (National Academy of Public Administration, 2001).

This chapter introduces public managers to IT outsourcing. It consists of three parts. The first defines IT outsourcing and discusses recent trends and developments. Against that background, the next part examines the benefits and risks associated with IT outsourcing. Knowledge about the costs and benefits can empower public managers to make an informed decision to realize the full potential of IT outsourcing. The third part presents a practical methodology for thinking systematically about management issues and strategies related to IT outsourcing, including the evaluation of costs and benefits. The proposed methodology is process oriented. This process is composed of five phases—starting with aligning IT outsourcing to organizational strategies and ending with the management of its implementation. Examples and illustrations are provided.

Defining IT Outsourcing

IT outsourcing is the utilization of external organizations for provision of information technology services. A wide range of services is available from IT vendors. Currently, the information technology services outsourced by federal agencies include network services, data center services, desktop, call centers, web hosting, and application services.

Although the types of IT services outsourced are easy to understand, they do not dictate a proper management strategy. Application services, for instance, are not necessarily more difficult to manage than web-hosting services. A more productive way of looking at an IT outsourcing arrangement is to examine the entire spectrum of relevant management tasks (see Figure 5.1). At one end of the spectrum, client agencies outsource the development, implementation, and coordination of IT services. For instance, if an agency wishes to automate and put its recruiting process on the web, it uses a vendor who has already developed the software program for that purpose and owns the facility to host the site. The agency's tasks are to provide content and monitor the service performance.

At the other end of the spectrum, the client agency is heavily involved in the development, implementation, and coordination of IT service. This service is then usually highly customized to the needs of the client agency.

Figure 5.1: Spectrum of IT Outsourcing: A Managerial Perspective

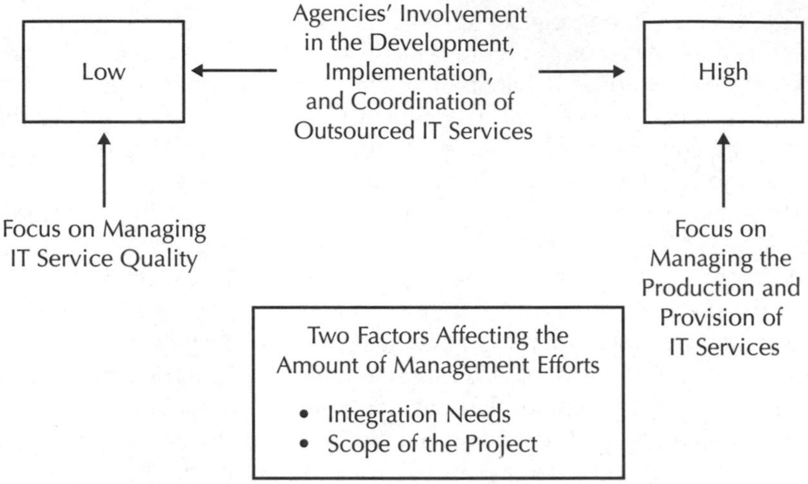

```
┌──────────────┐      Agencies' Involvement        ┌──────────────┐
│              │      in the Development,          │              │
│     Low      │ ◄──  Implementation,          ──► │     High     │
│              │      and Coordination of          │              │
└──────────────┘      Outsourced IT Services       └──────────────┘
        ▲                                                  ▲
        │                                                  │
        │                                                  │
 Focus on Managing                                     Focus on
 IT Service Quality                                  Managing the
                                                     Production and
                    ┌────────────────────────┐      Provision of
                    │  Two Factors Affecting the │    IT Services
                    │  Amount of Management Efforts │
                    │                            │
                    │  • Integration Needs       │
                    │  • Scope of the Project    │
                    └────────────────────────┘
```

In addition, the client agency is left responsible for support and maintenance of the IT services as well as the integration of hardware, software,
information, people, and support. As agencies move toward this end of the
spectrum, they usually face longer timeframes for development and deployment and higher costs for coordination and support.

In addition to the extent of outsourcing, the management challenge continues to grow with the integration needs and the scale of the project. Information technology services involve the use and management of hardware,
software, people, information, maintenance, and support. The more comprehensive and integrated the services provided by a vendor, the less work on
the side of the client in bringing different components together. For example,
if the network service providers offer only the hardware installation and
upgrade, the client organization needs to pick up the software and support.
Cross-functional integration of information systems may further strain agencies' resources. The outsourced IT service is more easily managed when it
can function independently or interface easily with the rest of the information systems. If this is not the case, the client organization, at the very least,
needs to play the role of system integrator. As a result, the organizational
resources required to carry out the integration can be overwhelming.

The scale and complexity of the IT outsourcing arrangement also have
bearing on the management effort. The larger and more complex an IT outsourcing arrangement gets, the more resources there are involved in coordinating, preparing for transition, and monitoring later on.

Trends and Recent Developments

Public managers need to understand trends of IT outsourcing to manage outsourcing effectively. Both the IT outsourcing marketplace and the client organizations' utilization have seen significant changes over the past few years. The IT outsourcing market has gone through a shake-out period and become more mature. The most visible example is outsourcing application services (also known as ASP). Initially, a large number of new and established companies entered the market for application services in late 1999. After over two years of severe competition and market change, only a small number of vendors remain in the market. The successful vendors in the federal outsourcing marketplace are those well-established major contractors of government services who have established new IT service areas to meet the changing needs of their federal customers. After the shake-out period, the IT outsourcing market has become more mature. The vendors who provide value to customers and have a sound business model are able to survive and prosper.

Two types of vendors have become the main forces in the IT outsourcing market. The first type is the total solution provider, who offers an integrated solution for network or other services. It acts as a single service point for all IT service needs that an organization is willing to outsource. These total solution providers integrate various information systems, providing hardware and software, and training and support. The second type of vendor includes those that are highly specialized in one type of service and have the capability of integrating with all remaining systems.

Two recent developments in the federal IT outsourcing marketplace are the emphasis on security services and the move to a partnership model. Information technology has taken on an important role in defending the country against terrorist threats. The use of biometrics for authentication and advanced encryption-standard codes for secure transmission of information are just two examples. The projected growth in IT security spending is evidence of this development. Out of $15 billion allocated for IT in the current administration's 2003 budget, $4 billion is earmarked for IT security projects.[4] Moreover, the emphasis on security matters is also seen in

---

Two Recent Developments of IT Outsourcing

- Growing emphasis on security (information assurance)
- Move to a partnership model of outsourcing

some traditional government contractors that wished to capture some piece of the market.[5] Government contractors have added security features that analyze the vulnerability of every part of IT services provided.

The other development is the growing popularity of partnerships between government and the technology industry. The Bush administration, in its effort to combat terrorism, is creating public-private partnership models to protect the nation's critical infrastructure.[6] This partnership model has been fueled by its success in e-government efforts. The quick deployment of the General Services Administration's electronic payment systems for government is a case in point. Partnership models also provide a wide range of financial options for the Interagency Public Key Infrastructure.[7] (Interagency Public Key Infrastructure is a federal effort to provide the hardware and systems, standards, and policies necessary to secure electronic transactions across federal agencies.)

To cope with the changing IT market and service needs, a growing trend among client organizations is the use of large integrated service providers or system integrators as their vendors. This use is prompted by the risk associated with merger and acquisition, or sometimes even bankruptcy, of small vendors. Another advantage of working with large system integrators is the flexibility in using most advanced technologies. System integrators are not bound to any technology, and they integrate various technologies as they help improve services. A complementary strategy is to build management capability to scan the market horizon and understand developments in technology and service needs as they arise.

An understanding of the recent developments and trends makes public managers aware of emerging issues. However, deciding on and managing an IT outsourcing project is a complicated undertaking. A thorough examination of value propositions and potential drawbacks is critical for determining the utility of outsourcing. Therefore, the next section offers public managers comprehensive lists of advantages and disadvantages of IT outsourcing to facilitate an informed decision.

Benefits and Costs/Risks of IT Outsourcing

The successful management of IT outsourcing arrangements requires an understanding of their benefits and the associated costs/risks. Realizing the full potential of IT outsourcing involves maximizing the benefits and minimizing the risks. As a result, this section examines both the advantages and disadvantages of IT outsourcing. The rapidly changing landscape of the IT outsourcing market poses challenges to public managers, which requires long-term planning.

Benefits

IT outsourcing, if properly managed, has several advantages over in-house provision of services. First, IT outsourcing gives client organizations access to experienced advanced technology and experienced personnel. Client organizations usually start to consider an outsourcing arrangement when planning a significant upgrade of IT services. The advanced, proven technology available from vendors can assist client organizations in accomplishing their missions. Client organizations are likely to get the best-of-the-breed technology services.

IT outsourcing also addresses one of the main problems facing federal agencies in carrying out large IT projects—the shortage of IT personnel. Because vendors have a specialized IT workforce for the services they provide, they are able to meet the demands for skilled IT personnel.

Quick deployment is regarded as another advantage of IT outsourcing over in-house service provision. As far as new and significantly expanded IT services are concerned, outsourcing has an advantage over in-house provision. In-house provision requires hiring a large number of new IT personnel, integrating old and new systems, establishing the IT infrastructure, and making procurement decisions for various components that go with the new services. This can be a daunting task. In comparison, vendors can provide a packaged solution that comes with personnel, infrastructure, integration services, and support. If the vendors are experienced in particular types of services, many systems are tested and potential problems are better anticipated. The deployment time can often be less than half of the time required for in-house provision. Moreover, deployment is critical when new IT capabilities need to be acquired quickly. For example, some IT systems and infrastructure need to be quickly updated to ensure security.

Benefits of IT Outsourcing

- Access to advanced technology
- Greater ability to meet the demand for skilled IT personnel
- Quick deployment
- Flexibility in the choice of technology and modules
- Improvement of cash flow management
- Cost savings

IT outsourcing also provides client organizations with flexibility in the choice of technology and modules. One of the biggest drawbacks of in-house IT service provision is the fixation on the purchased technology. The large capital investment in IT equipment for in-house service provision sometimes forces the continued use of obsolete technology due to financial reasons. Given the fast-changing nature of technology, outsourcing allows for better risk management. The risk is shifted to vendors because they are responsible for technology upgrades.

In addition, outsourcing usually helps client organizations with cash flow management. An outsourcing arrangement typically charges client organizations on a fee-for-service basis, and client organizations subsequently do not need to make a large initial capital investment.

Cost savings are another reason for IT outsourcing. Economies of scale may allow vendors to provide services at a lower rate than that of in-house provision. Multiple client organizations may share the same IT infrastructure as the vendor. The cost of maintaining a specialized support crew is also shared by a number of client organizations. The cost savings are especially significant when acquiring a highly specialized service, which is usually expensive.

Costs/Risks

IT outsourcing can expose client organizations to a number of costs/risks. One of the primary concerns is the loss of control over service level and service quality. Once an IT service is outsourced, the project scope, technologies, costs, and IT direction of the client organization are some of the factors that may be beyond the direct management control usually available to in-house service provision (Ware, 2002). Control is particularly difficult when a large gap exists between the client organization's knowledge of services and the vendor's. Client organizations have difficulty validating any claims that vendor organizations make, because they may not have access to critical information possessed by the vendor for claim validation.

Security is another risk factor. Critical data may be stored in a facility outside the client organization. The network-connected information systems of the client organization and those of the vendor may be subsequently subjected to security threats. If the main technology infrastructure of vendors is shared by multiple client organizations, there can be multiple sources of security threats. Security can also be an issue when security practices are problematic. Personnel training and background screening of IT personnel are important in addressing security threats.

The stability of vendors is considered by many client organizations as a major risk factor. Unlike public organizations, the survival of vendors is

> ## Costs/Risks of IT Outsourcing
>
> - Loss of control over service quality
> - Possibility of compromised security
> - Possibility of service disruption due to instability of vendors
> - Increased complexity of managing and monitoring the outsourcing contract
> - Prolonged procurement process
> - Union pressure and budgetary uncertainty

dictated by the rules of the marketplace. Vendors that provide IT services may go out of business without clear warning signs. When that happens, client organizations may need to start the outsourcing process all over again. Merger and acquisition also pose problems for client organizations. It is commonplace in the information technology industry to go through an initial boom and then shake-out period. Merger and acquisition are ways of restructuring the industry. If there are no terms and conditions specified in the outsourcing contract, client organizations may find themselves renegotiating them.

Managing and maintaining an outsourcing contractual relationship poses some risks. After the contract is negotiated, client organizations need to transfer their technical and personnel resources to the vendor. Client organizations, if not properly prepared, will likely run into problems of poor service quality or a mismatch between organizational needs and service delivered by vendors. The complexity of relationship management is usually underestimated. If the transfer of knowledge about the existing system or needs for a new system at various levels of the organization is neglected or done poorly, the IT outsourcing arrangement may function efficiently but not in alignment with the organization's strategic goals. Lack of proper monitoring of service level by the client organization may put it at risk of running into major service disruption. Poor communication and lack of a joint problem-solving mechanism may cause missed opportunities for early problem detection and continuous improvement.

In addition to the aforementioned ones, two additional risk factors are relevant to public sector IT outsourcing projects. Compared with in-house provision, government outsourcing must go through the procurement process. Complex rules and procedures could drain a client organization's resources. Another complication associated with the lengthy procurement process is the possibility of changing technology and leadership. The key piece of technology identified in the initial contract may have to be re-examined and some of the service terms may need to be renegotiated. Leadership may change if the procurement process takes a long time. This all adds to the challenge of maintaining a working relationship with vendors. Moreover, complex rules and procedures can create entry barriers and limit the selection available to client organizations.

IT outsourcing is even more complicated in the public sector when union pressure and uncertain budgetary support are present. The treatment of IT personnel involved in an IT outsourcing deal has a great impact on the success of the project. The importance of this issue is reflected in several recent IT outsourcing projects. The state of Pennsylvania's outsourcing project, for example, guarantees that nobody will be laid off (Tungate, 2002). An additional example is NMCI, which has a transition program to help their employees change from the public sector to the private sector work environment.

Key Features of Pennsylvania's Data Center Outsourcing Contract

- No need for restructuring or disrupting current IT workforce

- Service-oriented contract with flexibility and benchmarking

- Use of service-level agreements

- Services for making transition from the state to the vendor

- Disaster recovery as a priority

A Tool for Managing IT Outsourcing: A Process Methodology

IT outsourcing usually goes through various stages from the initial decision to evaluate the viability of IT outsourcing to the implementation of an outsourcing contract. A process model can help in three ways. First, it is comprehensive enough to capture operational and management issues that could otherwise be ignored. For example, if managers think through the transition and management involved in an outsourcing project, they will have a better chance to succeed. The other advantage is the general applicability of the model. Despite the fact that situations may be different for various client/vendor arrangements, the process model is able to capture the management issues that are common for all IT outsourcing arrangements. For example, the need for organizational input in transition management is probably the same for all arrangements. Lastly, a process methodology is adaptive to change. The main process remains relatively stable over time. The new service priority, such as security and business continuity, can be included as items, for example, in the service contract.

The recent development of IT outsourcing highlights the need for a shift in perspective. Traditional IT procurement should be replaced with service-based relationship management. A comparison of the old and new models is detailed in the following section.

Shift in Perspective

A successful IT outsourcing arrangement requires a shift in perspective. Traditionally, an IT outsourcing arrangement has been treated as a procurement deal. With this approach, it is the equipment or software that a client organization is getting. Most of the efforts go into crafting contracts, finding an appropriate vendor, and negotiating contracts. There seems to be little effort put into what happens after the contract is finalized and equipment delivered.

However, to fully realize the potential of an IT outsourcing arrangement requires a different perspective. It is no longer the IT equipment but the service that is the center of management. As a result, the new direction

Table 5.1: A Comparison of Traditional and New Approaches

	Traditional Approach (Procurement Model)	New Approach (Outsourcing Model)
Methods of Obtaining Equipment and Services	Buy	Lease
Management Relationships	Directing and Commanding	Partnership
Objects of Management	Goods	Services

Two Imperatives for the New Managerial Perspective

- Partnership approach to managing service outsourcing arrangement
- Integration of security concern throughout the IT outsourcing life cycle

---

should be on a relationship management that secures the quality and level of services provided by the vendor.

A partnership approach to relationship management becomes an imperative when the risks and uncertainties are high (Ware, 2002). A partnership helps both parties stay on the course of mutual benefits, and the long-term perspective helps find win-win solutions to risks and uncertainty. Contracts are probably unable to anticipate all contingencies. Given the possible disparity between client organizations and vendors regarding specific knowledge about an IT operation, client organizations need to rely on vendors to be forthcoming about potential problems or better solutions. In this case, a partnership can go a long way.

Another imperative is the integration of security concerns in the IT outsourcing arrangement. Security should not be treated as an afterthought. Rather, it should now be the centerpiece of IT outsourcing arrangements. As a result, the process model presented here will incorporate information assurance concerns at every phase. This should be done in a partnership approach. Client organizations and vendors need to work together to identify all security risks and jointly develop measures for minimizing them.

Critical Success Factors for the Process Model

Strong management support and involvement throughout the entire life cycle of an outsourcing arrangement is key to the success of this process model. IT outsourcing is a process with integrated steps and components. To properly address these interrelated issues at various stages, management support needs to be there at every stage of the process. A recent GAO report on desktop outsourcing has confirmed the importance of high-level management support (GAO, March 2002). Top management involvement is particularly helpful in the transition from existing in-house service provision to a vendor. At minimum, there should be a management team that oversees the entire process of the outsourcing arrangement.

Moreover, management should allocate enough time and sustain resource input for all stages of the outsourcing process. One of the common problems for IT outsourcing is underestimating the time and resources involved. A successful outsourcing project requires an intensive analysis of organizational needs, which is time consuming and resource intensive. The subsequent contract negotiation, transition, and implementation are equally demanding for time and resource input if the goal is to have a structured contract with smooth implementation. Moreover, public sector outsourcing, due to procurement requirements, may take a long time and require budget approval. Another time- and resource-consuming stage of the process is the transition from in-house to vendor service provision.

The IT outsourcing management team needs to have strong procurement and relationship management skills and knowledge. IT outsourcing demands that the management team has the appropriate knowledge and skills about vendor selection, contract negotiation, and contract implementation. The relationship-based nature of successful outsourcing requires a partnership perspective. The outsourcing of desktop services has demonstrated this point (GAO, March 2002). A management team needs to update its knowledge and skills continuously. For example, an IT outsourcing management team needs to learn about the implementation and update of Circular A-76 to do a successful outsourcing procurement.

The fast-changing nature of technology forces the management team to constantly learn about the best service model and adapt to it. Managers at various agencies have been developing new management tools, such as flexible payments based on service use. Given that, utilizing a learning network through professional organizations is a good way of keeping the management team updated. For example, human resource staffs across federal agencies can learn from one another about best practices in IT outsourcing for HR services. This is particularly the case in the information assurance area, which has a short history of development. With a new understanding of security vulnerabilities, public managers need to devise a better service management strategy.

Critical Success Factors for IT Outsourcing

- Top management support and involvement

- Ample time and resource input

- Strong procurement and relationship management skills

- Continuous learning and service benchmarking

- Frequent communication between agencies and their service providers

Frequent communication of technical and management issues should occur at all phases. This is critical for maintaining a partnership that hinges on a common understanding of the long-term mutual benefits. The constant exchange of vital information helps manage the IT outsourcing relationship. Moreover, frequent communication is the main mechanism to address changes in priority and service needs. Information assurance was not a priority of information technology service a few years ago, but it is a top priority today. Service needs may change significantly in about a year and may warrant a refinement of the performance matrix (Dorobek, 2002). Since change is the only constant, frequent communication is required for agencies and vendors to work together to focus on results that are responsive to new needs. Although the focus may be different at different stages, the main principle stays the same—frequent and open communication.

A Process Model

A process-oriented model is an effective tool for public managers to manage IT outsourcing from start to finish. A graphic illustration of the model is captured in Figure 5.2. The process begins with a clear definition of organizational goals and how a sourcing strategy would help achieve these goals. Within that framework, in Phase 2, sourcing needs are analyzed and the operational relationships are designed to meet those needs. Phase 3 follows and focuses on vendor selection and contract negotiation. In the process model, there is a strong emphasis on analysis and design of service needs and the contract because they lay the foundation for actual implementation. The fourth phase is the transition to the external service provider, and the last phase is the management of service performance. There could be an overlap between the last two phases when the transition is done incrementally.

Phase 1: Determining a Sourcing Strategy

When is a good opportunity for government agencies to consider IT outsourcing? There are four plausible scenarios. First, the existing IT outsourcing contract is up for renewal and the service level is unsatisfactory. An agency is probably going to continue using IT outsourcing but needs to look for a vendor with a better fit. Another opportunity is the major upgrade of the existing IT infrastructure. This is usually a good time to think about the advantages and disadvantages of outsourcing IT infrastructure. The third possibility is a mandate from Congress to quickly acquire new capabilities that are very difficult to acquire with existing in-house personnel. The last main scenario is when an agency is planning on reengineering its business process and may try to take advantage of capabilities available at vendors.

Figure 5.2: An Illustration of the Process Methodology for Managing IT Outsourcing

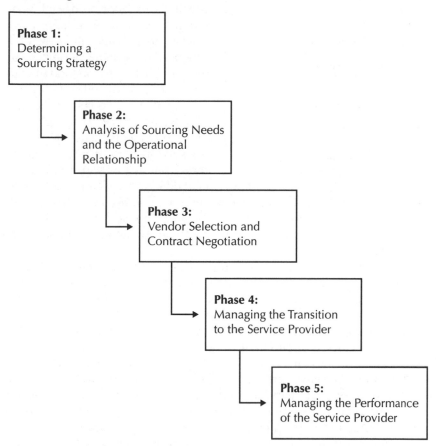

The sourcing decision should be in alignment with the organization's long-term strategy. Client organizations need to integrate IT outsourcing into their strategic goals (McIvor, 2000). IT outsourcing should not be treated as an afterthought or last-minute solution to an immediate problem, but should be an integral part of organizational efforts to achieve long-term strategic goals. A strategic intent can be the improvement of existing IT services or acquisition of new service capabilities for business impact.

Strategic alignment is the extent to which the proposed outsourcing arrangement helps achieve the strategic objectives. For example, one of the main strategic goals behind the Federal Aviation Administration's (FAA)

Issues Related to Sourcing Decisions

- Strategic objectives

- Extent and nature of organizational change

- Labor implications

- Management capabilities

---

decision to outsource part of their cost-accounting system was to gain specific cost-accounting information on each of their four main service areas. The alignment of a proposed outsourcing arrangement, then, is whether it is a good fit with what the FAA wanted.

Another common strategic goal of outsourcing is to focus resources on core competence. When an in-house IT service is not central to the organization, outsourcing it can help free up IT personnel to focus on the core. Network and application support, for instance, may not be central to a human resources department. In this case, it is of strategic value to outsource network and application support to a vendor and transfer in-house IT personnel to assignments on core business activities.

The process of deciding a sourcing strategy should also be thorough. A useful strategy is to go through the lists of benefits and costs associated with IT outsourcing mentioned in the previous section. In the list of benefit and cost items, emphasis should be placed on security and business continuity. For public managers, one main question is whether vendors have a stronger capability than their agencies in meeting stringent security requirements for IT services to be outsourced. An IT outsourcing project is justifiable only when security concerns can be properly addressed. Business continuity should also be one top item on the strategic evaluation of an outsourcing project. The preparedness for disruption or changing priorities should be factored into an outsourcing project. Without a contingency plan, government may be compromising its mission of serving its citizens.

Lack of thoroughness in checking all the cost/risk items may have serious consequences later on. One common problem is the underestimation of resource needs for managing an IT outsourcing relationship. Monitoring service performance, collaborating on service problems, and negotiating for changing service needs all require management and IT resources. A useful way of mapping main benefits and cost items is to think through the cost of the entire IT outsourcing process, even the cost of ending the contract (Bendor-Samuel, 2002).

A careful analysis of sourcing strategy should go beyond checking the value proposition based on the advantages and disadvantages of IT outsourcing to address the full range of organizational implications. Organizational change, personnel change, and management capability are three main implications of IT outsourcing in the public sector. An IT outsourcing arrangement usually implies a particular organizational change, such as closing an existing office or establishing a team working with vendors. Continuation of an existing outsourcing project with a different vendor does not involve a major shift of organizational culture or resource allocation. In comparison, outsourcing a service currently done within the organization may be a greater challenge due to the need for management practice and personnel changes.

Another outsourcing concern is labor. Government needs to abide by civil service rules that govern the hiring and firing of civil servants. For a public sector project, for example, job security for existing IT workers is usually a main issue that needs to be addressed. A sourcing plan should include a clear strategy for managing the IT workforce. One way to deal with labor concerns is to ensure job security for current IT employees. For example, the state of Pennsylvania's outsourcing project has a provision for job guarantees for the existing IT workforce. In general, public managers can either restructure the responsibilities of their IT employees or help them make the transition to the private sector.

Building the management capability should be an integral part of a comprehensive sourcing strategy. Government agencies need either to rely on their in-house expertise for evaluating IT outsourcing arrangements or to work with an IT consultancy when they need advice. At any rate, a strong base of technical knowledge and management know-how should be formed at this phase to carry out the tasks delineated at the second phase.

A related management effort for public managers is to gauge or gain organizational support. Public managers should get key stakeholders involved in the process. Stakeholders include the affected IT employees, top management, interest groups, and Congress. These stakeholders should be involved even at the early stages in the outsourcing process. They will offer great insight into the strategic fit of the IT outsourcing project, labor issues, and the level of support.

The deliverables of this phase include a preliminary assessment of the strategic fit of proposed IT outsourcing arrangements and the formation of a management team. The assessment should address security and business continuity. Moreover, it should also explore the labor and political implications of the proposed project ideas. The formation of a management team is the first step for committing organizational resources. This commitment is necessary for a thorough analysis of both sourcing needs and the operational relationship, which will be discussed next.

Key Strategic Goals

- Service improvement
- Security
- Business continuity

Phase 1: Best Practices

- *Achieve alignment of sourcing decisions to the strategic goals of the organization.* The main justification for an outsourcing project should be its strategic importance.

- *Anticipate and manage the organizational change implied by the outsourcing decisions.* Labor issues are paramount.

- *Build management capability and organizational support.* These are important organizational preparations for entering the next phase of IT outsourcing decision making.

Phase 2: Analysis of Sourcing Needs and the Operational Relationship

The primary objective of this phase is to develop a more detailed analysis of sourcing service needs and the operational relationship structure for meeting those needs. The identification of sourcing needs should be an elaboration of the strategic role of sourcing options, and organizational concerns should therefore be at the center of the analysis. For agencies that begin an IT project, having help from veteran IT outsourcing agencies is critical. A client organization, when crafting an operational relationship, should first consider a partnership model, which is a preferred method for addressing risks and uncertainty in the area of information technology.

Analyzing sourcing needs

Sourcing needs go beyond their conventional meaning as a set of functionalities of IT services. Service needs should include a quality aspect. Government should formulate its service need assessment based on strategic concerns. Security, business continuity, reliability, service integration, and other indicators are the main areas of service needs in addition to specified functionalities.

The need for security has become the central concern of IT outsourcing projects due to the protection of homeland security. The security need is high when mission-critical or high-security information is exposed by the proposed IT outsourcing arrangement. For instance, a defense network outsourcing contract is likely to command a high-security requirement. In contrast, an agency that is not involved in any of the critical information infrastructure may not need to meet stringent security requirements.[8] There are naturally variations in security needs for an IT service within an agency. Desktop support probably requires less security measures than application services for a personnel information system holding confidential information.

Business continuity should also be a top item on the list of sourcing needs. Business continuity is usually measured by uptime—the percentage of time that a particular service is available. Common examples of uptime are 99.99, 99.9, or 99 percent. The other aspect of business continuity is about providing uninterrupted service either by the creation of redundant service units or by immediate backup-and-restore services in the face of major disruptive events. Again, the level of business continuity required for a particular IT service may vary with the service needs. A communication network that supports a defense agency has no allowance for any downtime. Built-in redundancy may therefore be a requirement. In comparison, an e-mail service system for a transportation agency may not be as critical. The preparedness for disruption or changing priorities should also be factored into an outsourcing project.

In addition to security and business continuity, reliability is another main service criterion. A reliable service provider is responsive to agencies' service requests and meets them in a timely manner. In analyzing an agency's sourcing needs, the agency needs to determine the level of reliability required. One complaint of outsourcing agencies is that vendors may give a service request a low priority. If not specified contractually, a service request may take days or weeks to be filled. Moreover, reliability means that the vendor anticipates potential risk factors and addresses them. Vendors need to have mechanisms for analyzing vulnerability in the service and a scheduled plan for addressing potential problems.

Service integration is the final important criterion of service quality. It is the level of collaboration between client organizations and vendors for service production and delivery. A client organization may outsource their desktop services. However, client organizations must make clear how much integration between them and the vendor is required to cover all service needs. For example, a desktop service may include the hardware, software, maintenance, and help-desk support. Vendors may be responsible for all of these aspects of general software programs. However, they may not wish to support a more specialized software program. In that case, client organizations and vendors need to have a service integration plan to provide seamless service, where all service needs are met regardless of who bears the major responsibility.

Analyzing the sourcing needs involves a thorough cost/benefit

---

Topics to Be Addressed in Analyzing Sourcing Needs

- Specific functionalities of proposed IT service

- Security

- Business continuity

- Reliability

- Service integration

analysis. Meeting the service criteria stated above comes with a price tag. Public managers need to determine the proper service level by conducting a financial analysis of service needs. Public managers need to specify a level of service quality and service integration while balancing financial and service concerns. A slight increase in service quality may incur a significant cost. For example, to improve server uptime by .1 percent (i.e., from 99.99 to 99.999 percent uptime), an agency may need to pay as much as 5 percent more of the total project cost. This may not be financially justifiable for a personnel management application.

Security also comes with a price tag. For instance, a dedicated network, although more secure physically, usually costs more for the agency than a network infrastructure shared by multiple agencies. Whether the additional cost is justifiable depends on how important security is to the proposed network. With respect to the level of service integration, agencies also need to perform a balancing act between cost and performance. Agencies need to specify how integrated the service provider should be and how much they are willing to pay for a higher level of integration.

What further complicates the analysis of sourcing need is change. Service needs will probably change over time as well as the financial condition of the outsourcing agency. Managers should explore a wide range of service scenarios to map possible service needs. In addition, managers need to adopt a mechanism to monitor, anticipate, and address changing service needs. Failure to anticipate a possible change in service needs may result in a service-level contract that has very limited flexibility. To cope with change, a scalable IT service infrastructure is preferred, and a provision in the contract to address change is necessary.

Mapping operational relationships

After clarifying the sourcing needs, an outsourcing management team needs to develop a plan for an operational relationship. The mapping of an operational relationship should keep its focus on partnership opportunities. The relationship should be consistent with the client organization's long-term strategic direction and proper allocation of human resources outlined in the first phase. This operational relationship needs to delineate the working relationships among different units involved in the delivery and use of IT services (GAO, November 2001).

The composition of the management team should include key members of both the client organization and the vendor. At the client organization, an IT department and functional user groups are natural candidates. An IT department is able to bring in its knowledge of current IT operations and the technical components of the transition. User departments, such as a human resources department, can communicate their service needs to the vendors. Vendors are then responsible for the actual production and provision of IT services.

In addition to determining the departments or units involved, a management team needs to decide the level of organization that is appropriate for the joint effort and the appropriate team members. If the IT services support the entire organization's IT function and serve multiple departments, a high-level manager should be a member of the IT outsourcing team. The appropriate level of management is usually a function of the services outsourced.

One key management task at this phase is to assess the resource requirements. An IT outsourcing project team needs to estimate the human and financial resource requirements for operational tasks. Taking a process-oriented and holistic view of IT outsourcing helps cover all potential resource requirements. Public managers need to think about the resource needs beyond the first two phases of determining sourcing strategies and needs. They need to budget resources for all remaining phases of IT outsourcing. Building and maintaining an operational relationship involves intensive vendor selection, service agreement negotiation, transition, maintenance of ongoing IT service projects, and performance evaluation and service adjustment. Moreover, the management team at this phase should continue involving key stakeholders, particularly the user department and IT personnel.

The deliverables of this phase include a request for proposals (RFP), an internal operational plan, and the formation of an IT outsourcing project team to carry out tasks for the next phase. This proposal will have guidelines for the service requests developed in this phase and the criteria for appropriate vendors developed in the first phase. This detailed planning up front is necessary for a client organization to harvest the fruits of a strategic

Phase 2: Best Practices

- *Cover multiple dimensions of sourcing needs.* Security, business continuity, reliability, and service integration needs are the main ones.

- *Determine the level of service needs.* A cost/benefit analysis is useful for assessing the proper level of service for each dimension.

- *Anticipate the change in service needs.* Public managers need to anticipate any possible change in service needs and usually prefer a scalable IT solution.

- *Build a team-based operational relationship that meets the sourcing needs.* Resource requirements as well as operational relationships should be clearly stated and aligned with sourcing needs.

partnership with a vendor. An internal operational plan will give a clear indication of the organizational resources involved and the composition of team members in order to build a relationship with potential vendors. The formation of an IT outsourcing project team can then help oversee the vendor selection and subsequent intensive contract negotiations.

Phase 3: Vendor Selection and Contract Negotiation

Vendors respond to an agency's request for proposals by submitting proposals. The agency then reviews these proposals and undertakes the formal procurement process. It should be understood that vendor selection sometimes interacts with the actual contract negotiation. During the contract negotiation stage, agencies may request more details about the service package provided by the vendor.

Both vendor selection and contract negotiation should follow the general guidelines and parameters established in phases 1 and 2. These guidelines and parameters should serve as the working framework in which the IT outsourcing team operates. For example, if security and improvement of current IT service are the top two strategic concerns of the outsourcing agency, then it should look for a vendor that has strong security measures for their IT services and that delivers a state-of-the-art service package for improvement of existing services within the agency. On the other hand, if an outsourcing agency operates in a relatively uncertain environment, the contract negotiated should have a provision dealing with that uncertainty of service needs.

Vendor selection

Several general criteria are important for selecting the right vendor. The first important one is the alignment between the business solution for the client organization and the vendor's business objectives (Embleton and Wright, 1998, p.1). The mutual long-term benefits will help sustain a long-term relationship. Since the specific type of IT service is the major strength of the vendor, the vendor is more likely to maintain its market position. As a result, the outsourced agency is more likely to have stable and quality service from the vendor.

Another important criterion is having the appropriate skill set available at the vendor for achieving the agency's strategic objectives. For most public agencies, the main reason for outsourcing is to gain an advanced IT capability that is not available in-house. Therefore, it is important to ensure that the skill set available at the vendor is appropriate for providing the advanced IT capability needed.

Reliability is also key to successful IT outsourcing (Ware, 2002). Client organizations should look for market leaders and established players to ensure some level of reliability. Public agencies need to validate the relia-

Criteria for Vendor Selection

- Good strategic alignment between the agency and its vendors

- Appropriate skill set on vendor side

- Reliability

- Availability of security and information assurance package

- Ability to integrate various systems and deploy new technologies

bility claim made by the vendors competing for the IT outsourcing contract. One method is to conduct on-site visits with vendors to have them demonstrate the reliability of their services.

Moreover, a qualified vendor needs to have a good security package for the IT services it offers. A security package includes both technical and managerial aspects. The hardware, software, and facilities that secure production and delivery of services are considered the technical aspects. For technical considerations, one good source of information on information assurance products is the information assurance directorate detailing the national policy regarding the evaluation of commercial information assurance (IA) products. The management system deals with a comprehensive vulnerability analysis, security warning system, and procedures safeguarding security. A vulnerability analysis establishes an inventory of sources of threat to the information system and/or network in question, including external and internal threats. The vendor should have an information security policy in place and documentation that such a policy is actually being followed.

To address the risks associated with market and technological changes, system integrators or providers offering comprehensive packages are preferred. System integrators are useful for cushioning against constant changes in technologies and are likely to be more independent in choosing the appropriate combination of software programs for their clients. Their independence is particularly strong when compared with software vendors who also play the role of service providers. System integrators are able to upgrade IT services based on what is available on the market because their business focus is on meeting client organizations' needs rather than pushing for a particular solution. Total solution providers are preferred because of their integrated services.

Contract negotiation

Successful contract negotiation needs to adhere to the following guidelines. First, negotiations should focus on finding win-win solutions (Foster, 1996). This is consistent with the spirit of strategic partnership, which fosters flexibility and cushions against risks and uncertainty. Open and frequent communication of service needs and organizational concerns are a prerequisite for crafting a win-win solution. Outsourcing agencies and vendors need to identify the areas of complementary skills and resources. Public agencies need to avoid a single focus on the lowest cost. This approach has proven to be problematic in pursuing long-term gain from outsourcing arrangements (Bendor-Samuel, 2002).

Second, flexibility is a premium in service contracts. As a result, scalable and modular solutions are preferred (Goldman, 1998). Flexibility is important for coping with changing service needs. One approach is to include a benchmarking provision in the service contract. This provision usually requires the vendor to benchmark best practices and constantly improve its service quality by taking advantage of new technology.

Third, the contract negotiated needs to have clauses that address the risk factors mentioned in the previous section. For example, the contract needs to include some safeguard for client organizations whose primary concern is lack of control. Some additional control can be achieved by offering warranty and liability, terms for terminating a contract, and dispute resolution mechanisms to the client organization (Lee, 1996).

Among all risk factors, security and business continuity need to be at the heart of a contract because they are government's primary concerns. In a service-level contract, agencies should require the statement of a security policy and practices that the vendor is going to take to maintain information assurance. One method is to set up incident reporting requirements, where the vendor must report incidents of security breaches in the information systems supporting IT services. In addition, to address the risk of unforeseen cost escalation, the service contract should also include pricing and payment terms for services (Lee, 1996).

Lastly, a properly drafted contract also needs to address transition and operational relationships, and the transfer of both assets and personnel must be specified. The operational relationship envisioned in Phase 2 needs to be part of the service-level agreement as well. Both parties should agree on a formal management structure that oversees the transition and contract implementation.

In this phase, the client organization has several ways of better managing the process. One is to continue utilizing a learning network to learn about innovative ways to address changing service needs and security issues throughout the entire phase. Managers need to budget time and resources for selecting vendors and subsequently negotiating items in the service-

---

Phase 3: Best Practices

- *Select vendors that can best meet the sourcing needs of an agency.* Public managers need to examine the alignment of business goals of the parties involved, the complementary nature of skill sets, the reliability of the vendor, and IT security.

- *Choose system integrators when available for minimizing risks.* System integrators have the advantage that they are flexible and also cushion against market instability.

- *Negotiate a contract in the spirit of building a long-term partnership.* It is better to seek a win-win agreement by engaging in open and frequent communication.

- *Produce a service-level contract that addresses risk factors and clearly delineates operational relationships.* The service contract needs to be specific and flexible, and operational relationships should be an integral part of the agreement.

---

level agreement. Managers should also require a demonstration of key capabilities such as business recovery (continuity) and security measures. A site visit should also be required before the client organization signs the agreement (Embleton and Wright, 1998).

Phase 4: Managing the Transition to the Service Provider

The transition of IT services from the client organization (or a previous vendor) to the contract winner is a demanding and time-consuming task. In addition to the general involvement of an organization in the development and implementation of IT services, the amount of transition effort depends on the scale of the project and independence of service units. The resource demand is high when the transition involves the servicing of a large number of units by the vendor. Transition is easier when the IT service in question is itself a more independent service unit.

Following some guidelines should help the transition. The overarching principle should be the building of a long-term relationship based on mutual interest. Information needs to be shared, and open communication should be the norm. Ample resources also need to be allocated for carrying out the transition. The joint management team should provide financial and personnel support. The blueprint for the transition is outlined in the service-level agreement. The transition of the IT workforce involves both operational and labor components.

Information assurance should be a top item in the transition plan. When the information and IT service change hands, they are likely to be more vulnerable to security breaches due to the involvement of multiple parties. Therefore, the management team, in making the transition, should first identify threats to information assurance in the transition stage. Threats may include, at a minimum, disgruntled employees, migration of data and documents, retirement of old IT equipment, and uncontrolled access to new threats.

Operational documentation is critical in smoothing the transition from in-house to an outside vendor. One of the main barriers to transition is lack of documentation of work procedure and inventory. Vendors need to have a good understanding of work procedure and user needs in order to provide services. Moreover, the inventory of existing information technology hardware and software related to the IT service in question is another critical document for the vendor. Another key piece of information for service provision is baseline data on past service performance. This will help document the performance improvement brought by the vendor.

The transition of the IT labor force is more critical for public sector organizations than for private companies. Job security for the transition period is very important. One way is to require the vendor to hire government IT personnel affected by the contract and to keep them for at least a year or two. During that transition period, client organizations should secure training programs for their affected IT personnel. These personnel should be trained in the new technologies and business processes brought in by the vendor. However, one problem with transition is the possible brain

---

Phase 4: Best Practices

- *Prepare proper documentation to smooth the transition*. Proper documentation is needed for the relevant information systems, service needs, and performance measures.

- *Devote resources to facilitating a transition*. Human and financial resources should be in place for a transition.

- *Help the transition of in-house IT personnel*. Public managers need to provide training and career help for the IT personnel displaced by the outsourcing project.

- *Manage the transition with a strong management team*. Strong leadership and management commitment are critical for the time of change.

drain of the client organization. The client organization should make a conscious effort to keep some critical IT capability in-house to monitor the vendor's performance (Hurley, 2001).

A smooth transition also requires the constant attention of the management team that oversees the transition. Senior management members from both organizations need to remain committed through the entire process of transition (Goolsby, 2002). Sustaining the management effort is important, because projects may take several years to complete the transition.

The management team should foster communication between the two organizations about problems associated with the transition and ideas about managing the transition. The management teams need to ensure that, at all steps of transition, actions taken should be in alignment with their strategic goals.

Phase 5: Managing the Performance of the Service Provider

Service delivery is the ultimate test of the outsourcing project, and management is the key to the success of an outsourcing relationship. Two principles guide the management of an IT outsourcing project. First, both the client organization and the vendor should take a collaborative approach. Public managers need to know exactly what motivates the other party to provide service and proactively ensure that their mutual objectives are met (Goolsby, 2002). Second, both parties should be open to changes. The vendor in particular should be in a position to continuously improve its service by benchmarking best practices. The client organization in turn should be prepared to reengineer its business process to address changing demands.

Performance management is the central theme of the working relationship between client and vendor. Previously ignored, information assurance is now a critical dimension of performance. The collection of reliable performance data, monitoring, and communication are three indispensable components of performance management. Performance data need to be collected based on the performance matrix developed in the service-level contract at the contract negotiation stage. Collection of data related to assurance information should include the documentation of security breach incidents, commonly referred to as incident reporting. Service uptime, response time, and user satisfaction are some good indicators of service quality.

Monitoring should be done at least on a daily basis. The outsourcing management team needs to monitor the key performance measures daily, including security performance. There should be some triggers in place to alert IT service managers of security vulnerability and poor performance. Quarterly and annual reports help identify trends and patterns. The team should measure performance against the level of user satisfaction. Periodic review of performance reports and the refinement of the monitoring mechanism should be part of performance management routines.

Frequent communication is another key to successful management of an IT outsourcing project. Client organizations and vendors need to communicate technical and management issues associated with the outsourced IT services. They can update each other in an ongoing effort to improve services or jointly resolve management concerns.

A management team and structure need to exist during implementation of IT outsourcing contracts. One common problem with IT outsourcing projects is the lack of management support in dealing with ongoing problems. The outsourcing arrangement needs constant management and input of resources. A management team needs to be in place to keep the implementation consistent with the contract and to make sure the objectives are in line with the strategic goals of the organization. A stable management structure will help resolve any related technical and management concerns.

The deliverables in this phase are the performance review report and project plans for constant service improvement. A performance review should be done periodically with assessment of performance to see if a vendor is meeting service requirements. Project plans for service improvement include a service needs assessment project, methods to address service problems, and detailed steps to solve a service problem.

Phase 5: Best Practices

- *Take a collaborative approach*. A management system based on the principles of open communication and collaboration helps identify service needs and improve service quality.

- *Collect and monitor performance information*. A performance matrix needs to be in place, and the performance data should be communicated to the agency on a regular basis.

- *Be adaptive to change*. New service needs are likely to arise. Based on the collaborative model, public agencies and vendors can work together to turn change into an opportunity for service improvement.

Recommendations

IT outsourcing can be rewarding if properly managed. Recently, we have witnessed the growth of technology use in government for the delivery of information and services as well as for national security. IT outsourcing is emerging as a way of meeting the demand for the quick deployment of advanced technology. Access to skilled personnel, advanced technology infrastructure, flexibility, and cost savings are all driving forces for outsourcing. However, public managers face challenges when trying to fully realize the potential of IT outsourcing. Loss of control, instability of vendors, and complexity in managing an outsourcing contract are some of the barriers often cited.

The process model offered in this chapter gives public managers a framework for the informed management of IT outsourcing. This framework is designed to maximize the benefits while minimizing the risks involved, which can be accomplished by following both the recommendations and the best practices presented at the end of the discussion concerning each phase. The recommendations offer generic guidelines for the successful management of an IT outsourcing project from its very beginning.

Recommendation 1. Shift Focus to Service and Relationship Management

Public managers need to engage in a major shift of perspective to realize the full potential of an IT outsourcing project. Information technology needs to be treated as a service. As a result, public managers need to develop a performance matrix to measure and monitor service quality and take appropriate actions when service quality is in question. Moreover, the outsourcing arrangement should be treated and planned as a partnership. Partnerships with industry leaders are the best way to stay current with service and technological changes. To make a partnership work, public managers need to focus on relationship management throughout the entire process.

Recommendation 2. Provide and Sustain Resource Input

Service and relationship management will not work without proper resource input. One of the critical success factors for an IT outsourcing project is top management support. This support is necessary to provide needed resources. A main problem associated with IT outsourcing projects is the lack of proper and sustained resource input. Every single phase of the IT outsourcing process requires a significant amount of resource input to do quality work. As early as the planning phase, the agency needs to devote time and resources to identify a project with a good strategic fit for the agency. The resource input needs to be sustained through the contracting and transition phases. The resources involved in the transition may account for a significant amount of the total resource input due to its labor-intensive nature. At the management phase, a dedicated performance management team is still needed. The resource input cannot stop right after the transition is complete.

Recommendation 3. Develop and Upgrade Contract and Service Management Capacity

Contract and service management capacity is critical for the success of IT outsourcing projects. The service contract governs the relationship between the agency and its vendors. A poorly written contract is a recipe for disaster. The contract and service management team should be keenly aware of regulations and policies surrounding the IT project. Currently, competitive bidding, information assurance, performance measurement, and cost accounting are the main issues with which this team should be familiar. In addition, this team should be able to craft a service-level contract with provisions for benchmarking, technological change, penalty for poor service, and termination. Most of the service management concerns should be addressed when a service contract is negotiated.

Project management is another critical aspect of this management capacity, which ensures IT services are responsive to agency needs. The contract and service management team needs to upgrade its capacity to cope with new development. For example, the team needs to learn about the information assurance products and requirements under development to address issues in the contract under negotiation or refine performance measures in the existing service contracts.

Recommendation 4. Maintain and Foster Frequent and Quality Communication

Frequent communication of technical and management issues is usually overlooked by agencies. However, this is critical for partnership and service management. Communication needs to be carried out on a regular basis. Daily or weekly reports of service status based on a pre-set performance matrix should be available to the agency. Weekly or monthly meetings should be institutionalized for addressing both immediate concerns and long-term planning. Moreover, when there is a major change in service needs or technology, agencies and their vendors should follow an established protocol to address it. The quality of communication also matters. The level of organizational involvement and the inclusion of relevant information are two main aspects. Communication should be done not only between low-level but also high-level managers when a major shift of focus is introduced. Service performance information should be kept in a central depository and decision-support modules should be in place for informed decision making.

Appendix:
IT Outsourcing—Web Hosting as a Case Study

By Ranapratap Chegu, Principal Consultant, IBM Business Consulting Services

One type of IT outsourcing that has become popular in recent years has been web hosting. The following are types of web hosting that have emerged.

1. Virtual or Shared Hosting

In this model, the Internet Service Provider (ISP) provides the hardware, network, and, in some cases, database software for their clients on a lease basis. The managed services such as network management/monitoring, backup/recovery, operating system, server hardware, firewalls, and database administration are provided fully by the ISP staff. The clients are given limited access to the servers to maintain the application code and the website metrics data.

Advantages:
- Typically this solution is popular because it is cost effective.
- Customers do not need to integrate the infrastructure as well as maintain it.
- Leasing the infrastructure is always easier than procuring it.
- For the public sector, this is an effective solution for the unclassified type projects with limited budgets.

Disadvantages:
- Performance is a major issue as the servers and the network are shared among many clients.
- Security is also another big concern as the firewalls and web/application servers are shared.
- Configuration management becomes complicated.
- May not pass government security audits if the servers that host government applications are shared with non-governmental clients.
- Not a suitable solution for mission-critical applications as the system uptime is dependent on many shared activities.
- Risk of exposure if the ISP goes out of business.

2. Dedicated Hosting

In this model, the ISP provides the dedicated infrastructure—i.e., fire-walls, servers, backup—on a lease basis. The managed services such as network management/monitoring, backup/recovery, operating system, server hardware, firewalls, and database administration are provided by the ISP staff. Clients are given limited access to the servers to maintain the application code and the website metrics data.

Advantages:
- Superior system performance as the infrastructure is dedicated.
- Better configuration management and security.
- Customers do not need to integrate the infrastructure as well as maintain it.
- Leasing the infrastructure is always easier than procuring it.
- For the public sector, this is an effective solution for the unclassified as well as sensitive but unclassified type projects.
- With performance-based contracts, government can closely monitor the quality of the services provided by the ISP.
- Guaranteed uptime is achievable.

Disadvantages:
- This solution is expensive as the infrastructure is dedicated.
- Risk of exposure if the ISP goes out of business.

3. Co-Location Hosting

In this model, the ISP provides only physical space, bandwidth, power, and limited managed services. Clients bring their own server hardware, operating system, software, and database. Clients' staffs install and maintain their systems by themselves. In some cases the clients may use the shared backup and network monitoring/management services of the ISP to make the solution more cost effective.

Advantages:
- Superior system performance as the infrastructure is dedicated.
- Better configuration management and security.
- For the public sector, this is an effective solution for the unclassified as well as sensitive but unclassified type projects.
- With performance-based contracts, government can closely monitor the quality of the services provided by the ISP.
- Guaranteed uptime is achievable.

- Easily can pass government audits.
- The system can be transferred to another location easily if the ISP goes out of business.

Disadvantages:
- This solution is expensive as the infrastructure is dedicated.
- Longer government procurement cycles can delay the project deadlines.
- This solution is for clients who have bigger budgets as well as their own staff to maintain their systems.

Endnotes

1. This is based on the number by Input Inc., an information technology research and marketing firm.

2. For more detailed description about this project, see Murray (200).

3. Liza Porteus, "Legislation Driving Bush Administration E-Gov Efforts" *Government Executive,* April 2, 2002.

4. Liza Porteus, "Homeland Security Depends on New Technology, Rigde Says," *Government Executive,* April 24, 2002.

5. William New, "Tech Firms Look for Best Places to Pitch Security Products," *Government Executive,* April 1, 2002.

6. Porteus, *Government Executive*, April 24, 2002.

7. Bruce B. Cahan, "United States' Experience with Public-Private Partnership: Elements of Effective Public-Purpose Partnership," report prepared for OECD E-Government Project Seminar, June 21, 2002.

8. For a list of agencies that are considered lead agencies in protecting infrastructure, see General Accounting Office, *Critical Infrastructure Protection: Federal Efforts Require a More Coordinated and Comprehensive Approach for Protecting Information Systems,* Washington, D.C.: U.S. General Accounting Office, July 22, 2002.

Bibliography

Bendor-Samuel, Peter. (2002, May). "Building Relationship Around Service Provider Strengths." *Outsourcing Journal*. http://www.outsourcing-journal.com/issues/may 2002/everest.html [Accessed May 16, 2002].

Cahan, Bruce B. (2002). *United States' Experience with Public-Private Partnership: Elements of Effective Public-Purpose Partnership*. Report prepared for OECD E-Government Project Seminar, June 21, 2002.

Dorobek, Christopher. (2002, September 2). "Navy, EDS to Refine Performance Metrics." *Federal Computer Week*.

Embleton, Peter R. and Phillip C. Wright. (1998). "A Practical Guide to Successful Outsourcing." *Empowerment in Organizations* 6 (3).

Foster, E. (1996, September). "Outsource Sense." *Info World*, 8 (37).

General Accounting Office. (2001, July). *Electronic Government: Challenges Must Be Addressed With Effective Leadership and Management*. Washington, D.C.: U.S. General Accounting Office.

General Accounting Office. (2001, November). *Information Technology: Leading Commercial Practices for Outsourcing of Services*. Washington, D.C.: U.S. General Accounting Office.

General Accounting Office. (2002, March). *Desktop Outsourcing: Positive Results Reported, but Analyses Could Be Strengthened*. Washington, D.C.: U.S. General Accounting Office.

General Accounting Office. (2002, July). *Critical Infrastructure Protection: Federal Efforts Require a More Coordinated and Comprehensive Approach for Protecting Information Systems*. Washington, D.C.: U.S. General Accounting Office.

Goldman, Stan. (1998). *The Ultimate Outsourcing Study: A CIO's Guide to Best Practices*. Technology and Business Integrators, Inc.

Goolsby, Kathleen. (2002, May). "Co-creating Successful HR Outsourcing." *BPO Outsourcing Journal*. http://www.bpo-outsourcing-journal.com/issues/may 2002/hr.html [Accessed May 16, 2002].

Hurley, Margaret. (2001). "IT Outsourcing—Managing the Key Asset." *Information Management & Computer Security* 9(5): 243-249.

Lee, Matthew. (1996). "IT Outsourcing Contracts: Practical Issues for Management." *Industrial Management and Data Systems* 96/1: 15-20.

Lisagor, Megan. (2002, February 18). "Fine-tuning Outsourcing." *Federal Computer Week*.

Murray, Bill. (2000, December 1). "Joining Forces: The Navy and the Marine Corps have Connected to Launch One of the Biggest Technology Outsourcing Contracts Ever." *Government Executive*.

National Academy of Public Administration. (2001, August). *The Transforming Power of Information Technology: Making the Federal Government an Employer of Choice for IT Employees*. Washington D.C.: National Academy of Public Administration.

New, William. (2002, April 1). "Tech Firms Look for Best Places to Pitch Security Products." *Government Executive*.

Porteus, Liza. (2002, April 2). "Legislation Driving Bush Administration E-Gov Efforts." *Government Executive*.

Porteus, Liza. (2002, April 24). "Homeland Security Depends on New Technology, Ridge Says." *Government Executive*.

Tungate, David E., and Gregg Michael. (2002, March). "Pennsylvania Outsources to Save Millions." *PA Times* 25 (3).

Wait, Patience. (2002, March 4). "Government Outsourcing Grows Fastest of All Sectors." *Washington Technology* 16 (23).

Ware, Lorraine Cosgrove. (2002, May 3). *CIO Research Reports: Adventure in Outsourcing*. CIO.com. http://www2.cio.com/research/survey-report.cfm?id=78 [Accessed May 16, 2002].

PART II

Toward Partnerships

165

CHAPTER SIX

Contracting for the 21st Century:
A Partnership Model

Wendell C. Lawther
Associate Professor of Public Administration
University of Central Florida

This report was originally published in January 2002, revised January 2003.

Current Trends and Challenges
Influencing Contracting Out
and Contract Administration

Introduction

Current administrative and legislative efforts, especially those that have occurred since the George W. Bush administration took office, have focused a great deal of attention on the practice of contracting out or privatizing services/products. Recognizing that the dollar amount of federal spending on service contracts has grown from $70 billion in fiscal year 1990 to $87 billion in fiscal year 2000 (USGAO, 2001), these efforts are directed at capturing the purported increased efficiency and lower cost that can occur from public-private competition of existing services. Although these competitions may result in improved in-house service provision, those competitions that result in outsourcing are expected to lead to greater savings. At the same time, there is an interest in ensuring that federal contracting personnel have the requisite resources, skills, and numbers to: 1) effectively compete with the private contractors, and 2) maintain and increase accountability whether a service is contracted out or kept in-house.

The changes in federal procurement policy during the 1990s have led to increased flexibility for contracting officers, program managers, and related procurement personnel. While many feel there are still barriers to overcome in acquisition processes, such as an increased use of Performance-Based Service Contracting (PBSC), there is increasing awareness that contract administration has not received the attention it needs or deserves. The most effective changes in the function of contract administration have yet to be completely identified.

Conceptually, contract administrators need to alter their role, responsibilities, and behavior depending on a number of factors that primarily relate to the complexity of the services or products purchased. After reviewing present administrative and legislative trends and their impacts on federal contracting in this section, a conceptual framework is presented and discussed in the next section. A discussion of public-private partnerships (PPPs) follows. To be successful, PPPs may require radically different contract administration roles for services of highest complexity and/or uncertainty. Throughout, the focus is on achieving the most effective contract administration possible, given the nature of the service.

The Changing Environment

The environment for contracting out services and products for federal agencies continues to change, offering increased flexibility and concurrent challenges to agency officials in charge of choosing, awarding, and administering contracts. Agencies are beginning to feel the impact of the Federal Acquisition Streamlining Act (FASA) of 1994. FASA encouraged agencies to use indefinite-delivery, indefinite-quantity (IDIQ) contracts, and then to issue task and delivery orders when they needed more products or services. Governmentwide Acquisition Contracts (GWACs) are the preferred vehicle, creating competition among private contractors.[1]

There are signs, however, that federal agencies are not adequately prepared to deal with the increasing flexibility and complexity offered by this changing environment. Many of the changes allow for greater speed in obtaining services/products, but they have not provided much guidance for agency personnel involved in contract administration.

There are current pressures to implement the Federal Activities Inventory Reform (FAIR) Act, implying an increased emphasis on contracting out. Concurrently, the increased use of PBSC is touted as a realistic way to achieve greater efficiencies and savings when agencies do contract out.

A somewhat more cautionary message is sent by those who, as part of the General Accounting Office (GAO) Commercial Panel hearings, were concerned that there are sufficient skills and knowledge among agency personnel to effectively administer existing and future contracts. Similarly, others suggest that changes in overall contract administration functions and roles are necessary.

FAIR Act Implementation and Impact on Outsourcing

Currently there are various legislative and executive pressures on federal agencies to outsource or privatize existing positions. The FAIR Act requires all federal agencies to identify those functions that are "commercial in nature" and could be performed by private sector contractors. A March 9, 2001 memo from the Office of Management and Budget requires federal agencies to compete or directly convert at least 5 percent of their commercial activities by the end of fiscal 2002 (O'Keefe, 2001). This memo echoes the President's Management Agenda (USOMB, 2001), in which recent public-private competitions, as guided by the A-76 process, have

resulted in savings of more than 20 percent for work that stays in-house and more than 30 percent for work outsourced to the private sector (p. 18).

Although the FAIR Act does not require federal agencies to outsource those jobs listed as commercial in nature, there are many who would support a Bush administration push to use FAIR Act inventories as guides for outsourcing goals (Peckinpaugh, 2001). To the extent that public-private competitions result in increased outsourcing of "commercial in nature" services, the need for effective contract administration will rise.

Performance-Based Service Contracting (PBSC)

Performance-Based Service Contracting is another key element in the President's Management Agenda and in the March 9, 2001 memo from OMB. Agencies are mandated to use performance-based techniques for at least 20 percent of all service contracts worth more than $25,000.

PBSC provides an attractive alternative that potentially can facilitate bid processes and ease contract administration. Originally proposed in the early 1990s, there has been increasing opportunity and encouragement for federal agencies to use PBSC. In 1994, for example, the Department of Energy (DOE) began a process to change 18 of its 22 contracts with private companies and educational institutions to manage its laboratories. The change has been from cost-reimbursement contracts, with broad statements of work, to fixed-price contracts that are performance based (USGAO, 1999). Most of the use of PBSC, however, has been by Defense agencies.

Studies performed by the Office of Federal Procurement Policy (OFPP) indicate significant cost savings and increased customer satisfaction for both civilian and defense services. In 1994, 27 agencies pledged to participate in a pilot project; 15 of them changed 26 contracts to PBSC. The result was a savings of 15 percent, with a customer satisfaction increase of 18 percent (USOFPP, 1998a).

The savings can come from a variety of sources, all of which have an impact on the roles and effectiveness of the contract administration (CA). First, PBSC requires the agency to perform a job or work process analysis to identify performance indicators or standards that can be used as goals and/or incentives for the contractor. Where appropriate, historical data can be used. This analysis may lead to greater awareness of efficiencies that were not previously known. These indicators reflect both output and outcome measures.

Second, this analysis serves as the basis for the creation of Acceptable Quality Levels (AQLs). An AQL identifies the maximum percent or number of defective service units or products allowable. If the service/product does not exceed this percentage, then the service will not be rejected. It is assumed that the contractor will not intentionally deliver a defective service. It is also assumed that the contractor will correct the defective service whenever possible.

The existence of AQLs serves several purposes that can lead to savings. It can serve as a deterrent or incentive. The contractor knows that violations of the AQL may result in penalties. It sets a standard of performance. The contractor can use the AQL to determine the necessary work processes that will produce an output that meets the AQL. It thus serves as one basis by which the contractor determines the bid or cost of the project.

Another major result of the job or work analysis is the creation of a surveillance or quality assurance plan. This identifies the means and methods by which information concerning the extent to which the contractor is meeting the contract goals is identified. Periodic sampling, inspection, and other forms of review may comprise this plan (see USOFPP, 1980).

The role of CA staff in PBSC may include the following:

- **Job/work analysis performance:** The same individuals that participate in CA can assist with the studies necessary to establish performance standards and AQL.
- **Contract negotiation:** If the final contract is likely to contain different performance standards/AQLs than those found in the Project Work Statement, the CA should participate in these discussions.
- **Quality Assurance (QA) evaluation:** The CA creates the QA plan and carries out the evaluation/inspection of all services or products, determining whether they meet the AQL (USOFPP, 1980).

Ultimately, the more that acceptable levels of performance cannot be clearly and validly identified, the less viable PBSC becomes as an agency option. Although its use seems logical in light of interest in reducing contracting and procurement staff (e.g., USDOD, 2001), as well as reducing the costs of performing audits necessitated by cost reimbursement contracts, greater risks are possible if in-house CA knowledge is significantly lessened.

Other reasons may contribute to the current lack of adoption of PBSC among federal civilian agencies. First, contract officials lack training and familiarity with performance standards. Second, even though bidders specify how they will achieve the results identified in the Request for Proposal (RFP), those agency personnel charged with evaluating bidder responses must have sufficient knowledge about these processes and the appropriate private sector marketplace. This is a different kind of knowledge than has been required in the past (Drabkin, 2001).

GAO Commercial Activities Panel

The creation of the GAO Commercial Activities Panel (Federal Register, 2001) represented another major impetus that will most likely lead to reform of the A-76 process. Testimony held during the summer of 2001 indicates dissatisfaction from both those that favor greater outsourcing and those that oppose it. The lack of civilian agency usage of the A-76 process, for example, has led many to call for additional reforms, including suggestions of creating processes that replace or provide greater use of alternatives to the public-private competition presently supported by A-76.[2]

There were common themes running throughout the testimony presented to the GAO Panel that are relevant to the role of CA. Perhaps most important was a concern that agencies have enough skills and knowledge among in-house staff to adequately hold contractors accountable (e.g., Birkhofer, 2001). As stated by David Walker, United States Comptroller General and head of the panel:

> ... if you are going to contract out something, you've got to maintain an adequate number of public employees to manage cost, quality, and performance. That is absolutely essential. The failure to do that has put a number of programs and functions at high risk (Walker, 2001).

This comment echoes similar concerns found in the General Accounting Office Performance and Accountability studies of all major United States federal agencies (USGAO, 2001a). Agencies such as the Department of Energy, the National Aeronautics and Space Administration, and the National Parks Service were cited for weaknesses in contract management and administration.[3]

Changes in Contract Administration Roles

All of these past and present trends point to a need to change the role of contract administration. The Office of Federal Procurement Policy's *Guide to Best Practices for Contract Administration* (1994) identifies various weaknesses in civilian agency CA practices. Included in these are the "undefined Contracting Officer's Technical Representative (COTR) roles and responsibilities." This report calls for a wide variety of changes among those performing CA, including:
1. Updated training for COTRs and contracting officers;
2. Creation of a partnership between COTRs and contracting officers;
3. Greater sense of teamwork between program personnel and procurement staff; and
4. Greater understanding of agency missions and relevant goals.

In addition, other voices have called for changes. Martin (1995), for example, advocates that more flexible, broader responsibility and greater accountability be assigned to both the contracting officer and the program manager, encouraging greater teamwork in carrying out the contract administration function. More recently, Kelman (2001) has stated that "contract administration doesn't receive the emphasis it deserves." He calls for greater leadership in contract administration by: 1) giving more responsibility for performance measurement to those overseeing contracts, and 2) increasing contract management skills among top agency managers.

A Conceptual Framework:
Service/Product Complexity and Uncertainty

The most effective contract administration function is one in which the results of the service (or product) delivery by the contractor are characterized by high service quality, timeliness of delivery, under or at budget with a minimum of change orders, a lack of complaints, and a willingness to interact cooperatively with a variety of officials in the public sector. In other words, the goals of the service delivery are met to the satisfaction of public officials and the citizenry. The capability of contract administration to achieve this effectiveness depends in large part on the agency response to the nature of the service/product delivered by the contractor.

Basic Definitions

For the purposes of this chapter, it is assumed that the agency is the buyer of either services or products, and that the contractor is the private sector organization that contracts with the agency to deliver these services or products. The contract management process is assumed to include the entire process of collecting information about agency needs, deciding to outsource or privatize (if there is an already existing publicly provided service), writing an RFP, evaluating bids, and negotiating with the winning bidder. Contract administration is assumed to constitute those duties and responsibilities that occur after the contract has been awarded.

Depending on the size and nature of the contract, the agency may have several different personnel involved. The agency may create a team or steering committee consisting of a contracting officer and/or contract administrator, and technical and managerial personnel from the agency that will be using the service or product. A contracting officer's representative (COR)[4] and various purchasing agents may be involved. As part of the contract management and administration process, this team may continue to exist and act to oversee and manage the contract.

For clarity of understanding, much of the following focuses on the agency contract administration function, assuming that it is furnished by one individual. In some cases, one contract administrator will handle all CA functions. More likely, a government project manager will interact with the contractor on a daily basis, overseeing service delivery or system deployment activities. If a steering committee or team exists, it will provide more general oversight and monitoring functions. This analysis assumes that all personnel involved in the CA function fully cooperate, representing the agency with one voice. Realistically, this may not be accurate. Further analysis will be developed as appropriate to identify the areas of greatest impact for cooperation among all personnel that comprise the CA function.

The service or product described below can be both one that is delivered to customers or clients of an agency or to agency personnel. In many cases, consideration of both agency needs and client needs are appropriate, as a contractor may deliver hardware and software, for example, that will enable the agency to better serve its clients.

Factors Common to Contract Administration Effectiveness

The structure, roles, daily management activities, and needed resources of the CA function—as well as the likelihood of reaching contract goals—depend on a wide variety of factors. All of these factors are faced by both CAs as well as by the private sector contractors who have agreed to the terms of the contract.

These factors include:

Complexity/Uncertainty
1. Complexity of the service/product
2. Uncertainty inherent in choosing the best means to deliver the service or create the product
3. Degree of certainty of goal or outcome achievement
4. Degree of certainty that a specific service delivery means will result in the desired goal or outcome achievement
5. The amount of discretion given to the private contractor in choosing the means to provide the desired result
6. The degree of risk for both public officials and private managers that the service/product will not reach its goals

Knowledge and understanding
7. Knowledge about the service/product by the CA and contractors
8. Knowledge by the CA of federal rules and regulations, performance contracting, and other related laws and procedures
9. Knowledge by the CA of the contractor's organizational characteristics

Glossary of Key Terms

Acceptable Quality Level (AQL)—Usually identified as part of Performance-Based Service Contracting (PBSC), an AQL identifies the maximum allowable percentage or number of service units or products that are deemed defective. If a contractor does not meet the AQL, services/products will have to be corrected. Violations of the AQL may lead to sanctions against the contractor.

Competitive Negotiation—A formal request by the government soliciting bids that contain technical proposals and price quotations. Specific project goals and objectives are identified with only a very general scope of work, but bidders are requested to identify how these goals will be achieved. Extended negotiation is expected prior to contract award.

Contract Administration (CA)—The governmental or agency processes that occur after a contract with a private contractor has been signed. These include activities such as contract monitoring and review, inspection of delivered services or products, assessment and evaluation of the deliverables, amending the contract as needed, resolution of delivery problems, and application of sanctions and penalties as needed.

Contract Management—An overall concept that includes all activities performed by the government or agency that are relevant to contracts with private or nonprofit organizations. These include activities such as writing or creating the Invitation to Bid or Request for Proposal, devising a rating system for bid responses, rating the bid responses, awarding the contract, additional negotiations leading to a signed contract, and contract administration.

Contracting Officer—A person representing a federal agency who has the authority to award, administer, and/or terminate contracts. Contracting officers can also be described as a Contracting Officer's Representative (COR), Contracting Officer's Technical Representative (COTR), Government Technical Representative (GTR), or a Government Technical Evaluator (GTE).

Contractor-Customer Relationship (CCR)—The relationship between government agencies and private or nonprofit contractors that is generally found in the case of services or products of low to mid complexity.

Invitation to Bid (ITB)—A formal request by the government soliciting price quotations or bids from potential private contractors. Specifications and a scope of work are included. Awards are generally made to the lowest bidder without additional discussions or negotiations.

Project Manager—A person who represents the program or agency receiving the services or products delivered by a contractor.

Public-Private Partnerships (PPPs)—Relationships among government agencies and private or nonprofit contractors that should be formed when dealing with services or products of highest complexity. In comparison to traditional contractor-customer relationships, they require radical changes in the roles played by all partners.

Request for Proposal (RFP)—A formal request by the government soliciting bids that contain technical proposals and price quotations. Specific project goals and objectives are identified, and a general scope of work is usually included. Bidders are requested to provide greater detail concerning the means by which these goals will be attained. A limited degree of negotiation is expected.

10. Degree to which there is confidence that the contractor will not file for bankruptcy

Contract management process that occurs before contract award

11. Extent to which government officials have obtained appropriate information and knowledge prior to the completion of the RFP
12. The specificity and limitations imposed by the RFP, especially in the Statement of Work
13. Uncertainty and variation in volume of the demand or need for the service
14. Choice of bid type and process
15. Degree of competition from alternative private contractors
16. The timeline required to complete service delivery or project
17. The expectation of a long-term commitment
18. Nature of potential sanctions, default contingency plans, and potential incentives

Many of these factors are not mutually exclusive and overlap each other in the degree to which they influence each other in a causal fashion. In most cases, each factor can be placed on a continuum that ranges from "low to high." These factors will be analyzed in more detail, primarily focusing on the impact of service/product complexity or uncertainty.

The importance of different factors, in combination with each other, will determine the appropriate CA approach. Approaches will consist of efforts from incumbent CAs that will vary in terms of:

• The amount of time likely to be devoted to contract administration
• The nature and extent of the interaction with contractors or private partners
• The required knowledge and understanding of the CA
• The appropriateness of the training required for more specialized skills such as dispute resolution

These approaches will be grouped together in terms of three scenarios that relate primarily to the nature of the service or product. Simplistically, these are labeled Low Complexity, Mid Complexity, and High Complexity. These can be best viewed as falling along a continuum that runs from low to high complexity.

Additionally, it will be argued that in order to achieve maximum efficiency and effectiveness, traditional contractor-customer relationships (CCRs) are appropriate for Low and Mid Complexity scenarios, while public-private partnerships are required for High Complexity scenarios.

Specific Factors: Complexity/Uncertainty

Complexity of Service and Uncertainty about Service Delivery

The complexity of the service/product and the uncertainty about how to best deliver that service/product are two factors that are closely related. They are causally related, as the greater the complexity of the service, the greater the uncertainty about how to deliver it. The reverse statement is true as well, as uncertainty about means of delivery contributes to complexity.

A number of service delivery aspects can contribute to complexity. The amount and degree of technical expertise required to deliver the service, including the amount of training and/or education needed for those employees directly involved in service delivery, impacts complexity in a number of ways. The CA must review the extent to which private contractor service deliverers have the requisite knowledge, training, and education. This review occurs at a number of points in time: 1) prior to the approval of the contract, as part of the rating of responses to RFPs; 2) during the negotiation phase, especially if there are changes in those individuals identified as delivering the service; 3) after the contract is signed whenever there are changes in key personnel.

The CA must ensure that requisite expertise is continually provided. The contractor should not be allowed to hire technical personnel with much less expertise than that stated in the response to the RFP, using the contracted service as "on the job training" and then removing these personnel from the project (Kelman, 1990). If the contractor proposes to replace a financial manager with 10 years of experience making $80,000 per year with someone with only a few years of experience who will be paid $40,000, the CA should approve this change in personnel only after a review of the qualifications and knowledge of the proposed replacement.

This approval of personnel replacements may be necessary only for those service delivery processes of high complexity and/or uncertainty. If the desired outcome or output is not complex, such as janitorial services, then review of service delivery means and key personnel qualifications may not be necessary.

Also, if the service is routine—and the results of the service delivery, either in terms of outputs or outcomes, are clear, easily visible, and understood—then the CA can rely upon the contractor to provide appropriate means. These means could be outlined in the bidders' response or clarified in the negotiations phase prior to contract finalization. If viable competition[5] exists, and this fact provides enough of an incentive for the contractor to solve service delivery problems, then CA understanding of those means does not have to be thorough (see Figure 6.1).

The more complex the service delivery means, the more necessary it is for the CA to have an understanding of these means. This understanding

Figure 6.1: CA Understanding of Service Delivery Means

	High		
Uncertainty About Service Delivery Means		Not applicable	CA should have high understanding unless results are easily measurable
		CA understanding minimal	CA should have some understanding unless results are easily measurable
	Low		

	Low	High

Complexity of Service Delivery Means

does not have to be extensive or detailed, but it needs to be sufficient enough so that the CA can adequately perform the appropriate duties of review, monitoring, and evaluation.[6]

This understanding is needed for several reasons. First, the CA must have assurances that the contractor understands the service delivery process, both in terms of the technical expertise required and the management expertise required to deliver the service in the most efficient manner. Second, if problems occur in the service delivery process, with sufficient understanding the CA may be able to assist in the resolution of these problems. Third, if there are changes to the contract after implementation occurs, the CA will be in a better position to accurately assess the need for these changes and the appropriate amount paid to the contractor.

Clearly the more complex the service, the knowledge of the CA of the best means to deliver the service will be less than if the service is routine. To overcome this "shortfall," several options are possible. As part of the contract, during the initial stages of implementation, the contractor could educate or train the CA in the service delivery means, bringing the CA's knowledge up to date as much as possible. A different relationship needs to be established as more interaction and communication are required between the CA and the contractor during the service delivery process. More trust is required, with more flexibility in enforcing contract deadlines.

If agency institutional memory has been lost, and the contractor knows much more about the service delivery means than the federal CA, then the nature of the CA process must change to be effective. Additional CA personnel may be required to counterbalance the greater degree of dependency held by the federal government. Greater training in CA skills must be present.

Contractor Discretion to Choose Service Delivery Means

The extent to which the contractor should be given control over which service delivery means (or product creation means) to choose impacts the CA role in terms of the amount of time and effort—as well as knowledge—that must be spent. If the contractor can be given complete discretion over this choice, then review, monitoring, and problem-solving efforts by the CA could be much less than if the contractor's choice of means is constrained or limited. This degree of discretion or choice depends on:

- The complexity of those means
- The certainty that those means will produce the desired output/outcome
- The degree to which the output/outcome can be validly and reliably measured, e.g., the use of PBSC
- The confidence that a specific acceptable quality level or error rate will not significantly degrade service levels

The most significant of these factors is the degree of valid measurement that is possible. In one sense, if measurement is highly valid, the agency does not have to be concerned with the means by which outputs are obtained. Furthermore, if a PBSC is used, then it is assumed that there is sufficient incentive to ensure that the contractor will maintain service levels and quickly correct any errors for fear of losing a portion or all of the agency payment.

In reality, however, the first two factors must be considered, as they are likely to contribute to the validity of output/outcome measurement. If the service is of low complexity or routine, then high validity is likely (see Figure 6.2). For example, a contract for janitorial services could state that carpets in 100 percent of rooms in the building must be cleaned each night (output measure), with an AQL based upon a visible inspection by the CA of at least 10 percent of the rooms, at least once per week, resulting in a grade of at least a "9" out of a possible "10" points on a qualitative measurement scale (outcome measure). In this example, since the measures used to evaluate performance are highly valid, and the service delivery means are routine (low complexity), the contractor can be given the discretion regarding equipment to be used, scheduling the order in which rooms are to be cleaned, etc. Problems with service delivery are assumed to be unlikely since they can be easily and quickly noticed. Correcting these problems is also assumed to be easy.

For services that are not routine, but for which there is a reasonable certainty that chosen means will lead to desired outputs/outcomes, a variety of limitations and checks could be provided over contractor discretion. First,

Figure 6.2: Amount of Discretion Given to Contractor to Choose Service Delivery Means

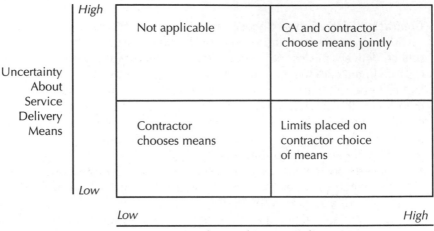

	High		
Uncertainty About Service Delivery Means		Not applicable	CA and contractor choose means jointly
		Contractor chooses means	Limits placed on contractor choice of means
	Low		
		Low	High

Complexity of Service Delivery Means

the scope of work/specifications in the RFP could prescribe a specific means. Contractor responses to this RFP would identify how the adoption of these means would lead to the desired output/outcome. Second, the scope could ask the contractor to choose and provide an introduction or brief description of the means. If this contractor is awarded the contract, the agency by implication has approved the contractor choice. Third, the scope of work could ask for an introduction in the response, with a complete description to follow within a specified time frame, e.g., 90 days after the contract start. This latter document would have to be approved by the CA, implying that: 1) approval may require several revised versions to be submitted; and/or 2) any changes desired by the contractor after contract start must be approved by the CA.

If the service is highly complex, and there is a high degree of uncertainty regarding how to best provide the service, then more than one option is available for the CA. If output/outcome measures are reasonably valid, and a performance contract is in place, then allowing the contractor more discretion over means choice results in a lower CA commitment in terms of time. The risk, however, lies in the amount of penalty assessed and the frequency that sanctions will be enforced if the AQL is exceeded. If there is little enforcement, then the absence of CA involvement in the means choice may lead to a significant lowering of service quality.

Alternatively, if the service can be delivered in "pieces" or "modules," each identifiable by a milestone that represents a "delivery date," then allowing the contractor complete discretion may be acceptable. This may be effective for the deployment of a system based on information technology (IT) expertise, for example, for which there is reasonable assurance that the means chosen will lead to the establishment of a workable system. The potential disadvantage is that the effective role of the CA in resolving difficulties that lead to missed deadlines or milestones may be limited.

A third option involves a greater commitment of the CA, as well as the commitment of technical and program manager personnel. If means are uncertain because of evolving technology, for example, and the link between means and results is also uncertain because of the need to "custom make" the software and hardware, then there must be an understanding by all parties that the choice of means will be an ongoing effort. The contractor must commit to training the CA and appropriate agency personnel about the means chosen, receiving feedback and altering those means as a result. The CA must play a much more active role, meeting frequently with the contractor and receiving updates regarding progress toward meeting milestones and objectives. The CA may be expected to work closely with agency personnel to assist in deployment efforts. There must be the expectation on the part of the agency and the contractor that a partnership is needed to provide the service or product.

The efforts of the Army to modernize its supply chain system by contracting with Computer Sciences Corporation (CSC) is one example. This 10-year $680 million contract, producing what is known as the "Log Mod" program, includes broad performance parameters, requiring CSC to use the latest technological processes in choosing appropriate software and hardware. CSC has hired over 200 of the 460 Army employees to create the Log Mod system. The Army has retained 77 employees, however, to monitor and administer the system (Cahlink, 2000). The complexity, size, and project length will require close cooperation between CSC and Army personnel to produce a successful system by the 2004 deadline.

The Degree of Risk

Risk can be defined in different ways for agencies and contractors. The likelihood that the service will not be provided, or the product delivered—either at all or to a much smaller degree—is a concern that at least conceptually is always present. In reality, for routine services, the amount of risk may be so small that it does not enter the consciousness of the CA or the private contractor.

Risk is dependent upon "subfactors" such as:
- The importance of the agency service delivery goal to the accomplishment of the agency's mission

- The degree of negative impact that will occur if the goal is not met
- The viability of satisfying the agency goal through means other than the contract at issue
- The existence of alternative contractors to deliver the service if the contract is canceled
- The ease of canceling the present contract and writing a new contract with another contractor
- The knowledge, skills, and ability of the CA to assist with finding solutions to service delivery problems

For low complexity or routine services (see Figure 6.3), risk is minimal. A contract for janitorial services in the General Services Administration Public Building Program, for example, falls into this category. Offices that are not clean will have little bearing on the overall agency mission. There will likely be little damage to the agency reputation if visitors experience "dirty" offices. Agency dependency on a given contractor is minimal, as other services can be easily located. Assuming that changing to an alternative contractor could occur with minimum disruption of service, or that a contingency plan is part of the RFP, the CA role is not influenced.

Figure 6.3: Influence of Risk on CA Activity

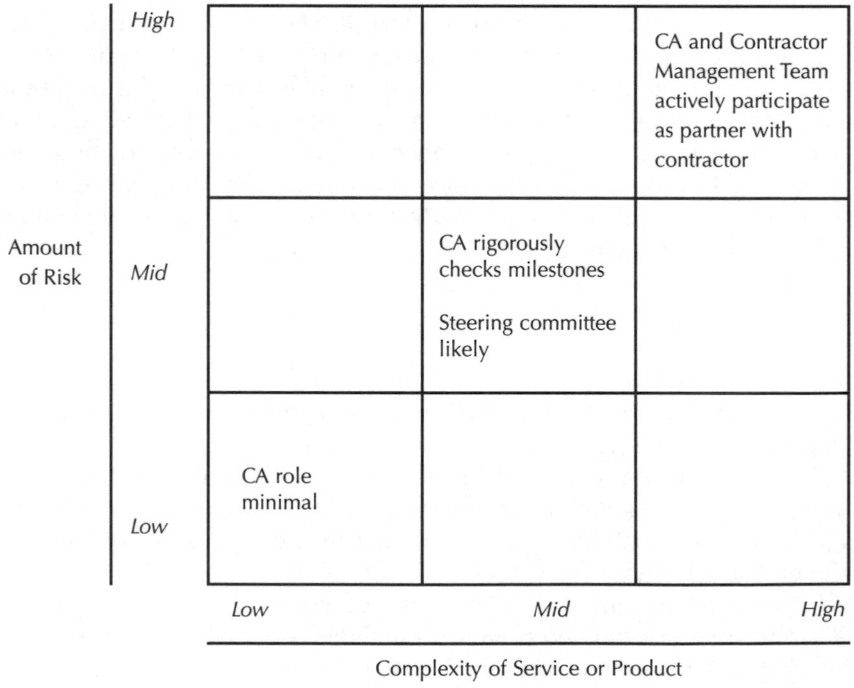

Amount of Risk	High			CA and Contractor Management Team actively participate as partner with contractor
	Mid		CA rigorously checks milestones Steering committee likely	
	Low	CA role minimal		
		Low	Mid	High

Complexity of Service or Product

For services of mid complexity, the risk is much greater. The adoption of IT services by an agency to provide faster, more convenient access to clients may fall into this category if "off the shelf" software and hardware can be used to establish the system. The importance of the IT system in meeting the agency mission is greater if it affects performance results efforts related to the Government Performance and Results Act, for example. The agency reputation could suffer, a large amount of money could be "wasted," and overall goals would not be met as well if this system fails. But if there are alternatives, as clients can still contact the agency for services by non-IT means, then the risk is lessened somewhat.

The higher degree of risk clearly influences the CA role. The dependency of the agency on the contractor is greater. Although other software/hardware contractors are likely to be available, issues such as intellectual property rights may greatly hinder the deployment of an alternative system. Still, as espoused by the Information Technology Investment Management (ITIM) system, for example,[7] milestones must be rigorously monitored and processes established that may lead to choosing alternative contractors. This process involves a review committee that consists of technical and managerial personnel as well as the CA. Also, a well-thought-out contingency plan needs to be part of the contract management process.

For services of high complexity, the risk is considerable and requires a change in agency contract management and CA policies, procedures, and even culture for the service goals to be achieved successfully. Even though a contract is awarded, there may be considerable uncertainty regarding how well the proposed service delivery means will work. If technology is fast changing, then technology "upgrades" are likely to be part of the contract, further adding to the complexity. The impact on agency mission and potential negative impact will vary with the nature and size of the contract, but clearly a successful project will require much more of a partnership relationship. In this role, the CA must involve a contract management team, acting in a proactive fashion to assist in the completion of the system deployment.

Specific Factors: Knowledge and Understanding

The amount and variety of knowledge required to effectively implement the CA function varies considerably. As indicated, there are at least four areas of knowledge that apply:
1. Knowledge about the service/product by CAs and contractors
2. Knowledge by the CA of federal rules and regulations, performance contracting, and other related laws and procedures
3. Knowledge by the CA of the contractor's organizational characteristics

4. Degree to which there is confidence that the contractor will continue operation or not file for bankruptcy

If there is a contract administrator and a project manager whose roles constitute the CA function, then the type and amount of knowledge needed can vary between these two individuals. The project or field manager should have much greater knowledge about the service provided by the contractor. This includes the means by which the service is delivered (discussed earlier), the milestones that the contractor should meet, and the knowledge that allows for valid inspection and testing of products and systems.

In contrast, the contract administrator should have much more knowledge about appropriate federal rules and regulations as well as laws. These would include appropriate steps to take in terms of applying sanctions and implementing change orders. In addition, there are a myriad of CA duties such as certification for payment, etc., that are appropriately the responsibility of the contract administrator.

The Federal Acquisition Requirements (FAR) spell out additional knowledge that can be categorized as information about the contractor and his/her management team, financial status, and organizational characteristics. This knowledge includes:

*   The contractor's financial condition, including commercial financing provisions
*   The capability of the contractor to comply with the contract in terms of technical performance and schedule
*   The capability of contractor management and engineering systems, including the purchasing system, traffic operations, and value engineering program where appropriate
*   The contractor's plans regarding small, disadvantaged, and women-owned small business master subcontracting plans
*   The existence of a contractor drug-free workplace program and drug-free awareness program
*   Contractor environmental practices (FAR 42)

This knowledge is the responsibility of the contract administrator. To some extent, the contractor can submit documents that would confirm the existence of appropriate programs and systems and which would require little review and evaluation. In other cases, the contract administrator may have to visit the contractor's facilities to gain enough knowledge to adequately evaluate.

To the extent that the knowledge about contractor operations is obtained several times throughout the life of the contract, the project manager can assist the contract administrator in identifying potential problems in contractor performance and capability. If a milestone is not met, for example, in the course of resolving the problem, the contract administrator may wish to perform an additional review of contractor engineering and management systems.

The degree of concern about contractor bankruptcy and capability to perform the contract impacts on the diligence in collecting contractor operations knowledge and the resulting alteration in CA roles and duties. The more concern about bankruptcy, the more important the existence of a performance bond and a contingency plan for the agency, as well as an assessment of the impact of service disruption. Another consideration is the existence of alternative contractors. If there are few—or no—other contractors that could deliver the service, then the CA function may have to engage in activities that assist the contractor in maintaining viability.

For routine services/products, especially those of small scope and amount, both contract administrator and project manager will likely spend less than 100 percent of their time on the CA function for a contract. Both may have sufficient knowledge about means prior to the contract award. Both have confidence that the contractor is fully capable of delivering the service. The project manager may resolve problems without much, if any, input from the contract administrator. If there are several alternative contractors, and the number of engineers and members of the management team are few, very little time and effort will be required to obtain this knowledge.

With increasing service/product complexity comes a much greater need for all who participate in the CA function to actively communicate and cooperate (see Figure 6.4). The existence of a steering committee is more likely, and some CA functions, including periodic monitoring of milestone completion and review of contractor operations, will be performed by this committee. The project manager and contract administrator are more likely to devote full-time effort to the contract, with knowledge gained and roles largely separate. When problems arise, however, there is a much greater need for these two to share knowledge and interact to resolve the problems.

For contracts involving highly complex services/products, there must be a much higher degree of overlap in the types of knowledge held by all those who perform the CA function. Those representing the agency must act as a team to a much greater degree. A greater sense of partnership must exist between the agency and the contractor. It is imperative that the contract administrator become much more aware of the service delivery means, as well as the extent to which milestones are met on time. The contract administrator may expect to play a greater role in resolving any problems or complaints. Ongoing information about financial conditions and organizational capability may be requested from the contractor.

If part of the complexity is due to an uncertainty that the contractor understands and is capable of delivering the service in the most efficient and effective way possible, then the project manager needs to have greater knowledge of contractor engineering and management systems. There is the

Figure 6.4: Knowledge of Contract Administrator and Government Project Manager

Complexity/Uncertainty of Service or Product		
Low	**Mid**	**High**
Government Project Manager has service process and content knowledge Contract Administrator is responsible for FAR and knowledge of contractor's organizational characteristics Little need for knowledge and role overlap Little need for teamwork No steering committee	Government Project Manager and Contract Administrator share some service content and FAR knowledge Steering committee created and meets periodically	High degree of knowledge sharing by Government Project Manager and Contract Administrator Both participate in dispute resolution Government Project Manager has greater knowledge of contractor management systems Steering committee closely monitors

expectation that this knowledge will evolve over the life of the contract, with the role of agency technical and managerial personnel changing depending on the efforts and capabilities of the contractor. The project manager needs to be much more aware of contracting policies and procedures, including the capabilities of the contract administrator in assisting with deployment issues.

If there is a great concern that the contractor may not be able to meet the goals of the contract, and it would be too expensive to change contractors unless extremely poor performance resulted, then the CA function may have to change drastically. The largely reactive nature of CA duties and responsibilities—i.e., monitoring and reviewing actions by the contractor—may have to change to a much more proactive one. Those participating in the CA function may have to assist the contractor in goal achievement. If the service to be provided is new, for example, then agency personnel should assist in marketing or publicizing the existence of this service, rather than rely completely on the efforts of the contractor.

Specific Factors: Contract Management Prior to Contract Administration

Contract management must be viewed as a process consisting of highly interrelated steps. These include writing the RFP, especially the Statement of Work, and evaluating bids to the RFP in addition to contract administration. The ease of contract administration and ultimately the achievement of agency goals are greatly dependent upon the earlier contract management steps. This section reviews the key factors that influence the part of contract management that occurs prior to contract administration.

The RFP Process: Statement of Work (SOW) Creation

In devising the SOW, the most significant "subfactors" include:

- The identification of the results—service/product—desired
- The degree to which the process of delivering the service should be specified
- The degree to which the bidders should be limited in their discretion to identify the process
- The review and approval of any part of the service delivery process prior to contract administration

Much of the same analysis concerning the degree of uncertainty regarding service delivery means discussed above is relevant to the SOW creation process. Without dealing with issues of uncertainty, one logical argument is that only results should be identified without mentioning service delivery, as the bidder may have a "better way" of service delivery than can be envisioned by the agency. To the extent that the service delivery process can be and should be limited by the SOW, however, the duties and responsibilities of the CA are eased.

The writer of a SOW requesting security guard services, for example, may understand that the employees providing this service should be "certified"—that they have undergone appropriate training and that the contractor has determined that they have successfully acquired appropriate knowledge as a result. There are various options in terms of what language will appear in the SOW. First, the SOW could request that all guards must be certified and identify the process that the winning bidder must adopt for training and certification. Second, the SOW could request the bidder to identify how they will hire, train, and certify those employees. Third, the SOW could request that all guards be certified, without mentioning the need for specific aspects of hiring and training, allowing the bidder to specify how this will occur. Fourth, the SOW could request a brief statement from the contractor that outlines the processes of hiring, training, and certification, with a provision that a more detailed plan/policy will be provided to the agency within 90 days of the contract award. This more detailed plan or policy must be approved by the agency. Fifth, there could be no mention of the need for certified guards, assuming that the bidder will understand that appropriate training is needed and will state this in the response to the RFP.

Which language appears in the SOW depends upon:

1. The degree to which the need for certified guards is an industrywide accepted practice or unique to the specific agency needs[8]
2. The degree to which there is a wide range of accepted training means and content—or there is a generally approved and accepted certification process
3. The extent to which the agency is confident that the winning bidder will have the understanding and capability of providing certified guards

If industrywide certification is generally accepted, there is one (or a few) accepted certification process, and the agency has high confidence in the winning bidder's capability, then the need for certified guards should be mentioned but no additional information may be requested (see Figure 6.5). If the need is unique, there is a wide range of potential certification practices, and there is a low degree of confidence in bidder capability, then the need for and additional information about hiring, training, and certification should be specified. If there is any doubt that all bidders would specify that guards should be certified, then there should be mention of that need in the SOW.

In general, the more information about the service delivery process that is requested in the SOW, the easier it will be for the CA to assure that the contractor is meeting the goals stated in the RFP. If the service is routine, however, and the amount of skills needed to deliver the service is small, then requesting information in the SOW about the service delivery process may not be needed.

With greater service complexity or uncertainty, the SOW should request information about process. For services of mid complexity for which few problems are anticipated, either the entire service delivery process could be described in the response or requested after the contract

Figure 6.5: Statement of Work: Specificity of Information Requested from Bidders

	Need for Qualifications or "Certification"	Range of Acceptable Practices	Confidence in Bidder
High Specificity	Unique to Agency	Wide	Low
Low Specificity	Industrywide Acceptance	Limited	High

award. The expectation here is that the CA would likely approve it without further discussion. For example, the existence of a drug-free workplace policy would most likely be reviewed and approved without much discussion from the CA.

For those services of highest complexity, the requirement of detailed policies after the contract award is essential, with the expectation that there may be a process of review, feedback, and approval over a longer period of time. In this instance, the SOW cannot specify many limitations regarding process, especially if there is uncertainty regarding how best to deliver the service. At best, through the request for post-award policy review, a partnership is begun that allows for continued discussion regarding policies and procedures.

To the extent that valid performance measures and Accepted Quality Levels can be identified, the need for the SOW to request process information lessens. The greater the knowledge of process, though, the more likely the CA can provide meaningful input to resolve any service delivery problems.

Choice of Bid Type and Process

There are three major bid types and resulting processes that have been discussed extensively. These are:
1. Sealed bids
2. Multi-step or two-step bids
3. Negotiated competition

The complexity and amount of discretion allowed by each bid type varies similarly with the complexity of the service delivered (see Figure 6.6). Sealed bids, the most commonly accepted bid type, is appropriate for routine services with low complexity/uncertainty. Along with the bid, potential contractors certify that they can perform the work identified in the ITB or RFP. The bidder with the lowest price receives the contract.

Multi-step or two-step bids, in which the response to the technical proposal is submitted separately from the cost or price response, are preferable for services of mid complexity. Bidders are required to demonstrate capability to deliver the service through their response to the technical proposal. The price bids of only those bidders whose response to the technical proposal is

Figure 6.6: Choice of Bid Type and Process

Complexity/Uncertainty of Service or Product		
Low	Mid	High
Sealed Bid	Multi-Step	Negotiated Competition

deemed "responsive and responsible" are opened, with the contract awarded to the lowest bidder.

This process is effective to the extent that the responses to the technical proposals are similar in the service delivery process that they identify. In other words, the responses must be comparable. The evaluation team must fully understand the processes as described in the response and be able to adequately judge their effectiveness. To the extent that one or more responses contain a service delivery process that is radically different from the norm, the use of the multi-step process may not lead to the best choice of contractors.

Also, since the decision regarding technical capability is made on a "pass/fail" basis, the bid process does not allow for different rating scores to influence the final selection of a contractor. Furthermore, there must be highly valid criteria to evaluate the technical proposal. Finally, there must be a fixed price (or fixed price with economic adjustment) contract type (Welch and Costello, 2000).

For services of high complexity, negotiated competition is the only appropriate bid type and process. If any of the stated conditions for the multi-step process cannot be met, then it is a significant viable alternative. After the technical proposals are opened, then discussions are held with those bidders whose response is deemed in a "competitive range." After discussions, each bidder proposes a "last and final best offer" regarding service delivery and price.

Negotiation offers several potential advantages for the agency. First, if there is any disagreement regarding completion of tasks, milestones, etc., in which the agency wishes changes from that proposed in the bidder response, these can be clarified and agreement reached. A highly tailored agreement that favors the agency can be reached. Second, to the extent the selection team does not fully understand the technical proposal, the negotiations may constitute a "training seminar" or educational experience via bidder answers to selection team questions. Third, these discussions are the beginning of a continuing dialogue that will characterize the partnership with the winning bidder after the contract has been awarded.

The major drawback of increased time and effort spent by agency personnel must be viewed as necessary to meet service delivery goals and choose the most effective contractor.

The Timeline Required to Complete the Project

The timeline in the bidder response and/or agreed to in subsequent negotiations has a direct bearing on contract administration. Influencing factors include:

1. The length of the timeline
2. The number of milestones/delivery dates
3. The degree of consistency or "sameness" in terms of deliverables

4. The expectation that milestones will be met
5. The importance of the project in meeting needs identified in the agency strategic plan

The complexity/uncertainty of the service determines the importance of these factors and the subsequent reaction of the CA to them. For services of low complexity, the length of the timeline—the contract award length—is less relevant because there is a high expectation that all services/products will be delivered on time. Likewise, if the same service/product is delivered repeatedly, then the number of delivery dates is less important. The priority of the service/product in meeting agency needs is most likely low as well. The Environmental Protection Agency telephone hotline contract (Laurent, 1998), for example, would fit this category.

With increasing service/product uncertainty, the relevance of the timeline becomes more important, requiring greater attention by the CA (see Figure 6.7). If it is a relatively long timeline, e.g., five years, the greater uncertainty suggests greater opportunity for problems or difficulties to occur. More consistent CA attention is required. Also, if the expectation of a long-term commitment is high, and the timeline for one project is likely to lead into another project —e.g., a contract for design leading to a contract for deployment—realistically the timeline becomes indefinite in terms of the agency contractor relationship. Although project timeline length is not likely to vary much given the outcome of negotiations, the discussions held at this point help to establish key partnership relationships after the contract award.

The number of milestones and delivery dates are directly related to what is promised to be delivered and the amount of time and effort the contractor pledges to meet a given milestone. To the extent these differences can be more clearly identified during negotiations, the CA will have an easier time in monitoring and reviewing contract progress. The agency is potentially able to: 1) persuade the contractor to agree on milestones that best meet its needs, while at the same time; 2) assist the contractor in more thoroughly assessing the time, effort, and resources necessary to meet each milestone.

The extent to which the project results in a product that will not be fully complete until the end of the timeline, e.g., an IT system, suggests that the deliverables identified at each milestone will be very different—e.g., development of software, installation of hardware, etc.—even though they are intended to be "building blocks" that result in an integrated whole. The CA must be very aware of all milestones, and much more thoroughly inspect and review the deliverables, assessing not only to what extent they are working, but also the extent to which a similar, if the not the same, deliverable can be produced by an alternative contractor.

For projects of highest complexity/uncertainty, there must be an understanding that milestones may be only approximate. If there is a high likelihood

Figure 6.7: Timeline Importance and Resulting CA Review

	Complexity/Uncertainty of Service or Product		
	Low	**Mid**	**High**
Length of timeline	Not applicable	More CA attention if contract renewal is anticipated	Greatest CA attention because partnership required and long-term commitment expected
Number of Milestones/ Deliverables	Minimal CA review if deliverables the same	More problems anticipated the greater the number of deliverables	Greatest CA attention because each deliverable unique
Sameness of deliverables	High: minimal CA review	More CA inspection and monitoring if different elements	Low: each deliverable reviewed and tested, especially if "building block" service or product
Expectation that milestone will be met	High: minimal CA review	Some problems anticipated Greater CA attention	Low: greatest CA attention because most problems expected
Importance to Agency Strategic Plan	Low: because problems easily solved Minimal CA review	Greater risk as problems more difficult to solve	High: risk and resource commitment likely to be greatest

that factors outside the control of the agency or the contractor will cause project delays, then milestones will have to be open to continual adjustment. The role of the CA is much more difficult and time-consuming, since the cause of each delay must be reviewed and investigated, with the CA providing assistance in resolving difficulties as possible.

At some point in the timeline, with projects of high uncertainty, the agency passes a "point of no return." After this point, the cost and effort of terminating the contract and seeking a viable alternative is greater than staying with the present contractor and resolving problems. The earlier in the time-line that this point exists, the greater the amount of time, effort, and resources the agency must commit to CA. A successful public-private partner-ship is the only agency-contractor relationship that will lead to the desired results, especially if the project is a high priority for the agency as defined by its strategic plan.

Expectation of a Long-Term Commitment

Much of what government does exists in terms of projects that have a clearly defined beginning and end, rather than the expectation of a long-term commitment between an agency and a contractor (e.g., Kelman, 1990). Traditionally, the short-term contractual relationship has been an essential part of American procurement culture for several reasons. First, there has always been the fear of corruption—that agency representatives may become too "cozy" with contractors, allowing costs to escalate and/or service quality to diminish. Second, the short-term view coincides with the philos-ophy that greater competition from contractors in the marketplace will lead to lower prices and better service quality. Third, the threat of contract ter-mination or non-renewal keeps current contractors always striving to deliver high service quality. Fourth, for some services or products that are uniquely governmental, there is the need to maintain competition over time by giving contracts to more than one contractor (Kettl, 1993).

In the private sector, a long-term commitment between buyer and seller is desired.[9] Both parties are more likely to establish a relationship that is flexible and that is expected to be dynamic and evolving. To achieve the goals set out by the contract, there will be less adherence to specific con-tract language, with the expectation that changes will occur and problems solved even if behavior is required that is not specified in the contract.

The 1994 Federal Acquisition Streamlining Act (FASA) recognized the importance of long-term commitment by acknowledging that agencies should consider contractor's past performance when evaluating bids received for future work. The following language is found in Section 1091 of FASA:

Past contract performance of an offeror is one of the relevant factors that a contracting official of an executive agency should consider in awarding a contract.

It is appropriate for a contracting official to consider past contract perform-ance of an offeror as an indicator of the likelihood that the offeror will suc-cessfully perform a contract to be awarded by that official (USOFPP, 2000).

The relevant assumption is that contractors will be more likely to perform at a higher quality under a present contract in anticipation of receiving future contracts. As a result, there is a greater likelihood of a long-term relationship and commitment when past performance is given greater weight in contract award decisions.

There are several additional potential advantages to the agency if it enters into a long-term commitment with a contractor. First, the contractor may be more willing to identify problems unforeseen by the agency and suggest means of improvement. This may occur within the boundaries established by the contract, or suggestions could be made regarding other aspects of agency policies and procedures. These suggestions may lead to change orders and additional profit for the contractor, but the agency benefits from greater efficiencies and higher quality service.

Second, the willingness to be flexible in establishing a long-term relationship may become significant if: 1) the volume of work needed by the agency changes from that identified in the original contract; and 2) unexpected variations in the service demand requires more or less effort from the contractor compared to what was identified in the contract. Under the short-term contract, if the agency discovers that it needs more service or greater amounts of a product than originally envisioned, then the cost of this additional work may be much higher. Alternatively, if the agency realizes it needs less than it originally contracted for, the contractor may insist that the agency accept and pay for the amount specified in the contract.

In some situations, even if the service is routine and the contract for the short term, a high degree of potential competition may be enough of

Figure 6.8: Desirability of a Long-Term Commitment (LTC)

	Complexity/Uncertainty of Service or Product		
	Low	Mid	High
Volume of Work or Service Demand Changes	Not applicable because of likely high degree of competition	If high: LTC more desirable especially if competition is moderate to low	LTC highly desirable if high change and contractor help is more valuable
Degree of Competition	Most likely high: LTC not needed because problems easily solved	Lower competition means greater risk and higher costs if LTC not made	LTC most desirable if competition is low and changing contracts has high costs

an incentive for the contractor to suggest improvements and be willing to solve problems without change orders. The contractor may wish to keep the contract for an extended period of time, and therefore will act in ways to elicit continued goodwill from the agency. The agency may not have the same interest in a continued relationship with a specific contractor, anticipating that other contractors could provide the same level of service if necessary. Problems that occur, however, may be infrequent and easily solvable, therefore limiting the contact between the agency and the contractor in ways not defined by the contract. The contractor may be willing to provide this "additional service" because it does not require much time and effort.

As service complexity increases, however, the value of a long-term commitment will increase. To the extent that a more efficient/effective means to deliver the service may be created before the conclusion of a given contract, the agency will wish to have the flexibility and provide sufficient contractor incentives to adopt this better means of service delivery. To the extent that the technology needed to deliver the service is uncertain, and would require extensive interaction between agency personnel and the contractor to effectively deliver the service, then this long-term commitment is even more desired.

There are various ways to increase commitment, even in the context of laws or regulations that may prohibit contracts beyond five years. One of the easiest may be to include a clause of renewal for another time period up to an additional five years, with possible additional renewal periods. This decision to renew would be at the discretion of the agency. An alternative would be to issue a new RFP, allowing for the incumbent contractor to bid. This alternative may be chosen if the agency feels there might be other contractors who would perform significantly better.

For highly complex services, the long-term commitment may be couched in phases. If a new customized IT system is to be deployed, one contractor could assist with planning the system. Once completed, a second contract could be let for design work. Third, installation could follow. In each case, a separate RFP could be issued. If the performance of the contractor who helped plan is high, this contractor would have an advantage in outbidding other contractors as long as evaluation criteria allowed for consideration of past performance.

From an agency perspective, there are risks to engaging in a long-term commitment. Costs may rise, either through change orders or at the time of renewal, as the additional services that the contractor provides may elicit additional costs if the services represent a significant change. The agency has to decide if potential increased costs are offset by potential increases in service quality. For highly complex services, the long-term commitment is necessary because of the risk that service quality may decline (see Figure 6.8).

Degree of Competition from Alternative Contractors

As discussed in the previous section, it is often desirable for an agency to be able to choose from among alternative contractors or potential contractors. A high degree of competition underlies much of the philosophy and reasoning associated with outsourcing or privatization, in that such competition drives down prices charged by contractors, which leads to increased efficiency.[10] For services/products of low to mid complexity in which certainty of results and process are at least relatively high, the agency should maintain viable alternative contractors (see Figure 6.9).

The challenge comes at the time that a contract must be renewed or an ITB or RFP issued. If the latter occurs, the agency must be able to convince these contractors that they have a reasonable chance of winning a contract. Otherwise, only the incumbent contractor will enter a bid. The agency has little choice but to renew the contract, even if higher costs are incurred.[11]

Performance-based service contracts can potentially assist, as it is more easily discernable if a given contractor is not performing acceptably, and therefore the decision to seek outside contractors can be made with more confidence that alternative contractors would provide a better service. Also, clearly stated valid results can allow other contractors to more confidently calculate costs and, therefore, increase the probability they would bid on a contract.

A major factor in the calculation made by alternative contractors is the ease with which an agency can change from one contractor to another. Various efforts can help increase this ease. To the extent that multiple contracts can be awarded for "parts" of the same service, the agency can maintain competition if one contractor is willing to assume the increased workload of another contractor who is not renewed. This arrangement has the increased advantage of more than one contractor becoming familiar with agency personnel and understanding agency needs.

If a significant expenditure of equipment is required, the agency can insist that the contractor lease agency-owned equipment. The agency could also require any operating policies and procedures to become the property of the agency, thereby increasing the knowledge held by the CA and making it easier for another contractor to assume services with limited interruption and change for clientele.

If sufficient institutional memory and personnel can be maintained so that the service could be reacquired by the agency, adequate competition can exist. This may be viable only in a limited number of cases.

The danger for the agency is that the service is not complex enough to warrant the creation of a public-private partnership but competition has lessened to the extent that the agency has become "captive" or overly dependent on the contractor. Over time, costs may increase without the benefits of a long-term commitment, as described earlier.

Figure 6.9: Impact of Competition from Alternative Contractors

Degree of Competition	High Mid Low	Very positive with minimal CA activity	Requires more effort to maintain as alternative contractors "disappear"	Unlikely
		Should be maintained through multiple contracts		High CA activity, long-term commitment, and public-private partnership needed to maintain service quality
		Unlikely	Higher risk that costs will rise at contract renewal	

	Low	Mid	High

Complexity/Uncertainty of Service or Product

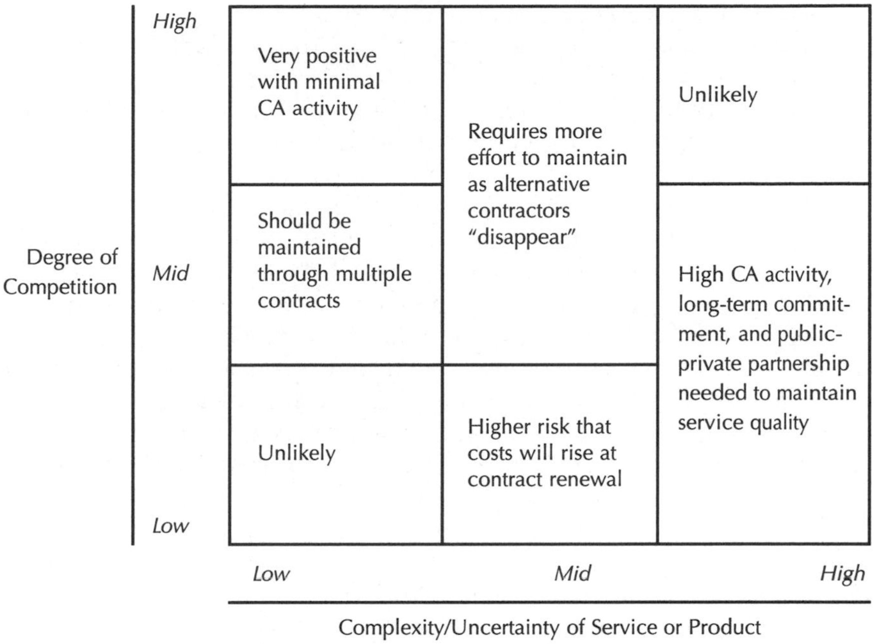

Nature of Potential Sanctions or Incentives and Default Contingency Plans

If the contractor does not meet performance standards, sanctions may be applied in terms of reduced payments. Alternatively, incentives could be offered to reward performance that exceeds expectations. If continued poor performance occurs, a default contingency plan should be put into place, and another contractor hired to continue the service.

The basis for sanctions or incentives must be valid performance measures. Given that it is unrealistic to expect perfect on-time delivery for the life of the contract, these measures must include an acceptable error rate, or Acceptable Quality Level. For services of low complexity or standard products, measures could be based on industry standards or past levels of performance. In some cases, clientele survey data could be used to establish a "satisfaction index" that determines acceptable performance. In other cases, percentage of delivery of services/products on time could constitute a viable performance measure.

To the extent that service delivery means are uncertain, and/or unexpected conditions or other factors result in missed deadlines, the issue of sanctions becomes much more complex. The importance of a contractor meeting the proposed timeline with appropriate milestones as identified in the bid and/or in subsequent negotiations depends on a number of factors. These include:

1. Delays that are the fault of the contractor
2. Delays that are caused by changing conditions, including increases in volume or need of services
3. The degree to which changing technology may mean changes in service delivery prior to the conclusion of the contract
4. The degree to which the CA imposes sanctions for missed deadlines

Contractor-caused delays in meeting milestones should be investigated by the CA to determine the cause and provide appropriate reaction. If the reason is human error by contractor personnel, then the CA must determine if additional oversight or review of personnel actions is required. The lack of appropriate experience may cause the CA to request a change in personnel, especially if the personnel identified in the bidder's response are not the same personnel that deliver the service after contract award. If poor management or planning is the cause, then the CA must determine if resolution of the immediate delay will correct the problem, leading to limited delays in meeting future deadlines.

If delays in meeting deadlines are the result of unexpected market conditions or unanticipated changes in the demand for services from clientele, then performance measures that refer to deadline delay may have to be discarded or changed. Likewise, performance standards may have to be altered. If service delivery means are highly uncertain, then it may be expected that changing technology, for example, will lead to the choice of different means as the timeline progresses. Deadlines or milestones may have to be changed if this occurs.

The choice of sanctions is always challenging, no matter how routine the service. This choice depends on several factors. In one sense, the agency never wishes to impose penalties, hoping high levels of quality will be maintained. From this perspective, the penalty could be a small amount, as it may never be imposed. Conversely, a large penalty amount may result in higher bids or may ultimately deter bidders.

Also, the dollar amount must be significant enough to provide an incentive for the contractor to meet the AQL. In other words, if the penalty is not high enough, the agency runs the risk of the contractor being more willing to "pay the fine" rather than maintain performance at acceptable levels. The choice of sanctions, as the choice of performance measures, depends upon the knowledge of service delivery means as well as on the results.

Three other factors to consider are: 1) the reason for the lack of compliance, 2) the degree to which a failure to meet the AQL can be corrected, and 3) the impact or effect of not achieving the AQL. If performance weakness is the result of human error and is not likely to be repeated, then the penalty may not have to be severe. However, if the response time is too high because of a lack of contractor staff and/or poor scheduling or staffing procedures, then the penalty needs to be severe enough to force the contractor to hire additional staff or correct what may be a pattern of undercompliance. If the penalty is too slight, then the agency risks repeated violations of the AQL, because it may cost the contractor less to correct the problem than to pay the penalty.

If the failure to meet performance standards is not significant in terms of its impact, then the penalty may not be severe. Waiting additional minutes to have a computer repaired may not cause any more harm than inconvenience. If a product that does not meet the AQL can be easily replaced by another, then the amount of the penalty may be low. However, if impacts are high, and the need for adherence to acceptable performance standards crucial to an agency's mission,[12] then the penalties must be much higher.

Finally, the penalties that are identified must be imposed. If not, they lose their effect as a means to stimulate consistent high-quality performance. The CA may feel that the imposition of penalties may have a demotivating effect, as contractor efforts to correct past errors may not occur (USDOE, 2001b).

If these problems can be successfully overcome, and contractor performance is maintained at acceptable levels, the amount of time/effort devoted to quality assurance can be considerably less with PBSC. As with any type of contract, though, the CA's role becomes more demanding the more problems that occur. A key assumption of PBSC is that the CA does not have to know much about how the contractor delivers the output. It does not matter, because if it is not delivered, a penalty is imposed.

However, if any action other than penalty imposition is considered by the CA, then it is to the advantage of the CA to understand the process. The CA may suggest solutions to the problem in lieu of penalties. If a shortage of qualified contractor staff is the likely cause of low response time, then the CA can suggest that more be hired. If the contractor claims that the AQL is too stringent, and performance problems are caused by changes in agency policies, for example, the CA may decide to change the AQL. Without an understanding of the work process, the CA may be dependent upon information furnished by the contractor in deciding what changes to make.[13]

The creation of a default contingency plan is a necessary part of the RFP creation process, and it should be fully communicated to the contractor who is awarded the contract. It can include the choice of the next lowest bidder, for example, and the present contractor can be notified that such discussions have taken place. If valid performance measures and sanctions exist, then there can be a clear link between these and the default contingency plan. For example, if the AQL is not met 50 percent of the time over a two-month period, then the contractor may be declared in default.

Although needed, the deployment of this plan may represent a failure on the part of the CA—as well as the contractor. It is best to make every

Figure 6.10: Imposition of Sanctions/Incentives by CA

	Complexity/Uncertainty of Service or Product	
	Low	High
Validity of Performance Measures Comprising AQL	High validity: sanctions imposed with little CA understanding of service delivery process necessary	Low validity: sanctions/incentives imposed with greater CA involvement in solving problems
Impact of Non-compliance on Agency Mission	Low impact: sanctions/incentives lower with corrections easily made Minimal CA involvement	High impact: sanctions higher but less likely to be enforced with extensive CA involvement in solving problems

effort to resolve problems. Sanctions may not be relevant for missed deadlines unless it is determined that the entire project is in serious jeopardy. This may be truer for highly complex services.

Summary: Characteristics of Low, Mid, and High Service Complexity and CA Roles and Responsibilities

Figure 6.11 compares and contrasts the functions of contract administration under the three levels of service complexity. A more detailed look at each of the scenarios follows.

Low Complexity

For services that are routine, with low uncertainty regarding how best to deliver the service, the ITB/RFP describes the service, including outputs, and specifies any restrictions. It does not specify choice of equipment or means, leaving that decision to the contractor. It may specify personnel either in the sense that all personnel must be "courteous to the customers" or that anyone the government wishes to fire will be fired. Otherwise, the contractor has maximum discretion to choose the best means in the response to the ITB/RFP and for the life of the contract. There is little need for the processes to be described in the bidder response, as price is the determining factor in awarding a contract. A sealed bid process is the most appropriate.

Understanding of the service delivery process by the CA can be minimal, although the routine nature of the service most likely means the CA will

Figure 6.11: Characteristics of Service Complexity Scenarios

Low	Mid	High
Contractor has maximum discretion to choose service delivery means. No equipment or personnel restrictions specified. No description of service delivery means in the bidder response. CA knowledge about service delivery means can be minimal. CA activities are minimal, using sampling or management by exception approach. Contract negotiations are minimal. No change orders are needed.	RFP describes services and scope of work in more detail. SOW may specify equipment and restrict personnel. Contractor discretion to choose service delivery means is limited. CA will have sufficient understanding of service delivery means. CA must check that milestones are met and deliverables are of appropriate quality. Performance measures are needed to ensure contract performance. Conflict-resolution skills are more necessary. Need for service may change over life of contract, leading to change orders.	Public-private partnership should be created, requiring all participants to be considered as equals. RFP provides general goals and results, inviting bidders to specify service delivery means. Competitive negotiations are expected. Long-term commitments are expected more frequently. CA staff need to work as a team, involved in all aspects of contract management. CA and contractor will jointly choose specific service delivery means, expecting that these may change over the life of the partnership. Education and training of CA is a continual process.

learn a great deal about the process through contract monitoring. A description of the service and or standard specifications of a product appear in the ITB/RFP. The CA may choose the "manage by exception" approach if competition is sufficient to ensure that another contractor would be quickly available. A complaint log is sufficient, with the contractor responding quickly to resolve the complaints.

Contract negotiations are easy, as there are few points of contention. Complex specifications are not necessary, as the scope of work is simple. No change orders are necessary.

Mid Complexity

In this scenario, the RFP specifies services and scope of work in more detail. There is a greater complexity of service and uncertainty in how to deliver the service because:

- Technological advances may refine or alter service delivery means.
- Full acceptance of service by citizens may not be assumed.
- There are potentially more problems in delivery and/or acceptance.
- The service may be more open to external influences to a greater degree, which would lead to changes in delivery schedules or processes.
- More technical expertise is required to understand the product/service.
- Result may not be easily visible or requires some inspection or testing.

The SOW may specify the equipment to be used, or it may request that the contractor specify the equipment. It will specify personnel in one or more of the following ways:

- Qualifications of management personnel may be specified;
- Any changes in management personnel or reorganization of management or non-management personnel must be approved by the government; and/or
- Anyone the government deems "unacceptable" will be fired and replaced.

The CA role is moderately complex and requires more time and effort. Milestones/dates of completion or delivery are important. The quality of the product/service needs to be checked, inspected, or tested. Performance measures are needed to ensure contract performance. There are likely to be conflict-resolution skills required. Change orders are possible. The need or demand for the service/product may change or fluctuate over the life of the contract.

It is anticipated that although the processes used to deliver the service or produce the product are moderately complex, the CA will have sufficient understanding to adequately check/inspect.

Training may be required for the CA on an as-needed, updated basis. This can occur through various means such as monthly meetings, manufacturing plant visits, or educational seminars.

For those projects of mid complexity, discretion given to the contractor to choose means may be limited or restricted by the CA. For example, approval of plans, schedules, policies, etc., may be required before implementation. The CA may monitor the degree to which changes have occurred once approved as the contract and related personnel evolve and change. The CA may have to require additional means changes in writing as part of the monitoring process. Understanding by the CA of the means will be established by initial training/education early in the contract process, along with the increased understanding that would occur as the CA manages the contract.

Performance outputs/outcomes are not as certain, and the requirement of a performance contract may be more focused on outputs than outcomes.

The service volume may be dependent on variables that are not fully predictable and thus open to uncertainty. The extent to which the choice of means and the resulting efficiency is dependent on the volume of the service must also be managed by the CA.

High Complexity

If the service is highly complex, and understanding of the service delivery means not clear, then the agency and the contractor should enter into a true public-private partnership. As described below, to be fully effective, the roles of both agency and contractor personnel must change from the traditional contractor-agency relationship that characterizes the low and mid complexity services. All participants must interact as equals. It must be recognized that the service to be provided will evolve in a dynamic manner, with changes likely to occur after the contract has been awarded. Whatever these changes, all partners must fully participate in their review and implementation.

The RFP provides very general goals and results, inviting the bidders to propose a service delivery means. Specifications may not be written. Instead, milestones will be identified that reflect "work packages" or service "segments" that can be identified. For example, software design may be completed by a given date. The scope of work is general, with few restrictions; or the only restrictions are those of delivery dates/milestones.

Competitive negotiation is the appropriate bid type and process, as the discussions involved begin the partnership. Those on the agency evaluation team should play a significant role in the PPP, acting as a steering committee or contract management team that coordinates and communicates frequently with contractor personnel, fulfilling the CA function. There is a long-term commitment, because it is recognized that to completely implement the IT system, for example, will take a number of years.

As the partnership evolves, the contractor and CA together will jointly choose and approve more specific means than what was originally identified. The contractor, with viable input from the CA, has maximum discretion to alter the means if greater efficiency or effectiveness can be obtained. There is the expectation that due to changing technology or other learning experiences, changes in means may be likely. This may be especially true to the extent that software, for example, must be custom-made to meet agency needs.

The duties of the CA include checking delivery milestones and approving means changes as they evolve. It is expected that the education of the CA will involve a continual process.

Ultimately, the effectiveness of the CA role is determined by the extent to which agency policies match resources in terms of personnel and time to the scenario as identified. Furthermore, in the most highly complex/uncertain services or products, the role of the CA may have to change more drastically. The creation of a public-private partnership is necessary to ensure success of the service/product.

The following sections discuss the major characteristics of PPPs, contrasting them with those of traditional contractor agency-customer, or CCR, relationships. The latter are clearly more appropriate for services of low or mid complexity. To the extent that the relationship between agency and contractor for a highly complex service does not take on the characteristics of a PPP, it is likely to fail.

Implementing Complex Contracts:
The Need for Public-Private Partnerships

For services/products of the highest complexity, government must consider entering into a public-private partnership. Although typically based upon a contract, it requires CA staff to play roles that are radically different from those relevant to low and mid complex service/product contracts. The CA staff must be much more proactive, working much more closely with the contractor to achieve project goals and objectives.

Increasingly, PPPs are found in a vast range of government-related products and services. It is a term that is politically popular, as it connotes greater efficiencies and higher quality services/products than if the public sector were the sole provider. It is also a term, though, that has several different meanings and is often applied inappropriately.

In the most general sense, PPPs can be defined as:

> An arrangement of roles and relationships in which two or more public and private entities coordinate/combine complementary resources to achieve their separate objectives through joint pursuit of one or more common objectives (National Highway Institute, 1999).

This generic definition does not provide a full understanding of the "separate objectives" and the "common objective" as it relates to agency and contractors.

Another definition of PPPs shifts the focus to the United States federal research and development field, defining them as:

> cooperative arrangements engaging companies, universities, and government agencies and laboratories in varying combinations to pool resources in pursuit of a shared R&D objective (*National Transportation Strategy*, cited in Smallen, 2000).

This definition provides a more specific example of separate and common objectives. The government agency wishes the university/private firm partnership to develop a product that can be marketed to better meet a pressing public need or achieve a public policy goal. The private firms wish to make a profit/return for their investment in developing the product.

These definitions do not suggest that the only goals of public and private partners are those as identified. The private contractor involvement may also lead to an improved reputation if the project is successful, as well as helping to meet a social or public policy need. Rather than a private firm, a nonprofit firm may become part of a PPP. The public agency may be in a position to collect revenue from a successful project as well. The partnership will not be successful, however, if the separate objectives of public and private partners are not met.

Contractor-Customer Relationships Versus Public-Private Partnerships

Since public-private partnership is a term applied to almost all relationships between public agencies and private firms, it is often used inappropriately. It is often applied to the traditional public agency—private contractor contractual or customer relationship. To more fully understand PPPs, characteristics of the more traditional low to mid complexity contractual relationships must first be understood.

First, the contract is to build a product or deliver a service that fits one or more of these categories:

- The product/service has relatively little complexity and uncertainty.
- There is a great deal of knowledge on the part of both public agencies and private contractors concerning the most widely accepted ways/ methods used to deliver the service.
- There is a generally accepted set of principles, methods, and materials used to deliver the service.

Second, the public agency pays the private contractor to deliver the product or the service. As a result, another characteristic of the traditional contract is that an institutional or organizational culture exists that recognizes that the private contractor is "employed" by the public agency. There is a hierarchical relationship that clearly identifies the public agency as the "boss" or the customer. Much of the public agency role is that of contract administrator. The public agency checks the work of the private contractor, inspects facilities, monitors progress, reviews deliverables, and resolves problems or enforces deadlines and penalties if they are not met.

Third, the relationship is viewed as project based and short term. A private contractor may provide janitorial services to an agency over many years.

But there is no expectation that the two-year contract to provide these services will be renewed in the future even though previous contracts have been renewed in the past. There is no expectation of a longer-term, continuous relationship, as the contract may be awarded to a competitor who provides better services at less cost.

Fourth, in terms of awarding the contract, a sealed bid or multi-step bid type and process is used to choose from among the private contractors that are qualified. Even though the rating system used to rate bids allows for better qualified contractors to achieve a higher rating, in most cases cost becomes the determining factor once all contractors are judged to be "responsible and responsive."

In general, the traditional contractual relationship is not characterized by a sense of commitment to a higher level goal or objective. There is no expectation that the employees of the janitorial service have any allegiance to the improvement of the agency's employees or United States citizens' "quality of life." They should be polite and professional in dealing with the public, but no more is expected.

Public-Private Partnerships

PPPs consist of partners from public and private sectors. They differ from traditional contractual relationships in several ways.

First, they involve providing a service or product that potentially can involve a great deal of uncertainty regarding how best to deliver that service. The service may be highly complex; changing technology may determine varying ways to deliver the service; and/or the service may require knowledge from service deliverers that is not present or difficult to obtain by one or more partners.

Second, all partners have discretion to identify ways/means of achieving goals. There is greater opportunity for innovation and creativity as a result. Third, risk occurs for each partner in a number of ways. For public agencies that contract out/partner an already existing service, there is always the risk that the private partner will not be able to deliver the same high quality service. Or, the private partner may not be able to achieve the initially agreed to stated partnership goals. From the private contractor's point of view, failure of the service, to the extent that the contractor leaves the partnership, means loss of profit, jobs, and reputation.

Public agencies, for example, may contribute a greater amount of financial support for the initial stages of a project. The private partner may contribute in-kind services as well as a line of credit initially. Risk may involve the loss of taxpayer dollars or private investment funds if the project is not successful.

Fourth, genuine cost-sharing is part of the partnership commitment. Private partners will make significant contributions, even if no funds are transferred. The "matching" can be in terms of contributing in-kind services and personnel time and effort, as well as in development costs of products, such as software, that are contributed to the partnership.

Fifth, partnerships are characterized by expected long-term commitments and relationships. The time period transcends the completion of one project with an identifiable product or outcome. It assumes that over time the products and/or services will evolve and change as new technologies are applied, or as problems are solved and improvements made. It also may be that return on investment may be many years after the product or infrastructure has been built.

Over all, there is the expectation that the PPP is based on trust, on commitment to problem or conflict resolution, and on the recognition that flexibility is necessary and that the relationship will evolve and change over time. If deadlines are not met, or public agency goals change with differing political climates, then the partners need to discuss the basis of the partnership and construct a different relationship.

The Agency-Contractor Relationship: Analysis

The relationship between public agencies and private contractors can best be viewed as occurring along a continuum. At one end is the traditional arrangement, where the private contractor works for the public agency on a specific project with a start and end date, with no expectation that there will be a continuing partnership relationship. At the other end is the ideal partnership relationship. As indicated in Figure 6.12, there are various dimensions that comprise the relationships that exist along this continuum.

Complexity/Uncertainty

The greater the uncertainty of how best to deliver the service, the greater the service will be "custom made" for the clientele who receive the service. Contributing to the uncertainty is the lack of knowledge on the part of both public and private partners. As a result, completion of the processes and infrastructure needed for service delivery may take a longer time than originally anticipated. The partnership must be willing to accept this outcome to remain successful.

The greater the likelihood that "off the shelf" software can be purchased and applied to delivery of IT services, for example, the less time it will take to design and implement the service, and the more a contractor-customer contractual relationship is likely. Compared to services such as janitorial services, however, the complexity of delivering IT services may mean that PPPs will always be necessary to ensure success.

Figure 6.12: Dimensions of Effective Contractor Agency Relationships

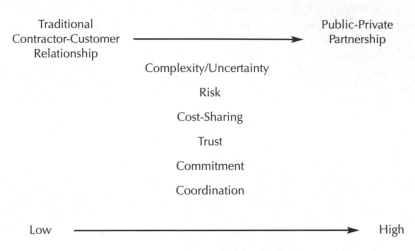

Risk

There is risk in any public-private relationship, as a private contractor may default on a contract and declare bankruptcy. With a PPP, though, the risk is much greater and much more varied. With a contractor-customer relationship, the janitorial services will be furnished and the telephone hot-line manned, even if different firms complete the task because the initial firms no longer exist. When a new service such as that provided by IT systems is the basis for a PPP, the uncertainty of technology and market may mean the service will not be provided at all if the partnership fails, with the loss of public and private investments that may be very difficult to recoup.

Since the continuum involves several dimensions, identified by the characteristics as discussed above, the relationship may "slip" or move from partnership back into contractual relationship on one or more of these dimensions, especially if there are difficulties. To the extent that this movement occurs, the partnership is not likely to succeed.

Cost-Sharing

The value of in-kind or "soft" contributions by the private partner may be difficult to calculate. The "overhead" or administrative costs typically added to the salaries of personnel in a contract with a public agency may be somewhat arbitrary. Alternatively, if, for example, the public partner contributes funds—and the private partner contributes software, hardware, and time of engineering personnel—then the profit of the private partner from involvement in the project may be less than that compared to other projects.

This situation may be acceptable to the private partner initially, as a lower return on investment may lead to gained knowledge and product success that will translate into additional projects and enhanced reputation.

The risk of uncertain, soft cost-sharing is that the PPP may not be that much different from a typical public-private contractual relationship. If the public sector spends a great deal of time in contract management, reviewing and responding to work performed by private contractors, then there is less of a partnership and more of the traditional CCR.

Trust

When trust breaks down because there are indications that a private partner may not deliver a specified project, then the public agency role must switch into a contract administrator role rather than a partner role. Additional communication and interaction must occur between the public and private partners in this situation. There must be a decision at some point to reconstitute the partnership, modifying roles and perhaps lowering expectations, or the relationship becomes predominantly a contractual one.

Coordination

There needs to be coordination of efforts between all partners. Too often, one partner may play a more passive role, allowing and/or expecting the other partner to provide information or services that may or may not be forthcoming. If the public partner plays the passive role, the danger is that a lack of coordinated effort may be perceived as the fault of the private partner, and contract administration efforts commence, sliding the PPP back toward the traditional contractor-customer relationship.

If the complexity of the service or product is high, and the uncertainty of how to achieve the desired outputs/outcomes is high, and/or the risk of failure is high, then a PPP is the only viable structure and relationship that will be successful. Under these conditions, a PPP is characterized by:

- The expectation of a long-term commitment
- Genuine cost-sharing
- A high degree of trust
- A high degree of coordination
- Commitment to a higher quality of service
- Commitment by the private partners to educate or train the public partners
- Flexibility/innovation in service delivery

The role of the CA function is much more proactive in a PPP. The nature of this role involves substantial change from the traditional CCR. There should be sharing of workplans, roles, and expectations that identify specific activities of the CA to help the private partners to achieve the overall project goals. To some extent, these can appear in the RFP process, and/or be identified and clarified during the contract negotiation process. In other instances, there may be a commitment before the contract is signed that recognizes the evolution of cooperative efforts.

To the extent that the PPP begins to fail and there is a return to the more traditional contractor-customer relationship along one or more continua, the role of the CA must change as well. For example, if trust begins to lessen because the private contractor has withheld information about problems with service delivery that have been subsequently discovered by the CA, then knowledge about the means must rise, and the CA must fall back on checking for process progress, changing the number of and date due of milestones identified in the RFP.

Recommendations

The function of contract management, including contract administration, may be undergoing additional changes in the near future. Revisions of the A-76 process, plus OMB policy statements that encourage and require adherence to the FAIR Act and likely greater contracting out, will place continuing focus on how effectively federal agencies contract for services/products.

To achieve maximum effectiveness in the contract administration function, there must be appropriate understanding of concepts such as service complexity and public-private partnerships. Accompanying this understanding should be changes in the roles of contracting officers, program managers, and others who monitor, oversee, and administer contracts. Especially for services of high complexity and uncertainty, such as information technology, successful delivery of services cannot occur without these changes.

1. Link contracting out decisions to agency missions and strategic plans as much as possible. The more complex the service, and the greater the impact of the service on the agency's highest priority goals, the more important it is to establish this linkage. Stronger top management support is a likely result, as well as greater appreciation of the need for sufficient CA staff and knowledge.[14]

2. Assess the amount of time and staff necessary for contract administration either when making the contracting out decision or early in the RFP creation. During the process that results in the decision to contract out an already existing service, valid consideration should be given to the amount of effort likely for effective contract administration. The more complex the service, the more staff will be needed. With careful calculations, efforts to reduce contracting or project management staff to levels that are too low for effective CA may be overcome.

3. Involve contract administrator staff in as many aspects of contract management as possible. Ideally, those involved in performing the CA function should also participate in the following key aspects of contract management:

- Knowledge or data gathering from industry representatives needed prior to RFP creation
- The creation of the RFP
- The review and evaluation of bids
- The negotiation process—either before or after the contract award

The greater the service complexity, the more valuable the participation in terms of avoiding potential difficulties that would occur during CA.

4. Identify early in the contract management process what level of knowledge of the service delivery means is necessary for effective contract administration. If the service is routine, the contract is a PBSC type, and/or there is a great deal of confidence in the validity of performance standards, the AQLs, and the system of penalties and/or incentives created, then knowledge of service delivery means by the CA can be minimal. This information will be established early in the contract award/management process.

With more complex services, or if there is uncertainty regarding the validity of the AQLs, then information about service delivery means should be gathered throughout the process leading up to contract award as much as possible. The importance of this effort becomes greater if there is an expectation that the service delivery means will change after the contract award.

5. Establish the means by which sufficient knowledge for the CA is obtained from the contractor. The contractor can provide training, workshops, inspections, and policies/procedures before the contract award and throughout the life of the contract. These specific means should be identified as early in the process as possible.

6. Establish clearly defined relationships among all members of the government contract administration team. As stated in USOFPP (1994), there are a variety of means to establish a well-defined relationship among all members of the team. For example:

> Some agencies have developed a joint partnership agreement that is signed during the preaward phase which defines how the parties will work together (p. 6).

In other cases, all team members can attend training together. Involvement in all aspects of contract management will also foster teamwork.

7. Ensure that all members of the CA staff have the requisite training and skills to effectively administer the contract. All members of the CA staff should have sufficient knowledge of the Federal Acquisition Requirements and other related policies and procedures prior to the start of contract administration. Training in conflict resolution is necessary. This determination is more important for contracts of mid to high complexity.

8. For contracts of highest complexity, realistically identify the need for changed efforts and relationships—those required by a public-private partnership. All of the recommendations above become more vital if a PPP will be established. All agency and contractor staff need to understand the nature of changed roles and efforts. The CA function must be much more proactive, engaging in activities that require much greater coordination with contractors/partners. Activities such as review, inspection, and monitoring may still remain, but they must be supplemented with additional CA efforts that are much more aligned with achieving agency goals.

9. For PPPs, trust and flexibility must be continually maintained by all partners. Both public and private partners must be open and honest with each other, especially if there must be significant changes in the original contractual agreement.

If, for example, the private partner finds that it is more expensive or difficult than originally thought to provide some aspect of what was promised, then the public partners must either accept this change and revise expectations, or find ways to assist the private partner in resolving difficulties.[15]

Likewise, the private partner must be honest about cost-sharing, for example, and other financial aspects of the organization. To maintain trust, the private partner must document all in-kind and dollar contributions in ways that are satisfactory to the public partners.

The partnership must seek to find the balance between flexibility that means lowered expectations or changes from original goals, and insisting that partners follow through on original promises even if costs are higher than expected. It may be that this balance depends upon the priority given to the item at issue, requiring a reallocation of funds and plans.

Again, the public partner cannot simply allow the private partner to not meet contractual obligations/partnership goals without interaction leading to a revision or reestablishment of the partnership. Each change from the original partnership agreement must be considered a new agreement, even if the formal contractual documents are not amended and the new agreement is documented in the minutes of a partnership meeting.

Otherwise, the partnership risks "sliding back" into a contractor-customer relationship and ultimately will face failure. If the public partners are paying the private partners and decide payments must be withheld because there is no agreement from the private partner on an issue, then the partnership is not likely to be successful.

Endnotes

1. With the passage of the Clinger Cohen Act in 1996, all restrictions for agencies to issue GWACs were lifted (Laurent, 1999).

2. The use of business and process reengineering techniques at the Naval Surface Warfare Center Division, Crane, Indiana, is one example. See Aucremanne (2001).

3. See also the discussions in USGAO, 1998; 2001b.

4. Other terms may be used to describe the COR including Contracting Officer's Technical Representative (COTR), Government Technical Representative (GTR) and Government Technical Evaluator (GTE). See USOFPP, 1994.

5. Competition is considered viable only to the extent that competing contractors exist in a given market, and that they would be willing to bid on an RFP and assume delivering the service.

6. If the contract is a PBSC type, then CA understanding can be less.

7. See USGAO, 1998.

8. See, for example, the discussion of Navy contracts for aircraft maintenance, in USOFPP, 1998.

9. This does not imply that all buyer-seller relationships would benefit from a long-term commitment. See the analysis in USGAO, 1994.

10. Many authors make this point. See Savas (2000), for example.

11. For a discussion of this point at the state and local level, see Lavery (1999).

12. In the Navy maintenance contracts, for example, the performance standard for meeting flight schedules is 100 percent. See USOFPP, 1998.

13. See USDOE, 2001b, for an example of changes in performance standards after the contract has been awarded.

14. See the ITTM system as discussed in USGAO, 1998.

15. See the discussion in USDOE, 2001a.

Bibliography

Aucremanne, Frank. 2001. *Strategic Sourcing at Crane.* Indianapolis, Ind.: Testimony before the GAO Commercial Activities Panel, August 8.

Birkhofer, William. 2001. *Testimony before the USGAO Commercial Activities Panel.* Washington, D.C.: Public Hearing, June 11.

Cahlink, George. 2000. "Supply and Demand." *Government Executive,* November 1. http://www.govexec/news/index.cfm?mo...t&articleid= 18735.

Drabkin, David. 2001. *Testimony before the Technology and Procurement Subcommittee,* House Government Reform Committee, May 22. www.house.gov.reform/tapps/hearings.htm

"General Accounting Office, Commercial Activities Panel." 2001. *Federal Register,* Vol. 66, No. 74, April 17: 19786.

Kelman, Steven. 1990. *Procurement and Public Management.* Washington, D.C.: The AEI Press.

————. 2001. "Contracting at the Core." *Government Executive,* July 30: http://www.govexec/news/index.cfm?mo...t&articleid=20714.

Kettl, Donald. 1993. *Sharing Power: Public Governance and Private Markets.* Washington, D.C.: The Brookings Institution.

Laurent, Anne. 1998. "Premium on Performance." *Government Executive,* August 1: http://www.govexec/news/index.cfm?mo...t&articleid=17637.

————. 1999. "The Buying Business." *Government Executive,* April 1: http://www.govexec/news/ index.cfm?mo...t&articleid=15902.

Lavery, Kevin. 1999. *Smart Contracting for Local Government Services: Processes and Experiences.* Westport, Conn.: Praeger Publishers.

Martin, Athuretta. 1995. "The Changing Role of the Contracting Officer." in Van Opstal, Debra. 1995. *Road Map for Federal Acquisition (FAR) Reform: A Report of the CSIS Working Group on FAR Reform.* Washington, D.C.: Center for Strategic and International Studies: 53-56 (Appendix B).

National Highway Institute. 1999. *Intelligent Transportation Systems Public-Private Partnerships — Participant Workbook.* Washington, D.C.: United States Department of Transportation, Federal Highway Administration, NHI Course No. 13603.

O'Keefe, Sean. 2001. *Memorandum for Heads and Acting Heads of Departments and Agencies, Subject: Performance Goals and Management Initiatives for the FY 2002 Budget.* Washington, D.C.: M-01015.

Peckinpaugh, Jason. 2001. "Bush Outsourcing Plan May Revitalize Fizzling FAIR Act." *Government Executive,* March 13: http://www.govexec.com/news/index.cfm?...t&articleid=19626

Savas, E.S. 2000. *Privatization and Public-Private Partnerships.* New York, N.Y.: Chatham House Publishers.

Smallen, David. 2000. "DOT's Vision for Transportation Research." *Public Roads* 63, No. 4 (January/February): 19-25.

Sochon, Gloria. 2000. "IT Acquisition and Management Reform: Has the Vision Become a Reality?" *Contract Management,* November: 32-36.

United States Department of Defense, Office of the Inspector General. 2000. *Contracts for Administrative, Management and Support Services Audit Report.* Washington, D.C.: Author, D2000-100, March 10.

United States Department of Energy, Office of the Inspector General. 2000. *The Departments Operating Contractor Make or Buy Program Audit Report.* Washington, D.C.: Author, DOE/IG-0460, February.

———. 2001a. *Bechtel Jacobs Company LLC's Management and Integration Contract at Oak Ridge Audit Report.* Washington, D.C.: Author, DOE/IG-0498, March.

———. 2001b. *Incentive Fees for Bechtel Jacobs Company LLC.* Washington, D.C.: Author, DOE/IG-0503, May.

United States Department of Transportation, Office of the Inspector General. 2000. *Technical Support Services Contract: Better Management Oversight and Sound Business Practices Are Needed Federal Aviation Administration.* Washington, D.C.: Author, AV-2000-127: September 10.

United States General Accounting Office. 1994. *Partnerships: Customer Supplier Relationships Can be Improved Through Partnering.* Washington, D.C.: Author, GAO/NSIAD-94-173: July.

———. 1997. *Assessing Risks and Returns: A Guide for Evaluating Federal Agencies' IT Investment Decision-making.* Washington, D.C.: Author, GAO/AMID-10.1.13: February.

———. 1998. *Measuring Performance and Demonstrating Results of Information Technology Investments.* Washington, D.C.: Author, GAO/AMID-98-89: March.

———. 1999. *National Laboratories DOE Needs to Assess the Impact of Using Performance-Based Contracts.* Washington, D.C.: Author, GAO/RCED-99-141: May.

———. 2000a. *DOD Competitive Sourcing: Results of A-76 Studies Over the Past Five Years.* Washington, D.C.: Author, GA0-01-20: December.

———. 2000b. *Information Technology Investment Management: An Overview of GAO's Assessment Framework.* Washington, D.C.: Author, GAO/AIMD-00-155.

———. 2000c. *Information Technology Investment Management: A Framework for Assessing and Improving Process Maturity Exposure Draft.* Washington, D.C.: Author, GAO/AMID 10.1.23

———. 2001a. *Major Management Challenges and Program Risks: A Governmentwide Perspective.* Washington, D.C.: Author, GAO-01-241: January.

_____. 2001b. *Contract Management: Trends and Challenges in Acquiring Services, Statement of David E. Cooper, Director, Acquisition and Sourcing of Management, May 22.* Washington, D.C.: Author, GAO-01-753T.

United States Office of Federal Procurement Policy. 1980. *A Guide for Writing and Administering Performance Statements of Work for Service Contracts.* Washington, D.C.: Author.

_____. 1994. *A Guide to Best Practices for Contract Administration.* Washington, D.C.: Author.

_____. 1998a. *A Report on the Performance-Based Service Contracting Pilot Project.* Washington, D.C.: Author.

_____. 1998b. *A Guide to Best Practices for Performance-Based Service Contracting.* Washington, D.C.: Author.

_____. 2000. *Best Practices for Collecting and Using Current and Past Performance Information.* Washington, D.C.: Author.

United States Office of Management and Budget. 2001. *The President's Management Agenda Fiscal Year 2002.* Washington, D.C.: Author.

Van Opstal, Debra. 1995. *Road Map for Federal Acquisition (FAR) Reform: A Report of the CSIS Working Group on FAR Reform.* Washington, D.C.: Center for Strategic and International Studies.

Walker, David. 2001. *Comments.* Washington, D.C.: US GAO Commercial Activities Panel Public Hearing, Outsourcing Principles and Policies, June 11.

Welch, Bob and Ann Costello. 2000."Five Tracks to Acquisition Success." *Contract Management,* August: 21-26.

CHAPTER SEVEN

Moving to Public-Private Partnerships: Learning from Experience around the World

Trefor P. Williams
Associate Professor of Civil Engineering
Rutgers University

This report was originally published in February 2003.

Understanding Public-Private Partnerships

Introduction

This chapter explores the concept of public-private partnerships and presents examples of how such partnerships have been created and implemented throughout the world. In the past, the predominant use of public-private partnerships has been related to highway and infrastructure projects. This, however, is beginning to change. The chapter presents examples of how public-private partnerships are now being used in the fields of health care and education.

In the decade ahead, a major challenge for government at all levels—federal, state, and local—will be to find and develop new ways to finance and implement large-scale projects. In the future, large-scale projects will not be limited to just highways and infrastructure as they will increasingly include large-scale technology projects. The use of public-private partnerships will offer an increasingly attractive alternative to traditional approaches to the financing and procurement of large projects. While many of the projects described in this chapter come from the world of highways, the challenge for all government managers in the future will be to find creative ways to extend the concept of public-private partnerships to sectors other than transportation.

This chapter is premised on the belief that government managers in the United States can learn much from the experience of others across the world. The chapter highlights the Private Finance Initiative in the United Kingdom, which is now applying the concept of public-private partnerships to many sectors. In addition to the United Kingdom, the chapter also presents examples of public-private partnerships from Europe, Argentina, Hong Kong, and the Philippines. Public-private partnerships are truly a worldwide phenomenon. Public sector executives in the United States have much to learn from their colleagues throughout the world.

Public-private partnerships (PPPs) are defined by the National Highway Institute as "an arrangement of roles and relationships in which two or more public and private entities coordinate/combine complementary resources to achieve their separate objectives through joint pursuit of one or more common objectives" (Lawther, 2002).

PPPs typically involve the use of private capital to design, finance, construct, maintain, and operate a project for public use for a specific time period during which a private consortium collects revenues from the users of the facility. When the consortium's term expires, title to the project reverts to the government. By then, the consortium should have collected enough revenue to recapture its investment and make a profit (Levy, 1996).

Reasons for Interest in Public-Private Partnerships

There are several reasons for the current interest in PPPs. One of them is greater efficiency in the use of public resources. Experience has shown that many public sector activities can be undertaken more cost effectively with the application of private sector management disciplines. It has been estimated that state and local governments experience cost savings of 10 to 40 percent through the use of PPP privatization schemes (NCPPP, 2002). Additionally, PPPs are a means of increasing investment in infrastructure. Economic growth is highly dependent on the enhancement and development of infrastructure, particularly in utilities and transport systems. There is an urgent need for new social infrastructure such as hospitals, prisons, educational facilities, and housing. Many governments see these as the most pressing areas for private involvement (Middleton, 2001).

As noted above, partnerships between government and the private sector address government needs in several ways:

- "… The private sector helps government to identify new user financed profit-making facilities or existing facilities in need of renovation or expansion. Private, profit-oriented businesses have a direct financial incentive to seek out new projects that would otherwise wait until government funds became available."
- Involvement of private sponsors and experienced commercial lenders assures in-depth review of the technical and financial feasibility of a project. Projects are subjected to more screening because of the private sector's need to assure profitability.
- "The private sector can access private capital markets to supplement or substitute for hard-to-get government resources."
- "The private sector builds more quickly and more cost effectively than government usually can. Construction is generally more rapid because private developers are more flexible and do not have to observe government procurement rules and bureaucratic constraints that delay planning and construction schedules." Government projects typically have more layers of bureaucracy that are required to approve construction activities than private-sector construction has.
- "The private sector usually operates facilities more efficiently than government can." The profit motive allows private developers to operate facilities more efficiently than government can. The need to reduce costs to increase profits spurs greater efficiency.
- "Private firms involved in a PPP provide a new source of tax revenue."
- "The private sector accepts risks that would otherwise be borne by the public sector."
- "The private sector transfers technology and provides training to government personnel during the course of a project" (Savas, 2000).

Government's role in PPPs is to identify and plan to satisfy the fundamental need for particular government facilities; investigate project feasibility; execute the many tasks involved in contract letting; assign monopoly rights by choosing a private partner; regulate prices; establish and monitor performance standards; and contribute to the financing (Savas, 2000).

Types of Public-Private Partnerships

Various types of PPPs are in use around the world. In general, in PPPs the constructor is not paid by the government agency to construct the project but instead obtains its own financing for construction. In some countries, Build-Operate-Transfer projects are often used. Under these agreements, a concession is granted to a contractor to design, finance, operate, and maintain a facility for a period, usually between 10 and 30 years. This is usually applied to large infrastructure projects such as highways. The contractor recoups the cost of the project by collecting tolls during the life of the concession period. Typically, at the end of the operating period, all operating rights and maintenance responsibilities revert to the government.

There are several contractual methods related to BOT. These include Build-Transfer-Operate (BTO), Build-Own-Operate-Transfer (BOOT), and Build-Own-Operate (BOO). With a BTO contract, a "private developer finances and builds a facility and, upon completion, transfers legal ownership to the sponsoring government agency. The agency then leases the facility back to the developer under a long-term lease. During the lease, the developer operates the facility and has the opportunity to earn a reasonable return from user charges" (Savas, 2000).

With BOOT, ownership of the facility rests with the constructor until the end of the concession period, at which point ownership and operating rights are transferred free of charge to the host government. BOO projects resemble outright privatization of a facility. BOO projects are sometimes let with no provision of transfer of ownership to the host government. At the end of a BOO concession agreement, the original agreement can be renegotiated for a further concession period (Smith, 1999). Figure 7.1 shows the spectrum

Figure 7.1: Range of Privatization

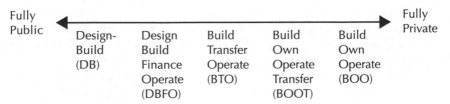

of privatization that is possible using PPPs. Design-build is the most public because it still requires government funds to finance the project. BOO is the most private because it involves the privatization of the facility.

The wraparound addition is another form of PPP. Using a wraparound addition, "a private developer constructs an addition to an existing public facility and then operates the combined facility for a fixed period or until the developer recovers costs plus a reasonable return on invested capital. The objective of this arrangement is to expand the facility despite the government's lack of resources or expertise to do so entirely with its own funds" (Savas, 2000).

There are a myriad of possible contractual relationships that can be employed using PPPs. Design-Build-Finance-Operate (DBFO) contracts are frequently used in Great Britain for highway projects constructed using the Private Finance Initiative (PFI). The PFI will be discussed in greater detail in a later section. A DBFO partner is responsible for the design, construction, maintenance, and operation of a facility. The DBFO partner also finances the project and is granted a long-term right of access, usually 30 years. The DBFO partner is compensated through specified service payments during the life of the project. For highways, this is expected to include traffic-related payments based on "shadow tolls." "Shadow tolls" are payments made by the host government to the contractor on the basis of traffic flows at predetermined points along the roadway.

A main difference between DBFO and a BOT arrangement is that no actual tolls are collected from road users. In a BOT arrangement, the private sector recovers its costs through toll or fee collection, and there is no cost to the government for the construction of the project. With DBFO, the cost of the project, in the form of annual payments, is still ultimately paid by the host government. This means that there is still a cost to the taxpayer with a DBFO arrangement. However, the cost of a DBFO project is less than the traditional method because efficiencies from private operation and construction reduce the overall cost of the project. A DBFO contract typically offers some protection to the private sector operator in the event that the public sector partner changes the conditions under which the road operates. This provides protection if other competing roads are upgraded during the contract period, thus reducing traffic flows.

Lease-Renovate-Operate-Transfer (LROT) is a partnership method that is used when a government already owns a facility that needs to be modernized. The private sector partner pays a rental to government and agrees to renovate the facility. In exchange, the private sector partner is granted a concession to operate the facility for a fixed period of time and to charge a fee for the service.

Table 7.1: Models of Public-Private Partnerships

DB	Design-Build	When one entity makes a contract with the owner to provide both architectural/engineering design services and construction services.
BOT	Build-Operate-Transfer	A concession is granted to a constructor to design, finance, maintain, and operate a facility for a period of time. The constructor recoups the cost of the project by collecting tolls during the life of the concession period.
BTO	Build-Transfer-Operate	A private developer finances and builds a facility and, upon completion, transfers legal ownership to the sponsoring government agency. The agency then leases the facility back to the developer under a long-term lease. During the lease, the developer operates the facility and earns a reasonable return from user charges.
BOOT	Build-Own-Operate-Transfer	Ownership of the facility rests with the constructor until the end of the concession period, at which point ownership and operating rights are transferred to the host government.
BOO	Build-Own-Operate	Resembles outright privatization. Projects of this type are often let with no provision for the return of ownership to government.
DBFO	Design-Build-Finance-Operate	A constructor is responsible for the design, construction, maintenance, and financing. The constructor is compensated by specific service payments from government during the life of the project.
BLTM	Build-Lease-Transfer-Maintain	In this type of arrangement, a facility is typically designed, financed, and constructed by the private sector and is then leased back to government for some predetermined period of time at a pre-agreed rental.
LROT	Lease-Renovate-Operate-Transfer	This model is for facilities that need to be modernized. The private sector constructor pays a rental to government and agrees to renovate the facility. In exchange, the constructor is granted a concession to operate the facility for a fixed period of time and to charge a fee for the service.

Understanding Models of
Public-Private Partnerships

Traditional Model

Before examining models of public-private partnerships, it is important to first understand the traditional model. In this model, the infrastructure is controlled by government agencies including many different types of facilities, such as roads, bridges, airports, hospitals, and prisons. The traditional manner of constructing government infrastructure includes a separate contract for design services, on a negotiated fee basis, followed by a separate contract for construction services, usually awarded on a competitive bid basis.

In traditional competitive bidding, the constructor with the lowest bid is selected to perform the project. The constructor is then obligated to perform the construction for the low bid amount unless design changes require change orders for additional work. Figure 7.2 shows the contractual arrangements found using the traditional format. Recently, many government agencies have sought out new project delivery methods due to the many inherent drawbacks of the traditional construction process.

Chief among the problems encountered with the traditional method is the potential to select a constructor that has made an unrealistically low bid. This may result in low-quality workmanship on the project because the constructor does not have the funds to properly complete the project. Additionally, the competitively bid project is often characterized by adversarial relationships between the government owner, the designer, and the constructor. Responsibilities are fragmented and shared, and the owner is placed in the position of being the arbiter of disputes. The traditional model

Figure 7.2: Traditional Contractual Relationship

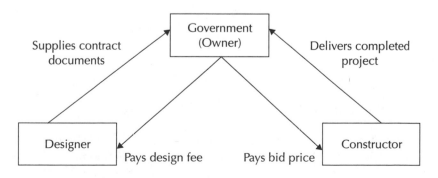

also has the significant drawback that construction cannot commence until after the design is completely finished.

Various factors, as discussed in the previous section, are driving government owners and the construction industry toward various non-traditional project delivery systems including public-private partnerships (PPPs). Government agencies are seeking alternative contracting procedures in response to quality and productivity concerns. These factors include:

- Demand for better quality and continuous improvement in project delivery
- Demand for more innovative services and products
- Desire to avoid the legal entanglements of adversarial relationships
- Desire for better handling of risk on projects
- Desire to have fewer delays and faster project delivery schedules (ASCE, 1992)

There are a number of methods available that can address the problems of competitive bidding. This paper discusses a continuum of methods from design-build through privatized procurement methods. The methods vary in the amount of risk they transfer from the government agency to the contractor. Under traditional methods, most risk is accepted by the government agency. With increasing privatization, the risk is more equally spread between the government and the contractor.

We are in an atmosphere where government agencies are considering the option to privatize government services in order to reduce cost and streamline government. The confluence of rising infrastructure needs and social demands, combined with governmental budget constraints and public resistance to tax increases, has made it essential for public authorities to consider turning to the innovative qualities and access to operating capital possessed by the private sector (NCPPP, 2002).

In the past, the focus has been on a government agency buying a project and then assuming full control for operations and maintenance. Now, new methods of procuring infrastructure projects allow the private sector to construct new facilities and then also maintain and operate them. PPPs are increasingly being employed as a technique of constructing projects. The new methods available tend to "privatize" more and more aspects of projects. These projects can be seen as partnerships between government agencies and the private sector. Thus the term PPP is often used when describing these projects.

Design-Build Model

With design-build, a single contractor is selected to provide both design and build services. This has several advantages over traditional methods of

Flexibility in Selecting Project Delivery Methods

Proper selection of a project delivery method is a major step toward achieving a successful project. Many owners find themselves faced with the dilemma of choosing a contracting method without being certain of the consequences resulting from the choice (BFC, 1995). In selecting the most efficient contracting method, government owners should consider the following major project elements:

- Ability to define the scope of work
- Concealed or unforeseen conditions
- Labor disputes
- Significant changes in the work
- Suitability of funding
- Project risk

An owner must select the most appropriate contract arrangement to prevent these factors from becoming a detriment to the project. Alternative methods of contract delivery provide the flexibility to handle many of the problems that arise. A barrier to the implementation of alternative techniques has been the slowness of public sector owners to adapt these techniques for infrastructure procurement. Federal agencies now have greater freedom to choose alternative methods of project delivery. The FY 1996 Defense Authorization Bill had provisions that established the procedures for the procurement of design-build projects. This allows federal contracting officers to use design-build whenever the situation merits its use (DSIA, 2000). However, many states are still tied to the traditional method of low-bid construction. The trend toward public-private partnership appears to be increasing the need to have alternative project delivery methods available for use in the public sector.

The Committee on Management and Contracting Alternatives of the Building Futures Council has concluded that the traditional project delivery process in which finance/design/construction and operation are treated separately may not be as efficient for owners in certain projects as alternatives like design-build or Build-Operate-Transfer (BOT) projects. The traditional method of procurement is not sufficiently flexible to accommodate the trend toward PPPs. The disadvantages of the use of the rigid traditional method, particularly by state governments, now outweigh the perceived benefits. Given the huge task of renewing the public infrastructure in the United States—and the limited resources available to do so—public agencies should be encouraged to develop and utilize alternative project delivery methodologies where they increase efficiency and decrease cost (BFC, 1995).

selecting a separate designer and contractor. The major advantage is that disputes between the design team and construction forces can be handled internally to one company. It is believed that this results in significant time savings on large, complex projects. Additionally, the coordination between the design and construction phases is enhanced by having one company responsible for both design and construction. Figure 7.3 illustrates the design-build contractual relationship, in which a single company is responsible for both design and construction. The owner pays the project cost and, in return, receives the completed project from the design-build contractor.

With design-build, the owner retains a single entity that provides both design and construction services for a project. The entity may be a consortium of a contractor and a designer, or a single organization, depending on the type of construction. U.S. federal agencies acknowledge two major differences between design-build and "traditional" project delivery. Most importantly, with design-build, project control is in the hands of a single entity from concept through design and construction. A second difference between design-build and traditional methods is that the project price is agreed upon at an early design level. With design-build, the price is often set at concept or early schematic design (10 percent to 30 percent design completion level). The traditional method of construction requires 100 percent completed design documents, and the contract price is not known until complete bids are submitted (ASCE, 1992).

For the design-build process to be used successfully, the owner must clearly define the needs and requirements of the project so that they are

Figure 7.3: Design-Build Contractual Arrangement

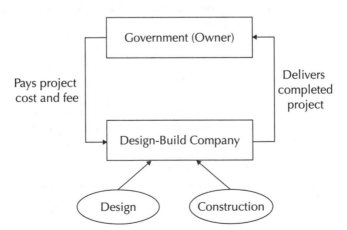

understood by the design-build contractors submitting proposals on the project. This may include some or all of the following: detailed space and equipment requirements, site surveys, soil borings, outline specifications, budget parameters, and scheduling requirements.

Benefits of Design-Build

There are several possible benefits that can be found in the use of design-build projects for government agencies. They include:

- Design-build projects establish a single point of contact for the government owner, which reduces disagreements over project responsibility.
- Design-build can potentially reduce project delivery time. Due to direct collaboration between the designer and constructor, construction on some phases of the work can begin while other phases are still in design. This can allow for fast tracking of projects.
- Design-build lowers the number of change orders versus traditional competitively bid construction. Because the same consortium performs design and construction, it eliminates the need for formal change orders that would occur using the traditional format.
- Design-build may lower project costs by reducing the time for construction and therefore reducing construction overhead costs.
- Design-build can foster innovative solutions because the design and construction teams are pursuing common goals (ASCE, 1992).

Data from the Department of the Navy shows that design-build can save 15 percent in dollars and 12 percent in time over conventional procurement. For projects using non-appropriated funds, the Department of Defense has saved 18 percent in costs and 14 percent in time over a three-year period (DBIA, 1996).

A study by the University of Florida of a Florida Department of Transportation design-build project showed that design-build under a single contractor actually reduced the duration of the project. Design time was 54 percent faster and construction time was 18 percent faster than traditional projects (Henk, 1998).

Possible Design-Build Drawbacks

One of the primary criticisms of design-build contracting is the possibility that inferior materials could be substituted. This is possible on projects where the government owner lacks the technical sophistication to assemble and coordinate a thorough project description (e.g., performance specifications in a scope of work package). The scope of work package is included as part of the Request for Proposals (RFP) for design-build projects. A contractor-dominated design team could encourage the owner to accept low first cost materials without regard to their life-cycle performance, particularly if the design-build selection has been based solely on price.

Loss of the independent professional designer can be a drawback for some owners. The owner may not receive the same type of advice from a designer who is part of a design-build entity and has a direct financial interest in the construction of a project (ASCE, 1992).

Federal Legislation and Design-Build

Recent federal legislation has legalized the application of a two-phase design-build process for federal procurement wherever it is deemed appropriate. The two-phase selection procedure enables federal contracting officers to use the design-build method of project delivery whenever the situation merits. Two-phase selection consists of proposers submitting qualifications in response to an RFP without including any cost or detailed design data. Then, three to five of the bidders chosen as most qualified by the agency are selected to bid in the second stage. The second stage evaluation includes price, technical approach, design solutions, management plans, and other criteria (DBIA, 2000).

Barriers to Design-Build Use

Some government agencies do not allow the use of design-build contracts. A 1996 Design-Build Institute of America study found that only 27 states permitted the use of design-build contracts (DBIA, 1996). Few if any laws expressly prohibit design-build. Generally, there are no statutes that prohibit state and local governments from engaging a single firm to provide both design and construction services. However, many states do indirectly preclude the use of design-build by requiring separation of design and construction, and by requiring that construction contracts be awarded to the lowest possible bidder only after a project is fully designed. The preference for separate design and construction contracts, as well as cost-based selection, is decades old and based on concerns over waste and abuse that now might be outweighed by requirements of efficiency, in addition to cost and time savings (BFC, 1995). Many organizations such as the Design-Build Institute of America continue to assert pressure on state governments to allow the use of design-build contracts.

Design-Build Examples

Design-build has mainly been employed for building projects. However, we have seen the recent application of design-build to some high-profile civil engineering projects. A primary example is the I-15 highway project in Salt Lake City, Utah. The $1.6 billion expansion project was completed under budget and ahead of schedule. A special permit was required from the Utah legislature to allow a design-build project. The project involved the reconstruction of the 17-mile interstate into a 12-lane superhighway for the Olympic games. A primary lesson learned by the government agency, the Utah Department of Transportation (UDOT), was to entrust the contractor with more flexibility. For example, UDOT had specified that a state road could not be closed at any time, but the contractor suggested it could complete rehabilitation a year early if allowed to close the road for four months. UDOT agreed and the strategy worked (Cho & Sawyer, 2001).

An example of a government building constructed using design-build is the U.S. Courthouse in Shreveport, Louisiana. Design-build was chosen because of the need to meet a strict budget and to expedite delivery within 24 months of notice to proceed to coordinate with the expiration of existing leases for the courts' space. The General Services Administration (GSA) utilized the services of an architect/engineer to develop an RFP. The RFP included schematic plans, a room-by-room statement of requirements for finishes, and technical performance specifications. The level of detail in the RFP reduced the number of unknowns during design, resulting in few changes to the budget and schedule as proposed.

The proposers were required to submit floor plans and narratives from the various disciplines, and exterior and interior renderings. An evaluation panel included representatives from every discipline. This was a one-phase selection process, with 14 teams submitting proposals. Selection was based on best value, not price. The winning proposal submitted more than the required drawings and renderings. The project was completed on a fast track schedule. The success of the project was due to the excellent working relationship between all project participants (DBIA, 2000).

Warranty Contracts

Warranty contracts are a form of performance-based contract where the contractor assumes post-construction performance risk. That is, for a project involving highway repaving, the contractor would warrant the paving work done, and return and fix any potholes or pavement distress for a specified number of years. Annual inspection of the end product replaces the typical quality control/quality assurance specification found in these maintenance projects. The purpose of warranty contracts is to improve quality, augment government agency expertise, redistribute performance risk, and reduce agency design and inspection personnel (Queiroz, 1999).

The state of Virginia has used warranty-based contracts in combination with design-build to form design-build-maintain contracts. The builder designs and builds the project and also includes long-term warranties for the maintenance of the project (Angelo, 2002). Combined with design-build projects, warranties offer a way of forming a PPP for the maintenance of a highway. The owner pays for the initial project and saves on maintenance costs, which are borne by the private sector.

Build-Operate-Transfer Model

Structure of Build-Operate-Transfer Arrangements

PPPs on large projects require consortiums of designers, builders, financiers, and other disciplines to form a concession company. The arrangements can be complex, and there is no fixed structure for concession companies or the form of contractual obligations between parties. Figure 7.4 shows the structure of a BOT project in which a contractor has several agreements with different parties. A bidding consortium of companies owns the contractor. The contractor also has a concession agreement with the host government that allows the contractor to take control of the facility for a given period of time. Loan agreements are obtained from various debt providers to finance the project. In the construction phase of the project, the contractor has a contract with joint venture construction companies to construct the project. Finally, the contractor has a contract with an operating company to operate and manage the facility during the concession period.

Typically, the contractor enters into four contractual agreements:

- A concession agreement with the host government.
- A construction contract, usually of the design-build type. The construction company may be a member of the bidding consortium.
- An operations and maintenance agreement with the firm that will be responsible for operating the facility. The operating company may be a member of the bidding consortium.
- Loan agreements. All loan agreements are entered into directly by the concession company. All funds from the banks flow through the concession company, not directly to the construction or operating companies (Hamilton, 1996).

Smith (1999) has identified five high-level factors that appear to be necessary for each major participant in a BOT project to have the maximum chance of achieving their goals. First of all, there must be a genuine desire for a win-win solution with common agreement among the parties as to their mutual and individual objectives. A BOT approach requires more teamwork than conventional contract types. Secondly, a complex BOT requires a strong, persistent, and persuasive project leader to fight for the project. Thirdly, there should be adequate and accurate data and risk assessment of both the procurement and operational phases, with responsibility for managing the risks placed with the party best able to control them. Fourthly, an accurate calculation of the project's economics is necessary, including length of concession, and assessments of the

---

Understanding Concession

A concession is a right, privilege, or property granted by the government.

Figure 7.4: Relationships in a BOT Concession Arrangement

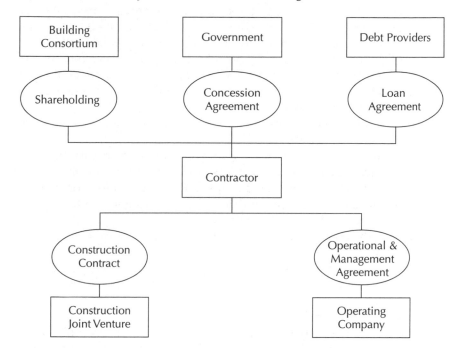

influence on income and expenditure of project risks. Finally, choice of the correct procurement methodology is important for the construction phase. Consortium contractors often perform the construction in a design-build format.

In BOT projects, the document that defines the relationship between the host government and the consortium building the project is the concession agreement. It establishes the concession rules and the contractual rights of the main parties. The principal issues that are dealt with in a concession agreement include:

- The nature and length of the concession, scope of the work, and operation of the completed facility
- A specification of what is to be provided
- The extent of permitted variations to the specification
- The performance standards to be achieved
- The tolls, prices, or payments to be charged, together with any arrangements for adjustments
- Provisions to ensure the concessionaire's rights in the event of changes to any enabling legislation and any payments that might accrue therefrom

- Provisions for the termination of the contract
- The circumstances in which the grantor of the concession will be permitted to take over the concession, and the rights of the parties should this occur before the end of the concession period (Smith, 1999)

The decision to create a concession requires a firm government policy. A successful concession requires a feeling of partnership between the government and the concession company. Government support of concession arrangements can be given in several different ways:

- Creating the appropriate legislative structure within which the concession can operate effectively.
- Providing an equitable regulatory environment in which tolls can be set in an objective manner, so that a reasonable return reflecting the balance between risk and reward can be earned by the concession company.
- Protecting the concession companies from competition, at least during the early years of operation.
- Helping the concession company to overcome bureaucratic opposition to the project.
- Developing a clear and effective program to allow public participation in the planning process and to deal with environmental issues.

Advantages of BOT Projects

BOT projects are typically applied to projects for the construction of utilities and transportation infrastructure. They have several advantages for the host government agency and its citizens:

- "BOT allows infrastructure projects to be obtained at little or no cost to taxpayers."
- "The government will incur little risk because there are generally sufficient bonds in place and sufficient letters of credit on hand to ensure completion of the project" in the event of default by the private sponsor before project completion.
- "The private sector can usually move preconstruction and construction along more rapidly than the public sector, and the construction cycle is more rapid."
- "The sponsors must operate and maintain the facility for a period of time exceeding 20 years," therefore the initial construction quality of the facility will be high.
- "General taxes will not have to be increased, nor will revenue bonds need to be sold to finance the project."
- "Only the users of BOT facilities pay the required tolls. The cost to society is borne by those who benefit from the project, not by the taxpayers. Citizens can elect alternate routes if toll rates are unreasonable, which exerts pressure on the BOT consortium" to maintain the facility (Levy, 1996).

Risks to BOT Concessionaires

Some members of a BOT consortium could make substantial profits from their participation in an infrastructure project. However, there are several risks that can occur, particularly for international projects in developing countries. Political instability in the host country is a concern at all stages of a BOT project. Because most concessions are from 20 to 40 years, long-term political stability is important. There is also the risk of significant cost overruns on a BOT project that may change a project's pro forma. If additional financing is not available, the project can come to a halt or end in default. There is also the risk of unfavorable currency devaluations that can cause a BOT consortium to pay back loans with devalued revenue.

Another risk is the level of the usage fee set for a facility. Toll rates for concession-type highways set by the Mexican government were about eight times higher than comparable tolls in the United States. This resulted in increased toll jumping. Finally, drastic changes in demographics over the concessionary period may substantially affect revenue. A BOT consortium's source of revenue is based upon projections of the number of consumers who will use a facility. If the number of consumers is less than projected, it can have disastrous effects on the profitability of the BOT venture (Levy, 1996).

Examples of Public-Private Partnerships around the World

Public-Private Partnerships for Highways in the United States

Most of the noteworthy BOT projects constructed in the United States have been toll highways. The environment in the United States is becoming more favorable for the development of toll road public-private partnerships due to the need to find innovative methods of providing funds for new highway construction. One of the primary impetuses for toll road development was the Intermodal Surface Transportation Efficiency Act (ISTEA) passed in 1991. The act expanded toll facility eligibility for federal aid to include construction of new toll facilities, reconstruction, resurfacing, rehabilitation, and conversion of some facilities to toll roads. ISTEA allowed the commingling of federal, state, and private funds and the sharing of responsibility between the public and private sectors. The act also allows both the public and private sectors to design, finance, construct, and operate new highway facilities and to participate in the repair and expansion of existing facilities (Levy, 1996).

The newer TEA-21 transportation legislation continues the encourage-ment of PPPs found in ISTEA. TEA-21 provides opportunities to utilize pri-vate funds through innovative financing methods. These innovative financing methods are intended to encourage PPPs for large highway and bridge projects by reducing costs and sharing risks between the public and private sectors (Ruane, 1998).

The construction of new toll highways by the private sector has several benefits. PPPs allow the construction of highways that could not be funded by the government. They transfer risks of delays and construction cost over-runs from the government and the taxpayer to the private developer. They also assure the highest quality construction because the private developer is responsible for maintenance for 30 to 40 years (Levy, 1996).

The Dulles Greenway Project

A primary example of a BOT project in the United States is the Dulles Greenway, which was opened in 1995. The Dulles Greenway is a toll road that was built in Virginia using the BOT concept. The road extends 14 miles from Dulles International Airport to Leesburg, Virginia. The roadway con-nects to the existing Dulles Toll Road. The road is a four-lane limited-access highway within a 250-foot right of way. It is financed, built, and operated by a private consortium.

The road required enabling legislation in the Virginia Assembly to establish the prerequisites for construction and operation of a toll road by a private company. A commission was set up to regulate applicants for toll roads, to supervise and control toll road operators, and to have responsi-bility for approving or revising toll rates charged by operators.

Autostrade International S.p.A. is a constructor, concessionaire, and operator of extensive networks in its home country, Italy. It is a general partner in the Greenway corporate entity and serves as the operator of the Greenway. Automated toll collection techniques are employed along with traditional manned toll collection booths.

The total cost of the project was estimated at $326 million. Of the ini-tial $68 million investment by the consortium partners, $22 million was for equity financing and the remaining $46 million provided access to various lines of credit that would serve as guarantees against project risks. A con-sortium of 10 lending institutions provided long-term financing in the amount of $202 million.

The Greenway's primary benefit is that it allowed the roadway to be constructed in a period when no government funds were available for the project. Without the use of private sector funding, the project would not have been constructed. In addition, the project is freestanding and requires no government support. Fees for the use of the facility are only collected from actual road users (Levy, 1996).

BOT Highway Projects in California

California has constructed several toll roads using the BOT concept. One project, the Riverside Freeway, involved the conversion of the median strip to an all-electronic-toll four-lane express highway with two lanes in each direction. Commuters can choose to take the stop and go lanes or pay up to $3.50 on the median "express" lanes. The median road is the world's first fully electronic toll road, with tolls that vary with demand (Poole, 2000).

Opened in 1995 with a 35-year franchise, the 10-mile lanes were developed for $126 million by a team led by a subsidiary of the general contractor Peter Kiewit Sons, Inc. In 1998, the team made plans to sell the lanes to a nonprofit corporation it helped create. The developer team was attempting to withdraw from the project after only a few years, even though it had a 30-year commitment. Public opposition ended the proposed $244 million deal, which would have refinanced the project with tax-exempt bonds, thereby reducing interest rates on the $100 million debt and allowing carpools to resume using the toll lane at no charge. Critics charged that the deal was not at arm's length so the price might have been high, resulting in excessive debt service and toll rates higher than necessary. The developer would have made double-digit returns on investment, even though the project had been only marginally profitable.

This example illustrates some of the dangers of BOT to governments. Although the road project is a success, the developer does not want to stay for the agreed-upon concession term. The government is left with a less-than-willing partner. The enabling legislation enacted by the state of California did not include provisions for the exit of a developer. Clear public safeguards are needed before infrastructure projects of this type can be sold.

Some states have more flexible laws than California for the establishment of these BOT ventures. In particular, some states permit a mix of public and private funds to leverage limited state funds with private capital. Also, such measures would permit the use of nonprofit corporations and tax-exempt debt (until Congress permits private infrastructure developer/operators to issue tax-exempt bonds).

Public-Private Partnerships for Infrastructure in Other Countries

Toll Systems in Europe

Toll systems are in widespread use in eight European countries for roads and/or bridges and tunnels: Austria, Denmark, Spain, France, Greece, Italy, Norway, and Portugal. It has been found in the European countries that a BOT approach and toll systems are increasingly recognized as the most efficient means of replacing taxpayer money with user money. The

State budget contribution to funding of the French national road system dropped from 56 percent to 22 percent, while toll revenue increased from 32 percent to 57 percent over the period 1973 to 1995. Toll roads allow the application of the user-payer principle. The European Commission as a matter of policy indicates that fees for infrastructure use should be linked directly to the costs that users impose on infrastructure and other citizens.

Europe has both public sector and private toll road concession companies. There are currently 63 state-owned concession companies managed by the public sector and 28 privately owned concessions. Out of a total of 17,009 kilometers operated under concessions, 4,548 kilometers are run by private companies (Bousquet, n.d.).

BOT Highway Projects in Argentina

Argentina has used BOT contracts to rehabilitate major sections of its road network. The goal of the program was reconstruction and maintenance of existing roads and a reduction of the public support required for highways. Bidding for the projects was competitive. In return for the right to collect tolls, the concessionaires were required to undertake a program of rehabilitation, maintenance, and capital improvements. There was some controversy with these projects because tolls were allowed to be collected before rehabilitation work was completed. The proper oversight mechanisms were not in place from the central government agency. This illustrates the importance of developing the proper relationships between the government and private sector to ensure project performance (Queiroz, 1999).

Hong Kong BOT Infrastructure

Several BOT projects have been constructed in Hong Kong. Four tunnels and a 10-kilometer toll road have been completed in Hong Kong since 1972. The government has identified a number of possible future schemes, and it would appear that the BOT method will be used for some time to come (Smith, 1999).

An example of a successful BOT project in Hong Kong is the Tate's Cairn Tunnel. In February 1988, the Hong Kong government passed a special ordinance to grant a 30-year franchise to a private sector consortium led by the Japanese construction company Nishimatsu. The project is the longest road in Hong Kong, a 4-kilometer twin tube tunnel with four lanes and approach roads. The project was completed two months ahead of schedule in June 1991. Total project cost was HK$2.15 billion (U.S.$276.5 million) (Pyle, 1996).

The tunnel was financed completely by the private sector. Shareholders contributed equity of HK$600 million. This translated to a relatively conservative debt-to-equity ratio of 2.6:1. The project's financing structure adequately addressed the major project risks. Precompletion risks ran for the relatively short 18-month construction period. The construction risk was low because the tunneling method used was well known. The contractor risk was mitigated by the good reputation of the contractor and by a delay penalty of HK$400,000 per day. The cost overrun risk was overcome by several guarantees from the shareholders. To ensure project quality, a 10-year performance bond put up by the contractor addressed performance risk.

The post-completion risks ran for the rest of the 12-year loan period. Interest rate risk was addressed by the purchase of an interest rate cap by the shareholders. Cash flow risk was mitigated by pre-approvals from the Hong Kong government to increase tolls over time.

This example indicates the many areas of risk transfer that must be considered with a BOT contract. It also shows that expertise and cooperation are required from experts in construction, finance, and design to successfully complete a large project of this type.

BOT Projects in Developing Countries

BOT projects are frequently used in developing countries as a means to obtain funds for much needed infrastructure projects. The types of projects funded are diverse. For example, the Philippines has undertaken BOT projects for shipping terminals, telecommunications, power generation, and industrial parks. With increased urbanization, developing areas require significant inputs of infrastructure investment. It is anticipated that much of this investment can be in the form of PPPs using a BOT form of contract.

Public-Private Partnerships for Health Care

Globally, health expenditures have risen from an average of 3 percent GDP in 1950 to 8 percent in 1999. Hospitals account for 30 to 50 percent of health expenditures. Public funding has not kept pace with the growth in spending. Constraints on public funding, combined with rising costs, have forced public hospitals to cut costs wherever possible while still trying to provide universal access to public patients. Some governments have turned to public-private partnerships to bring private sector efficiency into public hospitals (Taylor & Blair, 2002).

Hospital Partnerships in Australia

In Australia, federal and state governments have completed 15 BOO transactions in which a private firm builds, owns, and operates a public hospital. With a BOO transaction, the facility is constructed and operated by the contractor with no provision to return the facility to the government agency. It resembles complete privatization. One example from Australia is the Mildura Base Hospital. The government selected a private operator to design, build, own, and operate a new 153-bed hospital for a 15-year period. The operator provides clinical services to all patients who come to the hospital at no charge. In return, the provider receives from the government annual payments based on the forecast mix of clinical patients. For quality control purposes, the operator is required to maintain the hospital's accreditation, provide monthly reports on clinical indicators, and have high-volume treatments reviewed by external peers. The contract includes penalties for noncompliance. The ultimate sanction allows the government to step in and run the hospital. The results of the hospital's operations have been impressive. Capital costs for the new hospital came in at 20 percent below equivalent public sector comparators. All performance targets have been met, and patient volumes have been increased by 30 percent in the first year (Taylor & Blair, 2002).

Public-Private Partnerships in British Hospitals

The British government has used public-private partnerships in financing, construction, and management for many public hospitals over the past decade. Under the program, a regional health district requests bids for a private firm to finance and construct a new hospital, maintain the facility, and provide nonclinical services such as laundry, security, parking, and catering. The operator receives annual payments for 15 to 25 years for its capital costs and the costs of maintenance and services. In this model of PPP, the public sector remains responsible for all medical services.

The first hospital project constructed in Great Britain using a PPP approach was the New Dartford and Gravesham Hospital. The private consortium was required to design, construct, and finance a new 400 in-patient bed hospital and then to maintain the hospital and provide support services for a period of up to 60 years. The National Health Service Trust estimated the discounted cost of the contract would be £177 million over the first 25 years that the hospital is in use, after which the National Health Service Trust could terminate the contract without penalty if it decides to close the hospital. It is expected that cost savings of 3 percent, or around £5 million, will be obtained, compared with an equivalent project under conventionally funded procurement. Some hospital projects have higher levels of cost savings, but savings on this project were reduced by some errors made during procurement—in particular, only one final bid was received on the project (COPA, 2000).

Public-Private Partnerships for Schools

In the United States and abroad, PPPs have been adopted as an innovative means to allow communities to upgrade their public school facilities at substantially lower costs and in less time than purely governmental efforts require. School construction can be more timely using PPPs. PPPs are unencumbered by the multitude of regulations that govern public-sector bond offerings, voter approval, and review of competitive bids. One partnership school in Florida, Ryder Elementary Charter School, was designed and built in less than nine months compared to an average of five years for traditional elementary schools built in the state. The school is housed in a facility adjacent to the Ryder System corporate headquarters building. Introducing competition and the profit incentive into the process of school construction rewards expertise and efficiency. This can result in construction costs that generally will be much lower than the public sector construction process (Utt, 2001).

In recent years, public school systems in Nova Scotia, Great Britain, and some U.S. jurisdictions have implemented programs or pilot projects to encourage private investors to construct (and own) school buildings to the school system's specifications. In turn, the private partner leases the facility to the school system at rent levels below what the public school system would have incurred had it built and operated the school.

Nova Scotia offers an example of the use of PPPs for school construction. By the end of 1998, as many as 41 new schools had been completed or approved for construction under the Nova Scotia PPP program. The Nova Scotia projects are constructed using a Build-Lease-Transfer-Maintain (BLTM) format. In a BLTM arrangement, a facility is typically designed, financed, and constructed by the private sector and is then leased back to the government for some predetermined period of time at a pre-agreed rental.

The schools are completely operational when the lease begins, complete with all classroom furnishings and required computer equipment. The school system provides the staff for the school and maintains full control over curriculum and all educational services. The major advantages for the Nova Scotia school system are the speed with which schools can be upgraded and the average 15 percent cost savings achieved through leasing arrangements with the developer/owner. The school system leases the facilities for 20 years at a predetermined rent that is lower than the capitalized cost of construction and furnishing. The developer/owner covers the additional costs and earns a profit in the use of the facility during times when it is not used by the school system. In effect, the developer/owner leases the school to the school system during the daytime as negotiated. The developer/owner is then free to lease the school for other approved uses at other times of the day as well as on weekends and summer holidays. The purposes that the school may be used for are carefully spelled out in the lease with the school system and typically include education-oriented activities such as for-profit trade schools, and meeting space for civic or political groups (Utt, 1999).

The Pembroke Pines Public Charter School in Florida illustrates the significant construction efficiencies that can be achieved by a private developer. Pembroke Pines teamed up with Haskell Educational Services (HES) of Miami, a firm that specializes in designing and constructing assisted-living facilities, to build and operate its new facility. The cost of building the school was between 22 and 34 percent below other recent elementary schools built in Pembroke Pines. While HES designed and built the school, the community financed it (with tax-exempt borrowing), owns it, and leases it to HES to operate as a charter school. This differs from the Nova Scotia model, where the developer owns the school and leases it to the school system.

HES receives a state reimbursement of $3,750 per pupil per year, which is not sufficient to pay both school operating costs and the facility lease. HES generates the additional revenue to cover the remaining costs and earn a profit by offering fee-based after-hours programs at the school. At present, such programs include services like day care, enrichment, and other education programs for students. HES achieved construction cost savings through design efficiencies including reconfiguring special-purpose rooms that otherwise would stand idle during the school day into multipurpose rooms that are used more intensively (Utt, 1999).

Private Finance Initiative in the United Kingdom

Of special interest to those seeking examples of public-private partnerships is the Private Finance Initiative (PFI), now under way in Great Britain. The program was first announced by the British government in 1992 under a Conservative government and has continued by the current Labour government. The intention of the PFI is to bring the private sector into the provision of services and infrastructure that formerly has been regarded as "public." The PFI encourages joint ventures between the public and private sectors.

The purpose of the PFI is to increase the flow of capital projects against a background of restraint on public expenditure. It is aimed at bringing the private sector more centrally into the operation of capital assets, harnessing private sector management skills, and transferring risk away from the public sector to the private sector.

PFI is based upon the premise that rather than government committing capital investment to owning, operating, and managing the means of providing the necessary services, substantially greater economic efficiencies and lower costs might be attained by contracting out the services themselves to the private sector. Rather than owning a school or a prison, the government would simply buy the service it required from the private sector, such as education for a given number of children or custodial service for a given number of prisoners. The PFI would then leave it to the private sector to develop whatever mechanisms and facilities were necessary for the required level of service to be provided.

In a PFI arrangement, the public body becomes the project purchaser. The project is known to provide substantial capital investment, but what the government purchaser seeks to buy is not the facility (road or building) but the service conducted from it. The prime interest of a PFI purchaser is therefore to find an efficient and reliable operator of the facility. The operator is expected to procure the necessary facilities and to charge the public sector customer for the service. The cost of the service will include an element for amortization of the capital expenditure as well as elements covering profit and risk (RICS, 1995).

Three main types of PFI projects have been identified:

- *Financially freestanding projects*—where the private consortium recoups the full investment through user fees and charges. These arrangements are the same as the BOT format.
- *Joint venture projects*—funded through a combination of public and private sector funds with the private partner retaining a controlling interest.
- *DBFO projects*—where assets that provide public services are designed, built, financed, and operated by a private sector organization and paid for through service charges met by a public body (SP, 1999). DBFO differs from BOT in that the project is paid for by a public body. No user fees are collected in DBFO projects.

Most projects are constructed using some form of DBFO arrangements. This is typical for highways, hospitals, prisons, and schools. Some freestanding projects have been constructed, notably the Skye Bridge and the Birmingham North Relief Road. These freestanding projects collect actual user tolls.

The Construction Industry Council (CIC, 2000) has studied the perceived cost savings of design, build, and operate (DBO) in PFI projects. The median reported total DBO cost saving is in the range of 5 percent to 10 percent. Reported savings are highest (median in the range of 10 to 20 percent) in custodial and transport projects and lowest (median in the range of 5 percent savings to 5 percent increase) for education and health care projects. These are the subjective measurements of both private and public project managers.

PFI Theoretical Issues

There are several issues related to the application of PFI that are controversial. A major issue is the financial justification of PFI projects. It can be argued that PFI projects offer better "value for money" than a comparable government project because of the theory that private money brings with it better management plus greater incentives to finish projects on time and within budget. Others argue that there is no savings because of cost escalations during construction and that the private sector is no more efficient than the public sector.

Another justification for PFI is that it brings in new money for investments in areas that may otherwise languish, such as schools. That is, PFI can be used for projects where no public money is available and where there is no realistic prospect that a scheme could go ahead within a similar timeframe (Scott, 2001).

One specific element of PFI relates to the cost of borrowing. As the lowest-risk borrower, the public sector is traditionally able to borrow funds at a cheaper rate than private firms. It is then argued that investment funded through the traditional procurement routes will be cheaper than for a private borrower on a PFI project (SP, 1999). For a PFI project to be successful, it must counteract the increased cost of borrowing, adviser's fees, and private sector profit through innovation and appropriate risk transfer in order to save cost per unit value in the functions of design, construction, and operation. This can be done by reducing the costs of providing similar services, providing an improved service at the same cost, or a combination of both. The reduction of cost per unit value requires the transfer of risk and reward to the private sector, from either private sector efficiencies in production, requiring less input per unit of output, or the purchase or procurement of cheaper units (CIC, 2000). The required cost savings are produced by leaving choice in the project specifications for the private consortium to innovate on the construction and operation of the new facility.

Shadow Toll Concessions

A shadow toll contract enables the public authority to delegate the construction, funding, and operation to a concession company. In this case, the concession company does not collect a toll from the user. The public authority remunerates the concession company, with payment usually made on the basis of utilization of the facility.

The main advantages of a conventional toll concession contract—namely, optimization of the infrastructure with the risks and interim funding carried by the concession company—are maintained with a shadow toll system. Nevertheless, a shadow toll system does not solve the funding problem, as the government authority must pay shadow toll remuneration to the concession company in due course. Shadow toll contracts do not generate new sources of funding. Such an arrangement makes it possible to shift responsibility for the financial package to the concession company (so that the debt is non-public), but the final cost must be borne by the taxpayer ("delayed" budgetary funding) (Bousquet, n.d.).

DBFO on British Highway Projects

Several highway projects in Great Britain have been developed using the DBFO approach. The goals of the British Highway Agency have been to develop a private sector road operating industry and to transfer significant risk from the public sector to the private sector. Additional goals are also to minimize project cost and the risks to the public sector. Contractors on these trunk road projects are paid through a scheme of shadow tolling. The British National Audit Office (NAO, 1998) has produced a report analyzing the first four projects let using DBFO. Projects studied in the report ranged from the widening of 30 kilometers of expressway to the maintenance of 52 kilometers of highway. The report raises some interesting points concerning the DBFO procedures:

- The National Audit Office found that two of the four projects would provide better financial terms than traditionally procured and conventionally financed alternatives. These two projects involved a substantial construction component, whereas the other two principally involve maintenance work.
- The private sector takes significant financial risks on these projects including the entire risk relating to design building and roadway operation.
- The core technical requirements of the project specified by the government owner should not be so detailed as to stifle innovation and cost savings during construction by the builder.
- The bidding process was in three stages. There was a prequalification and then four consortia were selected to bid on each highway project. Bidders were then short-listed. Negotiations were conducted between the government and the bidders. Each bidder submitted a schedule of shadow tolls as a basis of negotiation. The bidder that minimized net present value of the shadow tolls was selected. This format of bidding requires the public sector bidder to estimate traffic flows over a 30-year period.
- A banded system was used to determine shadow tolls. The shadow toll per vehicle is higher for low traffic volumes and lower for high traffic volumes. There is a cap on the volumes for which tolls are collected. This removes the risk to government of traffic volumes being much greater than forecast, requiring a huge shadow toll payment.
- The cost of bidding is very high due to the complex nature of the bidding process.

The advantage of the DBFO method is found principally in the freedom of design left to the concession company, the transfer of risks to the concession company, and the enhanced efficiency resulting from private management. Otherwise, the DBFO method would have no advantage over budgetary funding and would cost more due to more substantial financial expenses, stemming in particular from the required return on invested capital (Bousquet, n.d.).

The Netherlands and Finland have also implemented shadow toll projects that are similar to the British DBFO technique. The Netherlands has adopted the scheme for the construction of tunnels in the western part of the country. The objective is to construct a larger number of tunnels than would be possible using budget sources alone. The "Noord" tunnel was the first for which private funding was adopted. The Dutch State Public Works Department allocated a lump sum of Fl 3.1 million for maintenance and operation over 30 years. This means that any increase in construction, maintenance, and operating costs is borne by the state. The concession company provided the funds for construction and will continue as owner of the tunnel for 30 years, receiving remuneration for the investment according to the number of vehicles using the tunnel and the agreed tunnel fee. The "Noord" tunnel has been in service since 1992. This form of concession system is under review in the Netherlands following construction of this tunnel, which has been criticized mainly because of excessive transaction costs (Bousquet, n.d.).

London Underground Controversy

The privatization of maintenance for the London Underground has caused significant controversy. One of the prime reasons for the partnership is the desire to provide sustained investment in the underground, which had not been possible using tax revenues. The proposed PPPs will drive private investment of £13 billion over 15 years, with £8.7 billion spent on enhancements and £4.3 billion spent on maintenance (NAO 2000). PPPs are being formed that will designate three consortia to maintain the London Underground. These infrastructure companies are planned to provide long-term investment planning, professional project management, and effective delivery of day-to-day maintenance for an annual payment. The trains and stations will still be run by the public sector. Payment is based on complex performance criteria. A primary fear of opponents of the scheme is that a divided management structure will ensue for the underground that will adversely affect operations and safety. It can be argued that the system will be parceled out to three private companies with little incentive to operate in a unified manner. It is feared that the government agency will lose control over the selection and management of major rehabilitation construction projects. Recent court challenges to the London Underground PPPs have been unsuccessful, and the projects are scheduled to move forward.

This is an example of a complex joint venture PFI project that will require skillful coordination between the public underground and the private contractors performing the maintenance work. It will be interesting to see how the various parties function in actual practice.

Conclusions

This chapter shows that there are various forms of PPP arrangements for acquiring government projects. Some of the conclusions that can be made include the following:

Conclusion 1. The traditional contractual arrangements of a separate contractor and designer have many drawbacks and do not allow for the application of the various forms of PPP. First among the problems encountered with the traditional method is the potential to select a constructor that has made an unrealistically low bid. This typically results in low-quality workmanship on the project because the constructor does not have the funds to properly complete the project. Additionally, the competitively bid project is often characterized by adversarial relationships between the government owner, the designer, and the constructor. Responsibilities are fragmented and shared, and the government owner is placed in the position of being the arbiter of disputes. Competitive bidding also has the significant drawback that construction cannot commence until after the design is completely finished.

Conclusion 2. Design-build has been used successfully on many government projects. Its main benefit is that a single organization both designs and builds a construction project. For those projects where government funding is available and a PPP is not desirable, design-build is an acceptable project delivery method. Some legal barriers have existed to the use of design-build by some states and municipalities. These should be removed.

Conclusion 3. There is a range of levels of privatization of construction projects, starting with little privatization with a design-build project to more complete privatization using a BOT arrangement. Privatization may provide greater efficiency and cost savings by bringing private sector discipline to new areas of project construction, operation, and financing.

Conclusion 4. BOT contracts are already widely used in the United States and internationally. They are mainly employed for major infrastructure projects such as roads and power generation. There appears to be an increasing interest in toll highway facilities. One of the unique features of BOT projects is that they attract new private investment in the infrastructure. Where projects are privately financed, this attracts new investment funds for projects for which no government funding may have been available. It is a way of building desirable projects without recourse to government funding. It frees up scarce government funds for other uses. Use of BOT avoids the need to increase taxes or effect budget cuts to build much needed infrastructure projects. BOT allows for more infrastructure projects to be constructed that act as an economic stimulus in the area in which they are constructed. BOT should avoid, or substantially reduce, the cost overruns experienced by government agencies when they build infrastructure via the traditional competitively bid method, because the contractual responsibility for design and construction rests with the contractor. Only the users of BOT facilities pay tolls. The cost to society is borne by those who use or benefit from the project, not by the taxpayers.

Conclusion 5. Shadow tolls used on the British DBFO projects have the disadvantage of requiring the government to fund a project. With BOT projects, the private sector pays for the project. The shadow toll projects require a high level of private sector efficiency to be successful.

Conclusion 6. Highways and large infrastructure projects are mostly performed using standard BOT and DBFO arrangements. Institutions like hospitals and schools tend to have different privatization arrangements such as BLMT, where the facility is leased back to the government agency. PPP can be used to acquire many different types of facilities. There are a variety of contractual arrangements possible. There are various lease and transfer options that can be used, if necessary, on a PPP.

Many projects are now using both design-build and PPP formats. It is clear that the many advantages of the PPP approach will see an expansion of its use on future projects. It is recommended that the use of PPPs to construct government facilities be increased due to the potential to save taxpayer dollars and increase the efficiency of project delivery.

Bibliography

American Society of Civil Engineers (ASCE) (1992). *Design-Build in the Federal Sector*. Report of the Task Committee on Design-Build. Washington, D.C.: Author.

Angelo, W. J. (2002). "VDOT Paves the Way," *Design-Build Magazine*. March 2002. http://www.designbuildmag.com/June2002/outsidetheboxJune02.asp (7/18/2002).

Bousquet, F. (n.d.). *Analysis of Highway Concessions in Europe: French Study for the DERD/WERD*. Washington, D.C.: World Bank. http://www.worldbank.org/transport/roads/tr_docs/hway_conc.pdf (8/21/02).

Building Futures Council (BFC) (1995). *Report on Design-Build as an Alternative Construction Delivery Method for Public Owners*. Georgetown, Md.: Author.

Cho, A. and T. Sawyer (2001). "Bulk of Ambitious $1.6-Billion I-15 Design-Build Job Complete." *ENR: Engineering News Record* 246 (19): 13.

Committee of Public Accounts (COPA) (2000). *The PFI Contract for the New Dartford and Gravesham Hospital*. House of Commons, Session 1999-2000, Twelfth Report, London: The Stationary Office Ltd.

Construction Industry Council (CIC) (2000). *The role of cost saving and innovation in PFI projects*. London: Thomas Telford Ltd.

Design-Build Institute of America (DBIA) (1996). *Survey of State Procurement Laws Affecting Design-Build*. Washington, D.C.: Author.

_____ (2000). *Guide to the Federal Design-Build Marketplace*. Washington, D.C.: Author.

Hamilton, M. J. (1996). *Privately Financed Road Infrastructure: A Concession Company's Point of View*. Sub-Saharan Africa Transport Policy Program, SSATP Working Paper No. 26. Washington, D.C.: World Bank.

Henk, G. (1998). "Privatization and the Public/Private Partnership." *Journal of Management in Engineering* 14 (4): 28-29.

Lawther, W. C. (2002). *Contracting for the 21st Century: A Partnership Model*. Arlington, Va.: The PricewaterhouseCoopers Endowment for the Business of Government.

Levy, S. (1996). *Build Operate Transfer*. New York: John Wiley and Sons.

Middleton, N. (2001). *Public Private Partnerships—A Natural Successor to Privatizations*. London: PricewaterhouseCoopers. http//www.pwcglobal.com/ uk/eng/about/svcs/pfp/ppp.html.

National Audit Office (NAO) (1998). *The Private Finance Initiative: The First Four Design, Build, Finance and Operate Roads Contracts*. HC 476 Session 1997-98. London: The Stationary Office.

_____ (2000). *The Financial Analysis for the London Underground Public Private Partnerships*. HC 54 Session 2000-2001. www.nao.gov.uk/publications/nao-reports/00-01/000154.pdf.

National Council for Public-Private Partnerships (NCPPP) (2002). *For the Good of the People: Using Public-Private Partnerships to Meet America's Essential Needs*. http://ncpp.org/presskit/ncpppwhitepaper.pdf.

Poole, R.W. (2000). "Don't Oversteer on Toll Roads." *ENR: Engineering News Record* 244 (11): 83.

Pyle, T. (1996). "Project Finance in Practice: The Case Studies." In *Infrastructure Delivery*, edited by A. Mody. Washington, D.C.: The World Bank, 171-190.

Queiroz, C. (1999). *Contractual Procedures to Involve the Private Sector in Road Maintenance and Rehabilitation*. Washington, D.C.: Transport Sector Familiarization Program, World Bank.

The Royal Institution of Chartered Surveyors (RICS) (1995). *The Private Finance Initiative: The Essential Guide*. London: Author.

Ruane, P. (1998). "What you need to know about TEA-21." *Better Roads*. http://www.betterroads.com/articles/brnov98b.htm.

Savas, E. (2000). *Privatization and Public-Private Partnerships*. New York: Seven Bridges Press, LLC.

Scott, J. (2001). "Is PFI a good deal." BBC News. http://news.bbc.co.uk/l/hi/in_depth/business/2001/ppp/1496562.stm.

The Scottish Parliament (SP) (1999). *The Private Finance Initiative*. Research Note 99/1. http://www.scotish.parliament.uk/whats_happening/research/pdf_res_notes/rn99-01.pdf.

Smith, A. J. (1999). *Privatized Infrastructure*. London: Thomas Telford Publishing.

Taylor, R. and S. Blair (2002). *Public Hospitals: Options for Reform through Public-Private Partnerships*. Viewpoint, Note 241, Washington, D.C.: The World Bank Group, Private Sector and Infrastructure Network. http://www.iedm.org/library/hospfinal.pdf. (7/02/02).

Utt, R. (1999). *How Public-Private Partnerships Can Facilitate Public School Construction*. The Heritage Foundation Backgrounder 1257. Washington, D.C.: The Heritage Foundation.

_____ (2001). *New Tax Law Boosts School Construction with Public-Private Partnerships*. The Heritage Foundation Backgrounder 1463. Washington, D.C.: The Heritage Foundation.

PART III

Toward E-Procurement

State Government E-Procurement in the Information Age: Issues, Practices, and Trends

M. Jae Moon
Assistant Professor
George Bush School of Government and Public Service
Texas A&M University

This report was originally published in September 2002.

Introduction[1]

There have been a great deal of criticism and negative perception that public procurement management is neither efficient nor effective at present. One study shows that the government spends about 5.5 cents to administer every procurement dollar while its private counterparts spend only 1 cent to do the similar procurement task (JTFIT, 1996). State governments spend about $75 to $100 administering a single transaction (JTFIT, 1996), which is perceived to be very inefficient. Such criticism and negative public perception force governments to find new and innovative approaches for promoting better, more efficient procurement management.

In the meantime, as information technology (IT) has become a possible solution for many administrative problems in the public sector, e-procurement has emerged as an innovative alternative to achieve a better, more cost-efficient system. E-procurement is defined as a comprehensive process in which governments either establish agreements for the acquisition of products/ services *(contracting)* or purchase products/services in exchange for payment *(purchasing)*, using IT systems.[2] E-procurement achieves these ends through various means, such as electronic ordering, purchasing cards, reverse auctions, and automatic accounting/procurement systems, among others.

Reflecting the dramatic emergence of IT applications in the information age, society has been flooded with literature based on various IT-related studies of business, sociology, and economics. Despite the wealth of information on IT-related issues and the increasing significance of IT for management and policy, surprisingly little research has been conducted in the field of public administration. Some studies suggest that public organizations, which tend to be late adopters of new technology, are perpetually behind in the technology diffusion curve. As this pessimistic view of the public sector suggests, such specific IT applications as e-procurement are neither well explored nor advanced in present studies.

Procurement management has had ample opportunities to improve through the phenomenal popularity of e-commerce (activities related to selling, transferring, and buying products and services using IT systems) and the availability of electronic transaction systems in the private sector. As large buyers, state governments search for managerial alternatives to streamline procurement procedures and reduce overhead costs. Often, IT is one of the most attractive alternatives. Of the many functional initiatives of e-government employed by state governments, this study is specifically designed to survey IT usages in e-procurement management.

State governments are the focal governmental unit of this study. Many state governments have adopted e-procurement management, following the federal government example and the compelling rhetoric of e-procurement. State governments are a good unit of analysis because of the wide variation in their practical implementation of e-procurement. Also, the experience of state governments represents a possible laboratory for local governments, which increasingly are interested in new alternatives for managing procurement.

The study explores general IT applications in the public sector from the perspective of e-government, specifically examining the evolution of e-procurement tools at the state level. Then state governments' adoption and implementation of various e-procurement technologies are examined. This is followed by several case studies of innovative initiatives that suggest the potential effectiveness of e-procurement practices in state governments. The study uses data collected by the National Association of State Procurement Officials (NASPO) in 1998 and 2000 and by the author in a 2001 follow-up survey. Overall, this study seeks to increase our practical understanding of and assess the future implications of e-procurement by surveying the current practices of state governments.

Information Technology and the Move toward E-Government[3]

IT appears to be the most significant technological factor in amplifying social (electronically networked society), economic (e-commerce), political (e-politics, e-campaigning), and governmental (e-government) dynamics through its unique properties of networked communication, data processing, and data management. In particular, e-commerce has become an increasingly popular practice for commercial transactions, thanks to the development of electronic transaction systems and Internet-based businesses. These practices have been reshaping the operation and content of businesses in the private sector.

Echoing the IT applications in the private sector, e-government has become a major reform buzzword for future governance in the public sector. A study by Hart-Teeter (2000) shows that both public and private managers are generally excited and positive about the prospects of e-government, though they raise some security and privacy concerns. IT has opened many possibilities for improving the internal managerial efficiency and the quality of public service delivery to citizens. For example, IT has contributed to dramatic changes in politics (Nye, 1999; Norris, 1999), bureaucracy (Fountain, 1999; 2001), performance management (Brown, 1999), reengineering (Anderson, 1999), red tape reduction (Moon and Bretschneider, 2002), democracy (Musso et al., 2000), and public service delivery (West, 2001) during the last decade. As part of the National Information Infrastructure (NII) initiative, the Clinton administration attempted to visualize electronic government as a means through which the government overcomes the barriers of time and distance in administering public services (Gore, 1993).

The Clinton administration believed that IT would enhance both the efficiency and the effectiveness of public organizations by simplifying administrative procedures and instituting reliable accountability mechanisms. On June 24, 2000, President Clinton delivered his first webcast address to the public and announced a series of e-government initiatives. A highlight was the establishing of an integrated online service system that put all online resources offered by the federal government on a single website, www.firstgov.gov. The initiative also attempted to build one-stop access to roughly $300 billion in grant and $200 billion in procurement opportunities (White House Press Office, 2000). This initiative reflected continuing governmental efforts to advance e-government at the federal level. For instance, the federal government has improved their websites and provided web-based services to promote better internal procedural management and external service provision (Fountain, 2001; West, 2001; Moon, 2002).

E-government includes four major internal and external aspects: (1) the establishment of a secure government intranet and central database for more efficient and cooperative interaction among governmental agencies; (2) web-based service delivery; (3) the application of e-commerce practices for more efficient transaction activities, as in procurement and contracts; and (4) digital democracy for more transparent accountability of government (Government and the Internet Survey, 2000). Various technologies support these unique aspects of e-government, including electronic data interchange (EDI), interactive voice response (IVR), voice mail, e-mail, web service delivery, virtual reality, and public key infrastructure (PKI).

For instance, after introducing Electronic Filing Systems (EFS) with custom-designed software that incorporates encryption technology, the U.S. Patent and Trademark Office (USPTO) substantially reduced the amount of paper the agency handles by allowing inventors or their agents to send any documents to the USPTO via the Internet (Daukantas, 2000). Due to various web technologies, 40 million U.S. taxpayers were able to file their 2000 returns via the web, while 670,000 online applications were made for student loans via the web-based system of the Department of Education (Preston, 2000). Some governments have also promoted virtual democracy by pursuing web-based political participation, such as online voting and online public forums.

In their research, some scholars have reacted to the introduction of IT and the evolution of e-government. Some early research (Bozeman and Bretschneider, 1986; Bretschneider, 1990; Cats-Baril and Thompson, 1995) attempted to understand distinctive managerial principles and unique characteristics of the public management information system (PMIS). Other research focused on information resource management at various levels of government (Caudle, 1988, 1996; Fletcher, 1997; Norris and Kreamer, 1996). Recently some scholars have researched the evolution of e-government (Weare, Musso, and Hale, 1999; Musso, Weare, and Hale, 2000; Fountain, 2001; Layne and Lee, 2001; West, 2001; Moon, 2002). Overall, we have a better understanding of the scope and volume of IT applications and advances in e-government, although not of how various aspects of IT affect specific administrative functions within government. This calls for a new set of studies to go beyond the impact of IT on governmental performance and examine the actual effects of IT on specific areas such as e-procurement.

As an e-government initiative, e-procurement has been widely pursued by many governments as a means of becoming "smart buyers." Public managers believe e-procurement both enhances the overall quality of procurement management through savings in cost and time and leads to a more accountable procurement system. The evolution of e-procurement will be explored in great detail in the next section.

The Evolution of E-Procurement

Procurement management is significant within governmental actions in terms of its monetary volume and managerial implications. Unfortunately, though, perceived as inefficient and wasteful in procurement practices, governments have suffered a decline in public confidence and trust in their performance. Even though state and federal governments have applied rigid procedural standards to prevent procurement abuses and enhance procurement management, the results have not always been successful—leaving room for further improvements in procurement management.

A study suggests that the total procurement cost to federal and state governments for purchasing from the private sector is an estimated $1 trillion. In fact, the federal government spent about $550 billion in 2000 (Neef, 2001). According to statistics from the General Services Administration (GSA), the federal government made about 28 million purchases during the 1998 fiscal year, and about 98 percent were valued at $25,000 or less. The sheer volume of transactions represents a great opportunity to use e-procurement methods for contracting and purchasing products or services because IT-based transactions can be processed much easier, faster, and cheaper. In particular, the government has fundamentally changed the old paper-based procedures and other forms of conventional management by introducing various elements of IT into procurement practices.

The Federal Acquisition Streamlining Act of 1994 required the federal government's procurement management to evolve into a more expedient process based on EDI[4] (Schriener and Angelo, 1995). This forced the federal government to develop the Federal Acquisition Computer Network (FACNET), which is the government's version of the EDI system. FACNET enables the federal government to disseminate its contracting information via online channels. President Clinton issued a presidential memorandum introducing the EDI system to all the federal government's contracting offices as a primary means for purchases in the $2,500 to $100,000 range. The initiative was taken to make federal procurement faster, more efficient, and more discretionary for federal agencies and employees in purchasing information technologies. Although FACNET's mandated use was repealed by a recent legislative action, many government and civilian agencies currently use it as a primary means of their procurement activities.

The Office of Management and Budget (OMB) has a strategic plan to incorporate e-commerce practices into government procurement management by reforming the buying and payment processes. Many public institutions are adopting innovative purchasing card systems, which are often credited with improving the procurement process for federal agencies and many state governments. Several states have participated in joint cooperative e-procurement systems to promote efficiency. Furthermore, state governments use IT in the form of financial models to support budget allocation, budget forecasting, and other related procurement management activities.

Following the federal and state model, San Diego County has practiced a similar e-procurement mechanism in which the county posts solicitation/bids and contract-award information on the web and integrates purchasing and accounting systems. To deal with increasing workloads and promote better procurement management, e-procurement allowed purchasing transactions under $100,000 through simplified procedures (Wood, 2000). To promote this system, the Purchasing and Contracting Office of San Diego County developed BUYNET, "a system that would integrate the existing online requisitioning system and the accounts payable system" (p. 38), with the technical assistance of the Department of Information Services. Wood (2000) reports that BUYNET represents a win/win situation to the county's procurement management by providing better information to suppliers, simplifying procurement procedures, reducing the workload of procurement specialists, and saving money for the county government.[5]

Proponents of e-procurement argue that it brings not only monetary savings to governments but also a more accountable, effective, and faster way to manage procurement. Figure 8.1 compares the prospective strengths and challenges of e-procurement. It also summarizes changes in a procurement manager's roles when procurement practices shift from paper-based to electronic.

Neef (2001) suggests that the various prospects of e-procurement are: (1) lowering transaction costs, (2) faster ordering; (3) greater vendor choices, (4) more efficient and standardized procurement processes, (5) more control

Figure 8.1: Prospects and Challenges in E-Procurement Management

```
┌─────────────────────────┐                    ┌──────────────────────────────────┐
│ PAPER-BASED             │                    │ E-PROCUREMENT                    │
│ PROCUREMENT             │   MOVE TOWARD      │                                  │
│                         │   E-PROCUREMENT    │ Prospects:                       │
│ Paper-based             │                    │ Cost savings                     │
│ catalog management      │   ───────────►     │ Time savings                     │
│                         │                    │ More vendor choices              │
│ Paper-based             │                    │ Increased efficiency             │
│ reconciliation and      │                    │ Control over spending            │
│ "order chasing"         │                    │   and employee compliance        │
│                         │                    │ Better reporting system          │
└─────────────────────────┘                    │ Increased buyer capacity         │
                                                │ Reduced paperwork                │
                                                │ Employee empowerment             │
                                                │ Streamlined work flow            │
                                                │                                  │
                                                │ Challenges:                      │
                                                │ Technical complexity             │
                                                │ Potential initial cost           │
                                                │ Relationships with online        │
                                                │   vendors                        │
                                                │ Relationships with               │
                                                │   independent ASPs               │
                                                │                                  │
                                                │ Procurement officer's roles:     │
                                                │ Electronic catalog and           │
                                                │   content management             │
                                                │ Internal purchasing policy       │
                                                │   development                    │
                                                │ Vendor management and            │
                                                │   service-level negotiation      │
                                                └──────────────────────────────────┘
```

Adopted from Neef (2001), e-Procurement: From Strategy to Implementation, *p. 58.*

over procurement spending (less maverick buying) and employee compliance, (6) more accessible Internet alternatives for buyers, (7) less paperwork and fewer repetitive administrative procedures, and (8) reengineered procurement work flow. Despite these positive aspects, government must still cope with technical, legal, and managerial challenges. These challenges include technical complexity, the potential financial burden involved in the initial investment, security issues, and sustainable relationships with vendors.

Moving toward e-procurement from traditional paper-based processes also brings great challenges to procurement officers. They need new technical and managerial skills, such as managing electronic catalogs, building relationships with online vendors and independent ASPs (portal site

providers), and developing strategic team-based purchasing with other purchasing entities, among others. To sustain the evolution of e-procurement,
state governments must provide appropriate technical training and assistance to procurement officers and develop closer working relationships
with vendors and various government buyers (state agencies, local governments, others).

Architectural Models

Models of e-procurement differ based on who is the focus of the procurement system (sell-side or buy-side), who manages the electronic catalog (suppliers, buyers, or third parties), and the types of portal sites
(one-to-many model or many-to-many model), among others (Neef, 2001).
Neef (2001) presents various models including the sell-side one-to-many
model, buy-side one-to-many model, independent portal model, and auction model.

The sell-side one-to-many model is a vendor-designed e-market Internet
site that allows potential buyers to browse and purchase specific products
from the site. As Figure 8.2 shows, public agencies can access the vendor-
designed e-commerce site and make purchases. This model is designed
mainly to meet vendors' interests and to promote the marketing activities
of vendors. The buy-side one-to-many model is closer to the generic e-
procurement concept than the sell-side one-to-many model, which is
closer to the concept of e-commerce.

As Figure 8.3 illustrates, a government can establish a buy-side one-to-
many model in which the government invites many vendors and provides
electronic catalogs for potential purchasing. Previously, buyers often
designed and maintained in-house electronic catalogs of many vendors for
various items. The buy-side one-to-many model incorporates electronic
purchase order, electronic invoice, electronic fund transfer, and enterprise
resource planning (ERP) elements into the system to enhance procedural
efficiency and convenience (Neef, 2001).

The independent portal model shown in Figure 8.4 represents both e-
commerce and e-procurement elements by having multiple vendors and
multiple buyers in a portal site that makes both electronic order and payment transactions.

The independent portal site is a central place where buyers and vendors are integrated to make online transactions. Current e-procurement
practices have shifted from the sell-side one-to-many model to the independent portal model. Many ASPs are third parties who design and provide
portal sites for web-based shopping malls, web-based auctions, and other
web-based marketing- and procurement-related services (Neef, 2001).

Figure 8.2: Sell-Side One-to-Many Model

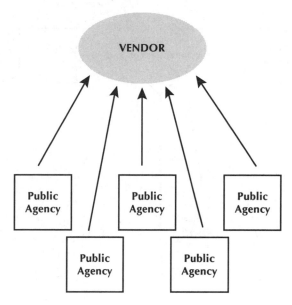

Adopted from Neef (2001), e-Procurement: From Strategy to Implementation, *p. 76.*

Figure 8.3: Government Buy-Side One-to-Many Model

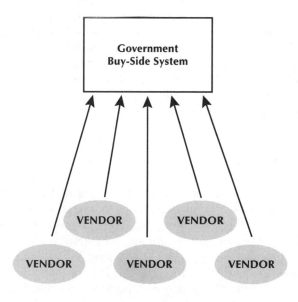

Adopted from Neef (2001), e-Procurement: From Strategy to Implementation, *p. 78.*

Figure 8.4: The Independent Portal Model

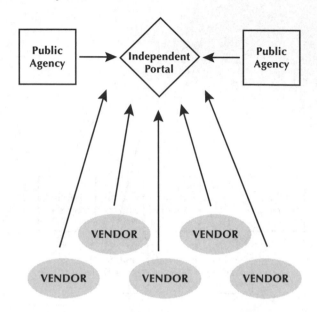

Adopted from Neef (2001), e-Procurement: From Strategy to Implementation, *p. 81.*

Many governments have favorably adopted this independent portal model, thanks to the potential benefits from the infrastructure that a private ASP readily provides. Many governments favor this model because, with low initial costs and little technical capacity, they can take advantage of commercial ASPs. Independent ASPs often proactively approach governments and develop e-procurement portal sites for them with an expectation of profitable business opportunities in the future.

Funding Approaches

Various funding approaches[6] have been presented and introduced by state governments for developing state e-procurement systems: (1) exclusive state-funded approach (Tennessee); (2) self-funded approach/reverse revenue approach (Texas, Connecticut, Colorado, and Utah); and (3) combined approach (Washington) (NECCC, 2000b). If a state has a designated revolving fund or funding flexibility, then the state-funded approach might be a good option. The state can then charge transaction fees to vendors and use them partially to fund the system.

Many state governments prefer the self-funded approach because it requires no initial funding. Private vendors often host the system and charge fees for providing e-procurement services, such as registration/subscription, ordering transaction,bidding transaction, and catalog service (NECCC, 2000b). The combined approach combines the self-funding approach with a government's paying partially for the system's initial development costs. As state governments and ASPs face substantial financial challenges with the exclusive state-funded approach or the self-funded approach, many states seem to prefer the combined approach (Sarkar, 2001b).

Governments need to consider legal and policy aspects in determining their funding mechanisms for e-procurement. States with statutory spending and revenue limitation (i.e., TABOR in Colorado) should deal with systems that charge a fee to the vendors, in the context of their statutory revenue limits. Limits on spending and revenue challenge the legal ability of state agencies to function like commercial entities. Also, they potentially could affect governments' efforts to provide equal opportunities to small businesses (NECCC, 2000b). There are several fundamental questions regarding funding sources of e-procurement systems: (1) Who should maintain the ownership of the system? (2) Who should be in charge of raising necessary funds? and (3) Who should pay the acquisition cost? To answer these questions, governments must deal with another set of legal, political, technical, and policy issues, such as a rigorous business and cost model, a fee-enforcement mechanism, a policy stating the mandated or optional use of the e-procurement system, political support, budget office support, and technical support (NECCC, 2000b).

Standardization

Standardizing e-procurement is another challenging task for both governments and vendors who want more efficient, more effective e-procurement systems. Standardization already has been an issue in terms of e-commerce practices, such as ordering integration with EDI, eXtensible Markup Language (XML), Open Buying on the Internet (OBI), as well as Vendor Centric Standards with XML and xCBL (NECCC, 2001b). Now, standardization includes several supplier concerns, such as catalog creation, external integration (punch-out,[7] channel consideration for co-branding, etc.), internal integration (supply chain automation), and order status as well as electronic invoicing and payment. It also incorporates specific commodity codes, such as National Institute of Governmental Purchasing (NIGP)[8] and the United Nations Standard Product and Services Code (UNSPSC),[9] among others.

In particular, EDI, a critical element of e-commerce, ensures the security of data transfer. EDI is often used between vendors and manufacturers when dealing with purchase orders, purchase order changes, invoices, and requests for proposals. Long used in the transportation industry, EDI has been adopted by many other industries. Its benefits include saving costs—reducing the amount of paper by transmitting electronic documents instead—improving quality through keeping better records and saving time, reducing inventory, and providing better information for decision making (Kalakota and Whinston, 1997). Among the standards for EDI are International Telecommunication Union (ITU) standards, the ANSI X.12 standard, and the United Nations EDIFACT standard (Gunyou and Leonard, 1998). Steps such as purchase order, purchase order confirmation, booking request, booking confirmation, advance ship notice, status report, receipt advice, invoice, and payment represent the basic EDI transactions (Kalakota and Whinston, 1997, p. 379).

Although closely associated with efficient, speedy adoption of e-procurement by governments and suppliers, standardization and interoperability still face many obstacles. Standardization often requires resources for training in such technical details as typography, lexicon, and structure. Considering the various standards currently used for state e-procurement systems, governments and vendors will have to give more attention and more resources to the difficult task of achieving a uniform standardization of e-procurement.

State E-Procurement in Practice

At the state level, NASPO along with the National Association of State Information Resource Executives (NASIRE) and the National Association of State Directors of Administrative and General Services (NASDAGS) conducted joint research and presented a white paper in 1996 to promote innovative procurement management. Their recently published report, "Buying Smart: State Procurement Reform Saves Millions," suggests managerial solutions and best practices based on a detailed examination of various procurement challenges.

Many state governments have already implemented some innovative procurement measures by reengineering the procurement process—reducing purchasing time, streamlining layers of review, allowing more discretion for small purchases, broadening relationships with vendors, and awarding bids based on best value (JTFIT, 1996). The joint study suggests five reform agenda items, in which e-procurement is emphasized as the future of procurement management:

- Simplifying the procurement of commodity items and services
- Building an infrastructure for electronic commerce

- Procuring based on best values
- Developing beneficial partnerships with vendors
- Solving problems with solicitations

A report by NECCC (2000b) summarizes the scope of e-procurement in state governments by presenting its six major elements: (1) passive bid solicitation systems, (2) web-based publication of state contracts and price agreements, (3) bid solicitation distribution systems, (4) catalog systems without bidding capability, (5) catalog systems with internal quote and bidding capability, and (6) catalog systems integrated with the state's accounting systems (p. 5). These elements reflect the evolution of e-procurement from the elementary stage—one-way, passive communication to disseminate public notices of bid solicitation—to the intermediate stage—proactive bid solicitation through the electronic mailing system—and onward to the highly sophisticated stage of integrating e-procurement into accounting systems. Some states (Connecticut, Washington, Colorado, and Utah) actually require that e-procurement systems be integrated with their existing accounting systems (NECCC, 2000b). As state governments take their technically sophisticated, extensive e-procurement systems to a higher level, they face multiple technical, legal, and managerial challenges.

Based on these preliminary observations, the next section surveys several e-procurement initiatives and presents innovative approaches for e-procurement market integration: single-state systems, two-state systems, a multistate system for horizontal integration, and a local-state system for vertical integration. The current status of various e-procurement applications among state governments is discussed, based on the three surveys conducted in 1998, 2000, and 2001.

Single State E-Procurement Initiatives

North Carolina (NC E-Procurement @ Your Service)

NC@your service
www.ncgov.com

In February 2001, North Carolina initiated an extensive e-procurement system for all public organizations in the state, including state agencies, schools, municipalities, and communities.

Unlike many of its counterparts, the North Carolina e-procurement system is mandatory for all state agencies. Two private companies developed the system. Its comprehensive online features include requisitioning, purchase order transmission, notification of electronic quotation requests, electronic quote response for informal bidding, and receipt of goods (for more information, see www.ncgov.com/eprocurement/asp/section/index.asp). The state also plans to integrate the e-procurement system with its financial system. Officials estimate cost savings to be about $50 million a year (Sarkar, 2001c). North Carolina chose a self-funding system, charging a 1.75 percent marketing fee to future vendors. Despite the bold e-procurement initiative, fewer online transactions have been made than the state and vendor expected, which puts more financial constraints on the self-funding model. This is an example of the unexpected obstacles that can follow the implementation of an e-procurement system in a favorable atmosphere and with great rhetoric on the part of a state government.

Virginia (eVA)

Leading an e-government initiative, Virginia's governor highlighted an e-procurement program with Executive Order 65 in May 2000. To actualize the state's e-procurement system, the Department of General Services collected information and feedback from vendors concerning the best design. The state organized a focus group to invite more specific input from vendors and then solicited designs of e-procurement systems (Sarkar, 2001c).

Virgina's system, namely eVA (www.eva.state.va.us), was designed to facilitate the automating and streamlining of procurement (Atwater, 2001). In addition to automated procurement procedures, it includes electronic receiving and invoicing as well as reverse auctions. The eVA system provides various procurement information services for public use, as well as exclusive information and services for registered vendors and agencies. Virginia charges $25 per transaction or an advance fee of $200 for registration, online access, vendor catalog posting, and other services such as electronic receipts and online bid submissions. Vendors also pay a 1-percent transaction fee per order, not to exceed $500. The eVA system is expected to benefit government buyers through better selection, buying, processes, and decisions. It benefits participating vendors through simplified administrative procedures, more opportunities, better processes, and better support services. Local governments and school districts in the state, as well as state agencies, can use the system for procurement.

Maryland (eMaryland M@rketplace)

Maryland initiated the eMaryland M@rketplace (www.eMarylandmarket-place.com) program and has been pushing e-procurement as part of an overall effort to become "the digital state." The state launched the program in 2000 and has already seen some progress. According to Pete Richkus, secretary of the Department of General Services:

> [The eMaryland M@rketplace] is already delivering significant savings for the State and our public sector partners. For example, Anne Arundel County saved almost $12,000 on 27 bid solicitations in its first month as a participating buying entity. Our eMaryland M@rketplace vendors are also realizing financial and resource efficiencies. In March 2000, Maryland began to move its $6 billion in annual purchasing to the Internet by taking a totally innovative approach: no new funding, no new bureaucracy, no multimillion dollar program development contract. The process begins with a creative, multistep request for proposal (RFP), well defined by requirements, and an aggressive outreach program to vendors throughout Maryland as well as to state and local government agency buyers. In its first year, eMaryland M@rketplace posted more than $10 million in purchases on its website, enrolled close to 3000 companies, and trained over 250 buyers (Maryland Department of General Services, 2001, p. 2).

Commenting on the eMaryland M@rketplace, Major Riddick, Jr., the state's former chief of staff under Governor Glendening and chairman of the Maryland Information Technology Board, said that the new e-procurement system will "save money, time, and eliminate duplicated efforts and our vendors can recover many of these same costs for themselves" (Maryland Department of General Services, 2001, p. 3). The annual report prepared by the Maryland Department of General Services (2001) for the eMaryland M@rketplace (2001) provides some evidence of growing popularity among public buyers in the state. The cumulative catalog-usage-by-dollar amount had jumped to $140,000 in March 2001 from $60,000 in March 2000, while the cumulative catalog-usage-by-transaction number had reached 175 in March 2001 from 25 in March 2000. As of March 2001, 262 government buyers (state agencies, municipalities, schools) and 280 vendors were participating in the eMaryland M@rketplace program.

Initiatives for Horizontal and Vertical Market Integration

Several states' innovative, collaborative e-procurement approaches demonstrate both horizontal (interstate) and vertical (intergovernmental) e-procurement collaboration for market integration. In horizontal market integration, two or more states combine their purchasing power to obtain better pricing and a more cost-efficient procurement system. In vertical market integration, local and state governments and quasi-governmental organizations collaborate by using the same electronic catalogs and the same e-procurement system. Figure 8.5 illustrates horizontal and vertical e-procurement.

Colorado and Utah Joint E-Procurement: A Cooperative System

In the 2000 meeting of the Western State Contracting Alliance, the governments of Colorado and Utah exchanged ideas about developing a co-operative e-procurement system that takes advantage of existing e-commerce and first-rate suppliers. Advancing the idea, the two states established a five-year contract for the joint system. They contracted with the NIC Commerce—a subsidiary of a nationally known portal vendor with 13 state portal implementations, including Hawaii and South Carolina—which has e-procurement catalog systems with NASA, the U.S. Air Force, and the Houston-Galveston Area Council of Governments (Utah Division

Figure 8.5: Horizontal and Vertical E-Procurement Market Integration

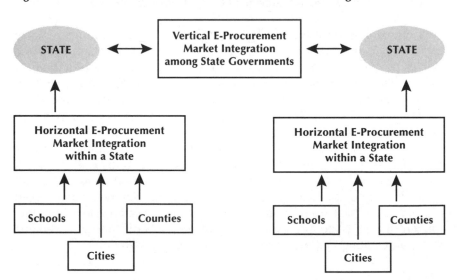

of Purchasing and General Services: www.purchasing.state.ut.us/eps/description.htm). The contract stipulates that the two state governments are not responsible for the development cost and that the NIC Commerce recovers its cost through a 1-percent transaction fee to successful vendors. Other states are allowed to join the system later.

This joint e-procurement system was designed to provide Colorado and Utah with a single catalog system for requisitioning and ordering small purchases, such as office supplies, computers and other commodities, as well as services on state price agreements and catalogs from other vendors in the NIC trading community. The system promotes various goals, as offered in its mission statement: (1) automating procurement processes, (2) collecting comprehensive expenditure data, (3) reducing procurement time with appropriate procurement oversight, (4) seeking improved pricing and cost savings, and (5) enhancing supplier exposure to state purchases (Utah Division of Purchasing and General Services: www.purchasing.state.ut.us/eps/welcome%20page.htm). Following a 270-day pilot phase, the system was to be fully implemented (Sarkar, 2001a). Unfortunately, the two states decided not to implement the joint e-procurement system because they viewed the pilot objectives (particularly in terms of demonstrated efficiencies and prospects of reduced costs through broad supplier adoption) as not having been met. Although Colorado and Utah did not see the tangible benefits of proceeding to full-scale production as outweighing the resource costs and risks involved, their joint effort offers a great possibility for future collaborative efforts between states.

Multi-State EMall™ Initiative: A Horizontal/Interstate Market Integration

To take advantage of the scale of economy—similar to better price deals at wholesale markets—several states joined the Multi-State EMall™ pilot project that the Operational Services Division of Massachusetts initiated at the end of 1997. Its private ASP, Intelisys Electronic Commerce (whose name was later changed to Metiom), was selected and asked to offer the applications of various e-procurement-related technical elements, including authentication and authorization, requisitioning, order processing, and receiving functionality.

In 1998, Massachusetts made online transactions for a statewide procurement contract. The pilot was later expanded to include four other states (Idaho, New York, Texas, and Utah) in the project. The Multi-State EMall team produced a comprehensive evaluation in 1999, suggesting the project to be successful and to exemplify the possibilities of online multistate cooperative procurement processes. In the report presented by the Multi-State EMall team (2000) to the NASPO 2000 Marketing meeting, the team forecasted its cost savings for the year to be between $4.3 million (conservative calculation) and $8.1 million (optimistic calculation). Despite its positive prospects, this initiative currently faces serious challenges as its ASP, Metiom, filed bankruptcy under Chapter 11 in May 2001 (www.state.ma.us/emall/). Despite the unexpected interruptions and challenges, the Multi-State EMall provides information and services via its own website (www.state.ma.us/emall/), and its executive committee plans to sustain the initiative.

State and Local Government Collaboration: A Vertical/Intergovernmental Market Integration

As seen in the eVA and Multi-State EMall initiatives, many single state e-procurement systems pursue vertical (intergovernmental) market integration to take advantage of economies of scale by combining the purchasing powers of local and state governments. California, Massachusetts, North Carolina, South Carolina, and Virginia invite local governments, school districts, and various quasi-public organizations to participate in their e-procurement systems and obtain price and procedural benefits. For example, the North Carolina e-procurement system attempts to generate a statewide vertical market integration to take advantage of cost savings by incorporating various vendors and buyers, including state agencies and institutions, universities, community colleges, public schools, and local governments.

Advances in State E-Procurement

Much of the following information was obtained from an e-mail survey designed by the author and from mail surveys conducted by NASPO, a non-profit organization of 50 directors from the 50 states' central purchasing offices. The NASPO surveys were conducted in 1998 and 2000 by the NASPO Research and Publication Committee, and their results were published in 1999 and 2001, respectively.[10] In 1998, 47 states[11] responded to the NASPO survey and provided their procurement information, while 43 states[12] responded to the 2001 survey.[13]

The NASPO surveys collected comprehensive information, including procurement authority, bidding practices, ethics codes, environmental issues, purchasing information technology, use of technology, automated procurement systems, purchasing cards, travel cards, and utility deregulation. In a follow-up (conducted by the author in October and December 2001) to update the 2001 NASPO survey, e-mail surveys were sent to procurement officers in 50 states. Thirty-five states[14] responded concerning the use of technology, automated procurement systems, and purchasing cards—information that helps us understand current e-procurement practices among the states.

This study basically combines the author's 2001 follow-up e-mail survey and the 2001 NASPO survey. The 2001 follow-up survey updates the 2001 NASPO survey and adds information for states that did not respond originally: Alabama, Delaware, Oregon, and Wisconsin. The combined 2001 data (the follow-up survey and 2001 NASPO survey) are analyzed and compared with the 1998 NASPO survey data to identify any particular trends in the adoption of e-procurement practices. It should also be noted that the 2001 surveys include much more detailed information than the 1998 survey regarding e-procurement, though many items overlap in the two surveys. The 2001 follow-up e-mail survey by the author includes questions regarding the effectiveness of e-procurement practices.

Adoption of Web Technology

Public agencies have adopted web technology widely in recent years. Agencies typically post a wealth of information regarding their missions, functions, contacts, public relations, and answers to frequently asked questions. Web pages for procurement offices often have more sophisticated and technical applications, such as electronic request for proposals, electronic ordering, vendor information, electronic catalog, reverse auction, and Internet-based bidding.

Despite variation in functions, as well as in degrees of sophistication and extensiveness, all state governments offer websites for procurement management. (The web addresses and major contact information are summarized in Appendix I.) According to the 2001 NASPO survey, all state governments utilized e-mail systems to support communication with vendors and internal buyers, but their computer systems are not well linked with other communication systems. For example, only 15 out of 43 states responded that they have integrated fax systems in which a fax is linked with central procurement's computer system. Only eight states (Arizona, Arkansas, California, Iowa, Nebraska, South Carolina, South Dakota, and Virginia) responded that they received incoming faxes via this system. This indicates that communication systems are not well integrated, although state procurement offices are fairly well equipped with various communication tools.

According to the 2001 combined survey data, while respondent states have their own web pages for their central procurement office, 42 states post solicitation/bid information and 41 states post contract-award information on the web. More state governments have come to rely on the web as a means of disseminating information for public notice. In 1998, for example, 39 states responded that they upload RFP information and 35 states responded that they post contract-award information on the web.

Posting Solicitation/Bids on the Web (2001)

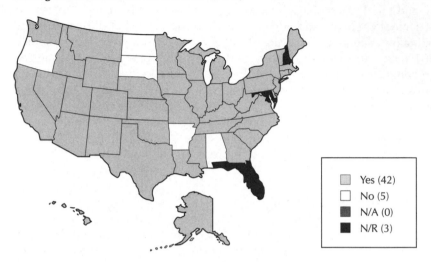

Yes (42)
No (5)
N/A (0)
N/R (3)

Posting Contract Awards on the Web (2001)

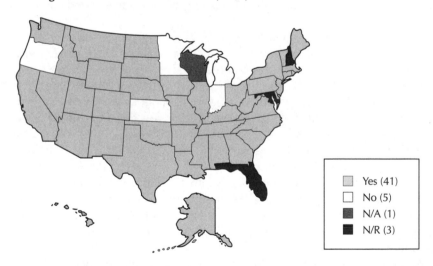

Yes (41)
No (5)
N/A (1)
N/R (3)

Adoption of Digital Signature

Digital signature is an electronic means of signing electronic documents that provides sender authentication using public-key encryption. Digital signature supports e-procurement and e-commerce by facilitating online financial and documental transactions. The authentication procedure of digital signature includes (1) combining private key and specific document and (2) computing the composite (key + document) and generating a unique number (digital signature).[15]

In 2001, only 31 states had enacted digital signature laws to facilitate online financial transactions. Only eight states (Illinois, Kentucky, Louisiana, Minnesota, New Mexico, South Carolina, South Dakota, and Tennessee) responded that their procurement management offices use digital signature to route and approve documents internally. Only seven states (Idaho, Maine, Minnesota, Pennsylvania, Tennessee, Texas, and Washington) responded that they accept as legally binding digital signatures from the vendor community on procurement documents.

The number of state governments enacting digital signature legislation, though, has increased. In 1998, only 21 states responded that they had digital signature legislation, and six states (Arizona, Maryland, Michigan, Nevada, Tennessee, and Texas) responded that they approved digital signature for internal documents. Only four states (Maryland, Ohio, Pennsylvania, and Washington) responded that they accepted digital signatures for procurement documents.

Digital Signature Legislation (2001)

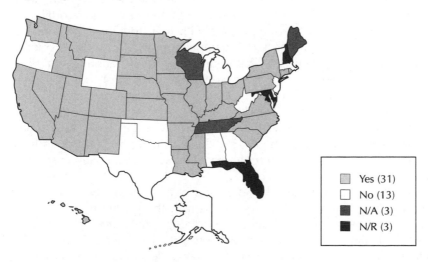

Yes (31)
No (13)
N/A (3)
N/R (3)

Digital Signature for Procurement Documents (2001)

▨	Yes (7)
☐	No (39)
▨	N/A (1)
■	N/R (3)

Internet-Based Bidding and Reverse Auction

Internet-based bidding, using e-commerce through online auctions, has become common practice. The practices of Internet-based bidding and even reverse auctions increasingly are being introduced to governments. For example, governments can specify the products they want to purchase with specific prices in a reverse auction, and vendors of these products compete to offer the best prices. At the federal level, the GSA's Federal Technology Service has introduced reverse auction through the Buyers.gov portal site. Often, bidders can bid more than once with their identities unknown to each other, which ensures dynamic competition and true market pricing (O'Hara, 2001). The Minnesota Department of Administration recently initiated reverse auction by allowing vendors to simultaneously compete with each other online for state contracts. The reverse auction system helps governments save costs because vendors tend to lower their bidding price to win the contracts. In fact, in its first auction on June 21, 2001, the Department of Corrections saved about $35,000 by buying 500,000 pounds of aluminum for license plates through MaterialNet (www.materialnet.com) (Morehead, 2001).

Despite the prospective benefits and rising popularity of Internet-based bidding systems and reverse auction in the private business area, they have not been widely introduced to state governments. Only 10 states (Colorado, Idaho, Maine, Minnesota, Missouri, North Carolina, Pennsylvania, South Carolina, Texas, and Wisconsin) have developed procedures or

Governing Procedures for Internet Bidding (2001)

Reverse Auction (2001)

statutes governing Internet bidding, while 13 states (Idaho, Kentucky, Maine, Massachusetts, Michigan, Minnesota, Missouri, North Carolina, Pennsylvania, South Carolina, Texas, Virginia, and Wisconsin) responded that their central procurement office has conducted electronic bidding. Only five states (Minnesota, Missouri, Pennsylvania, Virginia, and Wisconsin) currently conduct reverse auctions for their procurement. The 1998 NASPO survey did not survey the status of Internet bidding and reverse auction in state governments because they had not been widely introduced to state procurement management at that time.

Electronic Ordering

Like e-commerce practices in the private sector, electronic ordering—which governments can use to make purchase orders electronically—is a fundamental element of e-procurement. About 32 states have electronic ordering systems as part of their e-procurement systems. Of them, only four states (California, Ohio, Pennsylvania, and Virginia) responded that their systems are maintained by state governments, whereas 25 states responded that the systems are maintained by vendors. Four states (Idaho, Kentucky, Massachusetts, and Wyoming) responded that their systems are maintained jointly by the state and vendors.

The management of electronic ordering systems and procurement portal sites is often initiated, developed, and maintained by private businesses. This fact suggests two conflicting points. On the one hand, state govern-

Electronic Ordering (2001)

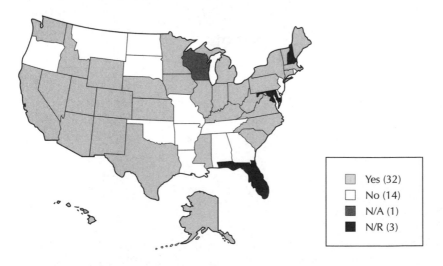

Yes (32)
No (14)
N/A (1)
N/R (3)

Electronic Ordering System Maintainer (2001)

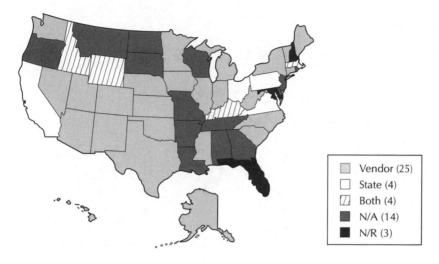

Vendor (25)
State (4)
Both (4)
N/A (14)
N/R (3)

ment have actively taken advantage of the existing private sector capacity to maximize the utility of e-procurement; on the other hand, a strong business interest exists in the e-procurement implementation process, which may cause concerns about potential accountability problems.

Electronic ordering has been rapidly diffused to many states over the last three years. According to the 1998 NASPO survey, only 21 state governments responded that they had an electronic ordering system. Similarly, a majority of the electronic systems (16) are maintained by vendors; the system is maintained by state governments in six states. The Florida state procurement office responded that the system was maintained jointly by vendors and state government.

Maintenance of Procurement Records

Strong managerial and technical capacities for maintaining and tracking procurement-related records—which allow the state to assess and audit its procurement decisions and cost-effectiveness—are critical to the overall quality of procurement. Many state governments seem to have a centralized record-keeping system in that central procurement offices maintain records of the overall dollar volume of purchases. According to the 2001 data, 31 state governments responded that they maintain those records in central procurement offices, while eight states responded that the records are maintained by other state agencies. Thirty-three state governments responded that their central procurement offices are able to track dollars spent by type

Record Keeping (Total Amount) by Central Procurement Office (2001)

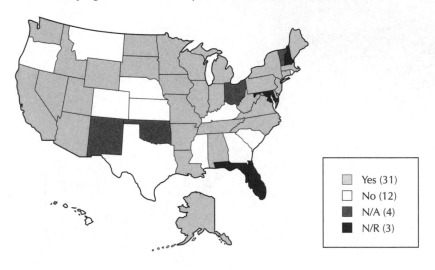

Yes (31)
No (12)
N/A (4)
N/R (3)

Tracking Records for Amount by Commodity (2001)

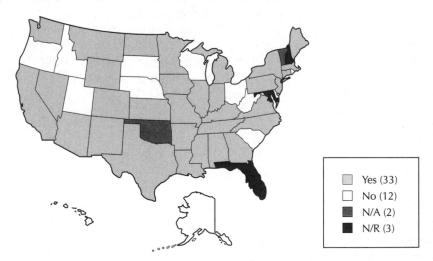

Yes (33)
No (12)
N/A (2)
N/R (3)

of commodity or service, while 36 states responded that they are able to track dollars spent according to vendor.

Little has changed in procurement record-keeping systems. The 1998 survey indicates that 30 states, specifically, their central procurement offices, recorded and maintained the overall dollar amount of purchases. Thirty-two state governments responded, in 1998, that they could track the dollars spent by type of commodity, while 36 state governments responded that they could track dollars spent according to vendor.

Automated Procurement Systems

Automation of the procurement process enables the state to make procurement decisions at the user level by providing vendors' information and catalogs on the web. The automated system often decentralizes procurement management, making the organization flatter, or less hierarchical. The system also helps save time and reduce total cost by providing comprehensive views of state procurement decisions and multiple procurement choices. Automated procurement systems offer various functions, from such simple services as provision of vendor's performance and order forms to such sophisticated services as lead-time analysis and asset management support.

In the 2001 survey, many states (42) responded that central procurement offices have automated procurement systems, but few states responded that they are equipped with a full range of capacities, such as automatic purging,

Automated Procurement Systems (2001)

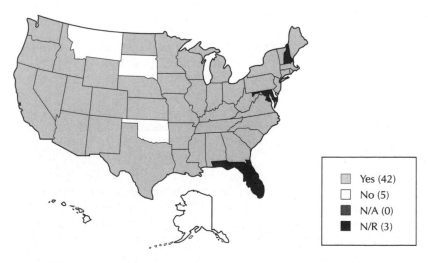

Yes (42)
No (5)
N/A (0)
N/R (3)

Automated Procurement Systems Integrated to E-Commerce (2001)

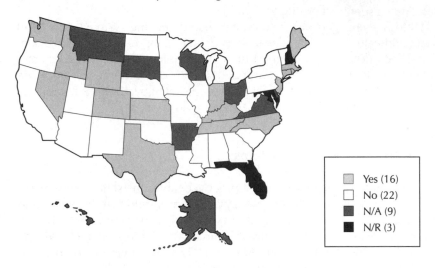

selection of vendors, vendor performance screens, lead-time analysis, and asset management. For example, 16 states have the capacity for lead-time analysis, and 18 states incorporate the EDI element in their procurement system. Sixteen state governments integrate their procurement system with the e-commerce system, and 26 have added asset management functions to the automated procurement system. These aspects of e-procurement were not included in the 1998 survey, so no comparison is made here.

Purchasing Cards

An electronic payment system (EPS) is defined as "a financial exchange that takes place online between buyers and sellers" (Kalakota and Whinston, p. 153). In fact, EPS is the critical part of e-commerce that enables online financial transactions. EPS includes electronic cash, electronic checks, online credit-card-based systems, the point of sale (POS), smart cards, and purchasing cards, among others. The federal government has developed a system to link e-procurement (ordering) and e-payment (paying) for goods and services. For example, an innovation from the GSA automatically links purchasing information and accounting information (Robinson, 2001).

E-procurement systems widely use purchasing cards, in particular, for small but frequent purchases. Many states have adopted purchasing cards to reduce processing costs and to enhance the quality of record keeping. It is common for the cards to be issued by major credit companies (such as

Visa, MasterCard, or American Express) so that public employees can purchase various goods and services directly through vendors. A recent NASPO (2001b) report highlights benefits that purchasing cards bring to procurement management, including administrative cost reductions, productivity increases, vendor flexibility, reporting improvement, and employee empowerment and convenience, among others.

> Presently, more than 50 percent of the items procured through purchasing cards are under $1,000. Quite often, these items can represent up to 80 percent of a government's transactions but less than 20 percent of that government's purchasing dollar. Using a government rule-of-thumb number that each purchase order costs $75 to $100 to issue, the potential cost avoidance for governments is substantial. Some users report up to a 90 percent reduction in processing costs (118).

In the 2001 survey, seven states (Alabama, Arkansas, Hawaii, Illinois, Indiana, Rhode Island, and Tennessee) responded that they do not use purchasing cards yet, although many states have flexible policies under which purchasing cards are optional. Forty, out of 47, states responded that they use purchasing cards as a tool for their procurement management. Most states that use purchasing cards have some sort of limit, such as a single purchase (often $1,000 or $2,500), daily purchase, or cycle purchase limit, to prevent abuse of the cards. Many states do not allow state employees to use purchasing cards for alcoholic beverages and travel. States vary greatly in monthly transaction volumes with, for example, South Carolina having

Purchasing Cards (2001)

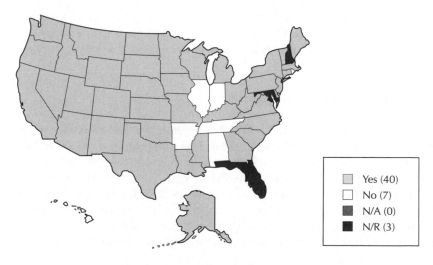

Purchasing Cards for Statewide Contracts (2001)

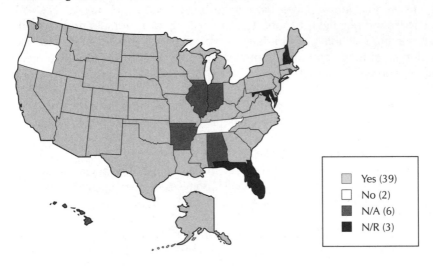

☐	Yes (39)
☐	No (2)
■	N/A (6)
■	N/R (3)

monthly card transactions of $35,000 and Washington spending $2.5 million per month on average.

Thirty-nine state governments use purchasing cards for statewide contracts and fleet management. Only five states (Arizona, California, Iowa, Pennsylvania, and West Virginia) responded that their purchasing cards are funded through a fee-based cost recovery. Only 17 state governments post purchasing-card transactions to their accounting systems.

Purchasing cards appear to be the major development in state procurement over the last three years. According to the 1998 survey, only 32 state governments indicated that they used purchasing cards for state procurement, 29 state governments used purchasing cards for statewide contracts, and 35 state governments had fleet management purchasing cards.

Assessment of Systems' Effectiveness

The 2001 follow-up e-mail survey by the author asked the states' chief procurement officers to indicate whether e-procurement management had yielded cost-saving and time-saving benefits. Only 13 states[16] out of 35 respondents indicated cost savings, while 11 states[17] indicated having saved time. Massachusetts indicated having saved $52–$108 per procurement transaction and having realized a 72-percent reduction in the time spent for procurement management. Despite rhetoric and some indication of positive outcomes, however, not many state governments could offer their specific,

Cost Savings through E-Procurement (2001)

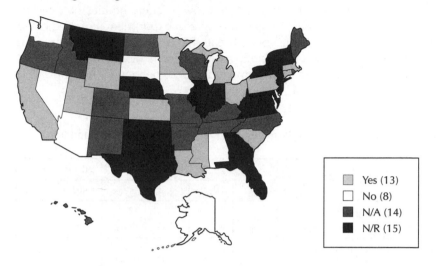

Yes (13)
No (8)
N/A (14)
N/R (15)

Time Savings through E-Procurement (2001)

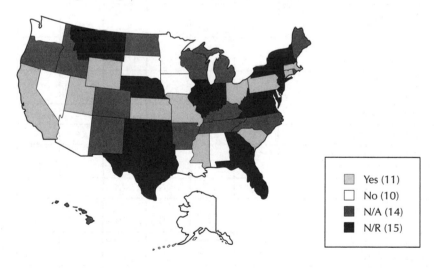

Yes (11)
No (10)
N/A (14)
N/R (15)

rigorous information about cost and time benefits. State governments, it seems, lack this information and cannot prove specific utilities of their initiatives because e-procurement is still new and experimental. As indicated above, however, many state governments have made steady progress in advancing e-procurement by adopting various elements. Table 8.1 summarizes the changes in state e-procurement practices between 1998 and 2001.

Table 8.1: Changes in State E-Procurement Practices between 1998 and 2001

	1998*			2001**		
	Yes	No	N/A	Yes	No	N/A
Posting solicitation/ bid on the web	39	8	0	42	5	0
Posting contract award information on the web	35	12	0	41	5	1
Digital signature legislation	19	28	0	31	13	3
Approving digital signature internally	6	41	0	8	35	4
Accepting digital signature for procurement documents	4	43	0	7	39	
Governing Internet-based bidding procedures***				10	35	2
Practicing Internet-based bidding***				13	33	1
Reverse auction***				5	42	0
Electronic ordering	21	26	0	32	14	1
Automated procurement system***				42	5	0
Purchasing cards	32	15	0	40	7	0
Purchasing cards for statewide contracts	29	18	0	39	2	6
Fleet management purchasing cards	35	12	0	39	6	2
Cost-saving benefit***				13	8	14
Time-saving benefit***				11	10	14

* Forty-seven state governments responded to the 1998 NASPO survey.
** Forty-seven state governments are included. The data from the 2001 NASPO survey and the 2001 follow-up e-mail survey by the author are combined.
*** The question is asked only in the 2001 e-mail follow-up survey, to which 35 state governments responded.

Conclusions and Recommendations

Conclusions

E-procurement, as an e-government initiative, is perceived to be an innovative alternative that leads to better, more efficient, and more effective procurement management by overcoming many traditional paper-based procurement problems. Based on this outlook, many state governments have implemented e-procurement initiatives to improve their procurement management, some even attempting to pursue horizontal and vertical e-procurement market integration.

Many state governments have adopted various e-procurement techniques: (1) posting solicitation and bids and contract-award information on the web, (2) electronic ordering, (3) automated procurement system, and (4) purchasing cards. Several others have also been implemented but less widely: (1) digital signature legislation and accepting digital signature as legally binding for procurement documents, (2) Internet-based bidding, and (3) reverse auction. E-procurement remains in the experimental stage, however, and most state governments have not reached the mature point of realizing benefits from their e-procurement practices.

A promising alternative rather than an instant panacea, e-procurement leaves state governments facing many technical, financial, legal, and managerial challenges. The following challenges should be resolved in order to sustain e-procurement as an initiative and obtain the prospective benefits and utilities.

1. Financial Issues

State governments often face considerable challenges in finding the financial resources required to develop e-procurement systems. With funding being a common problem, the exclusive state-funded approach is not being widely adopted. Many state governments rely on private companies' participation and private resources in developing the technical systems, and support a financial arrangement in which the private companies later recoup their investment by charging various fees. Accordingly, many e-procurement systems are developed, provided, and maintained by vendors and ASPs, which leads to the potential problem of private business interests overruling public interests. E-procurement systems driven by private businesses could be corrupted when those private interests lack appropriate accountability mechanisms.

Nor has the self-funded model met with success, as we saw in the North Carolina case. Sarkar (2001b) also reports that the private funding model has not been successful. A hybrid model has become more popular, one in which state governments invest some money and vendors recover their own costs through transaction fees. But state governments must continue to pay careful attention to the nature of funding mechanisms for e-procurement systems.

2. Technical and Standardization Issues

Lack of technical capacity is a major obstacle to e-procurement and other e-government initiatives. Procurement officers need such specialized technical skills as managing electronic catalogs, electronic ordering, Internet-based bidding, reverse auction, digital signature, purchasing cards, and automated procurement systems. Managing e-procurement demands a more comprehensive range of skills because the automated procurement system is often linked to budgeting and accounting systems. Similarly, standardization and interoperability pose continuing challenges to state governments as they pursue better, more efficient, and more effective e-procurement systems.

3. Vertical and Horizontal Market Integration

Collaborative initiatives for e-procurement market integration that several state governments have undertaken have failed to succeed. They face technical and managerial difficulties, and many local governments are not equipped with either the necessary technical capacities or the e-procurement officers. States have not acquired tangible benefits of horizontally integrated e-procurement systems partially because the potential for gaining efficiencies and reducing costs through broad supplier adoption are outweighed by the costs and risks involved.

4. Legal/Accountability Issues

Because there have been legal challenges with respect to digital signatures, state governments should have an appropriate legal arrangement that specifies when a digital signature is accepted as a legally binding signature for procurement documents. Posting RFP information on the web should also be treated as a legitimate public notice. Because, for instance, purchasing cards have been abused by many public officials who use them for inappropriate purposes (GAO, 2001), state governments need strong accountability mechanisms to reduce the possibilities of abuse, fraud, and mismanagement of the e-procurement system.

5. Internal/External Management Challenges

E-procurement offers various internal and external management challenges to state procurement offices. Internally, states should develop—and govern according to—policies that offer comprehensive institutional outlines for e-procurement decisions and processes, institute clear procedures and functions as well, and develop closer, more strategic relationships with vendors. Externally, state governments need to communicate with vendors and ASPs to update procurement items and prices and to negotiate with them for better options and prices.

Recommendations

1.   Develop Strategic Funding Mechanisms

In pursuing long-term, sustainable benefits of e-procurement, state governments should carefully assess both weaknesses and strengths of alternative funding models (exclusive state-funded approach, self-funded approach, and hybrid approach) and cost-recovery models. Assessments should be based on the governments' financial condition, the projected number and amount of e-procurement transactions, as well as cost-efficiency and public accountability.

2.   Provide Technical Assistance and Pursue Standardization

State governments should develop and maintain technical personnel, in-house or contractual, who can manage automated procurement and administer statewide procurement transactions and related data.

State governments should continue to introduce advanced e-procurement elements that are less diffused to governments, including Internet-based bidding and electronic ordering.

State governments should provide more technical training opportunities to state procurement officers and public/quasi-public officers who use advanced e-procurement systems.

3.   Promote Vertical and Horizontal E-Procurement Market Integration

State procurement offices should continue to carefully pursue e-procurement market integration, vertical and horizontal, and to form specific cooperative institutional arrangements.

They should invite more vendors to participate in e-procurement systems based on mutual interests, and they should also provide more technical assistance to local governments and other quasi-public organizations.

4.   Institute Legal/Accountability Mechanisms

State governments should enact digital signature laws and should proactively define announcements made via the web to be legitimate public notices.

State governments should institute strong accountability mechanisms to reduce the possibilities of abusive, improper, and fraudulent e-procurement activities.

State governments should promote accountability and efficiency by establishing and maintaining record-keeping systems and by integrating procurement systems with accounting systems to allow for systematic tracking and checking of procurement data.

5. Establish Collaborative Relationships with Vendors, ASPs, and Government Buyers

State governments should develop statewide procurement policies and procedures that govern many e-procurement activities, including electronic ordering, Internet-based bidding, and reverse auctions, among others.

Central procurement offices should develop closer, more strategic relationships among government buyers, vendors, and ASPs in order to build more cooperative relationships and ensure more updated price information and better price negotiation.

State governments should establish a systemic procurement arrangement for better prices with specific vendors through purchase agreements.

E-procurement offers both opportunities and challenges to state governments. To accomplish sustainable e-procurement, state governments should cope with these challenges proactively and strategically by enhancing appropriate technical and managerial capacities, improving the quality of systems, and establishing cooperative inter-sectoral and intergovernmental relationships among central procurement offices, state agencies, local governments, vendors, and ASPs. Such efforts will turn the rhetoric of e-procurement into real administrative results in the near future.

Appendix I:
Web Addresses and Contact Information
for State Procurement Offices
(As of September 2002)

Alabama
http://www.purchasing.state.al.us/
Director: Ran Garver (Acting)
Division of Purchasing
Department of Finance
P.O. Box 302620
100 N. Union Street, Ste. 192
Montgomery AL 36130
Phone: 334/242-7250
Fax: 334/242-4419
rgarver@purchasing.state.al.us

Alaska
http://www.state.ak.us/local/
akpages/ADMIN/home.htm
Director: Vern Jones
Division of General Services
Department of Administration
P.O. Box 110210
333 Willoughby Road
Juneau AK 99811-0210
Phone: 907/465-5684
Fax: 907/465-2189
Vern_jones@admin.state.ak.us

Arizona
http://sporas.ad.state.az.us/
Director: John Adler
State Procurement Office
Department of Administration
15 South 15th Avenue, Suite 103
Phoenix AZ 85007
Phone: 602/542-5308
Fax: 602/542-5508
John.Adler@ad.state.az.us

Arkansas
http://www.accessarkansas.org/dfa/
purchasing/index.html
Director: Joe Giddis
Office of State Purchasing
Department of Finance &
Administration
1509 West 7th Street
P.O. Box 2940
Little Rock AR 72203
Phone: 501/324-9312
Fax: 501/324-9311
joe.giddis@dfa.state.ar.us

California
http://www.pd.dgs.ca.gov/
Director: Ralph Chandler
Procurement Division
Department of General Services
1823 14th Street
Sacramento CA 95814
Phone: 916/445-6942
Fax: 916/324-2009
Ralph.Chandler@dgs.ca.gov

Colorado
http://www.gssa.state.co.us/
Director: Richard Pennington
Division of Purchasing
Department of Personnel
225 East 16th Avenue, Ste. 802
Denver CO 80203-1613
Phone: 303/866-6100
Fax: 303/894-7445
richard.pennington@state.co.us

Connecticut
http://www.das.state.ct.us/busopp.asp
Director: Jim Passier
Procurement Services
Department of Administrative
Services
P.O. Box 150414
165 Capitol Avenue
Hartford CT 06106
Phone: 860/713-5086
Fax: 860/713-7484
jim.passier@po.state.ct.us

Delaware
http://www.state.de.us/purchase/
index.htm
Director: Blaine Herrick
Division of Purchasing
Department of Administrative
Services
Wilmington Avenue,
Gov. Bacon Grounds
P.O. Box 299
Delaware City DE 19706
Phone: 302/834-7081
Fax: 302/836-7642
bherrick@state.de.us

District of Columbia
Director: Jacques Abadie, III
(Interim)
Department of Administrative
Services
441 4th Street, NW
Suite 800 S
Washington DC 20001
Phone: 202/727-0252
Fax: 202/727-6827
abadiej@ocp.dcgov.org

Florida
http://fcn.state.fl.us/fcn/centers/
purchase/
Director: David Minacci
Division of Purchasing

Department of Management
Services
4050 Esplanade Way, Suite 335M
Tallahassee FL 32399-0950
Phone: 850/488-3049
Fax: 850/414-6122
hosayr@dms.state.fl.us

Georgia
http://www.doas.state.ga.us/
Director: Debra Blount (Acting)
Statewide Business Services
Department of Administrative
Services
200 Piedmont Avenue, Suite 1304
W. Floyd Building
Atlanta GA 30334
Phone: 404/657-6000
Fax: 404/655-4528
rdkissel@doas.ga.gov

Hawaii
http://www.state.hi.us/icsd/dags/
spo.html
Director: Aaron Fujioka
State Procurement Office
P.O. Box 119
1151 Punchbowl Street, 230-A
Honolulu HI 96813
Phone: 808/587-4700
Fax: 808/587-4703
Aaron_Fujioka@exec.state.hi.us

Idaho
http://www2.state.id.us/adm/
purchasing/index.htm
Director: Jan Cox
Division of Purchasing
Department of Administration
5569 Kendall Street
P.O. Box 83720
Boise ID 83720
Phone: 208/327-7472
Fax: 208/327-7320
jcox@adm.state.id.us

Illinois
http://www.state.il.us/cms/purchase/
default.htm
Director: Robert Kirk
Procurement Services Division
Dept. of Central Management
Services
801 Wm. G. Stratton Building
Springfield IL 62706
Phone: 217/785-3868
Fax: 217/782-5187
robert_kirk@cms.state.il.us

Indiana
http://www.ai.org/idoa/index.html
Director: Rebecca Reddick
Division of Procurement
Department of Administration
Government Center South
402 W. Washington St.,
Rm. W468
Indianapolis IN 46204
Phone: 317/232-3032
Fax: 317/232-7312
rreddick@idoa.state.in.us

Iowa
http://www.state.ia.us/government/
dgs/Purchase/business.htm
Director: Patricia Schroeder
Customer Service, Admin. and
Purchasing
Department of General Services
Hoover State Office Building,
Level A
Des Moines IA 50319
Phone: 515/281-8384
Fax: 515/242-5974
Patti.Schroeder@dgs.state.ia.us

Kansas
http://da.state.ks.us/purch/
Director: John Houlihan
Division of Purchases
Department of Administration

Landon State Office Building
900 S.W. Jackson Street,
Room 102N
Topeka KS 66612
Phone: 785/296-2376
Fax: 785/296-7240
John.Houlihan@state.ks.us

Kentucky
https://ky-purchases.com/
Director: Mike Burnside
Division of Purchases
Finance & Administration Cabinet
Room 367, Capitol Annex Building
Frankfort KY 40601
Phone: 502/564-4510 ext. 248
Fax: 502/564-7209
Mike.Burnside@mail.state.ky.us

Louisiana
http://www.doa.state.la.us/osp/
osp.htm
Director: Denise Lea
Office of State Purchasing
Division of Administration
P.O. Box 94095
301 Main Street, 13th Floor
Baton Rouge LA 70804
Phone: 225/342-8057
Fax: 225/342-8688
dlea@doa.state.la.us

Maine
http://www.state.me.us/purchase/
homepage.htm
Director: Richard Thompson
Division of Purchases
Department of Administrative &
Financial Services
State Office Building
State House Station #9
Augusta ME 04333-0009
Phone: 207/624-7332
Fax: 207/287-6578
Richard.B.Thompson@state.me.us

Maryland
http://www.dgs.state.md.us/
overview/procure2.htm
Director: Mark Krysiak
Purchasing Bureau
Department of General Services
301 W. Preston Street,
Room M6
Baltimore MD 21201
Phone: 410/767-4430
Fax: 410/333-5482
gpwcmg@dgs.state.md.us

Massachusetts
http://www.state.ma.us/osd/osd.htm
Director: Ellen Phillips
Operational Services Division
John W. McCormack Office
Building
One Ashburton Place, Room 1017
Boston MA 02108
Phone: 617/727-7500 ext. 260
Fax: 617/727-6123
ellen.phillips@state.ma.us

Michigan
http://www.state.mi.us/dmb/oop/
Director: Kathy Jones
Office of Purchasing
Department of Management &
Budget
P.O. Box 30026
530 W. Allegan, Mason Bldg.,
2nd Floor
Lansing MI 48909
Phone: 517/373-0300
Fax: 517/335-0046
jonesk@state.mi.us

Minnesota
http://www.mmd.admin.state.mn.us/
Director: Kent Allin
Materials Management
Department of Administration
112 State Administration Building

50 Sherburne Avenue
St. Paul MN 55155
Phone: 651/296-1442
Fax: 612/297-3996
kent.allin@state.mn.us

Mississippi
http://www.mmrs.state.ms.us/
Purchasing/
Director: Don Buffum
Office of Purchasing & Travel
1401 Woolfolk Bldg, Suite A
501 North West Street
Jackson MS 39201
Phone: 601/359-3912
Fax: 601/359-2470
buffum@dfa.state.ms.us

Missouri
http://www.oa.state.mo.us/purch/
purch.htm
Director: Jim Miluski
Division of Purchasing & Materials
Mgmt.
Department of Administration
P.O. Box 809
301 W. High Street, HST Bldg.
#580
Jefferson City MO 65101
Phone: 573/751-3273
Fax: 573/526-5985
MilusJ@mail.oa.state.mo.us

Montana
http://www.mt.gov/doa/ppd/
index.htm
Director: Marvin Eicholtz
Procurement & Printing Division
Department of Administration
P.O. Box 200135
Helena MT 59620-0132
Phone: 406/444-3318
Fax: 406/443-2212
meicholtz@state.mt.us

Nebraska
http://www.das.state.ne.us/materiel/
Director: Don Medinger
Material Division
Department of Administrative
Services
301 Centennial Mall South
P.O. Box 94847
Lincoln NE 68509
Phone: 402/471-2401
Fax: 402/471-2268
dmeding@notes.state.ne.us

Nevada
http://www.state.nv.us/purchasing/
Director: William Moell
Purchasing Division
Department of Administration
209 E. Musser, Room 304
Carson City NV 89710
Phone: 775/684-0170
bmoell@govmail.state.nv.us

New Hampshire
http://www.state.nh.us/das/
purchasing/index.html
Director: Wayne Myer
Bureau of Purchase & Property
Department of Administrative
Services
State House Annex, Room 102
25 Capitol Street
Concord NH 03301
Phone: 603/271-3606
Fax: 603/271-2700
wmyer@admin.state.nh.us

New Jersey
http://www.state.nj.us/treasury/
purchase/
Director: Janice DiGiuseppe
(Acting)
Procurement & Contracting
New Jersey State Purchase Bureau
Department of Treasury

33 W. State Street, CN-230
Trenton NJ 08625-0230
Phone: 609/292-4751
Fax: 609/292-0490
formica_j@tre.state.nj.us

New Mexico
http://www.state.nm.us/clients/spd/
spd.html
Director: Lou Higgins
Purchasing Division
Department of General Services
1100 St. Francis Drive
Joseph Montoya Building
Santa Fe NM 87501
Phone: 505/827-0480
Fax: 505/827-2484
lou.higgins@state.nm.us

New York
http://www.ogs.state.ny.us/
purchase/default.asp
Director: Paula Moskowitz
Procurement Services Group
Office of General Services
Mayor E. Corning, 2nd Tower,
Room 3804
Albany NY 12242
Phone: 518/474-6710
Fax: 518/486-6099
customer.services@ogs.state.ny.us

North Carolina
http://www.doa.state.nc.us/PandC/
Director: J. Arthur Leaston
Division of Purchase & Contract
Department of Administration
305 Mail Service Center
Raleigh NC 27699-1805
Phone: 919/733-3581
Fax: 919/733-4782
john.leaston@ncmail.net

North Dakota
http://www.state.nd.us/csd/
Director: Linda Belisle
Central Services
Office of Management & Budget
600 East Blvd., Dept. 188
Bismarck ND 58505-0420
Phone: 701/328-3494
Fax: 701/328-1615
lbelisle@state.nd.us

Ohio
http://www.state.oh.us/das/gsd/pur/
pur.html
Director: Mark Hutchison
General Services Division
Department of Administrative
Services
4200 Surface Road
Columbus OH 43228-1395
Phone: 614/466-2375
Fax: 614/466-7525
Mark.Hutchison@das.state.oh.us

Oklahoma
http://www.dcs.state.ok.us/okdcs.nsf/
Director: Tom Jaworsky
Central Purchasing Division
Department of Central Services
2401 N. Lincoln Blvd., Ste 116
Oklahoma City OK 73105
Phone: 405/521-2115
Fax: 405/522-6266
Tom_Jaworsky@dcs.state.ok.us

Oregon
http://tpps.das.state.or.us/
purchasing/
Director: Dianne Lancaster
Purchasing Services Division
Department of Administrative
Services
1225 Ferry Street, SE
Salem OR 97310
Phone: 503/378-3529

Fax: 503/373-1626
Dianne.Lancaster@.state.or.us

Pennsylvania
http://www.dgs.state.pa.us/purch.htm
Director: Joe Nugent
Department of General Services
414 North Office Building
Harrisburg PA 17125
Phone: 717/787-4718
Fax: 717/783-6241
jnugent@state.pa.us

Rhode Island
http://www.purchasing.state.ri.us/
home.html
Director: Peter Corr
Associate Director/Purchasing Agent
Division of Procurement Materials
& Information Management
Department of Administration
One Capitol Hill
Providence RI 02908-5855
Phone: 401/277-2142 ext. 123
Fax: 401/277-6387
pcorr@purchasing.state.ri.us

South Carolina
http://www.state.sc.us/mmo/mmo/
Director: Robert Voight Shealy
Materials Management Officer
Office of General Services
1201 Main Street, Ste. 600
Columbia SC 29201
Phone: 803/737-0600
Fax: 803/737-0639
VShealy@ogs.state.sc.us

South Dakota
http://www.state.sd.us/boa/pp.htm
Director: Jeff Holden
Office of Purchasing & Printing
Division of Central Services
Bureau of Administration
523 East Capitol
Pierre SD 57501
Phone: 605/773-3405
Fax: 605/773-4840
jeff.holden@state.sd.us

Tennessee
http://www.state.tn.us/generalserv/
purchasing/
Director: George Street
Department of General Services
Third Floor, Tennessee Tower
312 Eighth Avenue North
Nashville TN 37243-0557
Phone: 615/741-1035
Fax: 615/741-0684
gstreet@mail.state.tn.us

Texas
http://www.gsc.state.tx.us/
Director: Jim Railey
General Services Commission
P.O. Box 13042 Capitol Station
Austin TX 78711
Phone: 512/463-3444
Fax: 512/463-7994
jim.railey@gsc.state.tx.us

Utah
http://www.purchasing.state.ut.us/
Director: Douglas Richins
Division of Purchasing
Department of Administrative Services
3150 State Office Building,
Capitol Hill
Salt Lake City UT 84114
Phone: 801/538-3143
Fax: 801/538-3882
pamain.drichins@state.ut.us

Vermont
http://www.bgs.state.vt.us/PCA/
index.html
Director: Peter Noyes
Division of Purchasing
General Services Department
128 State Street, Drawer 33
Montpelier VT 05633-7401
Phone: 802/828-2211
Fax: 802/828-2222
peter.noyes@state.vt.us

Virginia
http://159.169.222.200/dps/
Director: Ron Bell
Division of Purchases & Supply
Department of General Services
P.O. Box 1199
805 E. Broad Street, 4th Floor
Richmond VA 23218-1199
Phone: 804/786-3846
Fax: 804/371-7877
rbell@dgs.state.va.us

Washington
http://www.ga.wa.gov/vendor.htm
Director: Bill Joplin (Acting)
Office of State Procurement
Department of General
Administration
201 General Administration
Building
P.O. Box 41017
Olympia WA 98504-1017
Phone: 360/902-7404
Fax: 360/586-2426
bjoplin@ga.wa.gov

West Virginia

http://www.state.wv.us/admin/
purchase/
Director: David Tincher
Purchasing Division
2019 Washington St., East
P.O. Box 50130
Charleston WV 25305
Phone: 304/558-2538
Fax: 304/558-4115
dtincher@gwmail.state.wv.us

Wisconsin

http://vendornet.state.wi.us/
vendornet/
Director: Leo Talsky (Acting)
Bureau of Procurement
Department of Administration
101 E. Wilson Street,
6th Floor
P.O. Box 7867
Madison WI 53707-7867
Phone: 608/266-0974
Fax: 608/267-0600
Michael.Cornell@doa.state.wi.us

Wyoming

http://ai.state.wy.us/GeneralServices/
procurement.asp
Director: Mac Landen
Purchasing Section
Department of Administration
& Information
Emerson Building,
Room 323E
2001 Capitol Avenue
Cheyenne WY 82002
Phone: 307/777-7253
Fax: 307/777-5852
MLANDE@state.wy.us

*Source: National Association of State Procurement Officials (NASPO)'s website
(http://www.naspo.org/directory/index.cfm#anchor236482), accessed April 22, 2002.*

Appendix II:
Summary of the Surveys

Table 8.A.1: 1998 NASPO Survey

	Alabama	Alaska	Arizona	Arkansas	California	Colorado	Connecticut	Delaware	Florida	Georgia	Hawaii	Idaho	Illinois	Indiana	Iowa	Kansas	Kentucky	Louisiana	Maine	Maryland	Massachusetts	Michigan	Minnesota	Mississippi	Missouri
PC for Travel	y		n	y	y	y	y	y	y	y	n	y	y	n	y	y		y	y	y	n	y	n	y	n
Fleet Management	n		y	n	y	y	n	n	y	y	n	y	y	y	y	y		y	y	y	y	y	y	y	y
PC for Statewide Contract	n		y	n	y	y	y	y	y	y	n	y	n	n	n	y		n	y	y	y	n	y	y	n
Purchasing Card	n		y	n	y	y	y	y	y	y	n	y	n	n	n	y		n	y	y	y	y	y	y	y
Record: Amount by Vendor	n/a		n/a	n/a	y	y	n/a	y	y	n/a	y	y	y	y	n			y	y	y	y	y	y	n	y
Record: Amount by Commodity	n		n	n	y	n	y	n	y	y	n	y	y	y	n			y	y	y	y	y	y	n	y
Record: Total Amount	n		y	n	y	n	y	y	y	y	n	y	y	y	n			y	y	y	y	y	y	n	y
EO Maintainer	n/a		n/a	vendor	vendor	n/a	state	vendor	combo	n/a	n/a	vendor	n/a	n/a	state	n/a		n/a	vendor	n/a	state	n/a	state	vendor	vendor
Electronic Ordering	n		n	y	y	n	y	y	y	n	n	y	n	n	y	n		n	y	n	y	n	y	y	y
DS for Procurement Document	n		n	n	n	n	n	n	n	n	n	n	n	n	n	n		n	n	y	n	n	n	n	n
DS for Internal Document	n		y	n	n	n	n	n	n	n	n	n	n	n	n	n		n	n	y	n	y	n	n	n
Digital Signature	n		y	n	y	n	n	y	y	y	y	y	y	n	y			n	n	n	n	n	y	y	n
Contract Award on Web	n	n	y	n	y	y	y	y	n	y	n	n	y	y	y	y		n	n	y	y	n	y	n	y
Web Solicitation	n	n	y	n	y	y	y	y	n	y	y	y	y	y	y	y		n	y	y	y	y	y	n	y

Table 8.A.1: 1998 NASPO Survey (continued)

	Montana	Nebraska	Nevada	New Hampshire	New Jersey	New Mexico	New York	North Carolina	North Dakota	Ohio	Oklahoma	Oregon	Pennsylvania	Rhode Island	South Carolina	South Dakota	Tennessee	Texas	Utah	Vermont	Virginia	Washington	West Virginia	Wisconsin	Wyoming
PC for Travel	y	y	y		y	y	y	y	n	y	y	y	y	n	y	y	y	y	y	n	y	y	y	y	y
Fleet Management	y	n	n		n	y	y	y	y	n	y	y	y	n	y	y	y	y	y	y	y	n	y	y	n
PC for Statewide Contract	y	n	y		y	n	y	y	n	y	n	y	y	n	n	n	y	y	n	y	y	y	y	y	n
Purchasing Card	y	n	y		y	n	y	y	n	y	n	y	y	n	y	n	y	y	n	y	y	y	y	y	n
Record: Amount by Vendor	y	n	n		y	y	y	y	n	y	y	y	y	y	y	y	y	y	n/a	y	y	y	y	y	y
Record: Amount by Commodity	n	n	y		y	y	y	y	n	y	y	y	y	y	y	n	n	y	y	n/a	y	y	y	y	y
Record: Total Amount	y	n	y		y	y	n	y	n	y	y	y	n	n	n	y	y	y	n/a	n	n	y	n	y	n
EO Maintainer	n/a	vendor	n/a		n/a	n/a	vendor	n/a	n/a	state	n/a	vendor	state	n/a	n/a	vendor	n/a	n/a	n/a	vendor	vendor	n/a	n/a	vendor	n/a
Electronic Ordering	n	y	n		n	n	y	n	n	y	n	y	n	n	n	y	n	n	y	y	n	n	n	y	n
DS for Procurement Document	n	n	n		n	n	n	n	n	y	n	n	y	n	n	n	n	n	n	n	n	n	y	n	n
DS for Internal Document	n	n	y		n	n	n	n	n	n	n	n	n	n	n	n	n	y	y	n	n	n	n	n	n
Digital Signature	y	n	n		n	y	n	y	n	n	n	y	n	y	y	n	n	n	y	n	n	y	n	y	n
Contract Award on Web	y	y	y		y	y	y	y	n	y	y	y	y	y	n	y	y	y	y	y	y	y	y	y	n
Web Solicitation	y	y	y		y	y	y	y	n	y	y	y	y	y	y	n	y	y	y	y	n	y	y	y	y

Table 8.A.2: 2001 Combined Procurement Survey—The 2001 NASPO Survey and 2001 Follow-Up E-Mail Survey

	Alabama	Alaska	Arizona	Arkansas	California	Colorado	Connecticut	Delaware	Florida	Georgia	Hawaii	Idaho	Illinois	Indiana	Iowa	Kansas	Kentucky	Louisiana	Maine	Maryland	Massachusetts	Michigan	Minnesota	Mississippi	Missouri
Lead-Time Analysis	c	n/a	c	y	c	n/a	c	n/a		n/a	n/a	y	y	y	c	c	y	n/a			y	c	y	c	y
Automated Procurement System	y	c	y	y	y	y	c			y	c	y	y	y	y	y	y	y			y	y	y	y	y
Amount by Vendor	y	c	y	y	y	y	y			y	c	y	y	y	y	c	y	y			y	y	y	y	y
Amount by Commodity	y	c	y	y	y	y	c			y	c	c	y	y	y	y	c	y	y			y	y	y	y
Total Amount	y	y	y	y	y	c	y			c	c	y	y	y	y	c	c	y			y	y	c	y
EO Maintainer	n/a	vendor	vendor	n/a	state	vendor	vendor	n/a		n/a	vendor	combo	vendor	vendor	vendor	vendor	combo	n/a	vendor		combo	vendor	vendor	vendor	n/a
Electronic Ordering	c	y	y	c	y	y	y	c		c	y	y	y	y	y	y	c	y			y	y	y	y	c	y
Reverse Auction	c	c	c	c	c	c	c	c		c	c	c	c	c	c	c	c	c			c	c	y	c	y
Internet Bidding	c	c	c	c	c	c	c	c		c	c	y	c	c	c	y	c	y			y	y	y	c	y
Governing Internet Bidding	c	c	c	c	c	y	c	c		c	c	y	c	c	c	c	y			c	n/a	y	c	y
DS for Procurement Document	c	c	c	c	c	c	c			c	c	y	c	c	c	c	c	y			c	c	y	c	c
DS for Internal Approval	c	c	c	c	c	c	c			c	c	c	y	c	c	c	c	y	y	n/a		c	c	y	c	n/a
Digital Signature Legislation	c	c	y	y	y	y	y	c		c	y	y	y	y	y	y	y	y	n/a		c	c	y	y	y
Contract Award on Web	y	y	y	y	y	y	y	y		y	y	y	c	y	c	y	y	y			y	c	c	y	y
Web Solicitation	c	y	y	c	y	y	y	y		y	y	y	y	y	y	y	y	y			y	y	y	y	y

Table 8.A.2: 2001 Combined Procurement Survey—The 2001 NASPO Survey and 2001 Follow-Up E-Mail Survey (continued)

State	Lead-Time Analysis	Automated Procurement System	Amount by Vendor	Amount by Commodity	Total Amount	EO Maintainer	Electronic Ordering	Reverse Auction	Internet Bidding	Governing Internet Bidding	DS for Procurement Document	DS for Internal Approval	Digital Signature Legislation	Contract Award on Web	Web Solicitation
Montana	n/a	n	y	y	n	n/a	n	n	n	n	n	n	y	y	y
Nebraska	n	y	n	n	n	vendor	y	n	n	n	n	n	y	y	y
Nevada	y	y	y	y	y	vendor	y	n	n	n	n	n	y	y	y
New Hampshire															
New Jersey	y	y	y	y	y	n/a	n	n	n	n	n	n	y	y	y
New Mexico	y	y	y	y	n/a	vendor	y	n	n	n	n	y	y	y	y
New York	n	y	y	y	y	vendor	y	n	y	n	n	n	y	y	y
North Carolina	y	y	y	y	y	vendor	n	n	n	y	n	n	y	y	y
North Dakota	n	y	n	n	y	n/a	y	n	n	n	n	n	y	y	n
Ohio	n/a	n	y	n/a	n/a	state	n	n	y	n	n	n	y	y	y
Oklahoma	n	y	n	n	n/a	vendor	n	n	n	n	y	n	n	y	n
Oregon	n	y	y	y	n	n/a	y	n	y	y	y	n	n	n	n
Pennsylvania	n/a	y	n	y	y	state	n	y	n	n	n	n	y	y	y
Rhode Island	y	y	y	y	n	n/a	y	n	y	y	n	n	y	y	y
South Carolina	n	n	y	y	n	vendor	n	n	n	n	n	y	y	y	y
South Dakota	n/a	y	n/a	n/a	y	n/a	n	n	n	n	n	y	y	y	n
Tennessee	y	y	y	y	y	n/a	y	n	y	y	y	y	n/a	y	y
Texas	y	y	y	y	n	vendor	y	n	n	y	y	n	n	y	y
Utah	n	y	y	y	y	vendor	y	n	y	n	n	n	y	y	y
Vermont	n	y	y	y	y	vendor	y	n	n	n	n	n	n	y	y
Virginia	y	y	y	y	n/a	state	y	y	y	n	y	n/a	y	y	y
Washington	n	y	y	y	y	vendor	y	n	n/a	n/a	y	n	y	y	y
West Virginia	n	y	n	n	y	vendor	y	n	n	n	n	n	n	y	y
Wisconsin	n/a	y	n	n	y	n/a	n/a	y	y	y	n/a	n/a	n/a	n/a	y
Wyoming	n	y	y	y	y	combo	y	n	y	y	n	n	n	y	y

Table 8.A.2: 2001 Combined Procurement Survey—The 2001 NASPO Survey and 2001 Follow-Up E-Mail Survey (continued)

State	Time Saving	Cost Saving	Fleet Management	PC Linked to Accounting System	Cost Recovery for PC	PC for Travel	PC for Statewide Contract	Purchasing Card	Asset Management	Integrated to E-Commerce	EDI Element
Alabama	n	n	y	n/a	n/a	y	n/a	n	y	n	n/a
Alaska	n	n	y	y	n	y	y	y	y	n/a	n/a
Arizona	n	n	y	n	y	y	y	y	n/a	n	n
Arkansas	n/a	n/a	n/a	n/a	n/a	y	n/a	n	n	n/a	y
California	y	y	y	n	y	y	y	y	y	n	n
Colorado	n/a	n/a	y	n/a	n	y	y	y	n	y	y
Connecticut	y	y	n	y	n	y	y	y	n	y	y
Delaware	n	n	y	n	n	y	y	y	n	n/a	n/a
Florida				n/a					n/a		
Georgia	n/a	n/a	y	n/a	n	y	y	y	n	n	n/a
Hawaii	n/a	n/a	n	y	n	n	n/a	n	n/a	n/a	n/a
Idaho			y	y	n	y	y	y	y	y	y
Illinois	n	n	y	n/a	n/a	y	n/a	n	n	n	n
Indiana	y	y	y	n/a	n/a	y	n/a	n	y	n	y
Iowa	n/a	n/a	y	n	y	y	y	y	n	n	n
Kansas	y	y	y	n	n	y	y	y	y	y	y
Kentucky	n/a	n/a	y	y	n/a	y	y	y	n	y	y
Louisiana			y	n	n/a	y	y	y	y	n	n
Maine	y	y	y	y	n/a	y	y	y	n	y	y
Maryland											
Massachusetts	y	y	y	n	n	y	y	y	n	y	y
Michigan	n/a	y	y	n	n	y	y	y	n	n	n
Minnesota	n	y	y	n	n	y	y	y	n	n	y
Mississippi	y	y	y	n	n	y	y	y	n	n	n
Missouri	n	n/a	y	n/a	n	y	y	y	y	n	n

Table 8.A.2: 2001 Combined Procurement Survey—The 2001 NASPO Survey and 2001 Follow-Up E-Mail Survey (continued)

State	Time Saving	Cost Saving	Fleet Management	PC Linked to Accounting System	Cost Recovery for PC	PC for Travel	PC for Statewide Contract	Purchasing Card	Asset Management	Integrated to E-Commerce	EDI Element
Montana			y	y	n	y	y	y	n/a	n/a	n/a
Nebraska			y	n	n	y	y	y	n	n	n
Nevada	n	n	n	n	n	y	y	y	y	y	y
New Hampshire											
New Jersey	n/a	n/a	n	y	n	n	y	y	n	y	y
New Mexico			y	n/a	n	y	y	y	n	n	y
New York	n/a	n/a	y	y	n	y	y	y	n	n	n
North Carolina	n/a	n/a	y	y	n	y	y	y	y	y	y
North Dakota	y	y	y	y	n/a	n	y	y	n	n	n/a
Ohio			y	n	n	y	y	y	n/a	n/a	n/a
Oklahoma	n/a	n/a	y	n	n	y	n	y	n	n	n
Oregon	y	y	y	y	y	n/a	y	y	n	n	n
Pennsylvania	y	y	y	y	n/a	y	n/a	n	n/a	n	y
Rhode Island	y	y	y	n/a	n	y	y	y	y	y	n/a
South Carolina	n	n	y	n	n	y	y	y	n	n	n
South Dakota	n/a	n/a	y	y	n	y	n	y	n/a	n/a	n/a
Tennessee			y	n	n	y	y	n	n	y	n
Texas	y	y	y	n	n	y	y	y	y	y	y
Utah			y	y	n	y	y	n	n	n	n
Vermont			n	n	n	y	y	y	n	n	n
Virginia	n	n	n	n	n/a	n	y	y	y	n/a	y
Washington			y	y	y	y	y	y	n	y	y
West Virginia			y	n/a	n/a	y	y	y	n	n	n
Wisconsin	n/a	n/a	y	n	n	y	y	y	n/a	n/a	n/a
Wyoming	y	y	y	y	n	y	y	y	y	y	n

Appendix III:
Survey Instrument for the
2001 E-Mail Follow-Up Survey

Survey instrument is adopted from the 2001 NASPO survey to update information and fill in missing information.

1. Is the central procurement office posting solicitation/bids on the Web?
2. Is the central procurement office posting contract award information on the Web?
3. Has the state enacted digital signature law?
   1) If yes, what is the citation?
   2) If yes, please provide a summary of the law.
4. Does the state use digital signatures to route and approve documents internally?
5. Is the state accepting digital signatures as legally binding signatures from the vendor community on the procurement documents?
   1) If yes, which documents?
6. Has the state central procurement office developed procedures or have statutes governing Internet bidding?
7. Has the state central procurement office conducted bids via the Internet?
8. Has the state central procurement office conducted reverse auctions?
9. Does the state utilize electronic ordering?
   1) If yes, is the ordering system state or vendor maintained?
10. If the ordering system is state maintained:
    1) What standard do you use?
    2) What service provider does the central procurement office use?
    3) Is there a vendor fee or a fee to the customer?
11. Does the central procurement office maintain records of the overall dollar volume of purchase issued by central purchasing and delegated agencies (Yes, No, Other agency)?
12. Can the central procurement office tracks dollars spent by type of commodity or service (Yes, No, Other agency)?
13. Can the central procurement office track dollars spent by vendor (Yes, No, Other agency)?

Automated Procurement System

14. Does the central procurement office have an automated procurement system?

If yes, please indicate if the system supports the following capabilities:
1) a) Vendors automatically purged
   b) Vendors automatically selected
   c) Notice distribution of Invitation to bids and Requests for pro-
      posal via E-mail, Fax, Hard copy, or Other?
2) On demand electronic distribution of Invitation for Bids and
   Requests for Proposals (via Fax on demand, Internet download,
   Other)?
3) Vendor performance (via Vendor notes screen, Vendor performance screen, or Linked vendor notes and performance screens)?
4) a) Can purchase order form be easily modified?
   b) Do purchase orders look as they are printed?
   c) Can blanket purchase orders or contract be used?
   d) Can contracts be searched for goods and services?
5) a) Are Invitation to Bid templates available?
   b) What standard PC Suites software can be used in Invitation to
      Bid?
   c) Do you have the ability to use standard terms and conditions
      language in an Invitation to Bid?
   d) Do you have the ability to choose standard language for each
      Invitation
   e) Can the Invitation to Bid be downloaded from the Internet?
   f) Can the system handle sealed bids?
6) a) Can appropriate terms and conditions be copied to purchase
      orders and contracts?
   b) Can purchase order and contract be printed at remote location?
   c) Capable for online requisitioning from the agency customer?
   d) Is the system capable of electronic routing and approvals?
7) Is the system capable of workload assignment and status?
8) Will the system document purchasing process milestones or
   timelines?
9) Will the system provide lead-time analysis?
10) Will the system record and prompt for pending action?
11) Does the system have commodity code capability?
12) Does the system have keyword search?
13) Which commodity codes are utilized?
14) Does the program allow for forms to be downloaded?
15) Is the system EDI capable?
16) Does the system support online receiving?
17) Does the system provide integrated electronic commerce?
18) Does the system support delegated authority?
19) Is the system integrated with an asset management system?

Purchasing Cards

15. Does the state have a purchasing card?
16. What are the typical dollar limits placed on the card (Single limit, Daily limit, Cycle purchase limit)?
17. Does the state allow purchasing cards to be used for purchasing from statewide contracts?
18. What is the estimated monthly transaction volume using the purchasing card?
19. Which credit card and bank is the state using?
20. Does your state use a credit card for travel?
    1) If yes, is it the same credit card as for general procurement?
21. Is use of purchasing cards optional?
22. Does the state fund the purchasing card program through a fee-based cost recovery? If yes, what is the fee?
23. What products/services are disallowed for use with the purchasing card program?
24. Do the purchasing card transactions electronically post to your statewide accounting system?
25. Does the state remit monthly payments via wire transfer/ACH?
26. Do you have a fleet management purchasing card?
    1) If yes, what fleet card processor is the state using?
27. Is there a state travel office?
28. Is the travel office within the CPO? If no, where is it located?
29. Does the travel office administer contract for Travel Agency Service?
    1) If no, how are these services provided to the agencies?
    2) Does the state administer contracts for air fares?
30. Does the state administer contracts for car rental?
31. Does the state administer contracts for hotel/motel?
32. Have you made any cost saving through e-procurement?
    1) If yes, how much cost did you save last year?
33. Have you made any time saving through e-procurement?
    1) If yes, how much time did you save last year?

Endnotes

1. This research is supported by a generous grant from The PricewaterhouseCoopers Endowment for The Business of Government. The author wants to thank the excellent research assistance of Jwa Young Poo, Deserai Anderson-Utley, Hae Won Kwon, and Jongyun Ahn.

2. Definitions of related terms are available at the website of National Electronic Commerce Coordinating Council: http://www.ec3.org/InfoCenter/02_WorkGroups/2000_Workgroups/eprocurement/definitions.htm.

3. This section builds on a previous paper (Moon, 2002). Some parts of the paper reappear in revised form in this section.

4. EDI standards have been established to promote any commonly used data (documents) found in routine business transactions.

5. BUYNET can be accessed via the Purchasing and Contracting website: www.co.san-diego.ca.us/cnty/cntydepts/general/prchcntr/newfctns.hts.

6. Advantages and disadvantages of each model are well summarized in NECCC (2001a), *Electronic Procurement: Funding Models and Measurement to Success.*
Also see Johnson (2002), "Financing and Pricing E-Service." In Gant, Gant, and Johnson, *State Web Portals: Delivering and Financing E-Service.* The PricewaterhouseCoopers Endowment for The Business of Government.

7. Punch-out includes product selectors and product configurators. Product selectors refer to the technical applications that allow buyers to figure out specific applications of a product based on detailed characteristics of the product. It helps and supports selecting an appropriate product for a given application. Product configurators are a little different from product selectors in that they are equipped with the capacity to customize particular products within given criteria. For more details, see NECCC (2001b), p. 8.

8. There are 3-digit (class), 5-digit (item), 7-digit (group), and 10-digit (detailed item description) codes. For example, 615-45-29-028 is a 10-digit code. 615 indicates general office supplies, 45 is for file folders (regular, legal, and letter sizes). 615-45-29 indicates file folders, double tab, legal size, manila, standard height (overall 14-3/4 in. x 9-1/2 in.). 615-45-29-028 is file folders, one-third cut, 9-1/2 point, 100/box. The 3-digit level code does not require licensing but 5-digit and more upper-level codes require licensing. For more details, see NECCC (2001b), pp. 14–15.

9. The UNSPSC is accepted as the universal standard by the Electronic Commerce Code Management Association (ECCMA) and can be used without any licensing fees. There are four levels in the code hierarchy (segment, family, class, and commodity). Each hierarchical level has two to three digits for the code. For more details, see NECCC (2001b), pp. 15–17.

10. The NASPO surveys are summarized in NASPO Survey of State and Local Government Purchasing Practices (1998) and NASPO Survey of State and Local Government Purchasing Practices (2001a).

11. Nonresponding states are Alaska, Kentucky, and New Hampshire.

12. The seven states that did not respond are Alabama, Delaware, Florida, Maryland, New Hampshire, Oregon, and Wisconsin.

13. It should be noted that the 2001 NASPO survey reflects state e-procurement from 2000 since the survey was conducted in 2000 and published in 2001.

14. Nonresponding states are Florida, Georgia, Illinois, Indiana, Maryland, Montana, Nebraska, New Hampshire, New Jersey, New York, Oklahoma, Texas, Vermont, Virginia, and West Virginia.

15. For more details, see Kalkota and Whinston (1997), p. 142.

16. They are California, Connecticut, Kentucky, Louisiana, Massachusetts, Michigan, Minnesota, Mississippi, Ohio, Pennsylvania, South Carolina, Utah, and Wyoming.

17. The states include California, Connecticut, Kentucky, Louisiana, Massachusetts, Mississippi, Ohio, Pennsylvania, South Carolina, Utah, and Wyoming.

Bibliography

Anderson, Kim. "Reengineering Public Sector Organizations Using Information Technology." In *Reinventing Government in the Information Age,* New York, Routledge, 1999, pp. 312–330.

Atwater, Kristin. "Virginia Revolutionizes Virtual Sphere of Procurement." *Government Procurement,* June 2001, pp. 7–10.

Bozeman, B. and S. Bretschneider. "Public Management Information System: Theory and Perception." *Public Administration Review* (46) 1986, pp. 475–487.

Bretschneider, S. "Managing Information Systems in Public and Private Organizations: An Empirical Test." *Public Administration Review* (50) 1990, pp. 536–545.

Brown, Douglas. "Information Systems for Improved Performance Management: Development Approaches in US Public Agencies." In *Reinventing Government in the Information Age,* ed. Richard Heeks. New York, Routledge, 1999, pp. 113–134.

Cats-Baril, W. and R. Thompson. "Managing Information Technology Projects in the Public Sector." *Public Administration Review* (55) 1995, pp. 559–566.

Caudle, Sharon. "Federal Information Resource Management after the Paperwork Reduction Act." *Public Administration Review* (4) 48, 1988, pp. 790–799.

Caudle, Sharon. "Strategic Information Resources Management: Fundamental Practices." *Government Information Quarterly* (1) 13, 1996, pp. 83–97.

Daukantas, Patricia. "PTO Starts E-government Shift." *Government Computer News* (33) 2000, p. 198. http://www.gcn.com/vo119_no33/news/3327-1.html. Accessed September 7, 2001.

Fletcher, P. "Local Government and IRM: Policy Emerging from Practice." *Government Information Quarterly.* (14) 1997, pp. 313–324.

Fountain, J. "The Virtual State: Toward a Theory of Federal Bureaucracy." In *democracy.com? Governance in Networked Word,* ed. Elaine Ciulla Kamarck and Joseph S. Nye. Jr., New Hampshire, Hollis Publishing Company, 1999.

Fountain, Jane. *Building the Virtual State: Information Technology and Institutional Change.* Washington, D.C., Brookings Institution Press, 2001.

General Accounting Office (GAO). *Purchasing Cards: Control Weaknesses Leave Two Navy Units Vulnerable to Fraud and Abuse.* Washington, D.C., 2001.

Gore, Albert. *Creating a Government That Works Better and Costs Less: Reengineering Through Information Technology.* Report of the National Performance Review, Washington D.C., U.S. Government Printing Office, 1993.

Government and the Internet Survey. "Handle with Care." *The Economist* (8176) 355, 2000, pp. 33–34.

Gunyou, John and Jane Leonard. "Getting Ready for E-commerce." *Government Finance Review* Vol. 14, No. 5, 1998, pp. 9–12.

Hart-Teeter, Inc. *EGovernment: The Next Revolution*. Washington, D.C., Council for Excellence in Government, 2000.

Hiller, Janine and France Bélanger. *Privacy Strategies for Electronic Government*. The PricewaterhouseCoopers Endowment for The Business of Government, 2001.

Joint Task Force on Information Technology of the National Association of State Purchasing Officers and the National Association of State Information Resource Executives (JTFIT). *Buying Smart: State Procurement Saves Millions*. White paper. National, 1996. http://www.naspo.org/whitepapers/buyingsmart.cfm. Accessed October 13, 2001.

Johnson, Craig. "Financing and Pricing E-Service." In Gant, Gant, and Johnson. *State Web Portals: Delivering and Financing E-Service*. The IBM Endowment for The Business of Government, 2002.

Kalakota, Ravi and Andrew Whinston. *Electronic Commerce: A Manager's Guide*. Reading, Addison Wesley Longman, Inc., 1997.

Layne, Karen and Jungwoo Lee. "Developing Fully Functional E-Government: A Four Stage Model." *Government Information Quarterly* (2) 18, 2001, pp. 122–136.

Maryland Department of General Services. *eMaryland @ Marketplace 2001 Annual Report*. 2001.

Moon, M. Jae. "Evolution of Municipal E-Government: Rhetoric or Reality." *Public Administration Review* (4) 62, 2002, pp. 400–409.

Moon, M. Jae and Stuart Bretschneider. "Does the Perception of Red Tape Constrain IT Innovativeness in Organizations? Unexpected Results from a Simultaneous Equation Model and Implications." *Journal of Public Administration and Research and Theory* (2) 12, 2002, pp. 273–292.

Morehead, Nicholas. "Minnesota Tests Reverse Auctions." *Civic.com*. July 18, 2001.

Multi-State EMall™ Team. *Pilot Project Evaluation: A Multi-State Cooperative Procurement System on the Internet*. Office of the Comptroller, Operational Services Division, October 12, 1999.

Multi-State EMall™ Team. *Multi-State eMall: Procurement Powered by Intelisys*. Presented at NASPO 2000 Marketing Meeting. http://www.state.ma.us/emall/. Accessed April 10, 2002.

Musso, Juliet, Christopher Weare, and Matt Hale. "Designing Web Technologies for Local Governance Reform: Good Management or Good Democracy." *Political Communication* (1) 17, 2000, pp. 1–19.

National Association of State Procurement Officials. *NASPO Survey of State and Local Government Purchasing Practices.* 1998.

National Association of State Procurement Officials. 2001a. *NASPO Survey of State and Local Government Purchasing Practices.* 2001.

National Association of State Procurement Officials. 2001b. *NASPO State and Local Government Purchasing Principles and Practices.* 2001.

NECCC. 2000a. *Electronic Payments Primer.* National Electronic Commerce Coordinating Council Symposium 2001. Presented at the NECCC Annual Conference. Las Vegas, Nevada, December 13, 2000.

NECCC. 2000b. *Funding E-Procurement System Acquisition.* National Electronic Commerce Coordinating Council Symposium 2000. Presented at the NECCC Annual Conference. Las Vegas, Nevada, December 13, 2000.

NECCC. 2000c. *E-Government Strategic Planning: A White Paper.* National Electronic Commerce Coordinating Council Symposium 2000. Presented at the NECCC Annual Conference. Las Vegas, Nevada, December 13, 2000.

NECCC. 2001a. *Electronic Procurement: Funding Models and Measurement for Success.* National Electronic Commerce Coordinating Council Symposium 2001. Presented at the NECCC Annual Conference. Las Vegas, Nevada, December 10–12, 2001.

NECCC. 2001b. *Is the Lack of E-procurement Standards...a Barrier to Implementation? A Government and Supplier Perspective.* National Electronic Commerce Coordinating Council Symposium 2001. Presented at the NECCC Annual Conference. Las Vegas, Nevada, December 10–12, 2001.

Neef, Dale. *eProcurement: From Strategy to Implementation.* Upper Saddle River, New Jersey Prentice Hall, 2001.

Norris, Donald and Kenneth Kreamer. "Mainframe and PC Computing in American Cities: Myths and Realities." *Public Administration Review* (6) 56, 1996, pp. 568–576.

Norris, Pippa. "Who Surfs? New Technology, Old Voters, and Virtual Democracy." In *democracy.com? Governance in Networked Word,* ed. Elaine Ciulla Kamarck and Joseph S. Nye, Jr., New Hampshire, Hollis Publishing Company, 1999, pp. 71–94.

Nye, Jr., Joseph. "Information Technology and Democratic Governance." In *democracy.com? Governance in Networked Word,* ed. Elaine Ciulla Kamarck and Joseph S. Nye, Jr., New Hampshire, Hollis Publishing Company, 1999, pp. 1–18.

O'Hara, Colleen. "GSA Moves Ahead with Reverse Auctions." *Federal Computer Week,* June 6, 2001.

Preston, Morag. "E-government US-style." *New Statesman* (4517) 129, Special Supplement, 2000.

Robinson, Brian. "Down Payment on E-Procurement." *Federal Computer Week,* August 20, 2001.

Sarkar, Dibya. 2001a. "States Team up for E-Buying." *Civic.com.* August 22, 2001.

Sarkar, Dibya. 2001b. "States Premature on E-Procurement." *Government e-Business.* September 3, 2001.

Sarkar, Dibya. 2001c. States Buy into E-Buying." *Civic.com.* April 2, 2001.

Schriener, Juday and William Angelo. "Procurement Going Paperless." *ENR.* October 2, 1995, p. 13.

Sprecher, Milford. "Racing to E-government: Using the Internet for Citizen Service Delivery." *Government Finance Review,* (5) 16, 2000, pp. 21–22.

The Virginia Governor's Task Force on Procurement Assessment, 2000. *Report of the Governor's Task Force on Procurement Assessment: Recommendations to Improve Virginia Government's Procurement Systems.* February 3, 2000.

Utah Division of Purchasing and General Services. Description of the Utah/Colorado E-Procurement System. http://www.purchasing.state.ut.us/eps/description.htm. Accessed October 22, 2001.

Ventura, Stephen. J. "The Use of Geographic Information Systems in Local Government." *Public Administration Review,* (5) 55, 1995, pp. 461–467.

Weare, Christopher, Juliet Musso, and Matt Hale. "Electronic Democracy and the Diffusion of Municipal Web Pages in California." *Administration and Society,* (1) 31, 1999, pp. 3–27.

West, D.M. *E-Government and the Transformation of Public Service Delivery.* Presented at the American Political Science Association Annual Meeting. San Francisco, August 30–September 2, 2001.

White House Press Office. "President Clinton and Vice-President Gore: Major New E-Government Initiatives." *US Newswire.* June 24, 2000. http://web.lexis-nexis.com/universe...d5=0f245defaacf01afe17703e5dfd7da67. Accessed September 7, 2001.

Wood, Lawrence. "The Beginning of the End of Paper Procurement." Government Finance Review. June 2000, p. 38.

CHAPTER NINE

Transforming Procurement:
The Potential of Auctions

David C. Wyld
Associate Professor
Southeastern Louisiana University
Department of Management

Introduction

Overview

This chapter is a sequel of sorts, in that it builds upon the author's previous grant report for the IBM Endowment for The Business of Government. *The Auction Model: How the Public Sector Can Leverage the Power of E-Commerce Through Dynamic Pricing* was published in October 2000. This first report generated a great deal of interest, both inside and outside of government and in the popular and academic press, as it looked at the concept of dynamic (non-fixed) pricing and how government could employ auctions for better management of its resources. In the time since the publication of *The Auction Model*, the author has continued his research in the B2G (business-to-government) marketspace.

Despite the downturn in the economy and the death of many of the "dot-com" companies that helped usher in the "e" revolution, remarkable changes continue to occur across the economy—and in government as well. If the 1980s and 1990s had "megatrends," this first decade of a new century

---

A Cartoon about American Government Online Auction Sales That Originally Appeared in the German Business Daily, *Handelsblatt*

HAT VON EUCH JEMAND ÜBER' S INTERNET DIE FREIHEITSSTATUE BESTELLT?

Translated: "Did one of you order the Statue of Liberty over the Internet?"

Source: Hillenbrand, Thomas. "Der Staat Ist Der Beste Kunde." Handelsblatt (February 14, 2001): p. 52.

can be said to have what Paul Boutin (2001) coined "gigatrends." Certainly, e-government is such a gigatrend (as shown in Figure 9.1), being just one of the myriad of evident, tangible ways that the Internet is changing relationships between individuals, businesses, and the government. Over the past year, the e-government revolution has been accelerating, and interest has been growing at all levels of government and in how to best apply the Internet to government processes and services.

Figure 9.1: The Gigatrends of E-Government in the 21st Century

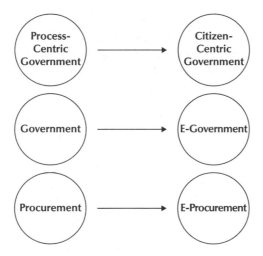

Mark Gibbs (2000) exclaimed: "E-government! Gad, but am I tired of 'e-this' and 'i-that'! Everywhere you turn, virtually and otherwise, it is e-something" (p. 1). In short order, however, e-government will likely prove that "This ain't your father's government!" (Schwartz, 2000, p. 187).

When we speak of e-government, there is really only one ultimate "customer" for government—namely the citizen. Much of the emphasis in the e-government movement has been turning the governmental paradigm upside down—and perhaps righting it in the process—to where there is a "citizen-centric" focus to governmental activities. Instead of agencies being focused on their missions and their operations, the goal of e-government can ultimately be said to bring a customer—or rather a citizen—focus to governmental operations. While outside of the scope of this research, a great deal of time, money, and attention is being directed towards designing "portals" that can enable citizens to better interact with the government in a seamless fashion across agencies—and even levels of government—in order to more easily interact with "the" government for their needs (Deloitte Research, 2000a).

E-government is thus a broad, all-encompassing term for efforts of all governments to make use of the Internet to connect with their citizens. The Gartner Group has defined the e-government market as actually consisting of three, distinct segments. These are:

1. G2C—Government-to-Citizen
2. G2G—Government-to-Government
3. G2B—Government-to-Business (or Supplier) (cited in Enterworks, 2000, p. 4).

In like fashion, the broader realm of e-commerce strategies can be viewed as either being:

- "Customer-facing," or
- "Vendor-facing" (Appell and Brousseau, 2000, p. 85).

Thus, e-government strategies, while ultimately of benefit to the public, can be viewed as being directed at citizen services (customer-facing) or supply-chain activities (vendor-facing).

While e-government encompasses many areas, with most focusing on *direct* government services to citizens, one of the areas drawing the most attention is what can be called the government's supply chain. Specifically, this research examines the e-sourcing activities at two critical "pain points" in the governmental supply chain—"touch points"—between governmental organization and its internal and external processes (Deloitte Research, 2001b). Attention in the B2G market has been increasingly directed at two areas where dynamic commerce can be applied in the governmental supply chain, specifically:

- E-procurement, and
- Asset disposition.

Up front, there is an important differentiation to be made between *dynamic commerce* and *dynamic pricing*. As Appell and Brousseau (2000) both demarcated and interlinked the terms:

> *Dynamic pricing* describes a process in which goods and services are traded in markets where price adjusts freely to supply and demand. However, pricing is just one of the data points used during the valuation of an offer. Since the exchange of goods and services often entails valuation of many variables beyond price, the notion of 'commerce' best captures the breadth and complexity of real-world business requirements…. Thus, *dynamic commerce* can be defined as the exchange of goods and services in electronic markets where not only price, but also other factors, fluctuate freely while all participants enjoy significantly lower interaction costs (p. 83).

This differentiation is graphically depicted in Figure 9.2.

Figure 9.2: Dynamic Commerce and Dynamic Pricing

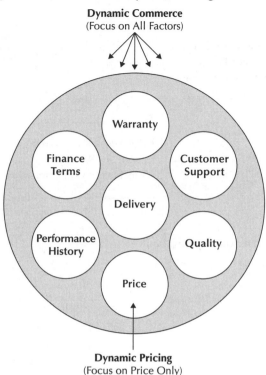

This chapter begins with an overview of both the business-to-business landscape and the trajectory of e-government to date. It then examines how dynamic commerce applications are taking hold in the public sector, helping to shape the e-government environment. Specifically, it looks in some detail at three broad areas where dynamic commerce models are currently beginning to be used in the public sector. These are:

1. *Reverse* auctions
2. Demand aggregation
3. *Forward* auctions

Two general auction archetypes form the basis of dynamic commerce models. From a definitional perspective, the differentiation between these two primary types of auctions—*reverse* and *forward* auctions—is provided in Figure 9.3. As can be seen in Figure 9.4, demand aggregation is another dynamic commerce tool that can be used to combine demand for similar products—and conceivably even services—both within and across organizations by pooling demand to make for larger purchases.

This chapter examines how each concept is being applied at various levels of government in the United States, with models and suggestions for how

Figure 9.3: The Two Types of Auctions

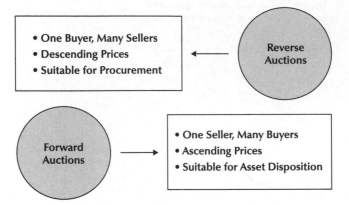

- One Buyer, Many Sellers
- Descending Prices
- Suitable for Procurement

Reverse Auctions

Forward Auctions

- One Seller, Many Buyers
- Ascending Prices
- Suitable for Asset Disposition

Figure 9.4: What Is Demand Aggregation?

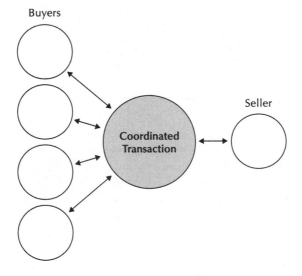

Buyers

Coordinated Transaction

Seller

to better implement the auction model in the public sector. Examples span the Department of Defense at the federal level and across the United States, from the State of Florida to the County of Los Angeles. We will see how online auctions are being used by government to buy everything from coal to computers and to sell everything from used cars to donkeys—literally. We will see that much of the implementation in all areas remains largely in the test and pilot project stages, still awaiting full-scale implementation. We will see how new adaptations of these models, such as multiparametric auctions, may work particularly well in public sector applications, given the complex and multifaceted nature of governmental procurement.

Additionally, the author has conducted interviews with:

- Leaders in e-procurement reform in the public sector;
- Individuals who are leading firms seeking to service the governmental e-procurement and asset disposition market; and
- Public policy analysts observing government's adoption of e-commerce techniques and technologies.

Excerpts from these interviews are interspersed in this chapter to lend additional insights into how e-procurement and online asset disposition fit into the overall movement towards e-government as we enter the 21st century.

In the recommendations section of this chapter, the author explores matters that will determine the trajectory and pace of growth in applying these dynamic commerce concepts in the governmental supply chain. The critical issues of assessing and funding such initiatives are looked at in detail. Then, attention is turned to aspects critical to successfully implementing not only aspects of dynamic e-procurement and online asset auctioning, but e-government in general. These include the questions of:

- How do we foster greater collaboration in government?
- How do we deal with a changing workforce?
- How do we contend with the technical needs?
- Why does effective leadership matter?

The author then examines areas in which future research should be conducted and suggests models and programs for the study of the B2G arena.

In sum, the message is hopeful. We will see that great progress has been made in developing not just a single auction model, but in creating implementable auctioning concepts throughout the e-governmental supply chain. We will see that this is not the final word, but the beginning. We will see that we are still in the early stages of putting these technologies into practice, on our way to making government—and governance—"faster, better, cheaper" for us all.

After the Fire ... The Internet Revolution

Because of the confluence of forces that have brought it about and the sweeping effect that it is having across business and society, borrowing on the book and movie analogy, the Internet has been characterized as "the perfect storm" (Tapscott, Ticoll, and Lowy, 2000, p. 1). Yet, this perfect storm has simultaneously brought about both great creation *and* destruction. Entirely new ways of doing business have rapidly emerged and totally new industries have been created. Yet, we have also witnessed a rapid decline in the value and numbers of firms in the so-called "New Economy."

Hammonds (2001) framed the matter very succinctly:

The Internet economy—a freestanding, all-techie economic zone—may never have existed. But there is *the* economy. And the Internet is one powerful force to transform it.... The new economy was truly defined by changes that were far more fundamental than the IPO explosion ... (and) that's what the new economy is all about, folks. The stock market was a sideshow, by definition a derivative of the real thing (emphasis in the original, pp. 117-118).

In the view of Litan (2001) and others, we should not let the burst of the "dot-com bubble" that has occurred—with the paring of fully two-thirds of the value of the NASDAQ index—cloud the reality of the revolutionary nature of the Internet. As he stated: "No one disputes the transformative impact of the railroad and the automobile, even though thousands of such companies that were once in business aren't anymore.... New technologies do more than just create new firms and consumer products. They change the way that firms throughout the economy do business" (Litan, 2001, p. 16). As Michael Bloomberg, mayor of New York City and former chairman and CEO of Bloomberg, LP, stated in an interview: "I don't think there is a new economy. I think there are new tools for *the* economy" (emphasis in the original) (quoted in Canabou and Overholt, 2001, p. 109). What we have seen, in the observation of Pravesh Mehra, a B2B specialist with Cap Gemini Ernst & Young, is that many have mistaken the tools and methods introduced in the Internet economy *as the* Internet economy, for a "method really doesn't add value" (quoted in Saba, 2001a, p. 29).

In the "post-Internet bubble" environment of today, the new reality is that "e" has a stigma attached to it. No longer is "e" regarded as inevitable or best—Internet technology is not being bought just because it is available, and there is a newfound demand for return on investment to come quickly. In the words of Cleary (2001), buyers of e-commerce applications are increasingly focusing on the question—"Tell me what I get out of this"— especially as *actual* returns have often been mere fractions of those promised by B2B vendors and analysts (Cleary, 2001).

As Hamm (2001) plainly characterized the present situation, "It's hard to ignore the economy when it comes up and slaps you hard across the face" (p. 126). Today's economic slowdown has been largely caused—in the opinion of many—by the extreme slowdown in the technology sector. As one writer put it, the personal computer industry is facing an environment equivalent to what the automakers would face "if everyone who already owned a car suddenly stopped buying new ones" (Spangler, 2001).

B2B has suddenly become "a scary place to be" (Ante and Weintraub, 2000). As a part of the overall Internet or "new" economy, today the B2B environment has done a 180 degree turn from the hype days of 1999 and early 2000, the heyday of public trading exchanges. We have witnessed what has been labeled the "dot-bomb" phenomenon, and certainly, as LaMonica (2001c) observed, "the bloom is off the rose" of B2B e-commerce (p. 5) and "it's now fashionable to say that exchanges—and the business-to-business market overall—are dead" (LaMonica, 2001b, p. 18).

"The Rocket-Ship Ride" of B2B E-Commerce

If only with a bit less thrust than it previously had, B2B e-commerce still appears to be on what has been described as a "rocket-ship ride" trajectory (Sostrom, 2001). After all, as Charles E. Phillips, a managing director at Morgan Stanley Dean Witter, observed, the move toward e-commerce is not likely to be deterred by the downturn in the economy. As he stated: "Even in hard times, I don't think that a single big company is prepared to say, 'Paper is fine. Let's keep doing it the old way'" (quoted in Canabou, 2001, p. 90).

As can be seen in Table 9.1 below, leading research firms still project rapid growth in the B2B sector of the economy, from under a trillion dollars this year (2001) to anywhere between approximately $3 and $6 trillion just three or fours hence. The four analyst firms' projections are graphically depicted in Figure 9.5.

Taking all these current projections into account, the consensus forecast (presented in Figure 9.6) is that B2B revenue should approach $4 *trillion* by 2004 and $5 *trillion* by 2005. However, Gordon (2001) acknowledged that while *excessive optimism* fueled the growth of B2B markets, today's environment may be characterized as being *excessively pessimistic*. Thus, the forecasts—especially in today's environment—may understate how fast and pervasive the movement of B2B transactions online may occur.

So what is the true state of the Internet economy? As Scott McNealy, CEO of Sun Microsystems, pointed out, the phrase "dot-com" is a misnomer,

Table 9.1: B2B Growth Forecasts (expressed in *trillions* of dollars)

	2000	2001	2002	2003	2004	2005
AMR Research	$0.40	$0.70	$1.20	$2.40	$5.70	
Gartner, Inc.	$0.20	$0.50	$0.90	$1.80	$2.70	$3.70
Forrester Research	$0.45	$0.70	$1.15	$1.85	$2.65	
Jupiter Research	$0.30	$0.90	$1.50	$3.00	$4.70	$6.25
Consensus Forecast	$0.34	$0.70	$1.19	$2.26	$3.94	$4.98

Source: The Wall Street Journal (Totty, 2001, p. R9).

Figure 9.5: B2B Growth Forecast

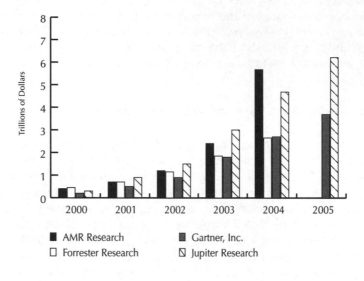

Source: The Wall Street Journal (Totty, 2001, p.R9).

Figure 9.6: B2B Growth Forecast—Consensus Estimate

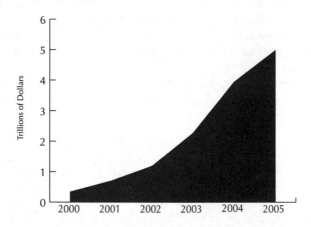

Source: The Wall Street Journal (Totty, 2001, p.R9).

as it should not be taken to connote only the fast-rising—and often fast-falling—Internet firms. Rather, *all organizations*—large and small, young and old—must take advantage of the power of being a "dot-com." "It (the Internet) is a more cost-effective way to run nearly every aspect of your company. It's all about moving business processes to open Internet standards to streamline interactions with customers, suppliers, and partners—and with your own employees" (McNealy, 2000, p. 47). As LaMonica (2001d) observed, the Internet economy—if not many of the companies who pioneered it—is clearly here to stay, as the "flameout" of the "dot-coms" "will not end the allure of the Internet for businesses and customers" (p. 5). Clearly then, the B2B concept, and the processes and technology supporting it, will be key to all organizations' success—both public and private—in the coming years.

The Current State of Affairs—The ISM/Forrester *Report on eBusiness*

How are B2B practices affecting business' procurement activities, and what is driving adoption of online acquisition processes? Perhaps the best barometer that we have on the status of e-procurement in the overall American economy is the quarterly *Report on eBusiness*. These reports come from research carried out jointly by the Institute for Supply Management (ISM, 2001a, b, c) and Forrester Research.

With three surveys of purchasing executives carried out in 2001, these reports lend perhaps the most credible insights into the current status of e-commerce in the B2B realm in the United States. Each quarter, ISM and Forrester survey 700 purchasing and supply management executives of both manufacturing and service industry firms. The surveyed firms, which are randomly selected each quarter, represent a broad cross-section of American business, as they are diversified according to:
*   Geography
*   Size
*   Industry—based on SIC (Standard Industrial Classification) Codes

From an overall standpoint, recent issues of the *Report on eBusiness* show that most organizations still are in the early stages of adopting Internet-based procurement. In increasingly larger numbers, organizations are making use of online capabilities for posting RFP's (requests for proposals) and RFQ's (requests for quotations) and for identifying new suppliers. Most procurement executives feel that the Internet—in time—will become central to their purchasing efforts. Yet, technological problems, most importantly the ability to integrate their internal procurement systems and collaborate their organization's systems with those of their suppliers, serve as a "roadblock" to fully adopting e-procurement (ISM, 2001a, b, c).

From this author's independent analysis of the data found in the ISM/Forrester Research-issued *Report on eBusiness,* several conclusions can be drawn.

Participation in Online Marketplaces

Participation in online marketplaces—both fixed and dynamic-priced environments—continues to rise. As can be seen in Figure 9.7, overall, just over a quarter of all firms now use online marketplaces as part of their move towards e-procurement. Throughout 2001, manufacturing firms were *less likely* than non-manufacturing companies to participate in online marketplaces. However, as can be seen in Figure 9.8, the gap between the manufacturing and service firms has actually been decreasing over time.

Yet, one statistic truly stands out in this area. This is the fact that larger organizations continue to pace the growth of e-procurement efforts. As can be seen in Figure 9.9, companies that purchase over $100 million annually far outpace their smaller brethren in their participation rates for online marketplaces. With the focus on large, private exchanges in specific industries, such as Covisint in automobile manufacturing (Schwartz, 2000a) and Exostar in the world of aerospace (Plyler and Shaw, 2001), this is not too surprising. Also, the previously discussed demise of many of the public exchanges—which may have made e-procurement more accessible to smaller organizations through the elimination of much of the upfront investment costs necessary to start up an exchange—may be another factor contributing to this significant—and steady—differential.

Figure 9.7: Overall Participation in Online Marketplaces

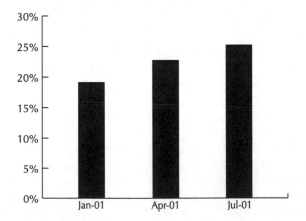

Source: *ISM/Forrester* Report on eBusiness *(www.ism.ws)–2001.*

Figure 9.8: Participation in Online Marketplaces: Manufacturers vs. Non-Manufacturers

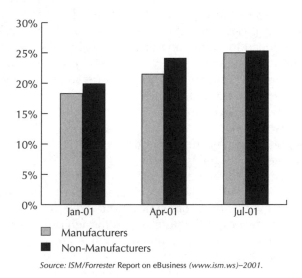

Source: ISM/Forrester Report on eBusiness (www.ism.ws)–2001.

Figure 9.9: Participation in Online Marketplaces: Size of Purchasing Organization

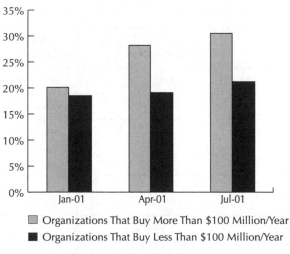

Source: ISM/Forrester Report on eBusiness (www.ism.ws)–2001.

Direct vs. Indirect Materials

What is the difference between direct and indirect materials? A good breakdown was provided by Eisenmann (2002), which is shown in Table 9.2. *Indirect materials* constitute what are typically referred to as MRO (maintenance, repair, and operating) goods, while *direct materials* are those that are closely linked to production or service delivery. Much of the high utilization rates seen in Figure 9.10 can be attributed to the fact that firms are increasingly making routine purchases for operating and office supplies (indirect purchases) through online sites, such as:

- Staples (www.staples.com)
- OfficeMax (www.officemax.com)
- Office Depot (www.officedepot.com)
- W.W. Grainger (www.grainger.com)
- FindMRO (www.findmro.com)

The exact breakdown on what is a direct purchase and what is an indirect one varies even within companies—and even depending upon the timing and circumstances of the purchase. Although purchases of indirect goods may, in fact, often outpace spending on direct materials, acquisition of MRO goods has heretofore not been looked upon as a strategic issue (Wendin, 2001). As can be seen clearly in Figure 9.11, this should be an area of attention for not only procurement executives, but for top officials of all organizations.

Table 9.2: Attributes of Purchasing Direct vs. Indirect Materials

	Direct Materials	Indirect Materials
Purchase Predictability	Volatile	Internally driven
Order Size	Large lots	Often small
Collaboration with Suppliers	Varies, usually high, but low for commodities	Varies, low for MRO supplies, high for equipment and services
Percentage of Total Dollars Spent	80%	20%
Percentage of Total Number of Purchase Orders	20%	80%
End Customer	External customer	Internal employees

Source: Adapted from Eisenmann, Internet Business Models (2002), p. 479.

Figure 9.10: Percentage of All Organizations Conducting Purchasing

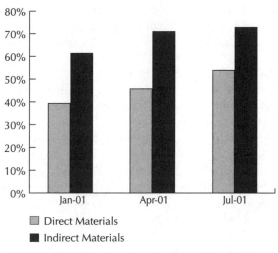

Source: ISM/Forrester Report on eBusiness (www.ism.ws)–2001.

Figure 9.11: Percentage of Total Procurement Dollars Being Spent Online for Direct and Indirect Materials

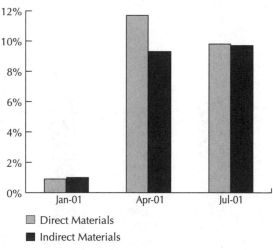

Source: ISM/Forrester Report on eBusiness (www.ism.ws)–2001.

As R. Gene Richter, former chief procurement officer at IBM, astutely acknowledged: "Everything is strategic to somebody. Talk about ballpoint pens. A secretary has spots all over her brand-new blouse because the pen you bought for a cent and half is leaking" (quoted in Anonymous, "E-Auction Playbook: What Top Supply Execs Say About Auctions," 2001, p. S2).

Use of Online Auctions for Procurement

With the present research being focused on dynamic commerce applications, the ISM/Forrester Research *Report on eBusiness* has yielded great insight into the pace of adoption of reverse auctions for e-procurement. What can be seen is that, overall, the penetration rate is probably surprisingly low to readers, who have heard much in the popular business press regarding the growth of online auctioning and could therefore be surprised at the approximately 15-20 percent participation rate for *all* companies, reflected in Figure 9.12.

However, a look behind these numbers is telling. First, as shown in Figure 9.13, manufacturing firms were far more likely to be online auction participants than service sector enterprises. In fact, only in the most recent survey (July 2001) did the participation rate of manufacturers not double that of their non-manufacturing counterparts. Also, when combined with the just discussed aspects of direct and indirect purchases, manufacturers are more likely to use auctioning for higher-dollar, more strategic procurement needs. Also,

Figure 9.12: Overall Participation Rates for Online Auctions for Procurement

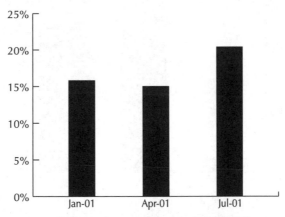

Source: *ISM/Forrester* Report on eBusiness *(www.ism.ws)–2001.*

Figure 9.13: Participation in Online Auctions for Procurement: Manufacturers vs. Non-Manufacturers

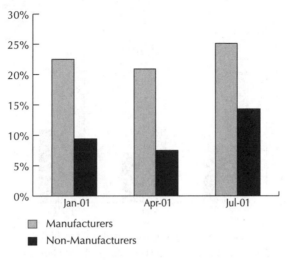

Manufacturers

Non-Manufacturers

Source: ISM/Forrester Report on eBusiness *(www.ism.ws)–2001.*

once again, size mattered, as organizations that had procurement budgets of over $100 million a year had far higher participation rates than those below this benchmark. As can be seen in Figure 9.14, while smaller organizations exhibited an increased likelihood to use online auctions for e-procurement, their participation rate never surpassed half of that of their larger counterparts.

Importance and Cost of e-Procurement

In the final area of analysis, the ISM data reveals, not surprisingly, that the vast majority of supply chain executives espouse the belief that the Internet will play an increasingly important role in the procurement task. From an overall standpoint, Figure 9.15 shows that—except for what might be viewed as the 10-15 percent "Luddite" faction of purchasing executives—those surveyed appreciate the growing importance of online procurement. Yet, in the most recent survey data reported (July 2001), there was a somewhat significant increase in the percentage feeling that the Internet was *not important*. It will be very interesting to see if this becomes a trend in future surveys of this organization and similar work done by others in the near future.

Figure 9.14: Participation in Online Auctions for Procurement: Size of Purchasing Organization

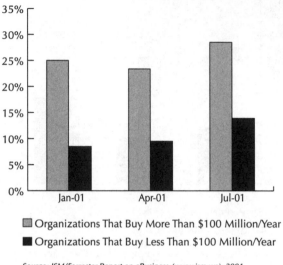

Source: *ISM/Forrester* Report on eBusiness *(www.ism.ws)–2001.*

Figure 9.15: Importance of the Internet to Purchasing Activities

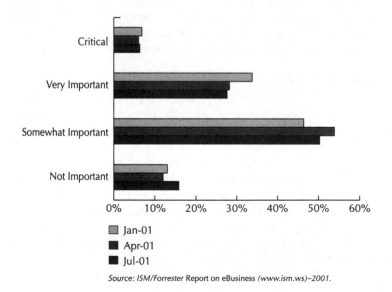

Source: *ISM/Forrester* Report on eBusiness *(www.ism.ws)–2001.*

A final area of concern arising out of analysis of the data underlying the ISM/Forrester Research reports is the fact that—at present—the vast majority of organizations are not yet seeing any significant cost savings as a result of their adoption of e-procurement. As shown in Figure 9.16, approximately two-thirds of responding procurement executives reported that they have seen no change in their "total cost" from shifting activities online. In fact, only a small minority of respondents (consistently less than 5 percent), saw actual cost savings from moving to e-procurement. And, in each quarterly survey, the number of respondents who did report significant cost decreases from moving to e-procurement has been less than those who have actually seen their costs increase. As will be discussed later in the public sector context, this view of e-procurement as being duplicative and an "incremental cost" is one that is proving true today—at least in the short term. If, over time, the shift does not produce cost efficiencies, this could be a significant driver *against* further adoption of e-procurement functions.

Figure 9.16: The Cost Impact of Shifting to E-Procurement

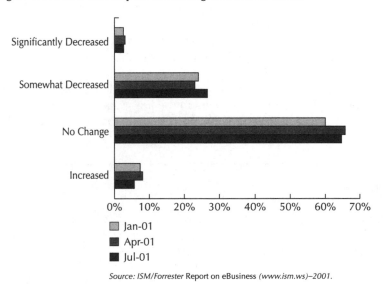

Source: ISM/Forrester Report on eBusiness (www.ism.ws)–2001.

The Two "E's"—E-Government and E-Procurement

Introduction

Rick Berry, CEO of ICG Commerce, observed that the net impact of e-procurement is that it "is stripping away all of the non-efficient factors that get in the way of a buyer making the right decision" (quoted in Baldwin, 2001a, p. 37). According to Stuart Turner, Oracle's vice president for public sector in the United Kingdom, "The public sector must increasingly address the same business issues as the private sector (quoted in Wait, 2001a, p. 1). One of the key areas to be "reinvented"—if you will—is the whole area of procurement. To cite just one example, the federal procurement process—particularly in the IT area—has been perceived as being "way behind Internet speed" (Bridis, 2000, p. B1).

Many in the public have begun to ask that if private sector companies can save tens of millions of dollars through online procurement, why can't the government? Former House Speaker Newt Gingrich (2000) advocated that: "Every government, at every level, should be rationalizing its purchasing system and moving on to the net to eliminate all paper purchasing. The savings in this area alone could be in the 20 to 30 percent range for most governments" (p. 10).

And what is government currently spending? According to data from the U.S. Department of Commerce compiled in the July/August 2001 edition of *The Public Purchaser*, total governmental procurement (inclusive of all levels)

Definitions

e-government: e-government is the inventive application of all forms of new information and communication technologies to improve the functioning of government itself, with the ultimate aim being to improve the delivery of governmental services to the citizen-customer served by the public sector.

e-procurement: e-procurement is the use of electronic means to improve sourcing of goods and services, both in the private and public sectors. E-procurement seeks to improve the workings of the acquisition process and the communications along the supply chain, while simultaneously reducing the costs of the purchasing operation. E-procurement encompasses a wide variety of tools, including purchase cards, online catalogs, electronic payments, *and* reverse auctions.

Surprise! Who's the Biggest Online Seller?

In a groundbreaking study, sponsored by the Pew Internet and American Life Project and *Federal Computer Week,* Judi Hasson and Graeme Browning (2001) conducted the first comprehensive review of online sales activities for the federal government. They found that the federal government has at least 164 websites that sell items directly to the public. Yet, as Hasson and Browning (2001) observed: "For all its success in establishing a digital marketplace, the (federal) government seems to be going about the job in a haphazard fashion … as there are few rules and even fewer standards for conducting business" (p. 3). However, as can be seen in the graphic below, the federal government's online sales exceed those of Amazon.com and eBay … combined (Brown, 2001)!

Comparison of Online Sales in 2000 (in Billions)

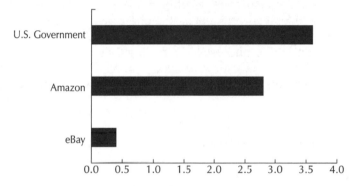

Source: Anonymous. "Survey: Government Web Sales Outpace Retailers." (May 28, 2001): (www.cnn.com)

For now, citizens seem to mostly be liking what government is doing online in the way of e-commerce applications and taking advantage of them. Hikers, for whom a road atlas map "just won't cut it," can now go to the U.S. Geological Survey's website (*www.mapping.usgs.gov*) and order highly detailed maps. Consider also how 80-year-old Doris Hennessy Winckler uses new online e-government services to accomplish something that previously was difficult and expensive. Before e-government arrived, for the past 25 years, Mrs. Winckler sent a check to a florist in Rome to have flowers placed on special days on the grave of her brother, Army Captain John Hennessy, who was killed in action in World War II and buried in the American Cemetery in Florence, Italy. Now she orders flowers five times a year through the American Battle Monuments Commission website (*www.abmc.gov*). Mrs. Winckler's response is quite simple—"This computer thing is marvelous!" (quoted in Hasson and Browning, 2001, p. 6).

in the United States is approaching $700 million (Figure 9.17). As can be seen in Figure 9.18, state and local governmental procurement has increased at a markedly higher rate than that seen in the federal government. Finally, when speaking of procurement at the federal level, as shown in Figure 9.19, the Department of Defense (DoD) still makes up the majority of the activity.

The private sector has shown that it is eager to partner with the federal government in the procurement realm. In fact, it has been said that firms are attracted to the B2G market at the federal level "like bees to honey," namely due to Uncle Sam's purchases of over $200 billion in goods and services through 31 million procurement transactions annually (Laurent, 2000). To put this in perspective, this amount represents more than the annual revenue of General Motors (Lynch, 2001)! Compounding the attractiveness of the public sector market is the stability the governmental market offers versus the turbulence of the formerly high-flying high-tech sector. As Birnbaum (2001) characterized the landscape, Washington is seen as a safe harbor, simply because the federal government is "the one place industry and individuals can turn when their own resources falter" (p. 52).

In interviews with this author, several leading thinkers on the subject expressed their beliefs on why e-procurement is a major part of the entire e-government movement. Excerpts from these interviews on this matter are on page 334.

Figure 9.17: Combined Governmental Procurement in America (1995-2001)

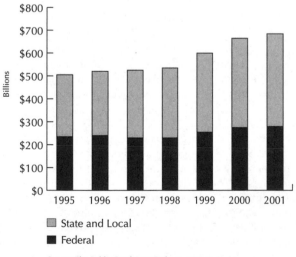

Source: The Public Purchaser (Perlman, 2001, p. 8).

Figure 9.18: Total Public Procurement Spending (1995-2001)

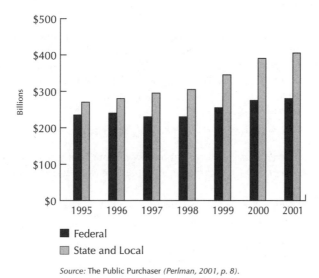

Source: The Public Purchaser *(Perlman, 2001, p. 8).*

Figure 9.19: Breakdown of Federal Procurement (1995-2001)

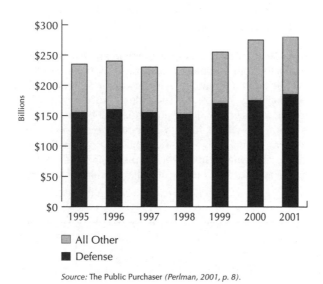

Source: The Public Purchaser *(Perlman, 2001, p. 8).*

Question: "How Does E-Procurement Fit with the Push for E-Government?"

E-procurement, I think, will be a major component of e-government. Though not as general an application as information kiosks for the public, e-procurement is the dominant topic within the procurement community. This is especially true at the state government level. In addition, e-procurement was really one of the initiatives at the forefront of the e-government movement. It was a pioneer and remains an important piece.

Larry Allen, Executive Director, Coalition for Government Procurement

Procurement requirements are a reality across all levels of government and offer a ripe test-bed for e-government applications and transaction-based measurable results.

Steve Cochran, Former Vice President for Technology, Council for Excellence in Government

E-procurement will be near the top of the e-government agenda, primarily because the procurement function lends itself to a number of electronic commerce solutions now available to government agencies. Agencies should be posting RFPs online, receiving bids electronically, and using innovative vehicles such as reverse auctions. In so many ways, e-procurement should be considered a "low-hanging fruit" item in the e-government movement, opening a major function of government agencies to the electronic world.

Carl DeMaio, Director of Government Redesign, Reason Public Policy Institute

I would say it is an excellent fit. Both e-procurement and e-sourcing create the types of efficiencies through automation and integration that are the goals of e-government. While there are many efficiencies and cost reductions through e-government by enabling services for individuals, such as vehicle registration, ticket payment, tax payment, there are actually substantially greater efficiencies for the nation as a whole through e-procurement and e-sourcing. This is because the government is such a large purchasing organization in terms of both dollar volume and total number of suppliers. Even a small saving in terms of percentage equates to a huge real dollar amount of savings.

Ray Letulle, Chief Technology Officer, Moai, Inc.

Why Adopt E-Procurement?

Stephen George, CEO of Epylon.com, sees there being more pressure on the public sector to move quickly in implementing e-procurement activities than in the private sector, precisely due to the fiduciary duty government has to spend the taxpayers' money wisely (opinion cited in Roberti, 2000).

According to Lawrence Herman, a managing director for BearingPoint: "With the tight economy, the need for savings from procurement is accentuated. So the question is whether states are going to step up their investment in order to increase their savings" (quoted in Welsh, 2001a, p. 2). Yet, a counterargument can very well be made, as was done by Seben (2001). He

---

Question: "What Is Driving the Public Sector's Adoption of E-Procurement?"

I think e-procurement will steadily gain momentum in the near term. There is still a lot that can be done to channel product purchases into e-procurement systems and, as users become more at ease with the technology, there will be more and more instances in which e-procurement can be used. The limit on the upward growth of e-procurement currently seems to be tied to the ability and desire of government buyers to place complex service buys on e-procurement systems. The federal government is now a net purchaser of services and, while some may be able to be competed in cyberspace, I think we're a long way from making e-procurement the dominant service acquisition method.

Larry Allen, Executive Director, Coalition for Government Procurement

The three most important drivers toward e-procurement are, in order: Budget, budget, and budget!

Schools want to put money into kids, not into procedures. Government, too, wants to invest in communities and the things that matter to them: safety, roads, and economic development.

Most public sector organizations are facing budget adjustments in some form or another, whether it is a downsized staff, less money for purchases, increased purchasing demand, or the search for increased budget efficiency. As the immediate and relatively simple method for governments to save money in both process and product costs, e-procurement is a natural choice.

At its core, e-procurement is about finding the best prices in the most cost- and time-efficient manner. That translates simply into real savings, freeing more money to be used on the people and communities that the public sector is charged to serve. This means more money available to fund sorely-needed road improvements, school building maintenance, or additional police officers.

Bill Perkin, CEO, Way2Bid

pointed out that if the downturn in the economy is serious and budgets shrink significantly due to shortfalls in revenue, the situation could get ugly. With history as an indicator, e-procurement will be less of an issue, namely because capital budgets—particularly in the IT area—will be slashed to where "buying" is not an issue, and government will again "be forced to milk the life out of existing technology and forgo new spending" (p. 2).

The Benefits of E-Procurement to the Public Sector

What are e-procurement's benefits, both to governmental agencies and the thousands of firms that supply them? Some of the benefits include reduced prices, lower costs, reduced errors, and increased speed in delivery.

In a July 2001 report, "States' eProcurement Road Map," Forrester Research (2001) put together perhaps the best investigative study done to date on the current status of e-procurement in the public sector. The Forrester study was a comprehensive study of electronic procurement at the state and local levels, but many of the findings can be generalized to all levels of government in the U.S. As can be seen in Figure 9.20, much of the benefit stemming from the shift to online purchasing methods centers around "process" savings, simply making the procurement process work better than it has in the offline world.

The soft-side savings from making purchasing processes electronic can be substantial. For instance, the State of Connecticut has been able to produce savings in the six-figure range in its procurement operations, with the majority of the savings coming from reductions in postage, printing, and advertising costs (Walsh and Dizard, 2000).

Figure 9.20: Benefits Realized by States from Shifting to Online Procurement

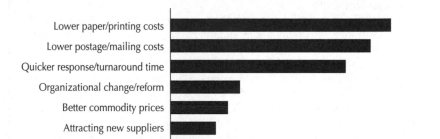

Source: Forrester Research. "States' eProcurement Road Map."
The Forrester Report (July 2001): (www.forrester.com).

Indeed, across the board, government agencies are finding that through the use of e-procurement, purchasing cycle times have been compressed from weeks or even months to a matter of hours (Roberti, 2000). As pointed out in a report from Deloitte Research (2000a), the public sector has a major motivation to use e-marketplace technologies to simplify the means through which they purchase goods and services, simply in order to stream-line the procurement process. This is a step that potentially could save bil-lions of dollars and millions of man-hours across the public sector.

In the private sector, purchasing process costs—namely, the cost of issu-ing and tracking purchase orders—have been shown to dramatically decline when procurement is made electronic. In one study, the average purchase order cost dropped over 70 percent (Wendin, 2001). Likewise, in the public sector, the costs of processing a purchase order have been shown to drop between 50 and 70 percent in an e-procurement environment. In some "best in class" examples, costs that formerly ranged from $100 to $150 per pur-chase order issuance have plummeted to around $20 (Terry, 2001). Some analysts have estimated the decline to be even more dramatic, with figures on electronic orders being as low as between $5 and $15 (Perlman, 2001).

On the other hand, what is hindering further adoption of e-procurement methods? The 2001 Forrester Research report addressed the flip-side issue, with the findings on this question being depicted in Figure 9.21. Chief among the obstructions to online purchasing adoption by states are lack of funding for e-procurement efforts and technological barriers—both on the part of the government agency and the vendors doing business with it.

Figure 9.21: Barriers Faced by States in Shifting to Online Procurement

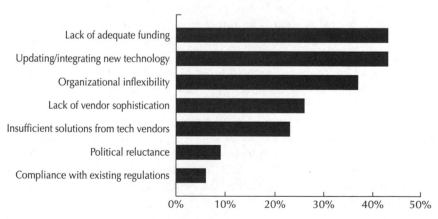

Source: Forrester Research. "States' eProcurement Road Map."
The Forrester Report (July 2001): (www.forrester.com).

Government as a "Role Model"

Perhaps most important of all—overriding the tangible factors—it has been observed that government's use of best practices in e-procurement will accelerate its vendors' adoption of B2B technologies, especially amongst smaller companies that are or seek to be governmental suppliers (Anonymous, "Governments Shop and Save Online," 2001). Indeed, governmental adoption of e-commerce techniques and models are especially important from the perspective that government can serve as a "role model" for how to make use of this new technology, serving as a catalyst for wider adoption of the Internet and web-based business practices throughout society and the economy (National Electronic Commerce Coordinating Council, 2000b).

The Public Sector's Adoption of E-Procurement

At present in the public sector, despite all the hype surrounding e-procurement, the actual execution of the concept seems to be lacking. This is especially true at the federal level. Matthews (2001b) cites statistics revealing that in the year 2000, only about 1 percent of total federal spending for goods and services was done online. The Coalition for Government Procurement found that at present, less than 1 percent of all goods and services purchased by various federal agencies through the General Services Administration (GSA) were bought online (Matthews, 2001b). And the numbers are not expected to rise exponentially any time soon, as Jupiter Media Metrix forecasts that e-procurement will only increase to 2 percent of the federal acquisition budget in the current year.

At the state and local levels as well, e-procurement is still in its infancy. As can be seen in the findings of Forrester Research's (2001) "States' eProcurement Road Map," summarized in Figure 9.22, much of what is being purchased through e-procurement is routine in nature (and largely would be seen as being indirect materials in the private sector). However, the state and local purchasing officials surveyed in the Forrester study expected to sharply increase their use of e-procurement across the board over the next two years for all categories of goods—and services. Larry Allen, director of the Coalition for Government Procurement, observed that "the $64,000 question is whether services can be bought online." However, Allen believes that, in the end, online purchasing is only well suited at present for low-dollar, commodity-type items (opinion cited in Matthews, 2001b, p. 2).

Figure 9.22: What Is Being Purchased Online?: Today (2001) and in the Future (2003)

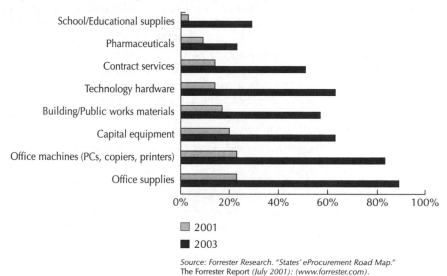

Source: Forrester Research. "States' eProcurement Road Map."
The Forrester Report *(July 2001): (www.forrester.com)*.

"Sticky" Pricing—and Purchasing Methods

According to Ray Letulle, CTO for Moai, a leading e-sourcing service provider (and one of those interviewed for this report), purchasing organizations today basically have four approaches available to them for buying goods and services:

1. They can use a *catalog* (online or offline) or a desktop procurement system to buy from a pre-qualified pool of goods;
2. They can use *reverse auctions*, typically for goods and services where price is the primary decision factor, to ensure better market value;
3. They can use more sophisticated online negotiation formats, such *as multiparameter auctions* or *weighted-score events*, when there are several factors beyond price or the purchases are for more complex bundles of goods and services; or
4. They can *negotiate* critical goods and services face-to-face with strategic suppliers (Letulle, 2001, p. S8).

Today, much of e-commerce in general—and in the B2G marketspace in particular—is still based on what has been alternatively characterized as:

- "Static" or "sticky" pricing (Moai, 2000b), or
- "Menu-driven pricing" (Appell and Brousseau, 2000, p. 85).

Question: "Where Is the Public Sector in Comparison to the Private Sector in Adoption of B2B E-Commerce Techniques?"

I actually see the federal government as being a little ahead of the private sector. A lot of this was initiated by the Reinventing Government project initiated by the last administration and the wave of procurement reform legislation that came through at about the same time. For much of the 1990s, government managers were adamant about using technology to make smaller workforces more efficient and deliver improved services at the same time.

Larry Allen, Executive Director, Coalition for Government Procurement

Private sector efforts are often focused on process efficiencies measured to improve the bottom line. They are far more results oriented than the public sector. And e-procurement in many large companies is focused on the total supply chain. It seems that the public sector, despite all the acquisition reform, is still focused on the procurement process as a separate support function. We are inching toward a more comprehensive role for the procurement professional, but it's still a few years off.

In defense of the public sector, there are some unique challenges it faces. For example, there is a need to seek full and open competition versus having one or two long-term partners. Also, the government sector must address socioeconomic factors. Clearly, the public sector's challenges are inherently more complex. In the e-government realm, fear-based cultures play an important role in the reluctance to accept and adopt new technology. Given the fishbowl that the public sector must operate within, it is difficult to push through change. However, I believe that shrinking budgets and smaller workforces will force many agencies to adopt e-procurement. Such constraints essentially have already forced the increased use of purchase cards, schedules, and GWACs (government-wide acquisition contracts) because the old way simply didn't work anymore. Over time, technological advancements will allow for e-procurement to be more of a mainstream tool.

Ken Buck, Executive Director of Business Innovation, GSA-FTS

This is a difficult question because there are so many factors that affect adoption in both the public and private sectors. The current economic slowdown has certainly affected adoption in the private sector. The public sector faces a tax cut that may affect spending, but if the economy stays weak, the government may increase e-government spending to increase growth in the tech sector. Additionally, many of the supply chain inefficiencies in the government are advantageous to special interest groups that may lobby against making the purchasing process more efficient and competitive. Initially, however, the organizations in the government who have taken advantage of e-sourcing are saving money and paving the road for others. I would anticipate the government to be a step or two behind private industry, but it won't stay far behind for long because the advantages are so compelling.

Interestingly, the federal government was one of our first e-sourcing users. We saw early adoption by the branches of the military. They were attracted to the 15-25 percent average savings our customers have seen by sourcing online. Overall, however, we have not seen the public sector—including state and local governments—as early adopters. This is more typical, given that the public sector often waits for risk factors in newer automated solutions to be ironed out before adopting them. Currently, the private sector is well ahead of the public sector, so the public sector has some catching up to do. The good news, however, is that the government organizations that have tried e-sourcing have saved significantly and therefore created a proven path for others to follow.

Ray Letulle, Chief Technology Officer, Moai, Inc.

I don't think they are directly comparable. Private and public sector organizations buy differently. Governments are more risk averse and of course more highly regulated. Also, private sector manufacturing companies concentrate purchases of raw materials or assemblies that become the products they sell. Efficiency in this area is far more important to them than indirect purchases, and they will go to great lengths to fund improvements since it helps their profit. Governments essentially buy indirect items—we don't make anything.

Jim Passier, Procurement Manager, State of Connecticut

The public sector's movement toward e-procurement will have a significant impact on the adoption of e-procurement by business constituents. The adoption of e-procurement methods by government will effectively introduce these savings to the economy as a whole, initiating positive changes that will have effects far beyond the savings of tax dollars.

If the public sector fails to adopt e-procurement, it may become difficult for progressive businesses to do business with the government electronically. Legislators would be inadvertently punishing those constituents who are striving for a more efficient operation. The public sector could unknowingly curb the tide of progress.

When the decision to adopt e-procurement is made, the public sector must make a firm decision and not back down under pressure. Caving in to the fears of businesses loyal to old-school practices will result in the loss of drastic savings of taxpayer dollars. Those vendors who are slow to adopt e-procurement will soon realize that to resist progress is to ask government to continue to spend tax dollars that could be better spent elsewhere.

Bill Perkin, CEO, Way2Bid

Recalling the distinctions between purchase of direct and indirect materials shown in Table 9.2 and discussed earlier, thus far, much of e-commerce has been directed at electronic purchases of what has been labeled indirect materials. Yet, this is just a continuation of the use of fixed pricing, transferred from the offline environment to wired markets. Indeed, the majority of *both* B2B and B2G e-commerce has been focused on developing sales through publishing electronic catalogs and automating processes for the purchase of fixed-price items. The fixed prices allow for standardization of prices across settings, but they are slow to respond to market condition changes. According to Allen, director of the Coalition for Government Procurement (and an interview subject for this report), e-procurement is best suited for high-volume, low-dollar purchases of indirect materials, as opposed to direct materials and more complex items (Matthews, 2001b).

Indeed, as can be seen in Figure 9.23, drawn from the survey findings contained in Forrester Research's (2001) "States' eProcurement Road Map," most e-procurement activities are based on the use of fixed-price mechanisms, namely online catalogs. Looking closely at this figure, it can be seen that *none* of the surveyed purchasing officials presently made use of electronic procurement auctions, and further, only 9 percent planned to do so in the next few years.

Figure 9.23: States' Use of Online Procurement Technologies: At Present (2001) and Projected for 2003

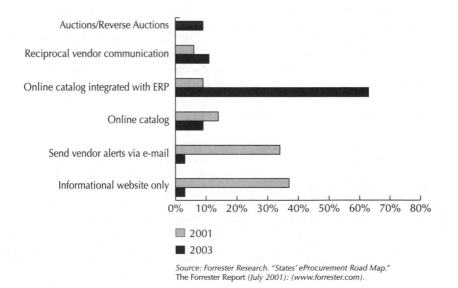

Source: Forrester Research. "States' eProcurement Road Map."
The Forrester Report *(July 2001): (www.forrester.com).*

So, where do Letulle's (2001) other "not so sticky" buying methods fit into the governmental e-procurement landscape? In the private sector, Kalin (2001a) has reported that by 2004:

- IDC Research predicts that 20 percent of all B2B e-commerce transactions will involve some form of dynamic pricing, including online auctions and price negotiations.
- Forrester Research predicts that half of all trade through B2B e-marketplaces will be dynamically priced.

Likewise, according to Zyskowski (2000), the two "most compelling" buying models for the public sector to employ to gain cost savings through the use of the Internet for e-procurement are reverse auctions and demand aggregation, both of which employ dynamic pricing.

Summary

In the next section of this chapter, we will explore the nature of dynamic pricing—and the larger issue of how dynamic commerce techniques can and are being applied in the public sector. Dynamic commerce can be seen as a subset of the entire e-commerce arena, encompassing only situations where pricing is fluid and flexible.

Specifically, we will examine how governments can and are beginning to make use of three dynamic commerce purchasing methods, namely:

1. Reverse Auctions
2. Demand Aggregation
3. Forward Auctions

Dynamic Commerce and Reverse Auctions

Introduction—Dynamic Pricing

In his first report for the IBM Endowment for The Business of Government, the author chronicled the history of dynamic (fluid or auction-based) prices (Wyld, 2000). Indeed, in historical terms, fixed pricing is a relatively recent phenomenon, brought about by the Industrial Revolution, with its accompanying standardized outputs and larger markets.

We have many countless examples where dynamic pricing has been employed in the economy. Some of these examples have become accepted business practices, such as yield management, which has been successfully employed across the transportation and hospitality industries, with everyone from airlines, hotels, rental car companies, and others employing the concept. Indeed, this is the business model behind Priceline.com, which acts as the intermediary to match supply and demand for perishable commodities—namely airline seats and hotel rooms—through dynamic pricing.

For all these successes, we are reminded that while dynamic pricing is tempting to use, on the consumer level especially, the concept is "tricky" to implement, simply because American consumers won't tolerate the practice when it is uncovered. There is the classic example where the chairman of Coca-Cola suggested—and then backed off of—the use of vending machines that could vary the price of drinks in the machine, based on the temperature. Davis (2000) recounted the uproar that occurred last year when Amazon.com experimented with dynamic pricing, charging different consumers different prices for the same DVDs and MP3 players. Still, major computer makers, including Dell, Compaq, IBM, and Hewlett-Packard, recently toyed with using dynamic pricing in their consumer markets as a means through which to optimize their pricing in order to reduce inventories and maximize profitability. This led Vizard, Scannell, and Neel (2001) to observe that customers will likely feel "cheated" if they find out that they were charged higher prices than other consumers.

There could be a similar backlash in the B2B arena. If we get to the point where dynamic pricing is over-employed and every nut and bolt has a variety of prices, then, as Eric Mitchell, president of the Atlanta-based Professional Pricing Society, cautioned: "You can just drown in prices for a product" (quoted in Kalin, 2001a, p. 4). William Brandel, research director at the Aberdeen Group, noted: "At the end of the day, it's always good for the market to find what is a fair price. So if you believe in that, then these are all great tools for the greater good, for finding the fine balance of capitalistic forces" (cited in Sanborn, 2001, p. 32).

Dynamic Commerce and Dynamic Pricing

Up front, there is an important differentiation to be made between *dynamic commerce* and *dynamic pricing*. While Appell and Brousseau's (2000) distinction was made up front in the Introduction, it is important to restate it again:

> *Dynamic pricing* describes a process in which goods and services are traded in markets where price adjusts freely to supply and demand. However, pricing is just one of the data points used during the valuation of an offer. Since the exchange of goods and services often entails valuation of many variables beyond price, the notion of "commerce" best captures the breadth and complexity of real-world business requirements.... Thus,

dynamic commerce can be defined as the exchange of goods and services in electronic markets where not only price, but also other factors, fluctuate freely while all participants enjoy significantly lower interaction costs (p. 83).

Likewise, according to Phillips (2001), *dynamic pricing* is characterized by "any environment where prices can change rapidly in response to changes in either the external environment (such as competitive price changes) or the internal environment (such as inventory changes)" (p. 8). *Dynamic commerce* is a broad, umbrella-like term, defined as "the buying and selling of goods and services through flexible pricing models that allow prices to change over time" (Moai, 2000a, p. 5). As such, dynamic pricing should be viewed as a *means* through which dynamic commerce is achieved, as "dynamic commerce manifests itself most commonly in exchanges and auctions" (Moai, 2000b, p. 5).

At present, there are three dynamic commerce methods that have been developed that can be applied in governmental e-procurement, namely:
1. Reverse Auctions
2. Demand Aggregation
3. Forward Auctions

As can be seen in Figure 9.24, these dynamic commerce applications have the potential to be instrumental in reshaping the first "pain point" in the governmental supply chain through their role in public sector e-procurement.

In this section, we will examine the "price only" dynamic commerce application—reverse auctioning—and how this tool can be used in governmental e-procurement.

Reverse Auctions

Historically, traditional auctions have brought buyers and sellers together for centuries (Miller, 2000). Today, *reverse auctions* are being employed in new ways in the electronic supply chain for e-procurement.

Definition and Characteristics

Formally, a reverse auction can be defined as "a supply-aggregating event that lowers the price of goods for a buyer" (Mattick and Brousseau, 2001, p. 133). Specifically, as can be seen in Figure 9.25, reverse auctions have certain key characteristics.

Additionally, the dynamics of *both* forward and reverse auctions are similar in two key characteristics:
1. Identities of bidders are *unknown* to all, and
2. Bid prices are immediately *known* to all (Marinello and Daher, 2001).

Figure 9.24: Dynamic Commerce Applications in the E-Government Supply Chain: E-Procurement

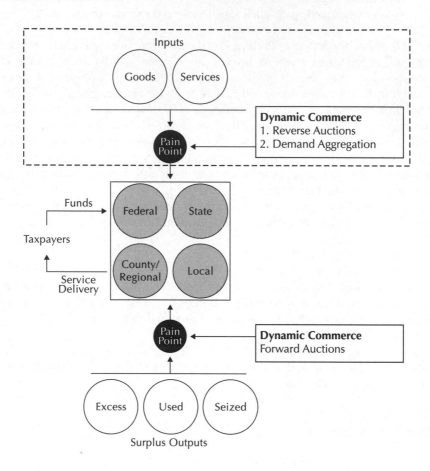

Figure 9.25: Characteristics of Reverse Auctions

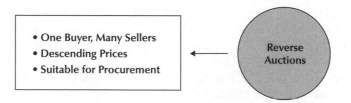

Through the pre-qualification process, all issues are generally settled between the procuring organization and potential suppliers before the time of the auction, with the only remaining issue to be settled being the *price* (Marinello and Daher, 2001). In most, but not necessarily all, reverse auctions, the buying organization is not bound—under the terms of the auction—to necessarily choose the lowest bidder (Kalin, 2001b).

Because the use of e-procurement auctions is so new—and because they are only now slowly creeping into mainstream utilization—much of the focus today is still on both the strategic question of when to employ auctions (and in what form and for what product). Also, first movers are gaining great tactical knowledge in how to carry out auctions and some of the pitfalls to avoid. However, because such e-market expertise can be the source of competitive advantage for private sector firms, there has been a relative dearth of published works sharing such information in the business press. Thus, much of the implementation of the electronic auction concept has been "under the radar" (Porter, 2001).

Benefits and Risks of Reverse Auctions

Reverse auctions have been accurately termed "accelerated Darwinism" by Niul Burton, e-Breviate co-founder and president, in that they enable organizations to "find out much more quickly who are the most competitive suppliers and who is going to win your business" (quoted in Waxer, 2001). In the area of reverse auctions, perhaps none has gained more attention than Covisint, the marketplace established by major automakers. In fact, in May 2001, Covisint hosted the largest online auction to date for DaimlerChrysler, in which the automaker procured $3 billion in parts in a single transaction, saving an estimated tens of millions of dollars in this event (Barlas, 2001).

What are the benefits and risks of using reverse auctions? According to Marinello and Daher (2001), the chief benefits of reverse auctions are:
* Increased numbers of potential suppliers
* Reduced procurement cycle time
* Lowered purchase prices

In a more comprehensive examination of the subject, Kyle Appell and Christopher Brousseau (2000) elucidated the benefits and risks of reverse auctions, both to the procuring organization and to their suppliers. A summarized version of their findings is on the following page.

Reverse Auctions in the Public Sector

Introduction

Reverse auctions have "no direct, singular antecedent in terms of a specific public purchasing principle simply because it has arisen due to the

A Breakdown of the Benefits and Risks of Using Buyer-Centric Dynamic Commerce Applications (Reverse Auctions)

Benefits to Buyer (Organization or Company):
- Opportunity to create or increase competition for buying dollars
- Better information about the marketplace
- Enhance the RFQ process and compress cycle time
- New supply management capability

Benefits to Seller (Vendor):
- Access to new customers
- New and timely information on state of the market
- Automated RFQ process
- New demand management capability

Risks to Buyer (Organization or Company):
- In the event sufficient competition does not materialize, the price could be higher than the buyer expected
- Risks of taking on new suppliers
- Potential effects on decision making and relationships

Risks to Seller (Vendor):
- In the event sufficient competition exists to ignite a bidding frenzy, the price may fall below that desired by the vendor
- Risks of taking on new buyers
- Potential effects on decision making and relationships

Source: Adapted from Appell and Brousseau (2000)
(http://www.ascet.com/documents.asp?d_ID=249).

emergence of a new technology which has provided the modern-day public purchasing officer with a capability that was not previously known" (National Electronic Commerce Coordinating Council, 2000a, p. 10).

Public procurement has operated for decades with the presumption that, in order to ensure the integrity of the process, sealed bids work best. However, according to the National Electronic Commerce Coordinating Council (2000a), the sealed-bid process inherently requires participants to make risk versus gain assumptions under great uncertainty. Thus, the prices generated through such processes carry a "risk premium," and they can potentially be higher than what could be achieved through a reverse auction. Michael Kelemen, director of the U.S. Army's Communications Electronic Command (CECOM) Acquisition Center at Fort Monmouth, New Jersey, stated:

Question: "What Is the Proper Role of Reverse Auctions?"

Reverse auctions seemed to have found a certain niche in procurement for now. What's interesting is that, generally, it's not nearly as big of a niche as was originally forecast. Reverse auctions continue to be used for the simplest of procurements: pure commodities such as road salt, relatively simple product purchases, etc. A few contractors, and agencies, who tried reverse auctions for other types of buys emerged with less than positive feelings about the process. This tells me that reverse auctions will be one arrow in a buyer's quiver of acquisition options, but not a dominant force.

Larry Allen, Executive Director, Coalition for Government Procurement

In the short term, reverse auctions have and will continue to demonstrate the viability of e-procurement through the use of dynamic pricing models. Eventually, they will become one of a number of strategic sourcing tools that will directly support an agency's mission. They are becoming more widely used for certain, tangible commodities, and I predict that in the very near term, many agencies will have this powerful pricing tool on their desktops and its use will become commonplace.

Again, there is a role for reverse auctioning for commodities, but it will be very difficult to apply it to the services realm, the area where we spend a lion's share of the money.

Ken Buck, Executive Director of Business Innovation, GSA-FTS

Once reverse auctions are understood, the public reaction is very positive—but much education needs to occur about what they are and are not—and when they make sense.

Steve Cochran, Former Vice President for Technology, Council for Excellence in Government

Reverse auctions are just one tool in a large toolbox of innovation available to government procurement professionals. It is not a panacea, but it is not a "flavor-of-the-month" either. In some areas, it works quite well and can lead to reduced costs and enhanced value. It depends on the product or service being purchased. Certainly, we'll see a dramatic increase in the use of reverse auctions over the next few years. But there are other tools that also deserve attention, such as share-in-savings contracts and award-term contracts.

Carl DeMaio, Director of Government Redesign, Reason Public Policy Institute

Reverse auctioning is a feature that is easy to grasp and implement, and it is intriguing to elected officials because it easily shows dollar savings to their constituents. As a result, more public sector organizations will probably use reverse auctions as their starting point in moving toward e-procurement. It appears to be growing in acceptance.

Bill Perkin, CEO, Way2Bid

A reverse auction keeps the industry posted of the prices while the bidding process is in progress, so there are no surprises, and industry can choose at any time to opt in or opt out. They're not just giving us what they think is their best shot; many times their best shot could be better, but they don't have the chance to change it (in a sealed-bid environment) (cited in Sanborn, 2001, p. 32).

Why choose to implement reverse auctions? The leaders interviewed for this report addressed what the proper role for reverse auctions in governmental e-procurement should be.

The Threshold Issue—Legality

The legal issues regarding the use of reverse auctions are multifaceted and complex (deserving of an entire study in itself). The legal challenges also pose great hurdles to the vendor community, who have to contend with a "maze of regulations for procurement," with federal, state, and local governments all having separate rules and regulations, some even conflicting amongst their own agencies (Roberti, 2000).

The revisions to the FAR (Federal Acquisition Regulation) in recent years have removed much of the controversy as to whether or not reverse auctions were permitted at the federal level (Schwartz, 2000). However, Congress has recently begun to focus on the propriety of what has been termed a "veritable procurement bazaar" with the advent of GWACs (government-wide acquisition contracts) and the outsourcing of procurement between agencies, such as the services provided by GSA's FTS (Federal Technology Service) and FSS (Federal Supply Service). Representative Tom Davis (R-Va.), now chairman of the House Committee on Government Reform, framed the issue by stating that "how the government buys billions of dollars' worth of goods and services each year is a small niche in government that not a lot of members (of Congress) have paid a lot of attention to through time" (quoted in Matthews, 2001e, p. 1). Yet, today, as Matthews (2001c) observed, Congress is beginning to ponder "whether too much of the business of government has become business" (p. 1).

What is emerging is the fact that changes in e-procurement have often also outpaced the laws governing purchasing in many states and localities. Many states are in the process of reviewing their purchasing regulations for conflicts that inhibit the move to e-procurement. For instance, in March 2001, Idaho Governor Dirk Kempthorne signed into law a modernization of the state's procurement guidelines—regulations that have been unchanged since 1974. This included elimination of cumbersome policies and procedures and modernizing others for the Internet age, such as enabling potential vendors to register with the state online—rather than through a paper process—before bidding on state contracts (Walsh, 2001b).

Question: "What Is the Status of the Legal Issues Involving Reverse Auctions?"

My experience in working with the states is that the legislative issues are really in the past. The laws that have passed work, and, in fact, FreeMarkets has been instrumental in going out and getting some of those laws changed on the state level.

Bill Bunce, National Account Manager—Public Sector, FreeMarkets, Inc.

There seems to be a complete paucity of authority or guidance in the FAR (Federal Acquisition Regulation) for reverse auctions. One must recall that prior to the FAR 15 re-write, "auctions" were expressly prohibited in negotiated procurements. "Price only" buying has always been done under "sealed-bidding" or an "invitation for bids" (IFB) procurement type. Reverse auctions are really an extension of IFB procurements, but with real-time, head-to-head competition. A new twist and danger is that some are hoping to apply reverse auctions to negotiated procurements for services without guidance or advanced thinking.

David P. Metzger, Partner, Holland & Knight, LLP

The Internet offers the public sector efficient methods unknown to legislators of the past, so some legislative policies unintentionally present challenges to the use of the electronic systems available today. But it is possible to maintain the spirit of the law while eliminating these unnecessary challenges.

For example, old policies requiring submission of multiple hard copies of bid responses are obsolete with electronic submission available today. Policy changes would also eliminate practices such as asking vendors to register separately with every organization within a state; electronic information exchange makes such duplication of information instantaneous and makes hard copies unnecessary.

Other challenges include policies that mandate that a bidding opportunity must be advertised in a newspaper or that a written bid must be placed in a sealed envelope. Perhaps the most beneficial addition to current purchasing statutes would be a clear understanding of how new technologies comply with existing purchasing philosophies, such as open competition and the search for the best value.

Finally, we recently presented the reverse auctioning feature to one state because they have specific legislation now that requires them to adopt reverse auctioning. I believe six states have similar legislation, and I suspect the trend will continue.

Bill Perkin, CEO, Way2Bid

Question: "What Are the Benefits of Using Reverse Auctions in Public Sector E-Procurement?"

A buyer and a supplier may have a longstanding relationship, in which case they are not as apt to reduce their price. A supplier would never say, "Hey, I've become more efficient over the past year so I'm going to give you a better price." But when you throw them into a transparent market and they have more margin to play with, you are able to extract more than you would have otherwise.

Bill Bunce, National Account Manager—Public Sector, FreeMarkets, Inc.

In many ways, the advantages for the public sector are greater than those for the private sector. Both sectors save equally from the automation of manual processes and the increased competitiveness of online bidding. Typically, these are 15-25 percent gross saving on cost, a 30-50 percent reduction in cycle time, and a 5 percent savings on administrative costs. There are other savings which are harder to quantify.

Ray Letulle, Chief Technology Officer, Moai, Inc.

There are at least three separate areas of benefit to government:
1. Productivity improvements in agency purchasing processes.
2. Better pricing due to increased volume (assuming political subdivision participation in the system) and elimination of data entry expenses for high transaction count vendors.
3. More competitive bidding as a result of improved management information regarding actual spending level.

Jim Passier, Procurement Manager, State of Connecticut

The advantages to government are really no different than what you see in the private sector. The number one reason they want to go with reverse auctioning is that they want to save money. In short, they want to reduce their bottom-line cost. They typically see afterwards that they can really increase their speed and velocity, and thus, there is actually a big efficiency gain that is gotten from it. Also, through this process, from a strategic sourcing standpoint, they are able to be more focused on who they deliver their business to. For example, running small disadvantaged business bids, we can actually run those types of events and make sure they are hitting the different goals they've got set up by the Small Business Administration or state and local government or whatever it might be in that particular entity.

Joe Quigg, FreeMarkets, Inc.

As discussed by the interviewees, the legal barriers to using reverse auctions have been eliminated at the federal level and are being quickly eliminated elsewhere, and the practice is even being encouraged in some state and local jurisdictions. Still, the simple question—"Can I do this?"— is certainly the first issue that has to be addressed by procurement officials in any jurisdiction in considering the potential use of reverse auctioning.

Benefits of Using Reverse Auctions in the Public Sector

It has been observed that online auctions for e-procurement offer three principal benefits to the public sector:
1. Financial savings versus traditional, manual sourcing,
2. Improved efficiency of the procurement process, and
3. Enhanced transparency of the procurement process (FreeMarkets, 2000, p. 1).

The interviewees gave their own opinions as to the benefits to be accrued through the use of reverse auctions.

After taking their input into account and reviewing the findings and research on the use of reverse auctions in governmental procurement, a new framework—the 3 P's of reverse auctions—will be utilized to analyze the benefits that reverse auctions can bring:
1. *Price* benefits
2. *Process* benefits
3. *Precision* benefits

Price Benefits

Michael Kelemen, director of the U.S. Army's CECOM Acquisition Center at Fort Monmouth, predicted that "I absolutely think it's going to revolutionize the way government procurement is conducted in the future" (cited in Sanborn, 2001, p. 32). It has been estimated that reverse auctions could shave anywhere from 10-60 percent off the "best" government prices—typically represented by the GSA Schedule price (Schwartz, 2000).

(1) Federal Level Examples

Although it is early to tell definitively, in reports of reverse auction pilots, savings have been reported in this range across government in the United States. In a variety of pilot tests held at the federal level, some of which are summarized in Table 9.3, this has been the case.

In one of the more notable tests of reverse auctions, the General Service Administration's Federal Technology Service (GSA-FTS) has conducted a series of auction events through its Buyers.gov operation (www.buyers.gov).

354 David C. Wyld

Table 9.3: Examples of Reverse Auctions at the Federal Level

Internal Revenue Service
In May 2001, the IRS saved 49 percent off the anticipated prices for an allotment of 11,362 desktop personal computers and 16,354 notebook computers to be installed over an eight-month period. The pre-bid prices started at $130 million, and the final bid price, submitted by the winners, PlanetGov.com and Dell Computer, was $63.4 million (Vasishtha, 2001).

Naval Supply Systems Command
In June 2000, the NSSC conducted a reverse auction, in conjunction with FreeMarkets, for components used in ejection seats utilized in several categories of fighter aircraft. The Navy estimated that its closing price of $2.4 million was 29 percent lower than the projected sales price (Roberti, 2000).

U.S. Navy
In April 2001, the U.S Navy saved $900,000 on an expected contract amount of $3 million for transporting the personal effects of military personnel between Hawaii and Guam (Terry, 2001).

U.S. Army
Michael Kelemen, director of the U.S. Army's Communications Electronic Command (CECOM) Acquisition Center at Fort Monmouth, New Jersey, reported that "we've procured everything from fax machines and computers to lumber and goats" through reverse auctioning, achieving an average 53 percent savings from the starting price over the course of 30 events (through March 2001) (cited in Sanborn, 2001, p. 32).

U.S. Postal Service
In a pilot test, conducted in the spring of 2000, the USPS conducted a reverse auction for leasing 4,600 mail-hauling trailers. The reverse auction event, conducted through FreeMarkets, enabled the Postal Service to save over 11 percent on its daily lease costs, producing an annualized savings of over $2.5 million (Schwartz, 2000).

In September 2000, the GSA-FTS held four reverse auctions for computers and printers for the Department of Defense Finance and Accounting Service (DFAS). The results of this auction are shown in Table 9.4. The savings from the four auctions, estimated at over $2 million, are based against what GSA-FTS describes as an Independent Government Cost Estimate (IGCE) for the items that were being procured. GSA-FTS followed up this series of auctions in November 2000 with online auctions for the U.S. Coast Guard to procure spare parts for HU-25 Falcon jets. The results of these auctions, which generated estimated savings—again versus an IGCE—of just over $300,000, are displayed in Table 9.5.

Table 9.4: Summary Results of GSA-FTS Reverse Auctions for the Department of Defense Finance and Accounting Service (DFAS)

Lots	IGCE Estimate	Ending Price	Total Savings	Savings
Lot 1 (500 Mhz Laptops)	$447,000	$360,000	$87,000	19.46%
Lot 2 (667 Mhz Desktops	$6,801,045	$5,997,000	$804,045	11.82%
Lot 3 (16 ppm Printers)	$1,250,666	$649,000	$601,666	48.11%
Lot 4 (24 ppm Printers)	$1,240,000	$637,000	$603,000	48.63%
TOTAL	$9,738,711	$7,643,000	$2,095,711	21.52%

Source: General Services Administration, Federal Technology Service–Office of Information Technology Integration (GSA-FTS). The Federal Technology Service Guide to Best Practices for Conducting Reverse Auctions. (April 2001): pp. 18-19 (www.buyers.gov).

Table 9.5: Summary Results of GSA-FTS Reverse Auctions for the U.S. Coast Guard

Lots	IGCE Estimate	Ending Price	Total Savings	Savings
1	$386,321	$210,000	$176,321	45.64%
2	$494,000	$459,062	$34,938	7.07%
3	$60,585	$35,045	$25,540	42.16%
4	$266,110	$249,833	$16,277	6.12%
5	$44,520	$35,925	$8,595	19.31%
6	$92,945	$53,291	$39,654	42.66%
7	$33,330	$31,462	$1,868	5.60%
TOTAL	$1,377,811	$1,074,618	$303,193	22.01%

Source: General Services Administration, Federal Technology Service–Office of Information Technology Integration (GSA-FTS). The Federal Technology Service Guide to Best Practices for Conducting Reverse Auctions. (April 2001): pp. 20-21 (www.buyers.gov).

Thomas R. Bloom, director of the Defense Finance and Accounting Service, was quoted as saying: "The Buyers.gov auction was tremendously success-ful and (the reverse auction) is a great vehicle to add to the competitive process. I think it has a great future in government procurement" (GSA-FTS, 2001, p. 19). As can be seen in the tables and is graphically depicted in Fig-ure 9.26, this initial series of auctions produced a cumulative savings of almost $2.5 million for the two agencies within the Department of Defense. To date, GSA-FTS has also reached beyond military procurement; in March 2001, it conducted reverse auctions for the National Institutes of Health for supplies, producing a 31 percent savings through the process.

Figure 9.26: Summary Results from Buyers.gov Pilot Reverse Auctions for the Department of Defense and the U.S. Coast Guard

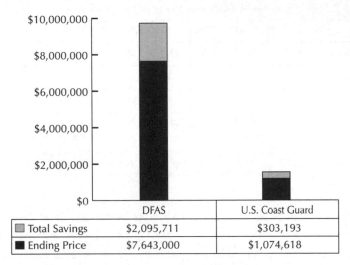

	DFAS	U.S. Coast Guard
▢ Total Savings	$2,095,711	$303,193
■ Ending Price	$7,643,000	$1,074,618

Source: General Services Administration, Federal Technology Service–Office of Information Technology Integration (GSA-FTS). The Federal Technology Service Guide to Best Practices for Conducting Reverse Auctions. (April 2001): (www.buyers.gov).

(2) State and Local Area Examples

At the state and local levels of government, the initial results coming from the use of reverse auctions show similar levels of savings to that achieved at the federal level. The state with the most experience in the area is the Commonwealth of Pennsylvania. Since 1999, the state has bid approximately a quarter billion dollars' worth of acquisitions through its FreeMarkets, based in Pittsburgh. To date, Pennsylvania has sourced a wide variety of items through FreeMarkets bidding events, including:

- Aluminum
- Capital equipment (such as loaders, back hoes, and paint trucks)
- Coal
- Electricity
- IT equipment
- Rock salt
- Sugar
- Telecommunications services (www.freemarkets.com).

The State of Minnesota conducted its first reverse auction in June 2001, on behalf of the Department of Corrections. The state bought half a million pounds of aluminum to be used for pressing license plates, saving an estimated $35,000 through the process (Morehead, 2001).

Many states, counties, and municipalities are observing the playing field, interested but letting others be the pioneers in this area. Thus, information such as that contained in Appendix I, analyzing the less-reported experiences of the State of Florida and the County of Los Angeles, California, should prove informative to the reader. Both of these jurisdictions' auctions produced tangible year-over-year savings against previously contracted amounts, making the cost savings much more tangible than in the federal cases covered earlier.

Process Benefits

The second broad category of benefits from the employment of reverse auctions in public sector e-procurement is in the area of the cost and execution of the acquisition process itself. It has been estimated that reverse auctions could shave 30-50 percent from procurement cycle times (Schwartz, 2000). CECOM Acquisition Center's Director Kelemen observed that the use of reverse auctions "save an awful lot of time ... and sometimes time is the most valuable piece of the process" (cited in Sanborn, 2001, p. 32).

In the federal government, as of the year 2000, the average time to award a contract stood at 268 days, according to a study conducted by the Logistics Management Institute. However, early examples of the shortened procurement cycle times experienced by the federal government are quite striking, as in the case of the U.S. Postal Service (USPS). In a pilot reverse auction program, the USPS' cycle time was reduced from approximately six months to less than one (reported in Schwartz, 2000).

Brandel of the Aberdeen Group noted: "What's driving reverse auctions right now is the time efficiency you get out of using them. Buyers, sourcers, and procurement agents are able to make their requests for service known to a much wider audience by combining reverse auctioning with matching engines and marketplaces" (cited in Sanborn, 2001, p. 32). On the other side of the equation, from the vendor's perspective, the process also eases the supplier's ability to work with the often laborious governmental procurement process. Phil Moore, vice president of sales at Egghead.com, observed: "I think reverse auctions are the future.... It's easier, from a supplier standpoint, to do this (the reverse auction) rather than sitting down and typing up a 40-page response (to an RFQ)" (cited in Sanborn, 2001, p. 32).

Precision Benefits

With auctions, dangers exist in ensuring the integrity of the process itself from a number of sources, including fraud, collusion, etc. This has been exemplified in the consumer-to-consumer markets, such as on eBay, where an estimated fraud rate of only 25 out of every million auctions has worked to taint the perceptions of many in the public that online auctions are "rife" with deceptive and illegal activities (Freedman, 2000). It has also been seen in the fine art market, where worldwide scandals involving the three major auction houses—Christie's, Sotheby's and Philips de Pury & Luxembourg—have resulted in investigations and charges of criminal collusions. These "backroom deals" have left people all over the art world asking: "What are the real prices for art?" (Peers, 2001, p. B1).

Yet, in contrast, the final area of benefit to governments making use of reverse auctions is the transparency inherent in the auctioning process itself.

As a society, we will have to learn how to deal with what Firmage (2000) characterized as capitalism doing a "full monty," coming in the form of the new and startling capabilities which bring us "total transparency" in transactions and trading. We will be able to gather a tremendous amount of information through the conduct of online auction events. As previously discussed, suppliers will be able to learn from their participation in bidding events a great deal about both themselves and their competitors. Likewise, governments will, over time, generate a wealth of information that can be "data mined" for patterns in both overall spending and e-procurement activities (Mattick and Brousseau, 2001).

For government, the benefits of such precision are immense. Instead of a paper trail supporting procurement decisions, the trail is electronic in nature. However, across the board, the use of reverse auction technologies provides a significant improvement in the ability of the procuring body to be able to indisputably demonstrate:

- Who bid
- What they bid
- When they bid
- Where they bid from

Further, according to FreeMarkets (2000), the concerns of governmental contracting officers to maintain a "fair and level paying field" in e-procurement activities can be greatly aided through the use of online auctions, due to the following characteristics of reverse auction events:

1. Potential suppliers are given identical information prior to the online auction.
2. Participating suppliers are given identical market information during the course of the online auction event.
3. Once the auction ends, buyers are able to make an immediate award decision, but they are not bound by price (p. 2).

This transparency and the ability to employ common metrics for measuring the success of all forms of dynamic-commerce, technology-based e-procurement efforts are a major focus of the recommendations section.

Illustrative List of Goods and Services Potentially Acquirable through Reverse Auctioning

IT Hardware and Peripherals
Computers & Monitors
Copiers & Fax Machines
Mobile Phones & Pagers
Modems
Printers
Routers and Switches
Scanners
Telephony Equipment
Video Systems
Wire and Cable

Electronics
Capacitors & Resistors
Circuit Assemblies
Motors
Printed Circuit Boards
Wires and Cables

Motorized Equipment
Aircraft
Earth-Moving Equipment
Forklifts
Generators
Landscaping Equipment
Passenger Vehicles
Trucks, Buses, and Vans
Watercraft

Office Management
Appliances
Copy Paper
Desk Phones
Furniture
Office Supplies

Food, Clothing & Health Care
Animal Feed
Athletic Equipment
Chemicals
Food Ingredients
Laboratory Equipment
Medical Equipment
Medical & Surgical Supplies
Prescription Drugs
Publication Subscriptions
Textiles

Uniforms
Vending Machines
Vitamins and Food Supplements

Services
Actuarial
Auto Repair & Maintenance
Building Demolition & Renovation
Building Maintenance
Call Center Services
Carpet Cleaning
Cellular Phone
Construction & Site Preparation
Debt Collection
Express Delivery
Food Preparation/Catering
Food Services
Janitorial
Landscaping
Laundry
Legal Services
Local & Long Distance Phone
Lodging
Machine Tool Repair
Marketing/Promotional Materials
Medical Waste Removal
Mine Reclamation
Paging
Pesticide/Herbicide Application
Photocopier Maintenance
Plumbing
Professional Counseling
Professional Printing
Relocation Services
Reproduction Services
Security
Tax Preparation
Telecommunications Installation
Temporary Services
Transportation
Utility Auditing
Vending Machine Services
Video Production
Web Hosting and Maintenance

Source: Adapted from American Management Systems and FreeMarkets (2000), p. 7.

What Can—and Cannot—Be Auctioned

Limitless ... or with Boundaries?

As can be seen through these examples, a wide variety of goods have been acquired through reverse auction processes. According to American Management Systems and FreeMarkets (2000), who enumerated a list of *potential* goods and services that could be procured through reverse auctioning, the potential range is quite wide.

Yet, as Dwight Young, director of National Mail Transportation Purchasing for the United States Postal Service, acknowledged, in actuality, reverse auctions are "not going to fit all commodities" (quoted in Schwartz, 2000, p. 199).

Reverse Auctions and Services

The list enumerated contains many potential services that could be subject to auctioning. Yet, according to Brenda Willard, acquisitions director for the State of Minnesota's Materials Management Division, reverse auctions are much more conducive to goods than to services, as you can easily specify *what* you want and *when* you want it (cited in Morehead, 2001). Certainly, one of the key issues that will influence the trajectory of reverse auctioning in the public sector is whether they are conducive to the acquisition of services as well. As can be seen in the interview exchanges, experts believe that it may prove difficult to use reverse auction technology for these purposes for anything other than the simplest—and least mission-critical—services.

Suppliers' Reactions to Reverse Auctions

Overview

One of the primary drivers of the Internet revolution is that commercial friction—delay, ignorance, transaction costs—continues to disappear as we evolve to transparent relationships across the economy. This trend changes the marketplace by providing participants with omnipresent information. There are many benefits of this—especially in enhancing the market power of the buyer. However, for the sellers, it is another story, "as one of the central business problems for years to come will be making money in a friction-free economy" (Colvin, 2001, p. 54). Thus, while transparency and the reporting capabilities of reverse auction technologies provide great benefits to the public sector, they provide a fundamental challenge to the other side of the procurement equation—the suppliers.

In the New Economy, it has been said that "value is created through ubiquity" (Commerce One, 2000, p. 1). In accordance with Metcalfe's law, the power—and value—of the network is increased with more participants.

To make reverse auctions *work*, having interested suppliers bidding in the auction events is a fundamental requirement. They simply must be there for the auction model to work. In fact, the use of the Internet in general—and, in particular, "innovative contracting models such as reverse auctions"— has actually worked to increase the number of potential vendors who are aware of and actually bidding on governmental procurements, helping to create more choice and more competition in public sector contracting (Reason Public Policy Institute, 2000, p. 32).

The "Squeeze Play"

Michael R. Katzorke, senior vice president, Supply Chain Management, Cessna Aircraft Company, stated: "I think reverse auctions are based on a faulty supposition that there are huge margins to be attacked" (quoted in Anonymous, "E-Auction Playbook: What Top Supply Execs Say About Auctions," 2001, p. S2).

As Birk and Macready (2001) observed, suppliers have to see potential for their own cost savings and revenue maximization to have a real incentive to participate in e-marketplaces and, in particular, reverse auctions. Otherwise, they will just feel that electronic markets are a means for buyers to squeeze margin out of them—which they may or may not have. Wilson Rothschild, a senior analyst with Metagroup, Inc., a Boston-based consulting firm, observed that, thus far, suppliers have felt that they have been "bullied" through their participation in online marketplaces to drive prices down. He feels that as long as judgments are primarily price-focused, the environment is one of "caveat vendor ... let the seller beware" (as quoted in Eure, 2001, p. R14).

As Jap (2000) explains, sellers can often end up feeling exploited through their participation in online procurement auctions. This is due to the fact that buyers, who may talk about creating partnerships with their suppliers, are perfectly willing to put their relationship on the line in a reverse auction. Eure (2001) states that foremost among the reservations that suppliers have to participating in reverse auctions is the fear that their product or service offering will be "commoditized," unable to be differentiated on intangible attributes such as service and quality.

Supplier Attitudes

How do suppliers feel about participating in reverse auctions? Certainly, reactions are across the board. New vendors have been brought in to participate in reverse auctions, but, on the other hand, existing vendors have seen their incumbent status and existing relationships threatened. As can be seen in the excerpts from the interviews conducted for this report on the subject, the attitudes of suppliers will be crucial in how reverse auctioning takes form across the governmental market.

Question: "Can Reverse Auctions Be Effectively Used for the Acquisition of Services?"

I think it will be more difficult to buy services under reverse auctioning. In limited cases, the buys should parallel that of commodities, with simple, indirect services being auctioned first. The difficulty with most services is that they are generally complex and require more of an evaluation process. Government is getting away from buying hours. I think the multiple award GWACs are better suited to the kind of responsible, fixed-price task orders that many procurement leaders are promoting. An example of where we've seen successful services procured with auctions is in the training arena. Training requirements can usually be well defined in terms of students, materials, location, amenities, etc. I don't ever foresee large-scale systems developments being auctioned.

Ken Buck, Executive Director of Business Innovation, GSA-FTS

Reverse auctions can possibly be employed for routine or repetitive services, such as lawn mowing, but not for sophisticated technical and professional services. As one moves along the continuum towards more complicated systems integration and complex professional services, the reverse auction technique is wholly inapplicable. The FAR calls for the exercise of independent business judgment by a source selection authority, which a price-alone technique—such as a reverse auction—cannot accomplish.

Take a systems integration requirement for shipboard communications, for example. Offers will differ as to technical approach, past performance, program management techniques, cost or price, and other evaluation factors and subfactors for award. To conduct a reverse auction, the technical approaches of the offerors would have to be disclosed to each offeror. Such disclosure is currently prohibited under the FAR. Even assuming this could be done, it is not clear how one firm would "bid" against the other on technical issues in a meaningful way. Technical offers would not match. Pricing or costing of one offer would not relate to the other. In technical areas, the auction is not "reverse" anymore. Each offeror would have to offer additional technical services for the same price or less. Thus, the auction would be reverse in one area (cost or price) and traditional "highest bidder" in the other (technical factors).

Objective changes in technical offers might be possible. More subjective changes, such as improved quality control, faster service, or clearer signals, may not be possible to track in such a reverse auction. Each offeror's unique approach to integrating services on the ship must be evaluated on its own, and against its own cost or price. A low price may indicate a lack of comprehension of the requirements, not a better price proposal. Additionally, classified issues may have to be dealt with and may prevent disclosure in the first place.

David P. Metzger, Partner, Holland & Knight, LLP

It is important to bear in mind the observation of Kambil and van Heck (2001), who stated: "Whenever someone is left worse off by the change to electronic markets, it is unlikely a new market will succeed, unless that party is initially subsidized or faces competitive pressures to participate in the market" (p. 7). As Eure (2001) cautions, there is great potential for online marketplaces, but only when *all* benefit from participation in e-procurement auctions (buyers and suppliers alike). Jap (2000) urged that reverse auctions be used strategically, perhaps to "wake up" their present supplier base and/or increase the number of participating vendors. However, they should also be complemented through the cultivation of long-term e-sourcing relationships with key suppliers. What if—as Sostrom (2001) and others have proposed—suppliers simply refused to participate in reverse auctions? Then, the whole supposition behind the value of these auctions could disappear.

Small and Minority-Owned Businesses

Some of the changes in the federal procurement process, particularly the emergence of government-wide acquisition contracts, or GWACs— which tend to favor large vendors—have diminished the effectiveness of the Small Business Administration's 8(a) program. This 8(a) program was specifically aimed at helping small and minority-owned businesses compete for federal contracts (Wait, 2001b).

In contrast, the development of e-markets may serve to actually enhance the competitiveness of small and minority-owned businesses. As noted by Sanborn (2001), one of the principal benefits of reverse auctions is that they somewhat level the playing field for small businesses, as they "can learn about the negotiation process and how to be competitive on the buying end" (p. 32). In most cases, all a company (or individual) needs to participate in a web-based auction is a computer—or access to one—equipped with a web browser (Mitchell, 2000). Small and minority-owned businesses, like all auction participants, can use their participation in online auctions as a way of learning if their production costs are in line with their competitors (Eure, 2001). There is also an emphasis on increasing the number of potential suppliers through the use of online acquisition auctions, which typically helps small businesses. For example, FreeMarkets maintains a database to match potential suppliers with buyers holding bidding events. They actively recruit small businesses to participate in reverse auctions and aid them through personal, hands-on training in the conduct of the auction process (through participation in training auctions using FreeMarkets' software) and in the calculation of their internal costs in order to make proper decisions on the extent of their bidding during the auction event (Kalin, 2001b).

According to Dizard (2001a), small and medium-size companies can greatly benefit from the increased exposure they get through participating in governmental e-marketplaces. Moreover, they may actually have a com-

Question: "What Are Supplier Attitudes Toward Reverse Auctions?"

Companies are in business to do business. They will generally pursue opportunities where the margins make sense for them to do so. While companies will usually be willing to take a hit on certain purchases to gain market access or some other business reason, at the end of the day they have to make their numbers to stay in business. Reverse auctions don't seem to provide a great opportunity for this.

Larry Allen, Executive Director, Coalition for Government Procurement

For buyers, the obstacles are straightforward. This will not be the first time that they have automated an aspect of their jobs. While there are some things to learn, the basic business behind negotiating with suppliers will not change. In many ways, this process makes the supplier better off as well—the cycle times are reduced, the negotiation process is automated, and they have the opportunity to win new deals that may not have been open to them—but the perception is somewhat different. The crux of the issue is around the fact that bidding online typically creates a more competitive environment. This is why buyers get better prices and terms. The first few events are difficult for suppliers because they are feeling the price pressure.

Here is what we have seen at Moai. As suppliers do more and more events, as they get away from straight, price-based reverse auctions and get more exposure to multi-attribute RFQs, they see the brighter side of e-sourcing. Many go on to become e-sourcing users themselves.

Ray Letulle, Chief Technology Officer, Moai, Inc.

Supplier reactions have been mixed. Suppliers fixate on transaction fees assessed by the application service provider and tend to overlook the benefits (such as "free" marketing to subdivisions, reduced maverick buying, etc.). Once vendors get on board and experience the advantages, the reaction becomes much more favorable. Vendors are now contacting us to get on the system.

Jim Passier, Procurement Manager, State of Connecticut

The sticking point is with the vendors, and my guess is it will cause them to cry a little. Some may argue that their products cannot be treated as commodities. In the long run, reverse auctioning can offer a faster, simpler method for public entities to obtain contracts while continuing to support the fairness rules now in place. Way2Bid makes every effort to consider vendor and fairness issues in the product it presents to buyers. That's one of the things we advise people to look at in evaluating an e-procurement provider: can they offer reverse auction capability and still meet fairness requirements.

Bill Perkin, CEO, Way2Bid

> You have got to make sure you have the buyer understanding and articulating the strategy behind what it is they do to their supply base. That is the most important. The second would be simple education of the supply base.
>
> If you think about it, if you have four or five suppliers that are going to be in an auction event, there is only one that is not going to be happy and that's the incumbent. The other three are bidding on business they currently don't have. What we have found, over time, is that the incumbent supplier starts to recognize that this is just another form of negotiations that just happens to be on an online platform and that if used properly, they could significantly expand this as a new channel for their business. Part of the savings comes from the fact the suppliers become much more knowledgeable in their business when it becomes more competitive. What we have found is that over the years, they become much more efficient as well, which means their costs go down. This gives us a better potential for additional savings over the years.
>
> Probably the best example I know of that is a large computer manufacturer. A while back, they were a bit reluctant to participate in this, but now I know they have a representative that is solely responsible for FreeMarkets. They see it as a channel. It was a combination of understanding the value of what we bring to the table and recognizing that there could be a whole new channel of business for them.
>
> *Joe Quigg, FreeMarkets, Inc.*

petitive advantage over big firms in that they do not face the "back-end" integration hurdles that large companies often face in dealing with public sector e-procurement systems.

Finally ... the Excitement Factor

One of the expressions heard time and time again in talking to those involved in reverse auctions—whether from the standpoint of the buying organization, the auction service provider, or the bidding vendors, is the excitement of the experience.

When the appointed hour arrives, the tension is usually thick in the buying organization, as weeks or months of preparation for the event translate into action—and usually tangible savings. There is also an "excitement factor" for the suppliers who participate in reverse auctions. One supplier quite honestly compared auction events to football games, as sometimes the early stages of the allotted time make "watching the computer screen like watching paint dry"—until the final minutes of the auction, when competition takes hold (Manciagli, 2001, p. S14). Suppliers who bid in online procurement auctions often describe their bidding experiences in terms like "wildly emotional" and "gut-wrenching" (Kalin, 2001b). Sellers have to beware getting caught up in an "underbidding frenzy," lowering their bids again and again in a competitive effort to "win" the auction.

As Kalin (2001a) points out, suppliers must determine—in advance of the auction event itself—how low they can *reasonably* go in their bidding. In other words, they must know what their "walk-away price" is. Indeed, as Ray Bjorklund, vice president of consulting services at McLean, Virginia-based Federal Sources, commented: "Spending the money and effort to get involved in a bidding scenario shouldn't be done before careful forethought. Suppliers should think carefully about their business model before they enter into an auction" (quoted in Schwartz, 2000, p. 199).

In sum, Phillips (2001) holds that pricing and revenue management decisions are amongst the most important decisions any firm can make. This is especially true when dealing with reverse auctions.

Reverse Auction Guidance

As can be seen, there are a multitude of factors that need to be considered before using reverse auctions as a *tool* as part of their overall e-procurement efforts. Some of the issues involved in making use of reverse auctions—and indeed all dynamic commerce mechanisms—will be discussed at length in the recommendations section of this chapter. At this point, where we have concrete, but limited, evidence as to how reverse auctioning has been used in public sector e-procurement, it is *vital* for decision makers in governmental procurement and the vendor community to remember that we are early in the adoption phase of reverse auctions and other tools. As such, they should endeavor to stay on top of the matter and look for models and success stories that they themselves can benchmark and model their own efforts after. Reverse auctions should be considered for a number of new, emerging e-procurement applications, including spot buys (Moai, 2000b), and to establish pricing for catalog-based items (FreeMarkets, 2000).

Unlike in the private sector, as discussed previously, where e-sourcing capabilities may be kept confidential as a source of competitive advantage, this holds no sway in the governmental marketspace. Thus, hopefully, through forums such as this, these success stories can be shared. Conversely, French Caldwell, research director at the Gartner Group, stated that there will be "a high rate of e-government project failures in the next several years (that) may be unavoidable" (quoted in Gibbs, 2000, p. 1). Hopefully, while the public sector is reluctant to publicize failures (as will also be discussed later in this chapter), governmental executives will share these stories as well when reverse auctioning seems to fail, so as others may not follow in their footsteps.

In ending this overview of reverse auctioning in the public sector, this author provides two general forms of guidance for those considering implementing this tool. First, in Table 9.6, guidelines are provided on when the use of reverse auctioning would be most appropriate. Also, an overall framework is provided for considering making use of reverse auctioning on the next page.

The "Price Only" Dilemma of Reverse Auctioning

When asked her opinions on reverse auctioning, Sarah Pfaff, co-founder and executive vice-president of eBreviate, recently responded bluntly, "Price-only auctions are dead" (cited in Waxer, 2001, p. 34). Certainly, price has been "the driving force" in the development of online e-markets and in pushing companies in the private sector and governmental bodies as well into e-procurement (Eure, 2001). Yet, the most severe criticism of reverse auctions is certainly their unidimensional focus on price alone. As Mattick and Brousseau (2001) observed: "As powerful a tool as reverse auctions have proven to be, not all sourcing events can be reduced to a single decision factor such as price" (p. 133).

Thus, the reverse auction model has been said to be incapable of capturing the true complexity that goes into procurement decision making, whether in the private sector or governmental purchasing environment. Indeed, at present, major companies operating in sophisticated e-market-places, such as Eastman Kodak, report that fully 80 percent of their e-pro-

Table 9.6: When–and When Not to–Use Reverse Auctions

Conditions Favoring Use of Reverse Auctions	Conditions Favoring Use of Alternatives
Many qualified suppliers	Few qualified suppliers
Commodity product	Specialized product
Buyer is important to suppliers	Buyer is small or transactional
Excess capacity in industry	Little or no excess capacity
Price is key selection criterion	Total-cost focus
Buyer is willing to award business based on results of reverse auction	Buyer wants flexibility

Source: Adapted from Desai-Sarnowski and Murzyn (2001), p. S16.

Factors to Consider in Implementing Reverse Auctions

According to the National Electronic Commerce Coordinating Council (2000a), governments seeking to implement reverse auctions as part of their e-procurement efforts should consider all of the following factors:

- **Saving Money:** The opportunity to discover actual market value of a commodity or service is more readily provided by a dynamic bidding environment, where interested suppliers can react to the bid activity of their competitors.
- **Security:** Fraud, confidentiality, authenticity of the signer and document, integrity of the message, and non-repudiation are typical starting points in discussions about the many possible Internet security issues.
- **Spoofing:** There may be more opportunities in an electronic environment for misrepresentations of identity. The impact in an auction environment is that artificial bidding might occur. Vendor registration, required by most jurisdictions currently, would likely remain a sound practice to minimize identity issues.
- **Collusion:** Many government procurement laws require bidders to affirm that they have not colluded in an attempt to influence the outcome of a competitive bid process.
- **Regulatory Environment (Legality of Auctions, Policy):** Each jurisdiction must determine whether it has the authority to conduct a buyer's auction. Other provisions, such as statutory conditions limiting the ability to make changes to a bid after initial submission, need also to be reviewed.
- **Disparate Impact on Suppliers:** Auctions, whether physical or electronic, require access. The impact of access is a significant one in public purchasing and often influences policies, if not statutes, which regulate that function.
- **Fail-Safe Technology:** Government should ensure the reliability of bid submission components and clearly specify and communicate the supported hardware and software required.
- **Training:** The advent of auctions as a procurement method may require new skills of public purchasing personnel.
- **Competition:** Assessment must be undertaken to ensure that if auctions are implemented, no potential supplier is unreasonably expected to modify their business practices to be required to compete.
- **Auctionable Materials:** Not all goods or services are candidates for auctions as the appropriate purchasing method. Guidelines are needed to ensure the procurement staff are familiar with the viability of auction in any circumstances.

Source: Adapted from the National Electronic Commerce Coordinating Council (2000a, p. 10-11).

curement auctions are conducted on a price-only basis, with cost being the sole driving factor. Yet, the remaining 20 percent may represent some of the most mission-critical procurements conducted by an organization (Orzell, 2001). ICG Commerce's CEO Rick Berry branded price as being "a takeoff point" from which you can use technology to enable transactions (cited in Baldwin, 2001a, p. 37). The goal will be to establish means through which buying organizations "will be able to consider many variables, not just price, to evaluate suppliers and their bids" (Jap, 2000, p. 3).

Aiming for the Lowest *Total* Cost

"The goal of any sourcing initiative should be to select the mix of suppliers, products, and services that best meets the organization's requirements at the *lowest total cost*, which is the sum of many parameters" (emphasis in the original) (Aberdeen Group, *e-Sourcing: Negotiating Value in a Volatile Economy—An Executive White Paper from the Aberdeen Group*, 2001, p. 1).

Kevin O'Marah, a senior analyst with AMR Research, believes that e-marketplaces will become more multidimensional and interactive over the next few years. Not only will e-procurements become based on "price-plus," there will be more two-way communication and collaboration. For instance, suppliers may be able to suggest product modifications or quantity/delivery changes that might be to the benefit of all parties. As he concluded: "The real promise of e-markets is not cost savings, though that is part of it. It's in the exchange of information and increasing the value of the product so that both the buyer and seller profit" (quoted in Eure, 2001, p. R14).

As an example of how "price-plus" e-procurement methodologies are being employed in the private sector, Whirlpool now holds online auctions based on "total costs," including financing terms. Over the course of five months, the company saved approximately $2 million through five events, while also doubling the grace period with its suppliers (Waxer, 2001).

Reverse Auctions and "Best Value" Procurement

Michael Kelemen, director of the U.S. Army's CECOM Acquisition Center, suggested that, over time, reverse auction technology will have to evolve to include "best value" considerations, "so that they will include a variable other than just the lowest bidding price" (cited in Sanborn, 2001, p. 32). According to Sherry Amos, vice president of marketing for Rockville, Maryland-based B2eMarkets: "The original premise of government exchanges was to pressure suppliers. Now, *total value* is the focus" (quoted in Terry, 2001, p. 3). Yet, if "best value" decisions are still heavily price based, vendors will be just as scared off as in price-only reverse auctions (Caternicchia, 2000).

Question: "How Can Reverse Auctions Be Reconciled with Best Value Procurement Decisions?"

Well, I think we've all seen and heard from reverse auction proponents that reverse auction buyers have always had the ability to use "best value" acquisition criteria. From the start, reverse auction providers and procurement executives have emphasized that no tool would require a user to make anything other than a best value determination. The reality is, though, that the starkness of the reverse auction model makes it extremely difficult for federal buyers to make a selection on any other factor than low price. The fear of protests and internal criticism means that very few procurement executives will have the fortitude to go with anything else. Best value determinations are the prehensile tail of reverse auction features—it's there, but it doesn't mean much.

Larry Allen, Executive Director, Coalition for Government Procurement

There seems to be some confusion in the marketplace around the relationship between reverse auctioning and e-sourcing. The fact is that reverse auction is just one of many tools used within e-sourcing to select suppliers and achieve payment terms. E-sourcing covers the whole sourcing process, from analyzing historical spend data, qualifying suppliers, determining key factors, and selecting suppliers and purchasing terms. In the private sector, reverse auctioning can be used as a tool to select suppliers and determine purchasing terms for about 15-20 percent of the total spend of a purchasing organization. These are the things for which price and quantity are most important. However, the other 80-85 percent of the purchases require more sophisticated capabilities. As the purchase becomes more complex, buyers need multi-

---

John Magnino, the Buyers.Gov engagement manager at IBM Business Consulting Services, reflects on his experience: "When the federal government first began using reverse auctions in online e-procurement, the lowest price and technically acceptable bid award was more common, due to its being simpler and more applicable to commodities. As reverse auction use has progressed, and more complex procurements are now occurring, it is evident that reverse auction solutions, with their multiparametric weighting capabilities, are an effective tool for promoting best value selection during the procurement process."

According to Enos (2001), public sector procurement rules often have had government officials "worry as much about fairness and equal access by bidders as they do about prices" (p. 1). As Laurent (2000) commented:

> While businesses buy to bolster the bottom line, government buys not only to provide goods and services to citizens, but also to achieve a host of

attribute and total cost model ("best value") RFQs that go beyond the simple price and quantity reverse auctions. Because rules and regulations often dictate price as the primary factor, I would expect this percentage to be higher for governments. Yet, the relatively low adoption rate means that it will be a while before we can say exactly what this number will be.

Ray Letulle, Chief Technology Officer, Moai, Inc.

At FreeMarkets, we do provide best value procurements. This is one of the "great myths" of e-sourcing and reverse auctioning. Purchasing people often think: "We are going to do this and our supply base is going to be all mad at us. We are going to put them in a box and beat them over the head with a stick and try to reduce their costs." This is not what we are all about. We provide—through our technology and services—numerous paths for our customers to be able to use transformational bidding and present value bidding, so that buyers can make educated decisions by using our platform to do their negotiations. The interesting thing is that during the negotiations, all suppliers are also dealing with each other, as opposed to one on one with the buyer. It helps drive the market price down, but at the end of the day, that buyer is going to make a decision. The decision is going to be based on whatever the best value is. This could include a number of different factors—financial terms, payment terms, or lease vs. buy. There are a number of different ways we have built this into our bids, and it is a very accepted practice for those who have taken the time to really understand what we do.

Joe Quigg, FreeMarkets, Inc.

social and economic goals. Supporting small, women-owned and disadvantaged businesses, keeping certain industries afloat, making sure veterans have jobs, favoring American enterprises, keeping felons from pocketing taxpayers' dollars, ensuring fair competition and a long list of other policy goals make federal procurement a rule-bound and confusing exercise—even now, when the government's purchasing system has been reformed and streamlined (p. 28).

As can be seen in the excerpts from the interviews, the general sentiment is that price-only reverse auctions are incompatible with the best value considerations that must be made in governmental purchasing. Thus, the challenge will be to develop tools that both will be better suited to deal with the complexities of real world public and private purchasing decisions and, as Sostrom (2001) pointed out, will enable both parties in the procurement transaction to accomplish their strategic goals.

"Price-Plus" Tools

We are entering what Michael Dow, chief e-business officer at American Management Systems, termed "a period of adjustment," as various government agencies are really just experimenting with standard, price-based reverse auctions. However, he predicts that, in the near future, we will see many experiments with *different* types of auctions, which will form the "beginnings of the reverse-auctioning concept as a legitimate, mainstream approach" (quoted in Schwartz, 2000, p. 199).

In the following pages, we will examine two of these *different* "price-plus" applications of dynamic commerce methods in governmental e-procurement. These are:
1. Multiparametric Auctions
2. Demand Aggregation

Multiparametric Auctions

One of the trends likely to spur the spread of auctions in e-procurement is the move away from price-only-based reverse auctions to multiple variable-based (or *multiparametric)* auctions. In other words, these will be what at first glance appears to be an oxymoron—an auction incorporating aspects *other than price* into the equation. Such multiparametric auctions have been labeled in various ways, including:
- Multi-variable auctions
- Multi-attribute auctions
- Multi-stage auctions
- Transformational bidding
- Structured negotiations
  Factors such as the following may be included in the auction environment:
- Condition of goods
- Warranty
- Delivery dates
- Transportation methods
- Customer support
- Supplier performance history
- Financing
- Quality
  For example, if an agency was conducting an auction seeking a provider for a provision of copy machine services, the variables that could be included in a multiparametric auction could include:
- Price *plus*
- Toner and supplies
- Customer support

- Service terms
- Warranty
- Replacement parts
- Finance terms

How might multiparametric auctions work? First, let us take the copy machine service example. Under a reverse auction, the only variable that vendors would be competing on, assuming that they could all meet the needed product and service specifications of the RFQ, would be price. However, as shown in Figure 9.27, under multiparametric conditions, suppliers would be bidding on all specified aspects as laid out by the contracting agency.

Rather than having the complexity of handling all specified variables at once, more realistically, organizations can employ a multi-stage, multi-attribute approach. This enables the buying organization to winnow suppliers down by gaining the "best in class" at each stage of the auction, as all suppliers who continue on in the process must meet the standards established in the marketplace through the dynamic bidding. An example of such a multi-stage, multi-attribute auction is depicted in Figure 9.28. As can be seen, the three parameters were:

1. Price
2. Shipping terms
3. Quality level

Figure 9.27: A Multiparametric Auction for Copying Services

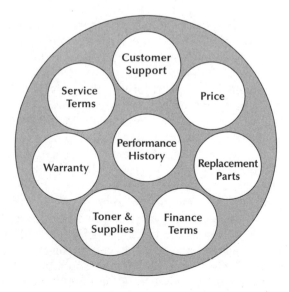

Figure 9.28: A Graphical Representation of a Multi-Stage/Multi-Attribute E-Procurement Auction

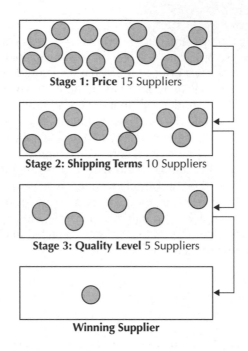

Stage 1: Price 15 Suppliers

Stage 2: Shipping Terms 10 Suppliers

Stage 3: Quality Level 5 Suppliers

Winning Supplier

While price was the initial "qualifying" stage of the auction—eliminating five bidders who could not, or chose not to, meet the market price established in the auction event—according to Moai (2000b), the first stage need not be price.

The panel of experts interviewed for this chapter was rather optimistic on the future applicability of multiparametric auctions.

As pointed out in the interviews, one of the major hindrances to the growth of such multi-variable auctions is the development of software—and level of built-in intelligence—needed to handle such events (Edwards, 2001). Fisher's (2000) review of the Toronto-based Bid.com's Dyn@mic Buyer Product describes how a buyer selects a series of selection criteria upon which the procurement decision is to be made, including price *and* other factors, such as delivery method, warranty, training, etc. These attributes are each assigned a value, and the supplier whose "bid" has the highest overall score (weighted according to the predetermined algorithm) "wins" the auction. Likewise, FreeMarkets uses sophisticated software that converts buyer preferences on between 50 and 200 buying attributes into an individualized algorithm that can be constructed to "transform" supplier bids, so that the competing bids can be evaluated on a total cost frame-work—in real time. Needless to say, one of the critical issues was how such weighting of factors should be done and how such decisions could be defensible in public sector e-procurement.

Three Next-Generation Auction Concepts

Certainly, different and more complex auction methodologies will not be necessary for all acquisition activities, and their nature ratchets up the costs and complexity of using dynamic pricing. Thus, one of the major challenges facing procurement executives in the coming years will be to find "the right tool for the job" (Edwards, 2001, p. 64). It will thus be necessary to develop tools and algorithms to make and automate such choices, pre-senting great opportunities for individuals and companies to develop expert-ise and marketability in this matter. As Sostrom (2001) aptly characterized the situation, the greatest challenge in implementing multiparametric auc-tions will be for procurement managers to be able to correctly identify and quantify non-price factors and to choose the "right tool for the job."

Total Cost RFQs

In the public sector, use of "Total Cost RFQs"—where all product or service characteristics are specified in great detail, so that only suppliers who can deliver this "price + other factors" mix can participate in the final, price-based auction—can achieve much the same results as a multi-variable auction. This can further be done without some of the "game day" complexity and possible contestability due to invariably having to monetize or convert product/service attributes to a numerical factor (FreeMarkets, 2000).

It is essential that organizations put the time into developing such Total Cost RFQs, as they not only aid the buying organization, but also the ven-dors. FreeMarkets Chairman and CEO Glen Meakem (2001) observed that the use of Total Cost RFQS allows for a "level playing field" amongst poten-tial suppliers.

The "Bot.com" Solution

Birk and Macready (2001) foresee the development of more and more "automated markets," which would strive for optimized procurement decisions through sophisticated matching engine software, employing multidimensional matching algorithms. Likewise, Appell and Brousseau (2000) similarly pre-dict the development of "continuous matching" marketplaces, which will be characterized by having "automated agents, comparable to current com-puterized stock-trading systems, perform matching in real time" (p. 88).

Question: "What Is the Future for Multiparametric/Multi-Stage Auctions?"

I would choose a different word than multi-stage. Perhaps "multi-faceted" or "dynamic" is more suitable. Multi-stage implies that there will be multiple rounds of proposals, which might suggest an increased burden on industry. There will certainly be pricing adjustments during the auction period. "On the fly" adjustments are viable, using technology like the e-Breviate tool. It automates, to some degree, the best value attributes. GSA has always championed the use of best value acquisitions and will continue to do so. We think that this methodology is in the best interest of both government and industry.

Ken Buck, Executive Director of Business Innovation, GSA-FTS

The key to what FreeMarkets terms "transformational bidding" is that on bid day, you actually have "apples and apples" being compared to one another.

For instance, in one event that I participated in, there happened to be multi-currency, rank bidding, and transformation. As a result, we had three different suppliers bidding three very different solutions. Thus, there was no way for the purchasing organization to be able to see—in a real-time event— something that was comparing apples to apples, unless they applied the right formula. One supplier needed a mark-up applied to it because of the way their bid was done. Now, you are getting out of a simple commodity, like "how much are you going to charge me for xyz commodity" to a more complex RFP, and if we go with this bidder, there are some issues related with it— not that we wouldn't go with it, but we just need to take them into account.

Bill Bunce, National Account Manager—Public Sector, FreeMarkets, Inc.

This is the direction of online sourcing. Buyers want to negotiate on more than just price and quantity. The multi-stage ability enables buyers to cost-effectively rationalize their supplier list from a large number to a smaller number through successive rounds by filtering out non-compliant suppliers.

Last year, for example, Moai was one of the first companies to pilot reverse auctions for the U.S. Army. The resultant system focused on "best value" auctions, where the lowest bidder doesn't necessarily win. For example, making sure the products delivered meet specific user specifications, and making sure that goods reach the field as soon as possible, are as important as saving taxpayer dollars. Following the success of the pilot engagement with the U.S. Army, Moai is now involved in integrating e-sourcing solutions for other defense agencies.

Ray Letulle, Chief Technology Officer, Moai, Inc.

From Multiple Parameters and Stages ... to Negotiations

According to the Aberdeen Group (2001, p. 11), total cost e-procurement solutions move away from the realm of the auctions arena and into a variety of online *negotiation* frameworks. These can take on three general forms, which are:

1. *Multiparameter negotiations*—enabling the negotiation and evaluation of suppliers based on multiple elements, including price, delivery, quality, warranties, and payment terms.
2. *Multi-threaded negotiations*—enabling iterative negotiations on a particular line item or selection criteria, such as delivery cycles. Such back-and-forth negotiations enable buyers to refine their requirements and suppliers to adjust their offers until they arrive at the optimal terms for both parties.
3. *Multi-round negotiations*—enabling the vetting of suppliers based on a particular criterion, such as quality, to determine which suppliers are qualified to move to the next stage of negotiations. Such multi-stage negotiations assist buyers in gathering details on all suppliers for use in future sourcing events.

Thus, we will see the progression from auction *events* to more ongoing, e-sourcing *relationships*. The discussion of the implications of these and other changes and challenges will be discussed in the recommendations section.

Dynamic Commerce and Demand Aggregation

Demand aggregation is one of the most promising concepts on the horizon for applying dynamic pricing concepts, both in private and public sector e-procurement. As depicted in Figure 9.4 in the Introduction to this chapter, demand aggregation simply is a way of pooling orders for similar goods—and conceivably services—between buyers. Jaroneczyk (2001) labels the demand aggregation model a "network auction," defined by the fact that prices are flexible, based on the convergence of supply, demand, and time (as pictured in Figure 9.29). This precise supply/demand configuration will be dependent upon the aggregation of buyers—the network—assembled at a given point in time.

The Mechanics of Demand Aggregation

How does demand aggregation work? Conceptually, the concept is easily understood. As shown in Figure 9.30, without demand aggregation, markets operate as an arena in which one-to-one transactions occur. Even if e-procurement methods are utilized—even the other forms of dynamic commerce previously discussed—still, the final transactions are direct, not being coordinated or aggregated in any way. However, with demand aggregation

Figure 9.29: The Convergence of Factors Present in Demand Aggregation

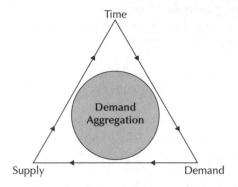

Figure 9.30: Marketplaces Operating without Demand Aggregation

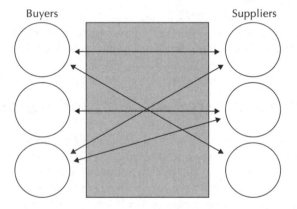

(as demonstrated in Figure 9.31), these individual purchase transactions are coordinated to gain higher volumes, better prices, and, perhaps, better purchase conditions on other factors as well. This is because these collaborative efforts bring more buying power to formerly disparate actors, while simultaneously making the transactions more valuable to the seller as well.

What are the plusses and downsides to demand aggregation? Largely the impact has been forecast to be positive. The benefits of demand aggregation to both procuring organizations and vendors are summarized below. On the other hand, demand aggregation has been characterized as having "asymmetrical benefits," in that one side achieves benefit at the expense of the other (Brooks, 2001). Yet, as one can see in the discussion conducted

Figure 9.31: Marketplaces Operating with Demand Aggregation

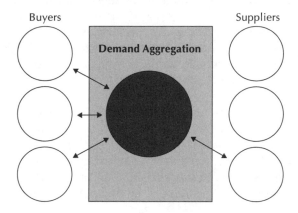

for this report with Greg Mesaros, founder, president, and CEO of eWinWin, a leading demand aggregation service provider, this is really an incorrect perspective. On page 382, Mesaros describes how both the procuring organization(s) and their suppliers can benefit from demand aggregation.

Use of Demand Aggregation in the Public Sector

How can demand aggregation work in governmental e-procurement? According to Manny DeVera, former deputy assistant commissioner with the GSA's Federal Technology Service, "auctioning may become a form of negotiation strategy ... (whereby) the government may get a lower price if all small buys are combined" (quoted in Frank and Trimble, 2000, p. 1). A B2G firm, FedBid.com, aimed at doing just that. Its goal was to aggregate federal government buyers' prospective purchases of less than the purchase card limit, which stands at $25,000 monthly, in order to drive better pricing (Caterinicchia, 2000). This is because far and away the lion's share of federal procurement is below this limit, and by aggregating this demand, the federal government could take advantage of volume savings and greater negotiating power (Robinson, 2000a).

We do have a good working example in the form of Buyers.gov's eFast program. According to Christopher Wren, chief technology officer in the GSA's Office of Information Technology, Buyers.gov is designed to aggregate purchases from several agencies into a single larger purchase, with the aim being to drive prices down in one of two ways (cited in Schwartz, 2000). Under the eFast program, suppliers post group purchasing offers in which prices fall as more orders are placed. Alternately, government buyers may post product requests, which other buyers may review and join. Pooled orders are then forwarded to suppliers for reverse auction bidding (GSA-FTS, 2001).

Figure 9.32 illustrates how the eFast program works. It depicts an example where four federal procurers submit requests for the same IT hardware, in this case laptop computers. Buyers.gov aggregates these requests into a single, larger purchase and attracts suppliers willing to bid on the entire allocation.

The principal challenge for demand aggregation is the speed and convenience of immediate purchases—many of which today are being handled through the ease of government purchase cards—versus the inherent delay that must come with any system that attempts to aggregate demand for common items, either within or across agencies. As Larry Allen, director of the Coalition for Government Procurement, bluntly put it: "Not everyone wants

Figure 9.32: Demand Aggregation in the Federal Government: eFast at Buyers.gov

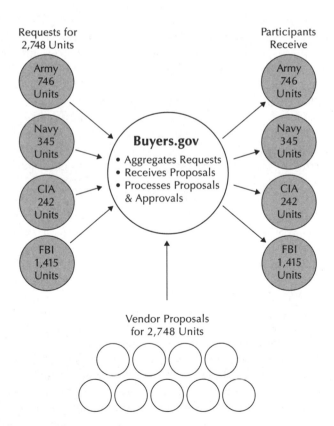

to shop at Price Club all the time. There are times when it's more appropriate for them (government employees) to shop somewhere else, and it doesn't mean they're getting a bad deal" (quoted in Frank and Trimble, 2000, p. 1). While demand aggregation unquestionably makes governmental agencies more of a "blue chip" buyer and could make governmental contracting even more attractive to suppliers (due to increased volume), the strategic question will be how it can be made more "real time" to encourage its use.

The future bodes well for more demand aggregation and cooperative purchasing in public sector e-procurement. On the state level, Betty Dillehay,

---

Benefits of Demand Aggregation

According to MobShop, a firm that specialized in demand aggregation, the benefits of demand aggregation can be broken down as follows:

Benefits to Buyers:
- **Reduce Product Costs**
  Optimize spend by leveraging the strength of the entire purchasing group.
- **Reduce Transaction Costs**
  Reduce the number of transactions, lower shipping costs, and achieve greater efficiency in the accounts payable process.
- **Reduce Maintenance Costs**
  Consolidate procurements around a smaller number of standard products.

Benefits to Suppliers:
- **Enhance Revenues**
  Increase the volume and velocity of transactions by generating high-volume aggregated orders.
- **Reduce Sales Costs**
  Complete multiple sales through a single transaction to reach buyers with greater efficiency. Demand aggregation also facilitates strategic sales by providing buyers with a powerful incentive to create larger purchasing groups.
- **Protect Margins**
  Maintain control of value/volume curves and compete on factors other than price by engaging in multiparameter negotiations.
- **Improve Supply Chain Planning**
  Gain valuable insight into future demand through visibility into purchasing group formation.

Source: Adapted from MobShop. The Value of Demand Aggregation in Public Marketplaces: A White Paper from Mobshop. *(2001)—(www.mobshop.com).*

Question: "How Would You Explain Demand Aggregation to a Non-Economist?"

The concept of demand aggregation is simple: What if a manufacturer could group multiple small and medium-sized buyers along a single production run with a single ship date? Most manufacturers attempt to do that now, receive orders and then plan a production schedule. However, what if a supplier posted a single production schedule for a product in pre-production, and let buyers group their orders around the single ship date? The supplier would have longer production runs with fewer changeovers, reduce inventory levels, and use far less working capital. The savings are immense. Also, this group of difficult-to-service customers could now become one of the supplier's most profitable segments. In this context, demand aggregation refers to a supplier's ability to group unrelated buyers for a standard product (with standard options) before the product is manufactured in a single production run.

Longer Run = Lower Per-Unit Costs

But, why would a buyer agree to the ship date indicated? The answer is simple—a lower price. In exchange for the buyer accepting the product at the specified time, the supplier shares a portion of the operating savings with the buyer. But, it comes with a twist: The buyer has the ability to group demand with other unrelated buyers to receive a lower price based on the total volume ordered.

Buyers using demand aggregation have realized savings ranging from **8 percent to 46 percent** on direct goods (i.e., plastics) and indirect goods (i.e., safety equipment)! Suppliers using demand aggregation have increased their profit margins while offering these lower prices.

Greg Mesaros
Founder, President, and CEO, eWinWin

deputy secretary of technology for the Commonwealth of Virginia, commented that one of the major benefits of her state's e-procurement system (eVA) is that it gives the state—for the first time—the ability to track the buying patterns of its agencies. This creates the database upon which to *begin* to look for volume-buying possibilities and to potentially aggregate demand (Sarkar, 2001c). Michigan has actually pilot-tested the MiBuy program, which aggregates demand across different state agencies to gain better pricing from vendors. The test involved 50 users and 10 vendors. In addition to price savings, the MiBuy program was geared towards producing softer savings by streamlining the procurement process, reducing duplication of efforts (Walsh, 2001a).

Representative Tom Davis, now chairman of the House Committee on Government Reform, is an advocate of "cooperative purchasing" between the federal government and state and local entities. While in its infancy still and facing some political opposition, the concept is being tested by allowing other levels of government to use the GSA Schedules (Matthews, 2001e).

Dynamic Commerce and Forward Auctions

Introduction—"The Usual Suspects"

How has surplus property typically been sold by government in the past? Across the country, on a daily basis, the "usual suspects"—a group of somewhere between 10 and 100 buyers—will show up at a city's property storage yard or the county courthouse steps to participate in a live auction. A portion of these buyers prefer this method and the opportunities it brings—and abhor having to bid online (Hasson and Browning, 2001).

How is this changing? Consider that San Diego County, California, is one of a number of governmental entities that, in addition to conducting traditional live auctions, are simply listing their surplus property, seized assets, and used equipment online on eBay (Monteagudo, 2001).

This is but one example of how the employment of electronic technologies is transforming the market for government auctions from one limited to the "usual suspects" to a new level of interest—and, indeed, a new audience. Bill Piatt, director of e-government strategy at Booz Allen & Hamilton Inc., observed that today, with the advent of online auctions of governmental assets, "many more citizens have access to property online than they do through the old approach" (Hasson and Browning, 2001, p. 2). Victor Arnold-Bik, chief of sales for the GSA, put it directly: "We recognize that John Q. Citizen does not have 24/7 to hang out at auctions, see the merchandise, and make bids. Now they can see pictures of the items, get information, and make bids at 3 a.m. or whenever they want" (cited in Colker, 2001, p. 1).

In this section, we will turn our attention to the second "pain point" in the governmental supply chain. This is what to do with literally tens of billions of dollars of what has been affectionately referred to as "stuff" and "junk," namely the government's surplus, used, and seized property and assets. As can be seen in Figure 9.33, dynamic commerce solutions can be

The Palm Beach Story

There is probably not a governmental asset today that has more baggage— and perhaps value—than the voting machines that ended up being the center of controversy between the George W. Bush and Al Gore camps in the disputed 2000 presidential election. Now, according to an Associated Press report, Palm Beach County, Florida, plans to auction up to 5,000 of the infamous "butterfly-ballot" punch-card voting machines.

Palm Beach County announced that the voting machines, which would include a copy of the ballot that "confused" voters on Election Day 2000, would be listed on eBay beginning November 7, 2001. That was the first anniversary of the election that brought so much controversy to Palm Beach County. The county's election supervisor, Theresa LePore, was unsure how much the machines would bring at auction, but viewed the decision to place the machines up for auction as an opportunity for closure on the controversy, stating: "I wish it would go away, but I know it won't. Out of everything bad that has happened, hopefully, something good will happen." Palm Beach County netted approximately $175,000 from the sale of 521 of the famous "butterfly-ballot" voting machines auctioned on eBay. (Anonymous, "Palm Beach County to Auction Infamous Punch-Card Machines," p. 13A).

applied at the "end" of the governmental supply chain to help the public sector better manage the disposition of these assets.

Asset Disposition

In the area of asset disposition, the Internet has been categorized as being "the greatest technological revolution for auctions since the microphone" (Voth, 2001, p. e6). Jeffrey M. Crowe, president and COO of DoveBid, a leading private sector firm blending offline and online auctions, stated that the equation for the auction provider is simple: "Any auctioneer will tell you if I get more people to come, I get more bidders, I get higher prices, I get paid a part of every transaction, I'll make more money (quoted in Voth, 2001, p. e6). DoveBid has proven this strategy to be correct, showing that online auctions increase recoveries by a range of 20 to 90 percent, driven by an increase of 40 percent in the ranks of bidders (Voth, 2001).

The dynamic commerce model appears to be especially suitable for the asset disposition process, enabling organizations to:
- Increase their recovery rates
- Hasten the timeline for the liquidations

Figure 9.33: Dynamic Commerce Applications in the E-Government Supply Chain: Online Asset Disposition Auctions

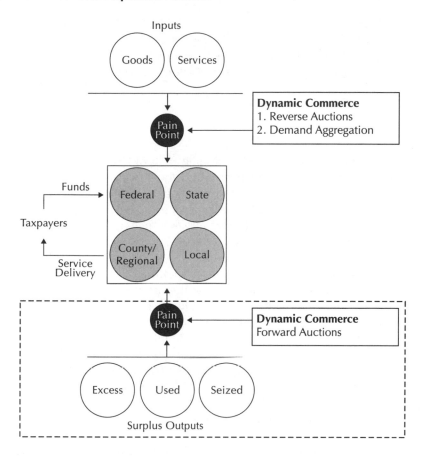

- Acquire new buyers (customers) for items (FairMarket, 2000).

Forward Auctions

The type of auction used for asset disposition is known as a *forward auction*. As shown in Figure 9.34, forward auctions are a bit more familiar to most people, as they follow the format whereby prices are "bid up" by competing bidders for the items being sold at auction. The benefits and risks of this type of auction are summarized on the following page.

Companies have found auctioning off excess goods, close-out items, and even returned merchandise a means through which to make a small return on items that would have otherwise "gathered dust in storerooms or ended up in the trash can" (Battey, 2001, p. 22). For example, the Burlington Northern

Figure 9.34: Characteristics of Forward Auctions

Santa Fe railroad recently began auctioning off its old locomotives online. The company has thus far auctioned off 47 of these 80-ton diesel locomotives online, six in a single afternoon. The new way of disposing of its old rolling stock has taken a complex, paper-laden process that used to span six weeks and compressed it into a single day (or less), netting Burlington Northern Santa Fe 11 percent higher returns in the process (Gaffen, 2001).

Governmental Use of Asset Disposition Auctions

One of the most intriguing areas for the development of e-government is the concept that the public sector should use online technologies to maximize its revenues through online auctions of surplus, used, and seized assets—goals akin to the private sector (Matthews, 2001d). According to Hunter Hoffman, company spokesman for Liquidation.com: "Surplus as a separate revenue entity is still being largely overlooked. Governments are looking at millions of dollars of unrealized money that can go back to the taxpayer (quoted in Sarkar, 2000b, p. 40).

Colker (2001) framed the issue by stating:

> Six years after the dawn of e-commerce, the federal government is jumping into the online fray just at the time when dot-coms are the investment equivalent of Florida swampland. But the feds, who are playing the Internet auction game to get returns on items ranging from surplus desks to luxury accouterments seized during the investigation of big-time criminals, have a big advantage. Like dot-coms in the e-biz golden age, Uncle Sam doesn't have to care about profit. Furthermore, it carries no inventory costs. No capital crunch. No stock options for uppity employees. Except for the relatively small expense of putting on the electronic auction, the government just collects the cash for items it needs to unload anyway (p. 1).

Judi Hasson, one of the researchers of the "Dot-gov Goes Retail" report discussed previously, commented: "Although it's nothing new for government to sell excess property and assets, using the Internet is changing the

A Breakdown of the Benefits and Risks of Using Seller-Centric Dynamic Commerce Applications (Forward Auctions)

Benefits to Seller (Organization or Company):
- Enhanced revenues
- Lowered costs and improved efficiency
- Access to a larger and more diverse group of buyers
- Real-time access to market demand information
- Stronger relationships with trading partners
- New channel to dispose of aged, unused, or idle assets

Benefits to Buyer (Trading Partner):
- Opportunity to lower price
- Lowered cost and improved efficiency
- Access to a larger and more diverse group of suppliers
- Better information about the market conditions
- Ability to participate in multiple auctions concurrently
- Means to smooth out supply and demand shocks
- Access to customer service

Risks to Seller (Organization or Company):
- Yield control over pricing to market mechanisms
- Exposure to new competition
- More complex logistics

Risks to Buyer (Trading Partner):
- Pay more than market value
- Credibility of product and/or supplier

Source: Adapted from Appell and Brousseau (2000)
(http://www.ascet.com/documents.asp?d_ID=249).

way the government does business" (quoted in Brown, 2001, p. 21). In the view of those interviewed, there is general support for this new way of conducting business—and the potential for increasing the recoveries on this property, while making these assets more available to the public.

In the remainder of this section, we will examine what is being sold online and who is—and should be—doing the selling. We will look at several companies that are successfully implementing this concept, partnering with governmental agencies to increase recoveries across the board. Finally, we will examine a critical legislative issue that needs to be addressed to fos-

Question: "Where Do Governmental Online Asset Disposition Auctions Fit into the Picture?"

I don't see a conflict at all in government trying to maximize its return on this property. The auctioning of surplus assets fulfills a market niche that will likely remain in existence for the foreseeable future. Under the traditional auctioning process, we attempt to obtain the highest price that the market will pay.

Ken Buck, Executive Director of Business Innovation, GSA-FTS

In my experience, surplus has not been a strategic initiative. It is not even the purchasing folks that have anything to do with it. It's some guy in the basement of the Science Building that's in charge of getting rid of surplus.

One of the most common questions I get when I talk to someone about surplus property is, "Will you take the junk away?" It is not, "Am I going to get the best price for it."

Bill Bunce, National Account Manager—Public Sector, FreeMarkets, Inc.

Public reaction is generally very positive, as [online auctions] help counter the "waste and abuse" perception of government. They provide a viable means of disposing surplus for dollars and revenue, rather than letting it languish or be tossed.

Steve Cochran, Former Vice President for Technology, Council for Excellence in Government

Why are government officials hesitant to shift to online markets for selling their surplus and used assets? It's like anything. It's change. And if you look at what we do, whether it involves reverse auctioning or forward auctions, change is the biggest obstacle that we have in moving forward to getting people to actually do something differently. The easiest thing is to have the local guy come down with his truck and pick stuff up and just take it away. "Take it off my hands and get rid of it for me. It's taking up my space, it has used up its usefulness and it's time for us to move on!" So, that becomes the easy thing to do. Whereas, what we would do is set up an actual marketplace and get them involved, specify what it is they are going to provide, share that information data with us, and actually go out and create a marketplace. It is additional work. So, I would say there is a change factor there that makes it a bit more challenging to get people to move off the dime, as opposed to making it something that's disposable, and it can be done in a very quick and painless fashion.

Joe Quigg, FreeMarkets, Inc.

ter the development of this practice for the betterment of both the government and its citizenry.

Public Sector Asset Disposition Auctions: The Fundamentals

What Is Being Sold Online?

The better question might be: What *is not* being sold online through governmental asset disposition auctions of one form or another? When the U.S. Customs confiscates an imported necklace, or the Department of Defense no longer needs a power tool, or the U.S. Marshals Service seizes a sports car from a drug dealer, all these items become available for purchase at government auctions. At the federal level alone, there is an amazing array of property for sale at any one time, as can be seen in Table 9.7.

Where Does This Property Come From?

Generally, the property being sold through online governmental auctions can be categorized as being one of the following types:

- Seized property
- Foreclosed property
- Unclaimed goods
- Surplus property
- Real estate
- Personal property

The reader will note that all of these sources are represented in the anecdotal tales of online asset disposition auctions, described on page 82.

Who Is Doing the Selling?

This is perhaps the biggest issue of all in terms of the development of online sales of governmental property. Organizations basically face the choice of setting up auctions on their own and running them on their own website, or they can choose to use an established online auction site (such as eBay) or a service provider (such as Bid4Assets, FreeMarkets, or Liquidation.com). Many organizations, however, both in the private *and* public sectors, may find that they do not have the infrastructure or the resources to conduct the auctions themselves. The process can be difficult and time-consuming, and if the auction cannot reach the right audience, it may bring low returns for the auctions themselves (Battey, 2001).

(1) GSA Auctions

For decades, GSA has held auctions at various locations around the country on all types of surplus federal property. By the year 2000, GSA was bringing in $300 million annually from these physical auctions.

Table 9.7: A Sampling of Property Auctioned by Various Federal Agencies

Agency	Property Auctioned
Department of Justice (DOJ): **U.S. Marshals Service (USMS)** **Drug Enforcement Agency (DEA)** **Immigration & Naturalization Service (INS)** **Federal Bureau of Investigation (FBI)**	residential and commercial real estate, business establishments, and a wide variety of personal property such as vehicles, boats, aircraft, jewelry, art, antiques, collectibles, and other personal property
U.S. Postal Service (USPS)	clocks, televisions, radios, tape recorders, jewelry, VCRs, clothing, vehicles, computers, workroom and office furniture, and electronic and hardware items for mail-handling equipment
Department of Treasury: **Bureau of Alcohol Tobacco & Firearms (ATF)** **Internal Revenue Service (IRS)** **U.S. Customs**	cars, boats, airplanes, real estate, carpets, electronics, industrial goods, jewelry, wearing apparel, and household goods
Department of Defense	tents, typewriters, computers, vehicles, aircraft components and accessories, engine accessories, office furniture and equipment, clothing, household paints and thinners, recyclable materials such as iron, aluminum, copper, paper, and much more
Dept. of Housing & Urban Development/Federal Housing Authority (HUD/FHA)	single-family homes (1-4 units)—including townhomes, condominiums, or other types of single-family dwellings—multifamily apartment projects, nursing homes, mobile-home parks, and hospitals
Department of Veterans Affairs (VA)	detached homes, townhouses, and condominiums
Department of Energy	office equipment, vehicles, furniture, trailers, generators, instruments and laboratory equipment, mechanical power transmission equipment, and heavy equipment

Table 9.7: A Sampling of Property Auctioned by Various Federal Agencies (continued)

Agency	Property Auctioned
Federal Deposit Insurance Corporation (FDIC)	real estate, undeveloped land, hotels, shopping malls, single-family homes, condominiums, and apartment complexes; personal property, computers, phone systems, furniture, fixtures, and plants; specialty items, crystal, china, and antiques
Government Printing Office (GPO)	printing and binding equipment, office furniture, and business machines such as copiers, calculators, and typewriters
General Services Administration, Federal Supply Service (GSA, FSS) (through gsaauctions.gov)	cars, trucks, boats, cameras and projectors, communications equipment, copiers, food preparation and serving equipment, hardware, jewelry and collectibles, medical and laboratory equipment, office machines, office and household furniture, recreational and athletic equipment, tools, and many other items
National Aeronautics & Space Administration (NASA)	computer equipment, printers, electronics, test equipment, office furniture, laboratory equipment, video equipment, computer tape, heavy vehicles, hardware, aircraft parts, communication equipment, recyclable materials such as metal, copper wire, waste office paper, wood pallets, aluminum cans, and much more
Small Business Administration (SBA)	real estate, commercial property, single-family homes, and vacant land, personal property, machinery, equipment, furniture, fixtures, and inventory used in business operations

Examples of Governmental Online Asset Disposition Auctions

Bid4Assets.com

- A 10 acre lot on the island of Hawaii, forfeited as part of a drug-related seizure, was sold for the U.S. Marshals Service (USMS) for $145,000. On the Bid4Assets site, potential bidders could view the "due diligence" report, showing photos of the property, a survey, an appraisal, and a map showing that the property was in one of the least-hazardous zones for lava flow on the island (Grenier, 2001).
- In another USMS auction, a 1983 Italian Augusta SpA executive helicopter, seized in a Florida money-laundering case, sold for $655,000. The auction received 11,000 page-views in four days (Grenier, 2001).
- Bid4Assets sold an entire commissary for the Department of Defense, with all the fixtures, including walk-in freezers and checkout counters (Hasson and Browning, 2001).

HanoverTrade.com

- The Department of Housing and Urban Development (HUD) earlier this year sold 6,000 loans made under the Section 312 program, which provided low-interest loans to rehabilitate single-family residences in low-income urban areas, for $109 million, making this the largest single governmental online disposition auction to date. HanoverTrade.com, compensated through a commission on the auction, provided a solution that enabled HUD for the first time to conduct this auction completely over the Internet, with no paper flowing to complete the transaction (Hasson, 2001a).

All Sold Out Internet Solutions

- Five regional GSA offices have begun listing real property holdings online and conducting online auction events for their sale. Through a private sector partner, All Sold Out Internet Solutions of Arlington, Virginia, GSA sells real estate across the nation (www.gsa.gov/pr/prhome.htm). Potential bidders can view property maps, photos, descriptions, and other pertinent information on this site, which even allows them to place money in escrow for the purchase. GSA offers the service for free, while the private sector partner collects both a website development and monthly hosting fee (Hasson, 2001b).

eBay

- The U.S. Postal Service sells undeliverable packages, many ironically from online sellers of books, CDs, and videos, such as Amazon.com and eBay (Hasson and Browning, 2001).

Today, through GSA Auctions (www.gsaauctions.gov), the agency is hoping to increase its returns by placing the auctions online in a system that is very "eBay-like." However, GSA Auctions offers more than eBay's electronic marketplace in that, according to Joseph Jeu (2001), assistant commissioner, Office of Transportation and Property Management of the GSA's Federal Supply Service, the site serves as "a single point of sale" and "a totally touchless property disposal system" to the public. GSA will even store the items sold at regional offices of the Federal Supply Service and even ship them (when possible) to the winning bidder (Schwartz, 2000).

GSA Auctions offers a wide variety of properties on its site. In the first six months of its operations, the GSA auction site generated $8 million in sales and had over 60,0000 registered viewers (Colker, 2001). In the view of GSA's Arnold-Bik, GSA Auctions is different from Internet auction sites, such as eBay and Amazon.com, in that: "We are doing business on behalf of the government" (cited in Hasson and Browning, 2001, p. 5).

Yet, the GSA effort is not being universally lauded. In fact, it has come under intense scrutiny in recent months. Why? There are both legal concerns and questions as to whether the site is the most cost-effective and efficient means of disposing of governmental property. In an anonymous letter to the editor of *Federal Computer Week*, an employee of the Defense Contract Management Agency issued a stinging criticism of GSA Auctions. He (or she) charged that:

> It only took GSA a year and a million dollars to do what any private citizen could have done in one hour at a cost of $2 or $3. Is this really "reinventing government" when bureaucrats fail to take full advantage of what is available commercially and insist on deploying a government-designed "clone" website? Former Vice President Al Gore's "golden hammer" could be put to good use in dealing with these decision makers (the Federal Supply Service commissioners) (Anonymous, Letter to the Editor, 2001, p. 1).

The letter writer went on to say that the fees charged by GSA Auctions were 10 times those of eBay and the potential audience reach of the auctions was far less than what could be found on eBay or other private sector auction sites, thus calling into question the business model of GSA Auctions and its ability to either cover its operating costs, let alone the investment made to set up the site (Anonymous, Letter to the Editor, 2001).

The cost question has led to legal concerns as well. In a May 8, 2001, letter to Acting GSA Administrator Thurman Davis, several leading congressmen contended that the GSA site "runs counter" to the approach mandated by Congress in the Federal Activities Inventory Reform Act of 1998 (FAIR). In this law, Congress attempted to separate, wherever possible, agency competition from commercial ventures. The letter was signed by

Dan Burton (R-Ind.), Tom Davis (R-Va.), Connie Morella (R-Md.), and Albert Wynn (D-Md.).

The letter specifically questioned the propriety of GSA Auctions, when FAIR called for the federal government to rely on private sector initiatives that can be shown to be faster and cheaper than public sector efforts (Hasson, 2001c).

(2) Private Sector Partnerships

In contrast to the GSA-led efforts at the federal level to be a governmental auction service provider, there are a number of private sector firms that are attempting to build on a business model of selling governmental property online. These include:

- eBay
- Bid4Assets
- FedWin
- FreeMarkets
- Liquidation.com

For example, Washington, D.C.-based Liquidation.com has recently signed an innovative contract with the Department of Defense to sell an estimated $23 billion of surplus equipment and goods over the next seven years. This represents all non-weaponry military items that actually reach public sale that have not been recycled or passed on to state or local governments. While excluding weaponry, the surplus items span a wide variety of categories, including:

- Military electronics
- Aircraft parts
- Medical equipment
- Clothing
- Textiles
- Industrial machinery (McCarthy, 2001).

According to Bill Angrick, CEO of Liquidation.com: "The Department of Defense is exiting the business (of selling surplus property). We're taking it on, and we're going to make it more efficient" (quoted in Brown, 2001, p. 1).

Until the present time, DoD surplus property was sold through the Defense Reutilization and Marketing Service (DRMS). On average, DRMS achieved a recovery rate of only 1.5 percent of the property's original value. Under the terms of this innovative contract, the government will receive 80 percent of the final auction price (less administrative and logistical expenses), and Liquidation.com will receive 20 percent. At the present rate of recovery, this would translate into sales (through 2008) of approximately $350 million, with Liquidation.com retaining $70 million. CEO Angrick was quoted as saying that this agreement represents "the single largest asset dis-

www.gsaauctions.gov

The GSA Auctions (www.gsaauctions.gov) website has been developed to complete GSA's transformation to an all-electronic asset management system. The site offers the general public the opportunity to bid electronically on a wide array of federal assets. The auctions are completely web-enabled, allowing all registered participants to bid on a single item or multiple items (lots) within specified time frames. GSA Auctions' online capabilities allow GSA to offer assets located across the country to any interested buyer, regardless of location.

GSA Auctions offers federal personal property assets, ranging from commonplace items (such as office equipment and furniture) to more select products like scientific equipment, heavy machinery, airplanes, vessels, and vehicles.

Currently, the categories of items offered on the GSA Auctions website are:

- Agricultural Equipment and Supplies
- Aircraft and Aircraft Parts
- Automobiles
- Boats and Marine Equipment
- Communication Equipment
- Computer Equipment and Accessories
- Construction Equipment
- Electrical and Electronic Equipment and Components
- Fire Trucks and Fire-Fighting Equipment
- Furniture
- Household/Personal
- Industrial Machinery
- Jewelry and Collectibles
- Lab Equipment
- Medical, Dental, and Veterinary Equipment and Supplies
- Miscellaneous
- Motorcycles
- Office Equipment and Supplies
- Photographic Equipment
- Trucks, Trailers, and Tractors

Source: GSA (www.gsaauctions.gov) 2001.

position contract in history," but that "the big winners here will be the Department of Defense and the U.S. Treasury" (cited in McCarthy, 2001, p. E5).

However, Liquidation.com, drawing upon its network of surplus buyers and its online auction capabilities, reasonably hopes to significantly increase the former recovery rate. If so, this would translate into millions more dollars going both back to the government and to its private sector partner. The company has set up a separate subsidiary, Government Liquidation, to handle the DoD contract, and it will hire more than a hundred people to handle this new business (www.liquidation.com).

Yet, with these new forms of collaboration come new forms of competition and conflict between the government's own efforts and its private sector partners (Roberti, 2000). An example of this can be seen at the federal level in the asset disposition arena, where public/private collaborative efforts, such as those of Liquidation.com and Bid4Assets.com—and even eBay—compete with the government's own GSA Auctions site.

Public Sector Asset Disposition Auctions: Success Stories

In investigating the realm of asset disposition auctions in the public sector, three exemplary cases stood out. These examples are presented here for the benefit of all in the public and private sectors who might model their own efforts on these examples.

The Long Reach Excavator Auction
First is the case study of a classic governmental asset auction. This auction was for a typically mundane item—a used piece of heavy construction equipment. What was *unusual* about this auction was the return that it generated. Conducted by Liquidation.com, this auction netted the State of Georgia more than double the expected amount.

While this may not be a glamorous item, it is representative of thousands of similar items being auctioned every year by governmental agencies across the United States. This auction thus stands as a good "best in class" example of how normal items can produce extraordinary returns for governments that are willing to partner with private sector experts in auctioning such items.

The Three Rivers Stadium Auction
The demolition of Three Rivers Stadium presented a unique opportunity for many parties to gain through the auctioning of literally thousands of items from the historic field. For the fans of the Pittsburgh sports teams, it presented a chance for them to purchase a piece of the stadium and its memorabilia. For other sports teams and even other governmental agencies, it imparted an

opportunity to gain items that they could put to use in their own stadiums and other venues. Yet, perhaps most importantly, auctioning the usable and noteworthy parts of the Three Rivers Stadium complex prior to its implosion gave the citizens of the Pittsburgh area the opportunity to produce significant amounts of revenue—$1.6 million—to help defray almost a third of the cost of the demolition.

While this is certainly not a "routine" event, the Three Rivers Stadium case shows how innovative thinking on the part of public sector leaders and their private sector partners can create unique opportunities for government not only to maximize returns in such situations, but also to choose appropriate—and, in this case, multi-channel—strategies to use auctioning to satisfy multiple priorities.

Dynamic Pricing ... and Donkeys?: The Bureau of Land Management

Burros—did you know that you can go online and buy a horse or a burro from the federal government? In perhaps the most extreme—and humane—use of dynamic commerce and Internet technologies, the Bureau of Land Management (BLM)—charged with managing millions of acres of federal range lands and the wild horses that roam them—now offers citizens the chance to bid online to provide homes for hundreds of the animals through its Wild Horse and Burro Internet Adoption Program. In all of the research conducted by the author, this process is the most interesting example found of how governments are making use of e-commerce techniques and models in their operations.

Summary

As has been seen in this review, there is a great deal of interest and activity in reinventing the whole area of the governmental supply chain. What had formerly been a sleepy area of activity is now looked upon as an area of opportunity. For those inside government, officials are now seeking to find ways to yield more revenue from what was formerly seen as a problem area. In the private sector, companies are seeking to partner with the public sector to make this possible through new and innovative business models.

On a final note, certainly one of the key issues in this area is money, namely, who gets the proceeds from the property sales. In most of the federal government and in many state and local governments, the revenue generated from asset sales—whether online or offline—goes to the "general fund." Thus, there is a "Catch-22" situation, in that the individual agencies do not have the incentive to be innovative in this area, because any actions they may take to put their asset auctions online will not be

David C. Wyld

rewarded with the ability to retain these funds. Additionally, many agency officials within government—both at the federal and even state and local levels—fear that any gains in revenue that they would see from increased recoveries on asset sales would be offset by funding cuts, leaving the status quo in place and robbing them of any incentive to shift to online asset disposition auctioning.

With this situation at the federal level, there is a general willingness across most agencies just to "give the stuff" to work through the GSA process, rather than to take steps to actively market the items. While this bodes well for the GSA Auctions initiative, it would dash any incentive for other agencies to move toward using outside partners. Indeed, there are a few agencies that by statute can retain revenues generated from asset sales, and these—like the U.S. Marshals Service and the U.S. Treasury—are the most aggressive in moving their sales online.

The issue is how to line up the incentives so that the taxpayer would see more agencies moving toward online auctioning to garner increased recoveries on property sales and, at the same time, allow for greater citizen access and participation in such sales. At the federal level, legislation was proposed to allow agencies to retain funds generated through property and asset sales. The proposal, the Federal Property Asset Management Reform Act of 2000, was not enacted by the last Congress. If enacted in the future, it will serve as a model for similar laws at all levels of government to foster the growth of online auctioning of surplus, seized, and used public property.

Recommendations

Introduction—the "e" Factor

In 1999, Stewart Alsop declared:

> The "e" in e-business will soon be irrelevant.... E-business is not so much e-anything as it is figuring out how to use technology to move stuff around efficiently. In the next wave, in other words, businesses will make "e" such a core part of their business that the difference between "e" and everything else will be nonexistent. Or they won't be businesses any more (pp. 86-87).

This was the embarkation point used by this author (Wyld, 2000) in discussing the conclusions of his first report on this subject for the IBM Endowment for The Business of Government.

Several years have passed since Alsop first offered his observation. Yet, still today, even in the wake of the collapse of the dot-com economy, the lure and the importance of the "e" factor *do* remain. As discussed at the outset of this chapter, the forces of the Internet Revolution—if not the companies and wealth accompanying it—live. Barb Gomolski (2001), a research director at Gartner, predicted that we are indeed close to the point where "the 'e' is going to fall off e-business, and it's just going to be business as usual" (p. 88). Likewise, CEO Scott McNealy of Sun Microsystems observed: "We hear a lot about e-business and e-commerce, but the extra 'e' is redundant" (McNealy, 2000, p. 47).

Today, we stand at a critical juncture in society, commerce, and governance, as the power of the "e" factor is indisputable. We are seeing e-commerce technologies reshaping our economy and society through thousands of applications of Internet technologies. As we have seen in this chapter, the migration of business-to-business commerce online is fast moving, despite the demise of many of the "new" economy companies and the wealth that accompanied them. The Internet Revolution clearly lives on, and, in the wider sense, e-business is simply becoming "the way business is done."

In like fashion, the business of government is also becoming increasingly electronic. As we have seen, there is great public support for these e-government efforts, evidenced by the findings from the Council for Excellence in Government's (2001) *The Next American Revolution.* We have also seen the beginnings of how dynamic commerce tools are being applied in e-procurement efforts in government.

The reality today is that e-government is fast becoming *government,* meaning that there is really no difference between an e-government strategy and *the* strategy for any governmental entity—and, in truth, *a strategy for governance.* Sayer (2000) emphasized that it is crucial to link e-government strategy with a philosophy for e-governance in general. Thus, the challenge that is today facing leaders at all levels of government in the United States—and indeed internationally—is what specific directions to take in forming an *overall* e-government strategy, for "today's public officials are stewards of the digital future" (Bowles, 2001, p. A2). As depicted in Figure 9.35, e-government strategies should be geared to "ramp up" quickly. Yet, most governments have not yet reached the point of scalability in *any* of their e-government strategies.

As Kaplan (2001) observed: "Before you can get e-government right, you need to get e-governance right. *Poor governance cannot be cured by e-elixirs*" (emphasis added) (p. 1). None of the tactics that have been proposed here are "e-elixirs" or "e-magic bullets," but they are solid building blocks for an e-government strategy. Almost all of the examples cited here are of pilots and tests, not permanent changes. The challenge will be to move beyond the pilot stages of e-procurement activities and online auctioning (as

Figure 9.35: The Strategy for E-Government

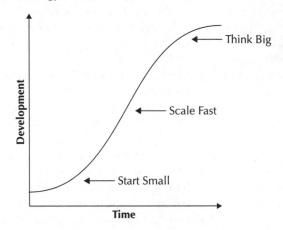

Source: Adapted from Hunter, David R. and Vivienne Jupp.
Rhetoric vs. Reality—Closing the Gap: A Study on eGovernment
Leadership from Accenture. (March 30, 2001): p. 12.
(www.accenture.com)

Figure 9.36: Where We Stand on Public Sector Adoption of Dynamic Commerce Applications

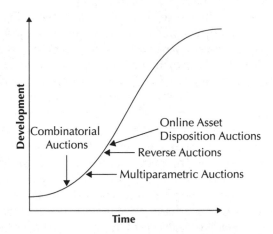

shown in Figure 9.36)—both for purchasing and for asset disposition—and to "ramp up" moves that make both financial and political sense.

Tapscott, Ticoll, and Lowry (2000) observed that the most important challenge facing leaders in all organizations today is not necessarily understanding the technology and social forces that are changing the economy today. Rather, the vital question facing each and every public official and manager is: "What should I do to respond to all these changes?" (p. 5). Don Tapscott (2000) framed the challenge in stating:

> Just as the Internet tsunami is causing turmoil and unprecedented innovation in the private sector, other facets of society are experiencing similar upheaval. In particular, our government, democratic institutions, and the state itself are in the early stages of what will be a dramatic transformation. The only question is whether existing governments will be willing participants or victims (p. 172).

Thus, as Martinez (2000) commented, today's principal strategic challenge facing *all* leaders is to have the ability to view the landscape through an "e-enabled lens." If one does so, the *only* boundaries for any organization in creating effective strategies are the creative limits of our imagination.

As pointed out by the National Electronic Commerce Coordinating Council (2000b), it is vital that any e-government effort—including those involving B2G applications—be aligned with the organization's mission and strategic plan. This means that e-sourcing strategies and applications such as those covered in this chapter will be vital components of any government's overall strategy in the years to come. As Chris Hummel, vice president of Oracle Asia-Pacific, framed the issue: "In five years, it won't be news to talk about e-government as a coming phenomenon. We won't be talking about whether governments are going to get online or not, we'll be talking about whether they have succeeded" (cited in Saywell, 2001, p. 2).

In looking forward, the leaders interviewed for this research effort were generally optimistic about where we will be five years down the road in terms of both e-government and e-procurement.

In charting e-enabled strategies to implement dynamic commerce concepts along the governmental supply chain, the author sees two critical issues that must be dealt with. First, how do we define and measure success in these areas? This issue centers around the question of what are the proper *metrics* to be employed in first determining where these dynamic commerce concepts can—and should—be employed, and then, how do we assess the gains and savings produced by them. If we can measure these with some degree of confidence, then the second key question—how we fund these initiatives—becomes easier to deal with, because we can actually discuss the tangible and intangible benefits of such applications. Much

of this section will be devoted to these two central—and interrelated—
issues.

Second, there are a number of specific implementation challenges facing
the application of e-procurement strategies in general and online auctioning
specifically, including:
- Cooperative efforts in government
- Technical issues
- Leadership and cultural change

While all of these are deserving of research reports in their own regard,
the issues will be briefly overviewed here to provide the proper context for
the difficulty of implementing dynamic commerce concepts and models.

Defining and Measuring Success: Return on Investment

In this section, we will address two key issues that are vital to successfully implementing and managing electronic procurement and asset disposition efforts in the public sector, but that are also applicable across
e-government in general. These center around:
- How do we measure returns on such efforts?
- Who will pay for these projects?

In short, these issues are intertwined in that public officials, their private sector partners, and, ultimately, individual citizens must examine the
relative worth of e-government initiatives. Here we will deal with dynamic
commerce applications specifically, but the discussions have relevance
across the whole of e-government.

Metrics for the Governmental Supply Chain
(1) Introduction to Metrics

> Traditional management adage: You cannot manage what you do not meas-
> ure. E-business addendum: You cannot measure what you do not define.
>   (Cutler and Sterne, 2000, p. 1).

ROI (return on investment) and metrics have been huge issues in the
area of e-business and e-government initiatives alike. With so much money
having been expended on e-commerce projects, both in the public and private sectors, there is a need to assess the worth of these investments. As
Heath (2001) commented: "Traditional methods for calculating return on
investment have been, for the most part, ill suited to measuring the strategic impact of e-business" (p. 1). Indeed, gauging the return on investment
for e-commerce projects and applications, in the view of Goldberg (2001),
presents decision makers with a "Gordian knot," as "the benefits are the

new processes they bring. Yet, because the processes are new, existing measurement tools may miss those benefits" (p. 1). Yet, even with the new methods come controversy, as what is a "hit" or a "page view" can be open to debate in the new economy (Goldberg, 2001).

According to analysts, very few companies have adequately measured the impact of e-commerce applications before, during, or after their implementation (Heath, 2001). Today, however, after "the go-go years of the dot-com demi-decade," return on investment is at the top of all factors in e-business decision making (LaMonica, 2001a).

In the public sector, the issue can be even more complex. Indeed, making the "business case" for e-government applications can be a difficult—if not impossible—task, requiring the tallying of both tangible benefits (such as reduced printing and postage costs and shortened cycle time) and intangible benefits (such as increased customer—or supplier—satisfaction and improved communications and accountability) (Harreld, 2000b). William Joplin, director of procurement policy and e-commerce for the State of Washington, emphasized the need "to build a business case for e-procurement policy" (opinion cited in Dizard, 2001a, p. 3). In making the business case, valid, defensible, standards based and meaningful will be critical for all the numbers. As Goldberg (2001) emphasized, there is a great need for baseline data to establish effective e-commerce metrics, along with consistency in the data collection process. However, all of this is vital in laying the groundwork for being able to demonstrate the return on such investments. It's vital in both proving the necessity and viability of e-procurement, both to policy makers and public officials and, ultimately, to the public they serve.

As OMB Watch (2001a) observed: "Because e-government in practice is still in its infancy, compared to e-government in concept, it is difficult to discern what minimum baseline standards to use in measuring the success of online government as implemented so far" (p. 2). Thus, government leaders have to be willing to learn from and benchmark successes not only from the public sector, but from private enterprise as well (Caterinicchia, 2001b).

For any e-government initiative, according to Stephanie Comai, director of e-Michigan, "There has to be a very strategic decision about how you're going to assess what the costs are and what the benefits are" (cited in Walsh, 2001a, p. 14). Citizens today are less willing than ever to have government "throw money at problems." However, they *do* want government to provide more services with reduced levels of resources (KPMG Consulting, 1997). Thus, there will be increasing demands on government to *prove value*. All of this highlights the importance of creating and using appropriate metrics to show the value of e-government initiatives, inclusive of the dynamic commerce applications featured in this chapter.

Question: "Where Do You See Public Sector E-Procurement in Five Years?"

E-procurement will continue to grow over the next five years. More and more users are becoming at ease with the use of technology in this manner, and the technology itself is becoming more and more user friendly. As e-procurement use widens, it will probably cease to be a separate phenomenon, becoming a practice that is considered commonplace. The trick, though, will be to adapt e-procurement systems to allow for acquisition of services on a broad scale. This will take both a technology and attitude evolution over the next five years. If the past is any guide, the technology will probably be there before the users are. Will federal agencies, for example, ever be thoroughly comfortable in acquiring engineering, diagnostic, personnel, and other services completely through cyberspace? It will be fun to watch.

Larry Allen, Executive Director, Coalition for Government Procurement

Over the next five years, government agencies have the opportunity to utilize the tools of electronic commerce to reduce administrative costs, improve the performance of procurement programs, and generally to buy smarter. These benefits are compelling, and I believe that we will see significant adoption of these programs across the public sector.

The key to success is to recognize that the tools of electronic commerce must be introduced incrementally, wisely, and in sync with market processes in use today. Government agencies that follow this path will achieve the significant benefits of e-commerce adoption.

Rusty Braziel, CEO, Netrana

E-procurement is simply a tool. As technology improves and people adapt, there will be commensurate improvements in process efficiencies and value buying. And like any other change, it's less about technology and more about changing behavior patterns. I see a bright future.

Ken Buck, Executive Director of Business Innovation, GSA-FTS

This stuff works! When you explain it to somebody who is not in the procurement world, they always have the same response: "Why wouldn't everybody want to do it? I just don't get it. Why does it take so long for these government folks to get it?"

Bill Bunce, National Account Manager—Public Sector, FreeMarkets, Inc.

I think we'll be in a much better, more efficient, more cost-effective, and more innovative place.

Steve Cochran, Former Vice President for Technology, Council for Excellence in Government

If we are as innovative as we need to be in this area, hopefully I have no idea what the future will look like in five years! At the most basic level, I hope we see 95 percent of contracted services and products (on a dollar-value basis) tied to performance measures, use of electronic vehicles to procure at least 75 percent of government products and services, and an adequately trained contracting workforce, motivated and capable of reaching and maintaining those goals. That would be a bright future.

Carl DeMaio, Director of Government Redesign, Reason Public Policy Institute

The government will move to automating the entire process of procurement and integrating these automated capabilities into many aspects of its supply chain. The government will adopt standard interfaces that will enable suppliers to seamlessly integrate with these automated solutions. The automated solutions will allow the government to find economies of scale across departments in order to further its purchasing power. Decision optimization systems will enable governments to make better purchasing decisions, and analytics systems will enable the government to curb purchases that fall well outside of current market prices.

Ray Letulle, Chief Technology Officer, Moai, Inc.

I hope in the future that reverse auctions are used only when bread-and-butter commodities and non-professional services are priced too high and can be brought back to reasonable price levels by such head-to-head competition. Reverse auctions constitute one tool that the federal government can utilize to reduce unreasonably high prices. Where prices are established and reasonable, reverse auctions may reduce profit margins to the extent that they discourage sources from participating in federal procurements.

Five years from now, the infatuation with this new technique will hopefully give way to an emphasis on its appropriate (and sparing) use. As that happens, I hope to see more efficient and extensive use of technology generally in procurements. When technology is appropriately applied to procurements, it will save paperwork and storage, shorten RFP-to-award cycles, increase the quality of proposals, and improve communications with serious offerors. That is where the federal government can make true savings from technology applied to procurements.

David P. Metzger, Partner, Holland & Knight, LLP

I believe we will see more open market buying for commodity items. Systems will increasingly make use of non-contract catalogs and automatically seek the lowest price among pre-approved suppliers whose catalogs are on the system. Buying will consist of electronically negotiating with a group of licensed suppliers who are free to adjust their catalog prices more or less at will. Contract buying will remain, but perhaps only for more specialized products and services.

Jim Passier, Procurement Manager, State of Connecticut

(2) Recommendations: Reverse Auction Metrics

Most experts agree that one of the primary benefits of reverse auctions—beyond the cost and procedural savings—will be the automated analysis that will be enabled through the conduct of the auction process itself. This should lead to greater understanding and better, more informed awards in the future (Schwartz, 2000). As discussed previously, this data can be used by both the procuring agency and by the vendors—even data mined—to produce greater understanding of the auction process itself and the savings derived from it.

(a) The Question of "Savings"

In regards to procedural savings, the author believes that reverse auctioning, especially that done by a third party, can not only produce cost savings, but also enhance the integrity of the process itself. As discussed earlier, the transparency of the process and the ability to generate data *on* the process is of benefit to the government, the auction service provider, and the vendors. Indeed, Kambil and van Heck (2000) proposed that in order for *any* online auction effort to be successful, all parties (auctioneer, buyer, and seller) must experience a "win-win-win," where they are better off with the new trading model than the previous trading model.

As recommended by the National Electronic Commerce Coordinating Council (2000a), in looking at the savings generated through reverse auctions, one must take into account the costs of conducting the online auction event itself to arrive at the "net savings" from e-procurement auctions. This author would agree with this assessment. In actuality, there are a variety of auction applications on the market, ranging from off-the-shelf, self-administered software packages to full-service outsourced solutions. What one chooses may be dependent on the internal capabilities of the organization and the desired levels of activity. However, one must look at what Miller (2000) labeled as the "true cost" of the application in terms of a price-value relationship.

A second recommendation from the National Electronic Commerce Coordinating Council (2000a) was that price results from reverse auctions should be benchmarked not only against historical past results in the same jurisdiction, but compared to similar jurisdictions holding sealed-bid procurements. This will allow public sector officials and analysts to see the actual differences achieved between reverse auctions and sealed-bid procurements. It will also enable agencies and jurisdictions that are procuring "new" goods or services (those not previously bid by them) to have benchmarks against which to appraise their level of savings. All of this spotlights the need for cross-jurisdictional data sharing to give policy makers the information from which to make informed judgments. While the need for more research is discussed later, this is an area where a formalized, permanent system of data sharing, both within and between levels of government, may be appropriate and necessary.

(b) The Long-Term Question

This author does believe that the year-over-year, event-over-event savings will be difficult to sustain through the use of pure, price-only reverse auctions. It simply will not be possible to drive costs down by 10-20 percent every time you conduct a reverse auction for a good or service. This echoes the views expressed by Sostrom (2001), who held that typically research has shown that the greatest level of savings is achieved in the first reverse auction for a good or service, not being replicable again. Further savings cannot be achieved unless market conditions change or unless demand is aggregated across buying groups.

Thus, one of the principal concerns this author has with much of the focus on the savings produced by reverse auctions is that the savings produced will not be sustainable over the long term. It logically will be impossible to achieve 10-20 percent lower prices auction-over-auction-over-auction over a series of years, as there will be points beyond which it will not be economically feasible for suppliers to participate in reverse auctions and bid down the prices any further. This echoes the feelings of Jap (2000), who predicted that continually looking for the lowest cost suppliers may lead to a withering away of willing suppliers and/or a consolidation of the supplier base. In fact, if the base of willing suppliers shrinks or disappears, either through poor financial performance and/or unwillingness to participate in e-procurement auctions, prices could actually stabilize or go up, thereby defeating the purpose—and expense—of conducting the auction itself. In the end, this could shift the balance of bargaining power back to the suppliers, reversing the cost savings achieved through reverse auction procurement buying and "ultimately eroding the economic performance of both buyer and supplier" (p. 3).

This author must make a point in conclusion that while there is no doubting the manner in which prices decline during reverse auction events, the concept of auction-based "savings" may be nebulous. When discussing reverse auction savings, most of the time, including examples cited in this report, the savings are calculated by comparing the price for the contract in question arrived at through the auction process versus the existing contract price. The illogic is clear—namely, what other exogenous variables might have also caused the price shift besides the endogenous factor of the auction? In just the past year, we have seen sharp price spikes and falls in the price of commodities such as oil and lumber. We have seen the prices of personal computers and laptops fall precipitously as demand slowed with a slowing economy. Further, every year, seasonality plays a huge role in the price of commodities such as heating oil and coal. Thus,

Question: "What Metrics Should We Use to Measure E-Procurement Success?"

Metrics should be applied in a balanced scorecard approach that best identifies to management the mission-related return on investment, process life cycle times, and how the socioeconomic and regulatory goals of each agency are met. Other metrics might include a concept such as "cost avoidance," where there are clear savings over the previous unit prices. Again, that can be tricky given that improvements may have been made that resulted in no price change but an increase in the value due to improved quality or performance.

Ken Buck, Executive Director of Business Innovation, GSA-FTS

If you talk to anybody who has been doing reverse auctions and getting benefits from it for some time, whether they be commercial or public sector, and ask them, "Tell me about this process and tell me what about it you see that's useful," I'm sure they would convey to you that there is a lot more to doing e-sourcing than the auction itself and that there is a lot more to it than the technology.

I was recently talking to one of the largest states in the country, and they said: "What I think we will do is probably go out with a schedule and issue a contract that will have probably three or four reverse auction providers on it. Then, whenever we need to do an auction, we will just pick one of the folks on it." After about an hour of discussion, we decided there is a lot more strategy involved than just on "game day" (the day of the auction event). You really need to have a partner that is in there with you—on a day-to-day basis—working on questions such as:

- "What are the right things to go to auction?"
- "What is the right auction strategy?"
- "What is the right lotting structure?"
- "What is the right auction format?"
- "Is the situation suitable for transformational pricing?"

Bill Bunce, National Account Manager—Public Sector, FreeMarkets, Inc.

Well, there are a number of "results" we hope to accomplish with e-procurement. First, we want better value and decreased prices for our products and services. That is the ultimate end-outcome. Sometimes that is hard to measure, especially in the absence of reliable baseline information. Second, you can look at intermediate outcomes of e-procurement, such as increased competition for government contracts, expanded choices for government, enhanced vendor knowledge of government RFPs, etc. Finally, we would want to measure the decrease in procurement costs as well as improving the simplicity of procurement processes.

Carl DeMaio, Director of Government Redesign, Reason Public Policy Institute

Because the savings are significant, there is a huge Return on Investment (ROI) driving large purchasing entities to online sourcing. We have seen the initial interest in the branches of the military and the GSA—all at the federal level. Due to the early success at the federal level, I expect states and then local governments to follow in the footsteps of the federal government relatively quickly.... In theory, reverse auctions should achieve both greater accountability and more cost-effective governance, but there are caveats to this. There are many factors that could produce unwanted results, including:

- The wrong suppliers are invited to the reverse auction.
- The rules of the event are unclear.
- The participants are not properly trained for the event.
- The wrong key factors are negotiated.
- A host of other process mistakes.

Overall, we have seen comparable savings and cost reductions between the private and public sectors, but the government sector can benefit more from the compliance and enforcement enabled by a flexible e-sourcing package. Last year, one of our largest private sector customers achieved a net savings of $150 million on a total spend of $2.4 billion. If the federal government were to achieve similar results, this would be a net savings of $112.5 billion on the $1.8 trillion budget.

Ray Letulle, Chief Technology Officer, Moai, Inc.

year-over-year or quarter-over-quarter savings may be quite questionable, perhaps even more so than comparing the auction price versus that of an "independent" estimate.

In sum, we must use caution—but not necessarily skepticism—in reviewing the results of reverse auctions. To assess the true level of savings, one must simply look below the surface to address three simple questions:

1. What is the auction's net savings—inclusive of the cost to conduct it?
2. What is the benchmark against which the savings are being compared and how was that figure calculated?
3. What were the process savings involved?

(3) Recommendations: Other E-Procurement Dynamic Commerce Metrics

The issues grow even more complex when looking for metrics that could potentially be used to assess—in monetary terms—the effectiveness of the other dynamic commerce methodologies. With the "price-only" focus of reverse auctions, price becomes *the* essential measure. However, what metrics should be used in assessing the success of "price-plus" applications?

Certainly, in multiparametric auctions, price should certainly be one of the metrics employed. However, because the former auction is multi-variable and perhaps even multi-stage in nature, a single-criterion success measure would be inappropriate. Thus, just as software that can handle the complexity of the event itself is an important issue, so to is the challenge of developing algorithms to assess the efficacy of the outcome.

In regards to demand aggregation, there are perhaps some more concrete measures that can be employed to assess the success of such efforts. First and foremost, there is a clear delineation between what the "market" price would have been at a given demand level and the "final" price paid with the aggregation of demand necessary to garner that price-point. Even if the final price to be paid by the aggregated group purchase is arrived at via a reverse auction mechanism, the "pre-post" comparison is perhaps more valid under these circumstances than when an agency holds a reverse auction only for its demand for an item or service.

As stated earlier, the challenge is to accomplish demand aggregation "in real time" and to know, to paraphrase Larry Allen's comment earlier, when to go to Price Club for an item and buy in bulk. Thus, both within and across government agencies, policy makers should examine their spend patterns to ascertain when demand aggregation could be accomplished. While this may be relatively easy to do in retrospect, the challenge will be to develop metrics and engines that can do this in real time. Finally, attention should be given to developing both velocity assessment metrics to examine how quickly these demand aggregations can be accomplished and targeting metrics to assess where the sources of aggregation are—or are not—coming from in a given agency.

(4) Recommendations: Forward Auction Metrics

At first glance, this area would seem easier to assess. After all, with all of the successes demonstrating increased recoveries on the used, surplus, and seized assets documented in this chapter and elsewhere, auctioning online would seem to be a clear choice.

There are two categories of metrics that should be used and developed. First, there should be activity metrics. Built around the author's "Five R" framework, these metrics would include:
1. Registration
    - How many registered users are there?
2. Reach
    - Who is bidding in the events?
    - Are new participants being attracted?
3. Range
    - How many bidders are participating?
    - Are bidders coming direct from your site or from links (and if so, where)?

4. Rates
   - How many times was the auction viewed?
   - What percentage of those who viewed the auction actually bid on the item?
5. Results
   - Are events ending in unsold items? (And if so, what are the cause(s) and categories of items affected?)

Secondly, metrics should be employed to measure the financial returns of the auction. As with reverse auctions, public sector officials should look at "net values"—less the cost of either in-house efforts to place the auction online or the cost of the auction service provider. Also, the spread should be analyzed carefully between the market price and the "value" of the item. This value can be a source of controversy, as several figures can be used, including:

- Original purchase price
- Book value
- Estimated market value

As their online asset disposition experience increases, governmental agencies can begin to compare their own returns from their online events versus that achieved through their former offline auctions. In this way, they can build a database upon which to assess the effectiveness of their own efforts. This is an area where collaboration would appear to be appropriate, as it would be very valuable to governments considering taking the step to have a consortium compile the experiences of various government agencies in their asset disposition activities. Certainly, the private sector partners who are providing the auction services will amass this type of information that can prove invaluable through analysis and even mining. Hopefully, they will be willing to share this information to encourage more and better auctions for increased recoveries on assets, rather than holding on to it for competitive advantage.

(5) Conclusion

In general, all e-government projects may be tough to justify on a cost-savings potential alone, making traditional payback and ROI models unusable. As Robb (2001) observed, "There comes a point in electronic government funding when financial models must be thrown out the window" (p. 4). Thus, in the end, decision making regarding e-commerce applications in general has been compared to baseball, where managers "work the numbers rigorously, but, in the end, trust their gut" (LaMonica, 2001a, p. 26).

Metrics will thus play a huge role in the development of e-government, simply because with the *right* measures it's possible to make more informed choices about the value of electronic applications in the governmental supply chain and to better make the business case—both within government and with the citizenry—for funding them. This would aid the comfort level of all with the specific application of dynamic commerce models and tools in particular. Thus, in the next section, we turn our attention to the issue of funding projects in this area.

Funding Innovations in the Governmental Supply Chain

In the author's on-the-record and off-the-record discussions with leaders in the public sector and with auction service providers, it is clear that initial funding—"seed money," if you will—is a difficult hurdle to overcome for most e-government initiatives. For example, in many instances, government officials have been unwilling or unable to shave $10 million, $20 million, $50 million or more off of their purchasing costs for lack of the funding commitment it would take to make the first step towards such savings through reverse auctions. Likewise, public sector executives may be unwilling to accept paying a share of savings for reverse auctions or a share of revenue on forward, asset disposition auctions, both of which have positive effects òn the overall budget of any governmental unit.

According to Robinson (2000b), there are three basic choices governments have in paying for e-procurement initiatives.

1. *Licensing*—They can license a vendor's software and conduct all operations themselves.
2. *ASP*—Using an ASP (application or, in this case, *auction* service provider) model, the agency pays a monthly usage fee to the vendor for hosting and/or managing the service or the software.
3. *Transaction fee*—A percentage fee is collected for each transaction made over the e-procurement site, to be paid by the vendor, the agency, or both.

The first two models are "funded"—financed through appropriations from the governmental unit, while the latter is the so-called "self-funded" or "reverse revenue" plan, whereby the exchange itself is funded through activities on the exchange. Table 9.8 gives a breakdown of states using each type of plan.

What we have seen is a great shift in funding for e-procurement initiatives at the state and local levels. In 2000, when there was a push for market share amongst private sector partnering firms, there was a great emphasis on self-funded models, where e-procurement initiatives were designed to be funded not by governmental appropriations, but rather by transaction fees, subscription charges, and other sources of revenue from participating vendors. However, due to both lower than expected transaction volumes and the "dot-com" shake-out (taking away some of the competitiveness of the marketplace), states are having to move to funded models. This is an expensive proposition, as according to Welsh (2001a), a statewide e-procurement

Table 9.8: A Breakdown of States According to Their E-Procurement Funding Model

State-Funded Plans	Exchange-Funded Plans
California	Arizona
Delaware	Colorado
Florida	Connecticut
Idaho	Maine
Massachusetts	Maryland
Minnesota	Michigan
Ohio	South Carolina
Vermont	Texas
Wisconsin	Utah
Wyoming	Virginia
	Washington

Source: Compiled from Dizard (2001a).

project's upfront costs will typically range from $5 million to $15 million, with ongoing needs for training and support. The need to tie these systems in with states' back-end financial systems will increase the value of such initiatives, while at the same time driving the costs up even further.

Another important consideration is scale, as the smaller the governmental entity (and hence the volume and size of transactions), the higher the transaction fees must be to cover the costs of the procurement site. This is exemplified by the self-funded e-procurement system recently established by the Minneapolis Public School System, hosted by Epylon, Inc. On the school district's site, vendors must pay a 2 percent transaction fee (Dizard, 2001b).

It is unlikely that "seed money" will come raining down to water the "e-government garden." While the George W. Bush administration has recently doubled its e-government requested budget to $20 million (Matthews, 2001d), others have called for far more. The Council for Excellence in Government has called for the creation of a strategic investment fund of $3 billion to be spent on e-government projects over the next five years (Matthews, 2001a).

While there are many innovative funding models on the table and on the drawing board, the traditional funding model of appropriations and acquisition still predominates in approximately 80 percent of all government technology projects. Thus, as reported by the National Electronic Commerce Coordinating Council (2000b), for most governmental bodies, e-government will be *an incremental cost* for the jurisdiction. As such, at a time when surpluses are shrinking to zero or turning to deficits due to a weakening economic situation, e-government funding will be forced to compete with other priorities at all levels of government. Dynamic commerce applications that could help to alleviate the budgetary crises could be shelved for lack of funding to initiate these programs. Also, more attention could be directed at reverse auctions to produce immediate savings and at moving asset disposition auctions online to quickly generate additional recoveries for an agency. Thus, in the end, the scope and direction of activities to improve the e-government supply chain will likely be significantly influenced by current budget realities.

This is where the author sees metrics and budgeting dovetailing. In short, *better metrics will facilitate better e-government decision making.* If elected officials and government executives can have better, concrete data to work from, dynamic commerce applications will be more likely to be funded through appropriations or a fee-based model, especially in an environment of perceived shrinking resources. As stated earlier in the metrics section, with an unwillingness to "throw money at problems" and with pressure to prove value, this puts the spotlight on the importance of properly developed, defined, and used measures in the whole realm of e-government. This also places a great deal of significance on future research efforts in the area of dynamic commerce applications in public sector e-procurement and online asset disposition as well, which will be discussed a bit later.

Implementation Issues

There are three areas of general concern that will be touched upon here that can impact the general success or failure of any e-government initiative and, specifically, the dynamic commerce applications looked at in this chapter. These are:
1. Cooperative efforts in government
2. Technical issues
3. Leadership and cultural change

Each of these—which, again, are huge issues in the area of e-government and public sector management in general today—will be briefly overviewed as they impact the development of dynamic commerce methodologies in e-procurement and online asset disposition auctioning.

Cooperative Efforts in Government
"Why reinvent the e-gov wheel 50 different times? Through collaboration and partnerships, the states can do so much more so much faster and at so much less cost to our citizens."
—Robert L. Childree, Alabama State Comptroller; NASACT (National Association of State Comptrollers, Auditors, and Treasurers) President (cited in National Electronic Commerce Coordinating Council, 2000b, p.4).

At present, there are several efforts that have already been established to form both formal and improvised cooperative, cross-jurisdictional procurement efforts. While, at present, none have used dynamic commerce concepts, certainly these groupings can employ reverse or multi-attribute auctions to bring lower prices and better value to their members. Likewise, they are particularly well-suited to using demand aggregation tools to band their purchase needs together to bring participating governmental bodies greater purchasing power.

At one level, we are seeing informal arrangements for cooperative purchasing emerge. The U.S. Communities Government Purchasing Alliance (www.uscommunties.org), for instance, offers states and local governments the ability to "piggyback" onto government purchasing contracts bid out by a lead agency. In one case, a contract entered into by Fairfax County, Virginia, for personal computers and peripheral equipment can be used by most states and localities. Such piggybacking can enable smaller governmental entities to enjoy the purchasing power of their larger counterparts, while also greatly reducing administrative costs by not forcing communities to go through the often burdensome bidding process (Walsh, 2000). Likewise, both South Carolina and California allow all counties, cities, school districts, and nonprofit agencies to make use of state-negotiated contracts for their own purchases, in effect, piggybacking on their e-procurement efforts (Enos, 2001).

The real potential in this area lies in making permanent joint purchasing arrangements between different jurisdictions, first on a localized or regional basis. Eventually, these could be developed into national and even perhaps international efforts. Among the most prominent of the formalized cooperative procurement programs at the state and local level are:
- COGBUY (Metropolitan Washington, D.C.)
- Colorado-Utah partnership
- North Carolina
- H-GAC (Houston-Galveston, Texas)

(1) COGBUY (Metropolitan Washington, D.C.)

Kulisch (2001b) commented that the COGBUY program of the Metropolitan Washington Council of Governments is the first e-procurement system that is both regional and multi-jurisdictional. The Metro Washington Council consists of over 20 local authorities that purchase a combined $100 million annually. COGBUY is aimed at eliminating rogue buying and gaining cooperative purchasing power by aggregating catalog purchases.

The Metro Washington effort is a good test case for regional cooperation. Toni Bansal (2001b), president of Digital Commerce Corporation, observed that if the Metro Washington effort is successful, it could be a model for state and local governments across America who are seeking to come together to enhance their purchasing power and prowess.

(2) Colorado-Utah Partnership
    The states of Colorado and Utah have established a web-based joint purchasing system that is the first such interstate system in the United States. Under a contract with NIC Commerce, the system first went live in August 2001, and the pilot will last for two years. In 2002, the system was opened up to include a variety of governmental entities in the two states, including counties, municipalities, school districts, and other political subdivisions (Sarkar, 2001d).

(3) North Carolina
    A model might also be found in North Carolina. On July 1, 2001, North Carolina launched a statewide e-procurement system, open to all state agencies, counties, municipalities, and educational institutions within the state. Annually, the state hopes to save approximately $50 million through the use of this system, which will hopefully lead to both process and price savings (Sarkar, 2001b).

(4) H-GAC (Houston-Galveston, Texas)
    One of the oldest cooperative purchasing efforts between governmental entities, dating back to 1973, is also one of the boldest and most promising. The Houston-Galveston Area Council's (H-GAC) Cooperative Purchasing Program has focused primarily on capital equipment for municipalities, having experience working as a conduit for such purchases across jurisdictions for years on an intrastate basis. Now, due to a recent change in the State of Texas' procurement regulations, H-GAC has entered into the online realm, developing an e-procurement site (www.hgacbuy.com/default.html). Leaders of the organization are opening up the program to governmental bodies outside of the state, and perhaps even internationally, with interest coming from the United Kingdom and other governmental entities abroad. The program now serves more than 1,300 local government, state agencies, and qualifying nonprofit corporations.

(5) Role of Associations and Other Organizations
    The author believes there is a great role to be played by organizations in developing informal communities and even formal, cooperative arrangements for e-procurement and/or online asset disposition between governmental agencies. This will put the spotlight in coming years on organizations such as:
• National Electronic Commerce Coordinating Council
• National Contract Management Association

Question: "How Do We Gain More Cooperation Among Governmental Entities in E-Procurement Initiatives?"

The single greatest challenge is that everyone wants to go their own way and develop their own system. While this spirit of entrepreneurialism is generally a good thing, it can also result in duplicative systems and become a justification to retain personnel and other infrastructure that otherwise could be re-channeled.

Having multiple systems is also very confusing for contractors. Even with the creation of central contract opportunity gateways, such as FedBizOpps, navigating inside each agency's own systems to find the actual business can be time-consuming, confusing, and costly.

This is the number one topic confronting public sector e-procurement, and it's a difficult one for procurement leaders to get their arms around. Organizationally speaking, I think the most critical thing is strong leadership. OFPP and others in OMB must exercise strong leadership to bring competing agencies and systems into harmony. Attitude-wise, I think agencies need to be shown that it is in their best interests to work collaboratively with one another.

As for working across levels of government, there is enough of the "not invented here" syndrome and pride of ownership at the federal level to contend with before getting state and local governments into the mix. From what we have seen from state government purchasers, it will be a long time before they embrace anything coming from their federal brethren. They would more readily extend their systems the other way, though it is unclear whether federal agencies would be interested in partnering in that direction on a large-scale basis. There have been a few incidents where this has happened, but nothing you could call a trend.

Larry Allen, Executive Director, Coalition for Government Procurement

We are more focused on the more strategic spend for the states, so we generally say a million dollars or more is the practical threshold. As you start moving from states down to cities and counties, you say, "Give me a list of all the bids you have coming up over the next 12 months that are over a million dollars." Well, that's an easy answer for them—they don't have any!

At the state and local level, what I have been focusing on is more a GPO (Group Purchasing Organization) Model—as is used widely in health care. So, if they are a county, having access to FreeMarkets' QuickSource or even a Full Source-type product through their state, they don't have to contract for it on their own. They might want to use it just once, and they should be able to do that through the state, or maybe through a group purchasing organization like the National Association of Counties. Also, in the metropolitan Washington, D.C. area, we have the Metropolitan Washington Council of Governments, and in Texas, they have the Houston-Galveston Area Council. These are models for the future.

Bill Bunce, National Account Manager—Public Sector, FreeMarkets, Inc.

- National Association of State Auditors, Comptrollers and Treasurers
- National Association of State Chief Information Officers
- National Association of State Procurement Officials
- National Association of Secretaries of State
- National Governors Association
- National Association of State Chief Administrators
- Information Technology Association of America
- National Automated Clearing House Association
- Western States Contracting Alliance

As will be highlighted in the discussion of research recommendations, these organizations can also play a key role in promoting research efforts that will prove crucial to information sharing, benchmarking, and persuading the public of the success of not only e-supply chain activities in the public sector, but e-government as a whole.

(6) A Procurement Portal?

To date, an e-procurement portal for the public sector has not emerged. As Walsh and Dizard observed (2000): "As yet, an Amazon.com or eBay has not yet proven to be the electronic salvation of the government procurement world the way these sites have in the consumer world" (p. 5). However, Fed-BizOpps could well be the site that could become the e-procurement portal, at least on the federal level. Currently, 29 federal agencies use the website (www.fedbizopps.gov) to post and receive procurement information via the Internet, with over 90,000 vendors registered with the site. Beginning October 1, 2001, all federal agencies were required to use the site to post all procurement information on contracts in excess of $25,000 (Brown, 2001).

(7) Summary

What is needed today is a new spirit of cooperation amongst governmental leaders in the area of managing supply chain activities in the public sector. When all is said and done, existing partnerships between governmental entities and new cooperative efforts should be undertaken to foster better management and practices in the realm of e-procurement and online property auctioning. While combinations will produce new problems with systems integration and other technical and standards-based issues, they also hold promise of scale and networking advantages for the participants. Thus, public sector officials should explore such cooperative arrangements and seek to find where dynamic commerce applications can be utilized within them.

Technical Issues

There are two general technical questions that need to be addressed to facilitate the development of e-procurement and auctioning activities in the public sector: basic computing needs, and standards and interoperability.

(1) Basic Computing Needs
One of the paradoxes of the e-business revolution is that in the private sector, younger, smaller companies had a distinct competitive advantage in that they can simply begin with a technological blank slate. In contrast, for established companies, "braving the world of e-business involves tearing up and replacing old systems" (Hamm, 2001, p. 130). Government, by nature, is not an "Internet start-up." In fact, it has many of the same profound systems problems of major corporations—only magnified and worsening with the advent of wireless technologies, from web-enabled cell phones to handheld devices (Caterinicchia, 2001a).

Bridis (2001) categorized the state of computing in the federal government as "the ultimate paradox" in that "the same government marching Americans into the next technology revolution has for years been mired in the Dark Ages" (p. B1). The "legacy" mainframe systems are holdovers from the '50s and '60s, an era when the federal government was indeed at the leading-edge of technology. However, with these systems serving as the informational underpinning for most federal agencies, they are often too expensive and foundational for wholesale replacement. Thus, over the past decade, a "Tower of Babel patchwork" has been set up within the federal government, trying to enable these mainframe legacy systems to be integrated with Internet and pc-based applications (Bridis, 2000, p. B1).

While the Year 2000 problem indeed prompted government to clear out some of its "digital deadwood" (and, in fact, almost a third of the oldest systems that could not have been made Y2K compliant were indeed replaced), it did not solve the legacy problem by any means. So, today, the federal government still has a "logistical nightmare" of stovepipes of information, housed in systems that cannot be made compatible with either the Digital Economy or even each other (Bridis, 2000). Clearly, the issue of stovepiped systems is beyond the scope of this research, but it is a concern that is receiving a great deal of attention, both in the press and in the federal government itself (Frank, 2001). Yet, as Terry (2001) pointed out, interoperability of systems will be a key issue to be addressed in moving toward more collaborative e-procurement activities, and without it, the stovepipes in government will be a significant hindrance. As Birk and Macready (2001) commented, the requisite starting point for e-commerce collaboration is to move beyond the information "silos" and "pipelines" that characterize so many organizations.

There is a major shift taking place in the way governments—at all levels—are directing their IT spending. According to Tom Davies, a senior vice president with Sterling, Virginia-based Current Analysis, Inc., "As the shift occurs, the dollars are being reallocated away from enhancing legacy mainframe and client-server based systems and toward web-based solutions" (quoted in Welsh, 2001b, p. 28). One of the dangers is that many e-government ini-

Question: "What Is the Proper Level of Public/Private Sector Collaboration in E-Procurement?"

In an ideal world, I think the public sector would focus on establishing common interface standards and data elements, and then let industry engineer around those standards. These elements and standards would run horizontally through government organizations, to the point that a procurement transaction would integrate seamlessly with finance, budget, and the program office. With seamless integration, there would be no need for reconciliation. Instead, government tends to focus on designing systems to meet its perceived unique requirements, which is wasteful.

In today's environment, the public sector needs to have unencumbered communications with the third-party service providers who possess e-procurement expertise as a core competency. These providers have the unique skill sets needed to help guide government leaders toward successful solutions. The bottom line, I guess, is for government to focus more internally on cleaning up its own processes, and then allow industry to design solutions around those streamlined processes.

Ken Buck, Executive Director of Business Innovation, GSA-FTS

One thing we have seen, and obviously this is probably more true in the commercial world than in government, is where we are moving the e-sourcing technology and process from the end of the procurement process to the beginning of the procurement process where you are designing a product.

In DoD, an example may be designing a new tank, or something like that. A statistic that has been around for a long time in the procurement process is that the costs of building a new product are defined during the design phase. By the time you get to the procuring process, the only thing you have left really is profit. If you start using the auction process, which we've begun now with some of our commercial customers, using it in the design phase and getting suppliers to bid against each other related to different designs, you can begin to extract huge chunks of savings out of the process versus just their profit at the end of the process.

Bill Bunce, National Account Manager—Public Sector, FreeMarkets, Inc.

I think there can be a high level of public-private collaboration in e-procurement, primarily because the establishment of an e-procurement system can itself be procured. The private sector has in many ways raced beyond government in e-procurement, building B2B (Business-to-Business) vehicles and systems for all kinds of products and services. It is time that government harness those lessons learned, systems, and innovations to serve the taxpayer.

Carl DeMaio, Director of Government Redesign, Reason Public Policy Institute tiatives, rather than harnessing the power of the Internet, will simply find agencies replicating "the same stovepiped, agency-centric bureaucracies they created in the paper world" (Matthews, 2000e).

The issue of the aging (or lack) of the government's IT infrastructure is by no means exclusively a federal one. Sarkar (2000a) called for the federal government to help with e-government funding for local governments out of fear that we may not only see a digital divide in society, but also one between the capabilities of large and small communities. Thus, it may be incumbent on government generally—with the federal government in the lead—to make a substantial investment in rectifying its computing infrastructure problems. If not, this may be a significant drag on the implementation of all e-government technologies and concepts.

Governments—in the end—will also need to adopt a "multichannel strategy" for service delivery to provide services and access to all. Sayer (2000) compared this to banking today. While there is a push for online services, there will always be customers who will interact with the bank in person, and not just in one method, as customers can still access services through the bank's facility or via the mail or telephone. This will likely prove true for e-supply chain efforts as well. Just as private sector firms, such as Liquidation.com and Bid4Assets, and the public sector, in cases such as the Bureau of Land Management's Wild Horse and Burro Internet Adoption Program, offer alternative means for bidding on governmental assets being disposed of (both online and offline), e-procurement efforts will likely operate on multiple tracks as well. Indeed, we will likely see allowances made for "traditional" paper bid submissions and for RFQs to still be mailed to potential vendors who desire to do business with the government in this manner. However, Kambil and van Heck (2001) urge just the opposite, namely either subsidizing participants to adopt the e-marketplace or making it more costly to use alternative (non-electronic) mechanisms.

(2) Standards and Interoperability

In the coming years, it will become increasingly necessary, as emphasized by Kambil and van Heck (2001), to make e-marketplace mechanisms—whether dynamically or fixed price in nature—to conform to technological standards and to be tied in with a variety of internal systems (both within government and within supplier's corporate systems).

Standards are necessary simply to reconcile different semantics used by different organizations (for instance, one organization may refer to an item as a "ballpoint pen," where another may call the identical article an "ink pen"). While "middleware" may be able to act as a bridge enabling organizations' differing systems to communicate with one another, translating data to meet their respective semantics and formatting needs, ultimately there is a need for standards. Large purchasing organizations can drive adoption of particular standards, and governmental bodies would be in a position to greatly influence standards. Still, suppliers who deal with multiple industries could face multiple standards between them (Sostrom, 2001).

This is a part of the need—overall—for there to be "consistency and standardization among government agencies, from the national down to the local level, in order to make e-government a workable proposition" (OMB Watch, 2001a, p. 3). The Clinger-Cohen Act of 1996 required all federal agencies to create an enterprise architecture, and if such systems can be made common and standardized across agencies, this would foster intergovernmental cooperation (Dorobek, 2001). The E-Government Act of 2001 called for the creation of "common and open protocols and standards" to facilitate the growth, accessibility, and interoperability of electronic government efforts both within the federal government and between levels of government (OMB Watch, 2001b, p. 1). Indeed, whereas open architecture and widely accepted and disseminated standards can help facilitate marketplace development, closed and proprietary applications inhibit growth, acting as barriers precluding network expansion and interoperability of systems between organizations (Commerce One, 2000).

What is the answer? Many believe that it lies in the area of XML—Extensible Markup Language—which allows systems to more easily communicate and organizations to exchange information (Kerstetter, 2001). It will be critical to look at e-procurement activities not in isolation, as integrating this functionality with both internal and external systems will serve to increase the adoption rate of the core electronic purchasing and asset disposition activities (Sostrom, 2001). All organizations—both public and private—must thus be able to automate processes throughout what has been termed "the extended enterprise"—linking the entire e-sourcing process from suppliers to customers (Active Software, 2000).

In the view of many, the primary source of savings *will not* come from driving down prices—and hence, supplier margins—through e-procurement. Rather, as projected by Deloitte Research (2000b), fully three-quarters of the potential savings will come from improving both collaboration and efficiency across the supply chain. According to Kulisch (2001a), the key to marketplace success may well be the ability of the e-procurement provider to enable public sector clients to integrate their purchasing and payment functions. William Brandel of the Aberdeen Group expects that, more and more, suppliers will want the auction technology to tie in both with their financial and procurement software (cited in Sanborn, 2001, p. 32).

On a final note, this author would recommend that it may not be government's proper role to *write* standards as a "blue-chip buyer." Yet, the government *collectively* could certainly exert power in setting standards, particularly if there can be consensus on standard language, metrics, protocols, and methods within and between levels of the American government, possibly even with international cooperation. Both software and middleware may be answers—or patches—but the real solution may come in the form of associations to set the standards. As with the governance of the Internet itself and with the model established by the ISO (International Standards Organization) in the area of quality, a new body may be able to establish standards for such interoperability and definitional agreement.

Leadership and Cultural Change
(1) The Need for a "Cultural Revolution"

This is *the* most important factor. For any of these changes to be brought about, *action* must be taken. Effective e-government, because of the level of coordination and synchronization needed, requires nothing short of an "in-house cultural revolution" (Bowles, 2001, p. A2). Yet, as Roberti (2000) put it bluntly, "government bureaucracies tend to resist change" (p. 2). In fact, "internal departmental fiefdoms" are the most cited obstacle by public officials to moving towards e-government—even more than funding issues (Carr, 2000, p. 1).

According to Geoffrey Segal, an analyst with the Reason Public Policy Institute:

> Internal politics and unwillingness to take risks can sometimes mean that vitally needed electronic government projects mark time while yet another feasibility study is conducted. What this boils down to is an unwillingness to take a chance. When you add all this up, it's easy to see why government has to become far more creative when it comes to funding electronic government (quoted in Robb, 2000, p. 1).

Zyskowski (2000) points out that government managers and policy makers "dwell in a separate universe" from the "dot-com" world. While the Internet is creating new ways for government to operate more efficiently and to be more responsive to the needs of the citizenry, there is not funding available to pursue every initiative—and, thus, priorities have to be set. Furthermore, as Zyskowski (2000) emphasizes, "Failure is generally not as easily tolerated in the government as it is in the private sector" (p. 1). Yet, he urges that government not "sit on the sidelines" during the transformation to the Digital Economy. Rather, the public sector "must be a cautious but vigorous participant in the transformation" (p. 1).

Kaplan (2001) acknowledged: "E-government threatens the status quo. Political elites and entrenched bureaucrats—particularly in places where government jobs have high profit margins—may resist" (p. 2). As Eisenhart (2001) points out, the "Washington culture" itself may be the greatest impediment to effective knowledge management, as it causes federal workers—at all levels—to avoid risk and, especially, to hide mistakes and missteps—even honest ones that could prove to be good learning experiences for other agencies. In contrast, in an "e-government culture," public officials and civil servants will be rewarded for "thinking outside of the box," as opposed to the bureaucratic mentality that encourages—both implicitly and explicitly—"play-it-safe" habits (National Electronic Commerce Coordinating Council, 2000b, p. 11).

(2) Leadership to Create an "E-Government" Culture
In its report *Transitioning to Performance-Based Government*, the Reason Public Policy Institute (2000) recommends that government—at all levels—should look to "blow up traditional 'brick and mortar' structures and fundamentally redefine how services are provided to the taxpayer ... [and] go beyond merely streamlining transactions and improving the efficiencies of existing processes" (p. 24). Yet, *nothing* will be changed without effective leadership and the active buy-in of all in government.

As Hamm (2001) observed, cultural barriers are *the* key consideration in making e-government initiatives work: "Just because technology is available to turn business processes upside down doesn't mean the folk who work there welcome the shake-up" (p. 128). In fact, it has been found that *up to 70 percent* of the effort it takes to put a technological solution in place involves coaxing cultural changes (Hamm, 2001). In *Transitioning to Performance-Based Government*, one participant in a forum on e-government stated: "I submit that the biggest challenge facing the procurement community is the need for a culture change among procurement officers" (Reason Public Policy Institute, 2000, p. 44).

One of the most surprising and pleasing things that this author has discovered in investigating this area of e-government is the number of entrepreneurial individuals within government who are trying to implement techniques to make the e-government supply chain "faster, better, cheaper," even without incentives—financial or otherwise. These are truly remarkable leaders, in that they have employed the ability to "think outside the box" without tangible or even intangible rewards to do so. Yet, to make the e-government culture work across entire agencies—let alone across the public sector itself—the rewards and incentives must ultimately be there. As Susan Hanley, consulting director of Bethesda, Maryland-based Plural, Inc., squarely addressed the issue: "If you are asking people to do something differently, you're going to have to create appropriate rewards and incentives so that they will do what you want them to do" (quoted in Eisenhart, 2001, p. 38).

We must remember that *people* are the key to the e-government equation. While the public sector may not have the ability to directly tie performance on key job indicators to financial incentives, this may be an area that needs to be looked at. With improved metrics, we may be able to say: Reward responsible individuals and teams for increased asset recoveries or decreased acquisition costs with financial bonuses while, most importantly, maintaining the transparency and accountability of these dynamic commerce-based processes. This is certainly a topic of interest, but far more complex than can be examined here.

Where governmental executives can take action *today* in aligning rewards to performance that fosters e-government, promoting *better government* is in the area of intangible rewards. Success stories should be triumphed— shouted and shared both within government and in public sector trade groups *and* in the wider media (especially media that reaches beyond the public sector audience itself). When procurement executives save millions of dollars by switching some items to acquisition through reverse auctioning, they should be recognized. When agencies band together at any level to overcome the NIH—*"Not Invented Here"* Syndrome and form demand aggregation groups to drive prices down for buying personal computers or coal, they should be applauded. When a local government puts its tax lien auctions online and reaches beyond "the usual suspects" to generate significantly more revenue in the process, it should be congratulated. When the military partners with the private sector to improve recoveries on surplus and unneeded items of all sorts, we should all be pleased.

Press releases and news stories should be generated. Awards should be given, both within government and by trade groups, such as is occurring with the E-Gov organization today (www.e-gov.com). Formerly, all of this might have been looked upon as a public relations or internal communications issue, but in actuality it is a strategic imperative today. Indeed, such intangible ways of promoting dynamic successes in improving the workings of the e-governmental supply chain will likely be the principal means through which to reinvent the government culture to better face the gigatrends changing governance today.

Lessons *to Be* Learned: Recommendations for Future Research

As can be seen by the scope of this research, there are a multitude of topics that come into play when assessing the development and impact of e-government. What is definitely needed as e-government and many of the e-procurement and other supply chain activities "ramp up" is a more comprehensive approach to the whole area of research in these areas. Even studies such as this are more anecdotal in nature, and as such, their limitations are many. However, they do serve a great purpose in informing leaders in the public and private sectors—as well as other stakeholders and, most importantly, concerned citizens themselves—about the status of e-government initiatives at present.

In this section, the author makes several assertions as to the need for research in the general area of e-government and, specifically, the dynamic commerce applications that are an increasingly important part of activities in the governmental supply chain.

Surveys of Potential

Some of the first research priorities should be attempts to simply assess the total potential for improving the government's e-supply chain activities. Governmental agencies at all levels should be examining where there is potential to gain savings and to produce additional revenue. This can be done internally and with the cooperation of outside parties, both interested potential partners and disinterested academic observers. On the procurement side, government leaders should be examining their total spend patterns in order to identify entire areas and pockets where they can apply *specific* dynamic commerce applications. Some acquisition areas will be potential areas for reverse auctioning, whereas others will be suitable for higher-order dynamic commerce tools, such as multiparametric auctions and demand aggregation. Getting a handle on where these tools can fit in the totality of procurement efforts is the requisite first step in the process.

On the other end of the governmental supply chain, it will be important to first study the exact size of the governmental asset disposition marketplace. Because so many governmental entities are constantly involved in disposing of unneeded, surplus, used, and seized assets and property, the exact market size is uncertain. This is further complicated by two factors. First, a significant amount of federal and state property never enters the sales process, as it is donated to other agencies and nonprofit organizations that can make use of the property instead (although some portion of the claimed assets may in fact be sold by the receiving agency, often in short order). Next, there is the question of the value of the property. As discussed earlier with respect to choosing and using appropriate metrics, how this property is valued is open to great debate—at least until a "market price" is established through the auctioning mechanism. Still, it will be critical that studies be carried out simply to "size" the market for online asset sales, both within and between all levels of government.

Surveys of Activities

Domestic

One of the principal recommendations of this author would be that more comprehensive research on the e-supply chain activities of government be conducted—and soon. What is needed is research—and the support and cooperation necessary to have it carried out—on the B2G side of the equation. We already have two excellent models to go by, both of which have been relied upon in preparation of this study.

First, there is the groundbreaking study that was sponsored by the Pew Internet and American Life Project and *Federal Computer Week*. Hasson and Browning (2001) conducted the first comprehensive review of online sales activities for the federal government, in which they surprisingly found that the federal government has at least 164 websites that sell items directly to the public, outselling leading retailers like Amazon.com and eBay in the process. While this study focused on the retail side of the equation, Hasson and Browning's (2001) painstaking methodology stands as a model by which comprehensive agency-by-agency reviews could be conducted to produce an aggregate picture of government's online activities in e-procurement and asset disposition.

For all of government, it will be important to undertake such comprehensive surveys of supply chain activities. As can be seen in Table 9.9, this would entail a number of studies at all levels of government in regards to their e-procurement and asset disposition activities, in order to capture the true picture of this aspect of e-governance. When repeated over time, a longitudinal database could begin to be assembled, and when repeated internationally (as will be discussed in the following section), this would facilitate cross-country comparisons and benchmarking.

Secondly, the ISM/Forrester Research (2001a, b, c) *Report on eBusiness* serves as a model for how surveys can be employed to assess both current sentiments on the status of e-commerce applications and, over

Table 9.9: Proposed Studies along the E-Government Supply Chain

	Federal	State	County	Local
E-Procurement (general)	XX	XX	XX	XX
Reverse Auctions	XX	XX	XX	XX
Multiparametric Auctions	XX	XX	XX	XX
Online Asset Disposition Auctions	XX	XX	XX	XX

XX=Study needed.

time, can be used to produce longitudinal data and studies on the growing use of online technologies and the reasons behind their growth. It
would be recommended that such studies should be commenced immediately to assess the current state of e-procurement activities (and continued
on a quarterly basis as ISM has done to produce longitudinal data), including at least representatives of the following stakeholders in the
survey database:
- Government procurement executives
- Contracting officers
- Public officials
- Auction service providers
- Vendors

In like fashion, an "ISM-like" survey should be instituted for the asset dis-
position side of the equation as well and continued indefinitely. The groups
that should be represented in this survey's population would include at least:
- Government executives overseeing asset disposition
- Public officials
- Auction service providers
- Vendors

International

One of the most critical areas for future research will be to expand
beyond the focus on the United States and to examine e-supply chain activities in the public sector around the globe. Again, a study much like the one
conducted by the Pew Center would be invaluable in this area to catalogue
and document the e-procurement and online asset disposition activities
occurring on a worldwide basis. Likewise, continuing survey-based
research projects should be instituted to capture international attitudinal
changes, facilitating cross-country comparisons.

It is very likely that the U.S. would be found to be in the lead pack—
but not necessarily in *the* lead—in e-government activities in the realm of
e-procurement. For instance, Saywell (2001) cites both the government of
Hong Kong and the State of Western Australia as exemplars of "world class"
e-procurement operations. In the latter case, Western Australia has
processed over half a million separate transactions between 19 state agencies and vendors through its Government Electronic Market in the six
months ending March 2001. In the United Kingdom, the British government's ambitious goal is to put 100 percent of all government interactions
online by 2005 (Trott, 2001). The estimated annual volume for public sector e-procurement in the United Kingdom is over $30 billion (Wait, 2001a).

Thus, it will be important to conduct individual country analyses of
e-procurement activities, both at the national level and by political subdivisions within each country. First, this is necessary simply to be able to

produce both national and cross-country comparative research. However, it will also enable researchers to find exemplary governmental units making use of e-procurement generally and dynamic commerce concepts in particular. Specifically, as applications such as reverse auctions, multiparametric auctions, and demand aggregation events take root in e-procurement on a global scale, governments will be able to benchmark on an international basis, which can produce even faster knowledge transfer of best practices and faster spread of these practices.

In a similar way, studies should be undertaken to examine the reach and spread of online asset disposition practices globally. While the United States seems to be the leader in this area, single-country and cross-country research can lend insight to government officials and potential private sector partners as they seek models to benchmark against for their activities.

The "Underground" Government Economy

In the future, it will be easy to track the growth of online property auctions through governmental sites (most notably GSA Auctions) and private sector partners (such as Bid4Assets, FedWin, and Liquidation.com). Yet, how much volume is there on eBay and other auction sites where government agencies at the local, state, and federal level simply list their items for sale? Such "unmeasured" sites will be difficult to track. This is especially true since, thus far, there has been hesitancy amongst public officials to publicize their online sales efforts. This has been observed to be out of a fear that the online processes, while producing good results, could have problems standing up to public scrutiny (Monteagudo, 2001).

This is a fascinating area for potential research, as one suspects that in the area of asset disposition in particular, there is likely much more activity ongoing or being developed than what is known about at present. If researchers can gain the cooperation of auction sites such as eBay, Yahoo, and iWon to compile metrics on governmental sales on their websites, then we will have a much more complete picture of governmental use of online auctioning as the "underground" aspects are brought to light.

Surveys of Public/Public Official Opinions

The Council for Excellence in Government's (2001) major study of public opinion regarding e-government, entitled *The Next American Revolution*, remains *the* best resource in assessing the American public's opinion on and reaction to e-government.

Beginning today and continuing into the future, further studies should be conducted to attempt to capture the opinions of the public and their officials on e-government generally and on the specific areas of e-procurement and online asset disposition discussed in this chapter. As with the Council for Excellence in Government's (2001) study, attitudes were measured generally and comparing those who had experience with and exposure to e-government versus those who did not. This would be useful in assessing how citizen and leader involvement in these e-supply chain activities might influence not only opinions on these specific activities, but attitudes toward e-government generally. As was found in the Council's study, the fact that a citizen had used e-government services was positively correlated with positive feelings and support for such initiatives. Thus, it may be found that efforts to involve small businesses in e-procurement efforts and to increase "John Q. Citizen" participation in online governmental auctions may produce spillover benefits in terms of support for e-government—and government—in general. It will be interesting to conduct such studies not only domestically in the United States, but internationally as well.

Conclusion—A Need for Information

As can be seen through the totality of this research effort and the suggestions for future research, there will be a need for continuing research of the phenomenon that is e-government and the dynamic commerce activities that take place along the governmental supply chain. *The critical need is information*. Research should be done on these evolving topics, not only within the public sector, but to compare governmental and private sector performance in e-procurement and online asset disposition activities.

Certainly, information sharing should be the buzzword. As discussed previously, governments do not have to worry—as do private sector firms—about maintaining proprietary methods in their supply chain functions as a potential source of competitive advantage. Indeed, sharing information, techniques, and methods should become standard practice across all of e-government. After all, governments do not have competitors in the same sense as private enterprise. Thus, this author would suggest a framework—perhaps even a national center or clearinghouse—for the exchange and study of e-supply chain activities. Such a center—*or centers*—could prove invaluable in promoting the development of e-government, not only amongst public officials, but in publicizing the successes of such efforts in the popular media to inform the citizenry. It is believed that these positive results will unquestionably meet with positive responses.

In the absence of such a center, it is imperative that both government leaders and their private sector partners continue to publicize their efforts in e-procurement and asset disposition activities. The trade press has done a great job of not just disseminating information, but analyzing the developments of e-government. This includes such online/offline outlets as:

- *Federal Computer Week*
- *Government Computer News*
- *Government e-Business*
- *Governing*
- *The Public Purchaser*
- *Government Executive*

Conclusion

A Final Note—The "Gus Pagonis Lesson"

In closing, noted management consultant and author Tom Peters (2001) recently observed:

> *Leaders win through logistics.* Vision, *sure*. Strategy, *yes*. But when you go to war, you need to have both toilet paper *and* bullets at the right place at the right time. In other words, you must win through superior logistics. Go back to the Gulf War. After that war ended, the media stories focused on the strategy that was devised by Colin Powell and executed by Norman Schwarzkopf. For my money, the guy who won the Gulf War was Gus Pagonis, the genius who managed all of the logistics.
>
> It doesn't matter how brilliant your vision and strategy are if you can't get the soldiers, the weapons, the vehicles, the gasoline, the chow—the boots for God's sake!—to the right people, at the right place, at the right time. Right now, Amazon.com and a hundred of its 'dotkin' are learning—or failing to learn—the Gus Pagonis lesson (emphasis in the original, p. 128).

In the end, just as with all governmental initiatives, the success of e-government *will depend* on the successful implementation of these ideas on e-sourcing and reinventing the governmental supply chain. Today, in the opinion of Representative Tom Davis (R-Va.), "Government ought to be asking every time we do something how this fits in with the information revolution" (quoted in Matthews, 2001e, p. 1). Dynamic commerce has the potential to substantially reshape the supply chain and to make government—*all government*—run "faster, better, cheaper." The people expect—and deserve—nothing less.

Appendix I:
Reverse Auction Savings from Coast to Coast

What kind of savings can be produced through reverse auctions at the state and local levels? To see how the concept actually translates into tangible savings, let's look at some representative results, provided by FreeMarkets, who conducted the reverse auction events for:

- The State of Florida, and
- The County of Los Angeles, California.

In each circumstance, the contracts put out for auction were existing ones. Thus, it is possible to look at the savings achieved through the use of the reverse auction pricing mechanism versus the historical price for the same good.

The State of Florida

In the case of the State of Florida, two of these auctions were classic examples of reverse auctions. In the first case, the results of which are shown in Figure 9.A.1, the reverse auction was for lamps. In the second case, the state was acquiring copy paper. The results of this auction event are shown in Figure 9.A.2. Both auctions produced savings of over $1.5 million, which represented a 20 percent and 9 percent savings, respectively, over the amounts expected to be paid.

There are two important points to be derived from examining the results of these two auction events. First, both of these auction screenshots demonstrate the high level of bidding activity during the auction event. Each "dot" on the slope line represents a unique bid submitted by one of the potential suppliers during the time frame of the auction. In the case of the lamp auction (shown in Figure 9.A.1), four suppliers submitted 62 total bids. In the copy paper auction (shown in Figure 9.A.2), only three bidders submitted a total of 105 bids during the auction event. Secondly, what can be seen in both cases—which is characteristic of most all reverse auctions conducted on a pure price basis—is the emergence of the "ski slope" curve. What is meant by this phrase is that there is a slow start to the bidding, then a frenzy of activity, where the price to be paid drops significantly at a point—and the reverse "S" shape takes form. At the end of the auction—or, more precisely, in the overtime period of the auction—there is often another peak of bidding activity. This can be clearly seen in the graphic on the lamp auction (Figure 9.A.1).

The final Florida auction to be reviewed was a "twist" on the traditional reverse auction format. Rather than potential suppliers competing with each other in the bidding process to drive the price down, the State of Florida specified a fixed amount that the state would spend for an allotment of personal computers. The PC specs were highly detailed, so it was assured that each of the six suppliers were able to provide directly comparable equipment. Thus, the point of competition was how many units the bidders would provide to the state for this specified amount.

As can be seen in Figure 9.A.3, this auction produced an upward sloping curve, as the competing vendors continued—rather constantly—to offer more and more units for the fixed amount. In the end, the state ended up obtaining 140 additional units through the auction event, representing a per unit savings of 37.3 percent over the starting amount.

Figure 9.A.1: Reverse Auction for Lamps for the State of Florida

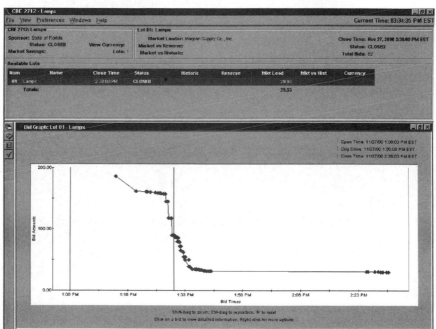

Figure 9.A.2: Reverse Auction for Copy Paper for the State of Florida

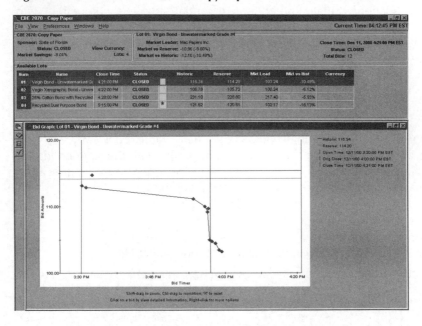

Figure 9.A.3: Reverse Auction for Personal Computers for the State of Florida

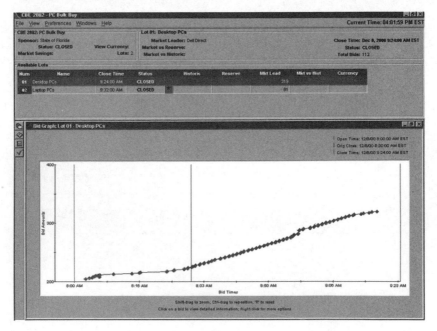

County of Los Angeles, California

The second group of reverse auction events to be reviewed were conducted for the County of Los Angeles, California, specifically for the L.A. County Independent School District (ISD). The screenshots for these events are shown as follows:

- Figure 9.A.4—Frozen Fruits and Vegetables
- Figure 9.A.5—Uniforms
- Figure 9.A.6—Metal Detectors

The results of these auctions are summarized in Table 9.A.1 below:

Table 9.A.1: Summary Results of Reverse Auctions Conducted for the County of Los Angeles

	Number of Suppliers	Number of Bids	Dollar Savings	Percentage Savings
Frozen Fruits & Vegetables	3	253	$28,145	13.05%
Uniforms	3	112	$58,670	16.88%
Metal Detectors	3	114	$512,300	64.04%

In these three events, the classic curve can be seen once again, but with higher levels of bidding activity. The most dramatic example is the final one, the auction for the metal detectors for the public schools (shown in Figure 9.A.6). Clearly, cost savings of this magnitude—over 60 percent—are beyond any norm for reverse auctions. Such an outcome can lead one to call into question both the propriety of prior contracts for the high amounts charged and/or the wisdom of the bidders, who might have gone below what should have been their "bottom-line price" in the frenzy of bidding.

Figure 9.A.4: Reverse Auction for Frozen Fruits and Vegetables for the Los Angeles County ISD

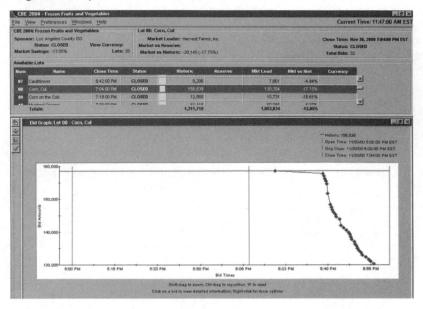

Figure 9.A.5: Reverse Auction for Uniforms for the Los Angeles County ISD

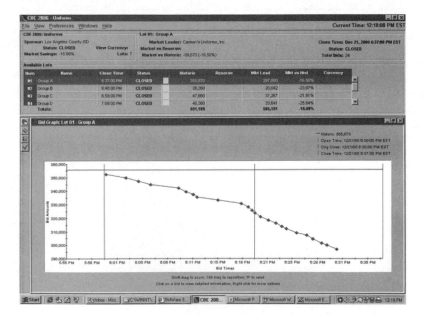

Figure 9.A.6: Reverse Auction for Metal Detectors for the Los Angeles County ISD

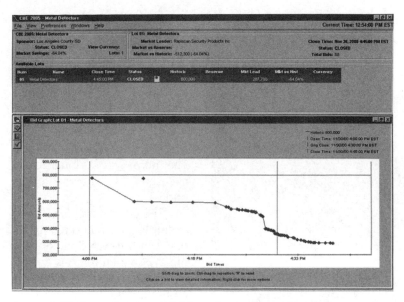

Source: Public Sector Overview—2001 (www.freemarkets.com).

Appendix II:
Case Study—Long Reach Excavator, Auctioned for the State of Georgia by Liquidation.com—June/July 2001

Between June 25 and July 13, 2001, Liquidation.com conducted a used equipment auction for the State of Georgia. The item was a long reach excavator, as shown in the photos.

The course of this auction exemplifies what often takes place in a forward auction of this type when there is a pool of qualified, active bidders on an item.

The long reach excavator went up for bid on Liquidation.com's site on June 25, 2001. The item received no bids for 16 days. Then, on July 12, one day before the close of the auction event, the first bid came in. Over the course of the next 24 hours, as can be seen in Table 9.A.2, five competing bidders combined to more than double the final price of the excavator over the minimum reserve price set for the auction.

As can be seen in Figure 9.A.7, this dramatic price increase came from a frenzy of bidding in the last 90 minutes of the auction.

In the end, as can be seen in Liquidation.com's screenshot of the auction outcome (Figure 9.A.8), the final price of $42,000 was quite pleasing to the State of Georgia. For its services, Liquidation.com received a transaction fee, paid by the seller—the state. However, this encompasses a wide range of services, including all due diligence, offering on-site inspections, handling payments, and arranging shipment of the excavator to the winning bidder.

Table 9.A.2: Bidding History on Long Reach Excavator Auction (Last Day)

Date/Time	Bidder	Bid Price
07/13/2001 03:10 PM	3 - WINNER	$42,000
07/13/2001 03:07 PM	3	41,000
07/13/2001 03:06 PM	1	40,000
07/13/2001 03:05 PM	3	39,000
07/13/2001 03:04 PM	1	38,000
07/13/2001 03:04 PM	3	37,000
07/13/2001 03:03 PM	3	36,000
07/13/2001 03:03 PM	1	36,000
07/13/2001 03:03 PM	1	35,000
07/13/2001 03:02 PM	3	34,000
07/13/2001 02:59 PM	2	33,000
07/13/2001 02:57 PM	3	32,000
07/13/2001 02:51 PM	2	31,000
07/13/2001 02:38 PM	3	30,000
07/13/2001 02:37 PM	5	29,000
07/13/2001 02:37 PM	3	28,000
07/13/2001 02:34 PM	5	27,000
07/13/2001 02:34 PM	3	26,000
07/13/2001 02:33 PM	5	25,000
07/13/2001 02:32 PM	3	24,000
07/13/2001 02:28 PM	4	23,000
07/13/2001 01:32 PM	3	22,000
07/13/2001 11:41 AM	2	21,000
07/12/2001 02:06 PM	1	20,000

Figure 9.A.7: Bidding Activity in Last 90 Minutes of the Long Reach Excavator

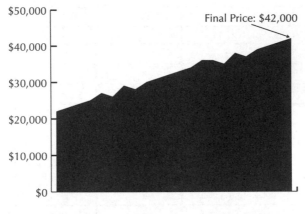

Source: LIquidation.com–2001

Figure 9.A.8: Liquidation.com Screenshot of Auction Outcome

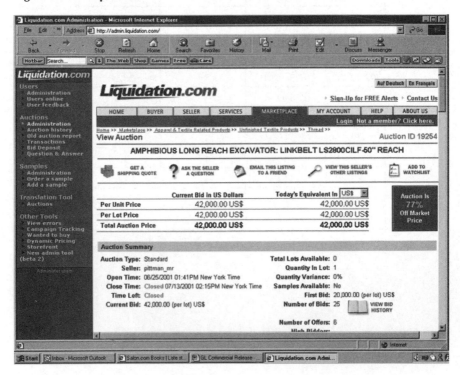

Appendix III:
Case Study—The Demolition of
Three Rivers Stadium

In the age of online auctions, one opportunity for governmental agencies is to take advantage of unique circumstances to conduct out-of-the-ordinary auctions to help defray the need for more taxpayer funding.

Such a prospect recently faced the Pittsburgh Sports & Exhibition Authority (SEA), a joint authority for the City of Pittsburgh and Allegheny County, Pennsylvania. Three Rivers Stadium had been the home for 30 years to both the Pittsburgh Steelers and Pirates. In the Steelers case, Three Rivers Stadium was the home of four Super Bowl champion teams (1975, 1976, 1979, 1980). One of the most famous plays in NFL history, Franco Harris's "Immaculate Reception," took place there. Likewise, the Pirates won two World Series (1971, 1979) while playing at Three Rivers.

Yet, like has occurred repeatedly across the nation, Three Rivers Stadium, a multipurpose facility, had grown old, eclipsed by new, single-sport stadiums built with more amenities and suites to meet the needs of today's sports economics. Thus, the City of Pittsburgh built both a new baseball stadium, PNC Park, which opened in April 2001, and Heinz Field, in which the NFL team began playing with the 2001 season. Three Rivers Stadium was thus slated for demolition, and the site, only 85 feet from the new Steelers Stadium, will be used for temporary surface parking and eventually will be developed as part of the mixed-use plan for the 25 acres of land between the ballpark and stadium.

In order to defray the over $5 million cost of demolishing Three Rivers on February 11, 2001, the Pittsburgh Stadium Authority (PSA) contracted with Pittsburgh-headquartered FreeMarkets to auction off usable assets and memorabilia from the old stadium. The strategy settled upon was to combine both online and on-site auctions of property from Three Rivers Stadium, both to maximize recoveries and to allow for high levels of participation from citizen fans of the two teams.

The online auction of "big ticket" items was held in November 2000. Buyers from across the United States and Canada participated in the auction. FreeMarkets identified potential buyers through the global network of buyers registered in the FreeMarkets® Asset Exchange, the leading B2B e-marketplace for selling surplus assets. The company also marketed the auction to minor league teams and other organizations that could use the assets. Each buyer qualified by FreeMarkets and invited by the Stadium Authority to participate in the auction was trained in the use of FreeMarkets' BidWare technology, which facilitates online, interactive bidding by allowing suppliers to see and respond to bids in real time. In preparation for the auction, FreeMarkets inspected and inventoried all items to be sold and coordinated site visits for interested buyers.

During the November event, over a half-million dollars was generated for the PSA, inclusive of these items:

- The stadium's Sony Jumbotron™ was purchased for $475,000 by Transit Image of New Jersey
- A block of 2,535 seats was sold for $22,688 to BlueChips USA, an Indiana-based developer of a Junior League baseball facility
- A block of 3,727 seats was purchased for $18,635 by the Long Island Ducks, a minor league baseball team
- A Whiteway Mini-Message Center was sold for $3,550 to the Butte Copper Kings, another minor league baseball team

In early January 2001, just prior to the scheduled implosion of the stadium, over 6,000 potential bidders registered to participate in the on-site, physical auction. Conducted by FreeMarkets, in partnership with Cowan Alexander Equipment Group, a leading international auctioneer, the auction generated more than $1.1 million for the Pittsburgh Stadium Authority. Buyers from across the United States participated in the auction, some traveling from as far away as Wisconsin. FreeMarkets and Cowan Alexander advertised the auction to potential buyers through both print and online channels.

On January 6, 2001, bidders and interested onlookers, totaling 12,000 in number, gathered at the Mellon Arena in Pittsburgh. In 10 hours of auctioning, all 4,321 lots were sold to 1,869 buyers. Among the items auctioned during the on-site event (and the prices paid for them) were:

- Home plate from the bullpen ($3,100)
- First set of lower-level floor-mounted stadium seats ($875)
- Game-used bases ($1,550)
- First 200 pieces of turf ($200 each)
- Locker room first aid kit ($800)
- Trash cans from Pirates' locker room ($175)
- Foul pole net ($650)
- U.S. flag that flew at stadium ($650)
- Stadium seating chart placard ($1,600)
- Framed Roberto Clemente photo ($1,300)
- Framed photo of Downtown Pittsburgh, circa 1929 ($650)
- New York Yankees banner ($1,000)
- Baltimore Orioles banner ($1,200)

Both the SEA and FreeMarkets were overwhelmed at the results of the on-site auction. "We are thrilled with the results of the auction," said Steve Leeper, executive director of the Pittsburgh Sports & Exhibition Authority. "We are amazed by the great turnout and the results of the bidding for the various items. We expected strong demand for the seats and turf, but some of the other items were truly remarkable." Doug Wnorowski, a senior vice president at FreeMarkets, remarked, "The on-site auction was a unique, once in a lifetime event that enabled Steelers and Pirates fans to participate in Pittsburgh history."

All sides seem to have benefited from this collaborative effort, which combined both the new technology of online auctioning with the traditional, on-site auction of the desired collectible items from the historic stadium. For FreeMarkets, Wnorowski commented: "We are very pleased to have helped auction the assets of Three Rivers Stadium and to have created value for the Stadium Authority and taxpayers in the Pittsburgh region in the process. By auctioning the assets of Three Rivers through both online and on-site auctions, the Stadium Authorities not only maximized their value—generating more than $1.6 million—but provided fans who wanted a piece of the Stadium with an opportunity to compete to get one." Speaking for the Pittsburgh Sports & Exhibition Authority, Steve Leeper remarked: "We are extremely pleased with the results. By selling the assets of Three Rivers through FreeMarkets, we were able to create a direct benefit for the taxpayers of the region by maximizing the value of our original investment and generating proceeds which will be applied to the cost of demolishing the facility."

Sources: Compiled from press releases from both the Pittsburgh Sports & Exhibition Authority (www.pgh-sea.com) and FreeMarkets 2001 (www.freemarkets.com). Photos courtesy of the SEA.

Appendix IV:
Case Study—"How Much for That Horse in the Pop-up Window"—The BLM's Wild Horse and Burro Internet Adoption Program

Congress finds and declares that wild free-roaming horses and burros are living symbols of the historic and pioneer spirit of the West; (and) that they contribute to the diversity of life forms within the Nation and enrich the lives of the American people...." (Public Law 92-195, December 15, 1971)

Within the U.S. Department of the Interior, the Bureau of Land Management (BLM) is charged with management of public lands. The wild horses and burros on the public rangelands are managed consistent with BLM's multiple-use mission, which takes into consideration natural resources such as wildlife and vegetation and other users such as livestock and recreationists. With the passage of the Wild Horse and Burro Act of 1971, the primary responsibilities of the BLM are to preserve and protect wild horses and burros and to manage for healthy rangelands. When an over-population of wild horses and burros exists on the range, the excess animals are removed and offered to the general public for adoption.

As part of its Wild Horse and Burro Program, the BLM offers horses and burros for adoption at several permanent field facilities and at numerous in-person adoption auctions. It also operates, on a regular basis, online auctions for wild horses and burros, captured on public rangelands.

The BLM operates several facilities to prepare the wild horses and burros that have been removed from the public rangelands for adoption. The animals are transported to preparation facilities from the rangelands. At the facilities, the animals receive veterinary care including inoculations and blood draws to ensure against equine diseases. The animals also receive identifying freeze marks on the left side of their neck. If desired by the adopter, the BLM will geld stud horses free of charge.

In order to participate in the online auctions, potential adopters must submit an electronic qualification to obtain an identification number. They must satisfy the same rigid standards as those who adopt animals from a BLM field facility.

The Adopter Must:
- Be 18 years of age or older.
- Have no prior violations of adoption regulations or convictions of inhumane treatment to animals.

- Not have adopted more than three animals in the past 12 months. Keep no more that four untitled animals at one facility at any time.
- Have received title to all eligible animals previously adopted.
- Be financially able to properly house, feed, and provide veterinary and farrier care for the animal(s).
- In terms of corral facilities, the adopter must have constructed:
    1. An outside corral with a minimum of 400 square feet (20x20) per animal. Corral should not be too large (more than 50x50), as animals gentle easier in smaller corrals.
    2. Fence must be at least 6 feet high for horses, five feet high for horses under 18 months of age and burros.
    3. Fencing material should be at least five wood rails or rounded pipes, or poles, 2x6 inch wooden planks or similar materials that do not pose a hazard to the animal. Small mesh, heavy gauge, woven wire fencing with a 2x6 inch board along the top, center, and bottom is acceptable. No barbwire, no electric wire, no T-posts. Once gentled, the animals may be maintained in pastures or in box stalls with daily turnout.

All of these requirements must be satisfied before an interested party can bid on and potentially adopt any animal through the BLM's program. Additionally, all individuals who adopt through the Wild Horse and Burro Program are subject to inspections of their facilities to ensure compliance. For all adopters, whether the horse or burro is acquired through in-person or online auctions, title to the animal is granted to the adopter, and the wild horse or burro is considered the private property of the adopter after one year of proven humane care.

Horses can be adopted at one of the BLM's Wild Horse and Burro facilities for a fixed price of either $125 (for males) or $250 (for females). At both the in-person and online auctions, however, prices may be raised significantly. For instance, as pointed out by Hasson and Browning (2001), some highly desirable horses, such as wild mustangs with Spanish-Colonial markings, yield, on average, $3,500 each in the BLM's Internet auctions.

Some examples from the August 2001 Internet adoption auctions were:

Sex: Mare
Age: 4 years
Winning Bid: $400
Color: Bay
Height: 15.0 hands
Necktag #: 2929
Captured: Paisley Desert Herd Management Area (HMA), Oregon
Pickup options: Elm Creek, Nebraska, and Cross Plains, Tennessee.

Sex: Mare
Age: 3 years
Winning Bid: $475
Color: Brown
Height: 14.2 hands
Necktag #: 1531
Captured: Black Rock HMA, Nevada
Pickup options: Elm Creek, Nebraska, and Cross Plains, Tennessee

Sex: Stud
Age: 4 years
Winning Bid: $260
Color: Bay
Height: 15.3 hands
Necktag #: 6894
Captured: Flanigan HMA, Nevada
Pickup options: Elm Creek, Nebraska, and Cross Plains, Tennessee

Sex: Filly
Age: 1 year
Winning Bid: $440
Color: Cremello
Height: 13.2 hands
Necktag #: 3371
Captured: Granite HMA, Nevada
Pickup options: Elm Creek, Nebraska, and Cross Plains, Tennessee

Sex: Filly
Age: 1 year
Winning Bid: $465
Color: Buckskin
Height: 13.2 hands
Necktag #: 3337
Captured: Granite HMA, Nevada
Pickup options: Elm Creek, Nebraska, and Cross Plains, Tennessee

How to measure the success of the program? What are the important metrics? As can be seen by the examples from the August 2001 Internet adoption auction, the online auctions draw significantly higher prices than the BLM's standard adoption rates. This does yield a greater return for the government in its efforts, while maintaining the strict control of the program (which even specifies the types of acceptable trailers and horse accessories than can be used). More importantly, however, the BLM places the vast majority of the captured horses and burros in settings which conform to their high standards—and the auctions merely widen the range of potential adoption families beyond those who can personally attend an event. The BLM is also experimenting with a program to provide satellite telecasts of its in-person events to expand the reach of these events as well.

In sum, this would appear to be an e-government initiative that works for all concerned.

Table 9.A.3: Animals Adopted by State—End of Year Statistics FY 2000 (Sept. 30, 2000)

State	Horses	Burros
Alaska	0	0
Arizona	217	71
California *	623	164
Colorado	309	45
Eastern States *	1,723	499
Idaho	156	45
Montana *	114	37
Nevada	39	7
New Mexico*	483	117
Oregon *	329	46
Utah	257	18
Wyoming *	438	25
National Program	392	48
Totals	**5,080**	**1,112**

Source: www.wildhorseandburro.blm.gov/population.htm (2001).

Table 9.A.4: Animals Removed by State—End of Year Statistics FY 2000 (Sept. 30, 2000)

State	Horses	Burros
Alaska	0	0
Arizona	3	752
California *	495	742
Colorado	141	0
Eastern States *	0	0
Idaho	94	0
Montana *	1	0
Nevada	4,022	132
New Mexico*	0	0
Oregon *	250	0
Utah	1,268	0
Wyoming *	733	1
National Program	0	0
Totals	**7,004**	**1,627**

Source: www.wildhorseandburro.blm.gov/population.htm (2001).

*Note: California administers the program in Hawaii; Eastern States administers the wild horse and burro program in the 31 states east of and bordering the Mississippi River and the District of Columbia; Montana administers the program in North and South Dakota; New Mexico administers the program in Kansas, Oklahoma, and Texas; Oregon administers the program in the State of Washington; and Wyoming administers the program in Nebraska.

Source: Bureau of Land Management's (BLM) Wild Horse & Burro Adoption Program (www.adoptahorse.blm.gov).

For more information on the Wild Horse and Burro Program, please call 1-866-4Mustangs, or consult the program's website at www.wildhorseandburro.blm.gov.

Bibliography

Aberdeen Group. *e-Sourcing: Negotiating Value in a Volatile Economy—An Executive White Paper from the Aberdeen Group.* (April 2001): (www.aberdeen.com).

Active Software. *White Paper: Business-to-Business Integration for the New Network Economy.* (2000): (www.activesw.com).

Alsop, Stewart. "E or Be Eaten." *Fortune* 141(5) (November 8, 1999): 86-87.

American Management Systems, Inc. and FreeMarkets, Inc. *Online Auctions in the Public Sector: A Powerful New Tool for Reducing Acquisition Costs.* 2000: (www.freemarkets.com).

Anderson, Brett. "Investing the Customer with New Value: As Organizations Tighten ROI Standards for e-Business, the Focus Shifts from Cost Savings to Managing Customer Value for Top-Line Growth." *E-Business Strategist* (May 2001): e8-e12 (www.destinationebusiness.com).

Anonymous. "Palm Beach County to Auction Infamous Punch-Card Machines." *The Baton Rouge Advocate* (September 1, 2001): 13A.

Anonymous. "E-Auction Playbook: What Top Supply Execs Say About Auctions." *Purchasing Magazine* (July 2001): S2 (www.purchasing.com).

Anonymous. "Governments shop and save online." *http://www.microsoft.com/europe/industry/government/features/2503.htm* (February 2, 2001).

Ante, Spencer E. and Arlene Weintraub. ""Why B2B is a Scary Place to Be: Too Many Business-to-Business Forums Are Chasing Too Few Dollars." *Business Week* (September 11, 2000): 34-37.

Appell, Kyle and Christopher Brousseau. *The Value Propositions of Business-to-Business Dynamic Commerce: A White Paper for the ASCET Project.* 1 (April 1, 2001): (www.appell.ascet.com).

Baldwin, Howard (a). "Applying The Network Effect To Purchasing: Q & A with ICG Commerce CEO Rick Berry." *Line56* (April 2001): 37-38.

Baldwin, Howard (b). "Who's Paying for All This?: Everyone Who Benefits from e-Business Should Share the Cost, But It's Not Easy to Determine Who That Is." *Line56* (May 2001): 65-67.

Barlas, Demir. "Not Dead Yet: Covisint's $3 Billion Online Auction May Quiet Some e-Marketplace Doubters." *Line56* (July/August 2001): 19.

Battey, Jim. "Afloat with Auctions: Online Auctions Offer Companies Another Sales Channel to Unload Excess Inventory." *Infoworld* 23(34) (August, 20, 2001): 22.

Berton, Elena. "Winners In UK Software Sector Target Govt Contracts." *The Interactive Wall Street Journal* (June 18, 2001): (http://interactive.wsj.com/archive/retrieve.cgi?id=DI-CO-20010618-003895.djm).

Birk, Brian and William Macready. "Beyond eMarketplaces: How Automated Markets Are Reinventing Online Trading." *Perspectives on Business Innovation from the Cap Gemini Ernst & Young Center for Business Innovation: Issue 6—Reinventing the Marketplace* (February 2001): 81-85 (www.cbi.cgey.com).

Birnbaum, Jeffrey H. "Move Over, Silicon Valley; D.C. Is Where It's At." *Fortune* 143(8) (April 16, 2001): 52, 56.

Black, Jason. "Back-Office Bonanza: E-Procurement Can Put the Unsung Heroes of the Back Office in the Top 40. Remember, Though: Rome Wasn't Built in a Day." *Internet World* (September 1, 2001): 22.

Blum, Vanessa. "All the President's Men ... Are Going Dotcom: Talent from All Around the Beltway is Driving Toward Washington's High-tech Industry." *Fast Company* (January 2001): 24-26 (http://www.fastcompany.com/feature/dc_migration.html).

Boutin, Paul. "GIGA Trends." *Wired* 9(4) (April 2001): 204-205.

Bowles, Jerry. "E-Government Meets E-Commerce." *Forbes* 167(6) (March 5, 2001): A1-A8.

Bridis, Ted. "Top Offices of Uncle Sam Make Do with Early-American Technology." *The Wall Street Journal* (October 30, 2000): B1, B4.

Brooks, Jeffrey D. *More Choice is not Enough: e-Markets Need to Do More than Aggregate Buyers and Sellers—A Research Note on eCommerce Networks from the Andersen Consulting (now Accenture) Institute for Strategic Change.* Issue 9 (July 31, 2000): (www.accenture.com/isc).

Brown, Richard. "E-Gov Outsells Amazon: Uncle Sam Presides Over a G2B Bazaar Online." *Line56* (July/August 2001): 21.

Canabou, Christine. "Best of the Best: Charles E. Phillips." *Fast Company* Issue 47 (June 2001): 90.

Canabou, Christine and Alison Overholt. "Smart Steps: What Smart Steps Should Business Leaders be Taking to Deal with Act II of the New Economy? Maybe the Smartest Thing to Do is to Take Stock of Act I: What Lessons Did We Learn in the First Five Years of the New Economy? *Fast Company* Issue 44 (March 2001): 91-101.

Carr, Laura. "E-government Services Elusive." *The Standard.com* (November 6, 2000): (www.thestandard.com).

Caterinicchia, Dan (a) "Wireless in the Wings: The Market is Waiting for Government to Catch Up." *Civic.com* 5(5) (May 2001): 38-39.

Caterinicchia, Dan. (b) "Reports Reveals e-Gov Lessons." *Federal Computer Week* (March 30, 2001): (www.fcw.com).

Caterinicchia, Dan. "Online Market Set to Go." *Federal Computer Week* (June 19, 2000): (www.fcw.com).

Caterinicchia, Dan and Natasha Haubold. "The Dot-com Invasion: Internet Companies Arrive in Droves to Help Feds Enter the New Economy." *Federal Computer Week* (May 22, 2000): 32-36 (www.fcw.com).

Clark, Aaron. "Public Life 2.0." *Wired* 9(5) (May 2001): 80.

Cleary, Mike. "ROI Is King: Net Managers Seeking Better Returns." *Interactive Week* 8(23) (June 11, 2001): 41-42.

Colvin, Geoffrey. "Value Driven: Four Ways the Revolution Continues." *Fortune* 143(4) (February 10, 2001): 54.

Commerce One. *The Global Trading Web—Creating the Business Internet: A White Paper from Commerce One.* (November 2000): (www.commerceone.com).

The Council for Excellence in Government. *e-Government: The Next American Revolution—A Blueprint from the Council for Excellence in Government.* (January 2001): (www.excelgov.org).

Craft, Lester. "Gearing Up to Go the Distance: Stamina and Preparation Will Prevail in the e-Business Marathon." *Line56* (July/August 2001): 9-10.

Cutler, Matt and Jim Sterne. *E-Metrics: Business Metrics For The New Economy—A White Paper from NetGenesis Corp.* (2000): (www.netgen.com/emetrics/).

Davis, Jessica. "Net Prophet: American Consumers Will Force e-tailers to Just Say No to Dynamic Pricing." *InfoWorld* 22(41) (October 9, 2000): 116.

Deloitte Research (a). *Through The Portal: Enterprise Transformation for e-Government—An e-View by Deloitte Consulting and Deloitte & Touche.* (2000): (www.dc.com/deloitte_research).

Deloitte Research (b). *The Future of B2B: A New Genesis—An e-View by Deloitte Consulting and Deloitte & Touche.* (2000): (www.dc.com/deloitte_research).

Desai-Sarnowski, Ami and Pat Murzyn. "When to Auction." *Purchasing Magazine* (July 2001): S14-S15 (www.purchasing.com).

Dizard, Wilson III (a). "E-Procurement: States Wrestle with e-Commerce Policy." *Government Computer News* (April 5, 2001): (www.gcn.com).

Dizard, Wilson III (b). "E-Procurement: Minneapolis Schools to Build Self-funded Procurement Site." *Government Computer News* (January 29, 2001): (www.gcn.com).

Dorobek, Christopher J. "HUD's Enterprising Effort." *Federal Computer Week* (June 4, 2001): (www.fcw.com).

Edwards, John. "Working the Wiggle Room: Online Negotiation Tools Can Help e-Markets Nail Down the Details." *Line 56* (April 2001): 51-55.

Eichmann, Don A. *E-Marketplace Participation: Reaching the Bottom Line: E-Marketplaces are Often Hailed as the Fountainhead of Great Efficiencies in Procurement and Collaboration. But e-Procurement-based Benefits Can Be More Elusive than Some Promoters Admit—A White Paper for the ASCET Project.* (May 2001): (www.eichmann.ascet.com).

Eisenhart, Mary. "Washington's Need To Know." *Knowledge Management* 4(1) (January 2001): 36-40.

Eisenmann, Thomas R. *Internet Business Models*. (2002) Boston: McGraw-Hill Irwin.

Enos, Lori. "Report: Public E-Procurement Mired in Red Tape." *E-Commerce Times* (May 31, 2001): (www.ecommercetimes.com).

Enterworks, Inc. *Virtual Government: How Process Automation and Data Integration are Revolutionizing E-Government Portals and Marketplaces—An Enterworks, Inc. White Paper.* (2000): (www.enterworks.com).

Eure, Rob. "Almost Sold: Many Suppliers Have Avoided Online Marketplaces, Fearing It's a Buyer's World. New Technology Is Changing That." *The Wall Street Journal (Special Report: E-Commerce)* (May 21, 2001): R14.

FairMarket, Inc. *The Power of Networked Dynamic Commerce Marketplaces: A White Paper from FairMarket, Inc.* (2000): (www.fairmarket.com).

Firmage, Joe. "Make Way for the Civil Economy." *Business 2.0* 5(18) (September 26, 2000): 142-148.

Fisher, Dennis "B2B Auction Services: More Goods on the Block—WayBid, Bid.com Open a Wider Range to Buyers." *eWeek* 17(51) (December 20, 2000): 37.

Frank, Diane. "IT Advice: Knock Down Stovepipes." *Federal Computer Week* (February 22, 2001): (www.fcw.com).

Frank, Diane and Paula Shaki Trimble. "GSA Looks to Online Auctions." *Federal Computer Week* (January 10, 2000): (www.fcw.com).

Freedman, David H. "Sleaze Bay: Snipers, Shills, and Scammers Are Working the Online Auction Game—Could They be Working You Over." *Forbes ASAP* (November 27, 2000): 134-140.

FreeMarkets, Inc. *Online Auctions in the Public Sector: Reducing Acquisition Costs for State and Local Governments—A FreeMarkets White Paper.* (2000): (www.freemarkets.com).

Gaffen, David. "The Ultimate Online Auction: Eat Your Heart Out, eBay." *Fortune* 143 (Special Issue—Technology Review) (Summer 2001): 36, 52.

General Services Administration, Federal Technology Service—Office of Information Technology Integration (GSA-FTS). *The Federal Technology Service Guide to Best Practices for Conducting Reverse Auctions.* (April 2001): (www.buyers.gov).

Gibbs, Mark. "Eh? E-? I-? Oh, you!" *Network World Fusion* (April 24, 2000): (http://www.nwfusion.com/columnists/2000/0424gibbs.html).

Gingrich, Newt. "A New Approach to Cutting Government." *Wall Street Journal* (February 27, 2001): A26.

Gingrich, Newt. *The Age of Transitions.* (April 4, 2000): (www.newt.org).

Goldberg, Aaron. "ROI Metrics: Building Empirical Metrics." *CIO Insight Magazine* Issue 1 (May 2001): (www.cioinsight.com).

Gomolski, Barb. "When the 'e' Drops Off: Who Cares Whether or Not e-Business Runs the Show? Thank Heaven We're Getting Back to Just Good Ol' Business-As-Usual." *Infoworld* 23(25) (June 18, 2001): 88 (www.infoworld.com).

Gordon, Leslie A. "A Look at e-Markets: Cheers or Sneers—What Works, What Doesn't, and Why Some Businesses Won't Touch 'em." *Line56* (March 2001): 26-27.

Grenier, Melinda Patterson. "The Curiosity Shop: Online Auctions Aren't Just About Office Supplies and Semiconductors. There's Also the Spock Ears and Ox Gallstones." *The Wall Street Journal (Special Report: E-Commerce)* (May 21, 2001): R16-R17.

Grygo, Eugene. "Exchange future mixed." *InfoWorld* 22(23) (June 5, 2000): 42-43.

Hamm, Steve. "E-Biz: Down But Hardly Out. Downturn Be Dammed. Companies Are Still Anxious to Expand Online Because the Net is a Way to Boost Sales and Shrink Sales." *BusinessWeek* (March 26, 2001): 126-130.

Hammonds, Keith H. "Looking Ahead: 2001-2006: If You Think The Past Five Years Were Something To Behold, Survive the Next Five Years." *Fast Company* (44) (March 2001).

Harreld, Heather (a). "Redtape.gov?: Governments Are Offering Their Services Online, but Will They Truly Streamline Processes or Will People End Up Waiting in Line Online?" *CIO Magazine* (September 15, 2000): 1-9.

Harreld, Heather (b). "Measuring E-GOV Value." *Federal Computer Week* (August 28, 2000): (www.fcw.com).

Hasson, Judi (a). "HUD Sells Loans Online." *Federal Computer Week* (July 3, 2001): (www.fcw.com).

Hasson, Judi (b). "Homesforsale.gov." *Federal Computer Week* (May 28, 2001). (www.fcw.com/fcw/articles/2001/0528/cov-pew1-05-28-01.asp)

Hasson, Judi (c). "Lawmakers Query Need for GSA Site." *Federal Computer Week* (May 21, 2001) (www.fcw.com).

Hasson, Judi and Graeme Browning. *Dot-gov Goes Retail: The Federal Government Has Become One of the Biggest Online Retailers in America—A Special Report from the Pew Internet & American Life Project and Federal Computer Week.* (May 28, 2001): (http://www.pewinternet.org/reports/toc.asp?report=35).

Heath, Peggy Sue. "ROI Metrics: Measuring the Future." *CIO Insight Magazine* Issue 1 (May 2001): (www.cioinsight.com).

454 David C. Wyld

Hunter, David R. and Vivienne Jupp. *Rhetoric vs. Reality—Closing the Gap: A Study on eGovernment Leadership from Accenture.* (March 30, 2001): (www.accenture.com).

Institute for Supply Management (ISM) (a). ISM/Forrester Research *Report On eBusiness—July 2001* (July 16, 2001): (www.ism.ws).

Institute for Supply Management (ISM) (b). ISM/ Forrester Research *Report On eBusiness—April 2001* (April 16, 2001): (www.ism.ws).

Institute for Supply Management (ISM) (c). ISM/ Forrester Research *Report On eBusiness—January 2001* (January 22, 2001): (www.ism.ws).

Jaroneczyk, Jennifer. "Sold on an Old Idea." *Internet World* (February 15, 2001): 22-23.

Jeu, Joseph. "Letter to the Editor." *Federal Computer Week* (March 12, 2001): (www.fcw.com).

Kalin, Sari (a). "How Low Can You Go?: If You're Smart, You'll Decide Your Online Pricing Strategies Before the Bidding Wars Begin." *Darwin* (April 2001): (http://www.darwinmag.com/read/040101/low.html).

Kalin, Sari (b). "Blood, Sweat, and Fears: If You're Going to Give Reverse Auctions a Try, Get Ready for Some Thrills and Chills." *Darwin* (April 2001): (http://www.darwinmag.com/read/040101/low.html).

Kambil, Ajit and Eric van Heck. *Successfully Implementing Electronic Auctions and Markets: A Working Paper from the Accenture Institute for Strategic Change* (2000): (www.accenture.com/isc).

Kaplan, Jeffrey A. "The Powers That E." *CIO Magazine* (March 15, 2001): (www.cio.com).

Kelmen, Steve (a). "Primer on High Performance." *Federal Computer Week* (July 9, 2001): (www.fcw.com). (http://www.fcw.com/fcw/articles/2001/0709/pol-Kelemen-07-09-01.asp).

Kelmen, Steve (b). "Don't Give Up on the Net." *Federal Computer Week* (June 11, 2001): (www.fcw.com). (http://www.fcw.com/fcw/articles/2001/0611/pol-Kelemen-06-11-01.asp).

Kerstetter, Jim. "When Machines Chat: XML IS About to Spark an Efficiency Revolution." *Business Week* no. 3742 (July 23, 2001): 76-77.

KPMG Consulting. *White Paper: Return on Exchange (ROE): A Unique Service That Rationalizes Exchange Membership.* (2001): (www.kpmg-consulting.com).

KPMG Consulting. *White Paper—Organizations Serving the Public: Transformation to the 21st Century.* (January 1997): (www.kpmgconsulting.com).

Kulisch, Eric. (a) "Two States Opt for e-Procurement." *Federal Computer Week* (February 1, 2001). (www.fcw.com).

Kulisch, Eric. (b) "D.C. Region Oks Buying Deal." *Federal Computer Week* (January 12, 2001) (www.fcw.com).

LaMonica, Martin (a). "Metrics and Instincts Shape IT's Rising Role." *InfoWorld* 23(10) (May 14, 2001): 26.

LaMonica, Martin (b). "Trading Exchanges May Outlast Their Critics." *InfoWorld* 23(24) (June 11, 2001): 18. (http://iwsun4.infoworld.com/ articles/op/xml/01/06/11/010611oprecord.xml).

LaMonica, Martin (c). "A Business Downturn Revives Supply Chain." *InfoWorld* 23(10) (March 5, 2001): 5.

LaMonica, Martin (d). "Cycling Down the e-Business Economy." *InfoWorld* 22(52) (January 1, 2001): 5.

Laurent, Anne. "E-invasion." *Government Executive* 32(6) (June 2000): 26-34.

Letulle, Raymond. "E-Auction Playbook: Maintain Contact." *Purchasing Magazine* (July 2001): S8 (www.purchasing.com).

Litan, Robert E. "The Internet Economy: The Markets May Have Soured on Internet Start-ups. High-tech Oases in Countries Like Malaysia and India May Not Lift Their Countries Out of Poverty. But All Those Dot-coms and Silicon Valley Dreams Never Had Much to Do with the Real Economic Impact of the Internet. The New Economy is Alive and Well." *Foreign Policy* (March-April 2001): 16-24.

McCarthy, Ellen. "Liquidation.com to Take Over Military Surplus: D.C. Company's Subsidiary Wins Sales Rights For 7 Years." *The Washington Post* (June 20, 2001): E05.

McNealy, Scott. "It's like...: Businesses Built on Metaphors Still Need Value" *Forbes ASAP* (October 2, 2000): 47.

Manciagli, Dana. "E-Auction Playbook: A Supplier's View." *Purchasing Magazine* (July 2001): S14 (www.purchasing.com).

Marinello, Michele and Michael Daher. "Reversal of Fortune: Turning the Tables with a Reverse Auction Could Hammer Down Procurement Costs." *Line56* (July/August 2001): 73-74.

Martinez, Pete. *Models made "e": What business are you in?—A White Paper from Centers for IBM e-business Innovation.* (December 2000): (www.ibm.com).

Matthews, William (a). "Council's Blueprint Upgrades e-Gov." *Civic.com* 5(4) (April 2001): 14.

Matthews, William (b). "Feds Eschew Online Buying." *Federal Computer Week* (June 1, 2001): (www.fcw.com).

Matthews, William (c). "Contracting Bazaar Draws Hill Scrutiny." *Federal Computer Week* (April 30, 2001): (www.fcw.com).

Matthews, William (d). "Bush e-Gov Fund to Double: But Tapping the Pot Won't Be Easy for Agencies." *Federal Computer Week* (March 26, 2001): (www.fcw.com).

Matthews, William (e). "E-gov's Point Man (Rep. Tom Davis)." *Federal Computer Week* (March 12, 2001): (www.fcw.com).

Matthews, William (f). "Worldwide Web." *Federal Computer Week* (August 27, 2001): (www.fcw.com).

Matthews, William (a). "Public Getting Impatient About e-Gov, Experts Say." *Federal Computer Week* (December 4, 2000): (www.fcw.com).

Matthews, William (b). "Experts: E-gov Examples Shine Abroad." *Federal Computer Week* (December 1, 2000): (www.fcw.com).

Matthews, William (c). "Blurring the Lines." *Federal Computer Week* (November 13, 2000): (www.fcw.com).

Matthews, William (d). "Poll: Public Hopes e-Gov Leads to Accountability." *Civic.com* 4(11) (November 2000): 14-16.

Matthews, William (e). "Federal e-Gov Forecast Is Gloomy." *Network World Fusion* (June 8, 2000): (http://www.nwfusion.com/news/2000/0608egovslow.html).

Mattick, Bradley and Christopher Brousseau. *Strategic Sourcing through Private E-Marketplaces: E-Procurement Systems and Reverse Auction-Based Services Have Proved the Validity of Applying Technology to Purchasing and Sourcing—A White Paper for the ASCET Project.* 3 (July 1, 2001): (www.mattick.ascet.com).

Meakem, Glen. "E-Auction Playbook: Know Your Market." *Purchasing Magazine* (July 2001): S7 (www.purchasing.com).

Miller, Sandra Kay. "Convenient Setup with AuctionBuilder 1.0: Able-Commerce Assembles the Tools for Companies to Cut Travel and Sales Negotiation Time with Online Auctions." *InfoWorld* 22(32) (August 7, 2000): 43.

Moai Technologies, Inc. (a). *Implementing Dynamic Commerce Solutions: A Guide to the Critical Success Factors for Creating Online Exchanges and Auctions—A White Paper from Moai Technologies, Inc.* (May 2000): (www.moai.com).

Moai Technologies, Inc. (b) *An Introduction to Dynamic Commerce and Negotiated e-Commerce: A Review and Analysis of Trends and Opportunities in Commerce on the Internet—A White Paper from Moai Technologies, Inc.* (May 2000): (www.moai.com).

Monteagudo, Luis Jr. "County tempts bidders online: Departments Turn to Internet to Dispose of Items in Default." *San Diego Union-Tribune* (May 14, 2001): (http://www.signonsandiego.com/news/uniontrib/mon/metro/news_1m14auctions.html).

National Electronic Commerce Coordinating Council (a). *E-Procurement Policy Issues: A White Paper of the National Electronic Commerce Coordinating Council Symposium 2000* (December 2000): (www.ec3.org).

National Electronic Commerce Coordinating Council (b). *E-Government Strategic Planning: A White Paper of the National Electronic Commerce Coordinating Council Symposium 2000* (December 13, 2000): (www.ec3.org).

OMB Watch (a). "Plugged In, Tuning Up." (March 2001): (www.omb-watch.org).

OMB Watch (b). "Building the Framework for Access to Government: An Analysis of the Information Management Components of The E-Government Act of 2001." (May 2001): (www.ombwatch.org).

Orzell, Daniel J. "E-Auction Playbook: Train Buyers Well." *Purchasing Magazine* (July 2001): S4 (www.purchasing.com).

Peers, Alexandra. "Secrets and Seurats: Value of Works of Art Is Hard to Tell as Auction Houses Negotiate Backroom Deals." *The Wall Street Journal* (July 2, 2001): B1, B3.

Pendse, Nigel. *Essential E-Analytics—The Essential Role of E-Analytics in the New Business Model: A White Paper from Brio Technology.* 2000. (http://www.brio.com/library/white_papers/pdf_files/e_analytics_wp.pdf).

Peters, Tom. "Rule #3: Leadership Is Confusing As Hell." *Fast Company* (44) (March 2001).

Phillips, Robert. *Pricing and Revenue Management—Driving Profit Improvement from CRM—A White Paper from Talus Solutions, Inc.* (April 2001): (www.crmproject.com/wp/phillips.html).

Plyler, Andy and George P. Shaw. *Exostar: The Trading Exchange Revolutionizing A&D. Exostar Provides an Open Internet Trading Exchange for Global A&D Suppliers and Buyers of All Sizes, from Commercial Aviation to Defense and Space Systems—A White Paper for the ASCET Project.* (May 2001): (www.plyler.ascet.com).

Porter, Anne Millen. "E-auctions: When to play, how to play, how to win." *Purchasing Magazine* (July 2001): S1 (www.purchasing.com).

Reason Public Policy Institute. *Transitioning to Performance-Based Government: A Report to the 43rd President and the 107th Congress* (November 2000): Alexandria, Va., The Reason Public Policy Institute (www.rppi.org).

Robb, Drew. "Financing Online Government." *E.gov* (June 19, 2001): (www.egovernment.govtech.net).

Roberti, Mark. "Government: The Stealth Market." *The Industry Standard* (June 12, 2000). (http://www.thestandard.com/article/display/0,1151,15826,00.html).

Robinson, Brian. "Texas Buying Site Goes National." *Federal Computer Week* (September 10, 2001): (www.fcw.com).

Robinson, Brian (a). "Strength in Numbers." *Federal Computer Week* (August 28, 2000): (www.fcw.com).

Robinson, Brian (b). "How Much Will e-Procurement Cost?" *Federal Computer Week* (August 28, 2000): (www.fcw.com).

Saba, Jennifer (a). "Dancing Giants at the e-Markets Ball: Cap Gemini Ernst & Young B2B Specialist Pravesh Mehra Tackles the Subject of e-Markets." *Line56* (March 2001): 29-30.

Saba, Jennifer (b). "Growth Trajectory: Executives Report B2B Adoption is Well Underway." *Line56* (June 2001): 22-23.

Sanborn, Stephanie. "Reverse Auctions Make a Bid for Business: Auction Technology Helps Companies Reach a Wider Audience and Save Time and Money." *InfoWorld* 23(12) (March 19, 2001): 32.

Sarkar, Dibya (a). "E-gov a Low Priority for Bush." *Federal Computer Week* (May 10, 2001): (www.fcw.com).

Sarkar, Dibya (b). "N.C. building Web-based buying." *Federal Computer Week* (March 7, 2001): (www.fcw.com).

Sarkar, Dibya (c). "Virginia Unveils e-procurement System." *Federal Computer Week* (March 2, 2001): (www.fcw.com).

Sarkar, Dibya (d). "States Team Up for e-Buying." *Federal Computer Week* (August 22, 2001): (www.fcw.com).

Sarkar, Dibya (a). "Study: E-gov can't stop now." *Civic.com* 4(10) (October 2000): 43.

Sarkar, Dibya (b). "Site Peddles Gov Surplus." *Civic.com* 4(12) (December 2000): 40.

Sayer, Peter. "E-government Not for Governments." *Network World Fusion* (November 6, 2000): (http://www.nwfusion.com/news/2000/1106egov.html).

Saywell, Trish. "Singapore Leads Asia In Embracing E-Government." *The Interactive Wall Street Journal* (June 13, 2001): (http://interactive.wsj.com/archive/retrieve.cgi?id=DI-CO-20010613-007237.djm).

Scannell, Ed, Matthew Nelson and Dan Briody. "IT Gets Back to Business." *InfoWorld* (November 15, 1999): 37.

Schwartz, Ephraim (a). "All eyes focus on launch of Covisint." *InfoWorld* 22(38) (September 15, 2000).

Schwartz, Ephraim (b). "E-business Gets Dynamic: On-the-fly Partnering Redefines Trading Relationships." *InfoWorld* 22(32) (August 7, 2000).

Schwartz, Karen D. "Patriot Gains: Online Reverse Auctions Give the World's Largest Bureaucracy New Power Over Its Pocketbook by Delivering a Less Costly, More Efficient Purchasing Process." *Business 2.0* 5(19) (October 10, 2000): 187-199.

Seben, Larry. "Digital River Flows into E-Government Sector." *CRM Daily* (June 13, 2001): (www.crmdaily.com).

Shapiro, Carl. "Will E-Commerce Erode Liberty?" *Harvard Business Review* 78(3) (May-June 2000): 189-196.

Sostrom, Carolyn Pye. "The Next Step in E-Commerce: Every Day, Professionals Are Deluged with Statistics and Promises about e-Commerce Tools and Trends. How Will They Affect the Supply Management Function and Its Leaders?" *Purchasing Today* (June 2001): 46-54.

Spangler, Todd. "Amid PC Industry Famine, Gateway Restructures." *Interactive Week* 8(34) (September 3, 2001): 14.

Tapscott, Don. "E Pluribus Connecto." *Business 2.0* (September 26, 2000): 172-173.

Tapscott, Don, David Ticoll, and Alex Lowry. *Digital Capital: Harnessing the Power of Business Webs*. 2000. Boston: Harvard Business School Press.

Temin, Thomas R. "E-government: Microsoft Stakes e-Gov Claim on XML." *Government Computer News* (June 2, 2001): (www.gcn.com).

Terry, Lisa. "Special Report: E-commerce in Government/E-business Procurement." (August 13, 2001): (www.wtonline.com).

Totty, Michael. "The Next Phase: Contrary to Rumor, B-to-B e-Commerce Is Showing Surprising Signs of Life." *The Wall Street Journal (Special Report: E-Commerce)* (May 21, 2001): R8-R9.

Trimble, Paula Shaki. "Not e-Gov, but e-Governance." *Federal Computer Week* (June 12, 2000): (www.fcw.com).

Trott, Bob. "Microsoft Details Enterprise Project for U.K. Government." *Network World Fusion* (March, 27, 2001): (http://www.nwfusion.com/news/2001/0327msuk.html).

Vasishtha, Preeti. "IRS Gets PC Bargains in Reverse Auction." *Government Computer News* (May 17, 2001): (www.gcn.com).

Vizard, Michael, Ed Scannell, and Dan Neel. "Suppliers Toy with Dynamic Pricing: Users Face Prospect of Daily Server Pricing Changes as Industry Pursues Profits." *InfoWorld* 23(20) (May 14, 2001): 26.

Von Hoffman, Constantine. "The Making of E-Government: A Research Project Has Brought Together Governments and Businesses to Study the Future of Government in the Digital Economy." *CIO Enterprise Magazine* (November 15, 1999): (www.cio.com).

Voth, Danna. "Dovebid.com Bets Its Assets on e-Business: By Taking an Established Business Online and Expanding Its Geographic Base, the Auction Company Bids Up Its Revenues Sixfold." *E-Business Strategist* (May 2001): e4-e6 (www.destinationebusiness.com).

Wait, Patience (a). "Oracle, British Company Join on U.K. Online Marketplace." *Washington Technology* (March 30, 2001): (http://www.washingtontechnology.com/).

Wait, Patience. (b) "Firms Worry About 8(a) Program's Long-Term Health." *Washington Technology* 15(24) (March 19, 2001): 16-18 (http://www.washingtontechnology.com/).

Walker, Richard W. "Buying IT over the Web is Convenient, Feds Say." *Government Computer News* 19(16) (June 19, 2000): 27.

Walsh, Patrick J. "Buying Strategies: Idaho's Rules Get in Step with Its Technology." *Civic.com* 5(5) (May 2001): 44.

Walsh, Patrick J. (a) "A Setup for Savings: Michigan Designs a Program to Gauge Whether e-Procurement Can Save Money." *Civic.com* 5(1) (January 2001): 14.

Walsh, Patrick J. "Buying Strategies: Shopping Network Boosts Local Government Clout." *Civic.com* 4(10) (October 2000): 42-43.

Walsh, Trudy and Wilson P. Dizard III. "Online Buying's a Boom or Bust Proposition: Hidden Costs, Red Tape Stall Growth of States' e-Procurement Efforts." *Government Computer News* (July 2000): (www.gcn.com).

Waxer, Cindy. "When Price Takes a Back Seat: Big Companies Test Auctions That Put More Than Pricing Up for Bid." *Business 2.0* (June 26, 2001): 34.

Welsh, William (a). "Companies Ditch Self-Funding Model for E-Procurement Demand Remains Strong." *Washington Technology* 16(2) (April 16, 2001): (http://www.washingtontechnology.com/).

Welsh, William (b). "E-Gov Drives State and Local Market." *Washington Technology* 15(22) (February 19, 2001): 26-35 (http://www.washingtontechnology.com/).

Wendin, Christine Grech. "Slash Purchasing Costs." *Smart Business Magazine 14*(5) (May 2001): 66-67 (www.smartbusinessmag.com).

Wyld, David C. "The Auction Model: How the Public Sector Can Leverage the Power of E-Commerce through Dynamic Pricing." Published by the IBM Endowment for The Business of Government, (October 2000): Arlington, Va. (http://www.businessofgovernment.com/GrantDetails.asp?GID=59)

Zyskowski, John. "Harnessing the Internet Economy." *Federal Computer Week* (August 28, 2000): (www.fcw.com).

About the Contributors

Mark A. Abramson is Executive Director of the IBM Endowment for The Business of Government, a position he has held since July 1998. Prior to the Endowment, he was chairman of Leadership Inc. From 1983 to 1994, Mr. Abramson served as the first president of the Council for Excellence in Government. Previously, Mr. Abramson served as a senior program evaluator in the Office of the Assistant Secretary for Planning and Evaluation, U.S. Department of Health and Human Services

He is a Fellow of the National Academy of Public Administration. In 1995, he served as president of the National Capital Area Chapter of the American Society for Public Administration. Mr. Abramson has taught at George Mason University and the Federal Executive Institute in Charlottesville, Virginia.

Mr. Abramson is the co-editor of *Transforming Organizations, E-Government 2001, Managing for Results 2002, Innovation, Human Capital 2002, Leaders,* and *E-Government 2003.* He also edited *Memos to the President: Management Advice from the Nation's Top Public Administrators* and *Toward a 21st Century Public Service: Reports from Four Forums.* He is also the co-editor (with Joseph S. Wholey and Christopher Bellavita) of *Performance and Credibility: Developing Excellence in Public and Nonprofit Organizations,* and the author of *The Federal Funding of Social Knowledge Production and Application.*

He received his Bachelor of Arts degree from Florida State University. He received a Master of Arts degree in history from New York University and a Master of Arts degree in political science from the Maxwell School of Citizenship and Public Affairs, Syracuse University.

Yu-Che Chen is a Visiting Assistant Professor of Information Systems and Public Affairs in the School of Public and Environmental Affairs at Indiana University. His current teaching and research center on e-government as well as the design and implementation of information systems. His particular focus is on the outsourcing of e-government services and its complex relationships with organizational innovations and performance.

Dr. Chen's broad research interest lies in the reinvention of government, particularly in the use of information technology and innovative policy instruments to improve performance. His most recent project examines the use of data warehousing and data mining to improve government decision-making capabilities. His work has appeared in peer-reviewed conference proceedings. He has published in such journals as *Public Administration Quarterly* and *Government Information Quarterly*. His articles deal with the use of application service providers and assess the potential of using an innovative policy instrument, voluntary programs, to better accomplish public agencies' missions.

Dr. Chen received his M.P.A. and Ph.D. degrees in public policy from Indiana University. He has been involved in developing and implementing e-government applications. His technical training includes both database management systems, such as Oracle and MS ACCESS, and development of information systems using CASE tools. Moreover, he has extensive experience in quantitative data analysis, such as logistic regression and panel data analysis.

Kathryn G. Denhardt is Associate Professor, School of Urban Affairs and Public Policy, and policy scientist, Institute for Public Administration at the University of Delaware. She works with public-sector practitioners to improve organizational performance and contract management, implement team-based approaches in complex work environments, facilitate decision making involving multiple stakeholders, and ensure accountability for achieving desired outcomes.

As a public service faculty member, Professor Denhardt blends this applied work with traditional academic pursuits in the university's School of Urban Affairs and Public Policy. There, she coordinates the organizational leadership specialization for the Master's in Public Administration Program, teaching in the areas of performance management, administrative ethics, human resource management, and civic engagement.

Professor Denhardt has maintained a strong interest in government ethics throughout her career. She has worked with government entities throughout the United States as well as internationally to help these governments create an environment in which high standards of ethics are integrated with highly effective public management. Her work spans a great variety of programmatic areas, including education, prisons, public works, transportation, IT, public personnel, community empowerment, and conflict resolution.

Professor Denhardt received her Ph.D. and M.A. in political science and public administration from the University of Kansas and her B.S. degree from Kansas State University.

Jacques S. Gansler holds the Roger C. Lipitz Chair in Public Policy and Private Enterprise at the University of Maryland School of Public Affairs. He teaches graduate school courses, and leads the School's Center for Public Policy and Private Enterprise, which fosters collaboration among the public, private, and nonprofit sectors to promote mutually beneficial public and private interests.

Dr. Gansler served as the Under Secretary of Defense for Acquisition, Technology, and Logistics from November 1997 until January 2001. In this position, he was responsible for all matters relating to Department of Defense acquisition; research and development; logistics; acquisition reform; advanced technology; international programs; environmental security; nuclear, chemical, and biological programs; and the defense technology and industrial base.

Prior to this appointment, Dr. Gansler was executive vice president and corporate director for TASC, Incorporated, an applied information technology company, in Arlington, Virginia. During his tenure there (1977-1997), he played a major role in building the company from a small operation into a large, widely recognized and respected corporation, serving both the government and the private sector.

From 1972 to 1977, he served in the government as deputy assistant secretary of defense (materiel acquisition), responsible for all defense procurements in the defense industry; and as assistant director of defense, research and engineering (electronics), responsible for all defense electronics research and development.

His prior industrial experience included vice president (business development) at I.T.T. (1970-1972); program management, director of advanced programs, and director of international marketing at Singer Corporation (1962-1970); and engineering management at Raytheon Corporation (1956-1962).

Dr. Gansler has served on numerous corporation boards of directors, and governmental special committees and advisory boards including vice chairman, Defense Science Board; chairman, Board of Visitors, Defense Acquisition University; director, Procurement Round Table; chairman, Industry Advisory Board, University of Virginia, School of Engineering; chairman, Board of Visitors, University of Maryland, School of Public Affairs; member of the Federal Aviation Administration Blue Ribbon Panel on Acquisition Reform; and senior consultant to the Packard Commission on defense acquisition reform.

From 1984 to 1997, Dr. Gansler was a Visiting Scholar at the Kennedy School of Government, Harvard University, where he was a frequent guest lecturer in executive management courses. He is the author of three books, contributing author to 23 other books, author of over 100 papers, and a frequent speaker and congressional witness.

Dr. Gansler holds a B.E. (electrical engineering) from Yale University, an M.S. (electrical engineering) from Northeastern University, an M.A. (political economy) from the New School for Social Research, and a Ph.D. (economics) from American University

Roland S. Harris III is Managing Partner, Americas and Global Public Sector, IBM Business Consulting Services. In this role, Mr. Harris leads business consultants, services, and delivery service experts specializing in helping state and local governments, federal governments, health care, and education industries leverage world-class technology to improve business performance. In January 1999, Mr. Harris was appointed as the IBM Global Services general manager, public sector.

Mr. Harris serves on the board of a number of technology associations, including the Enterprise Solutions, Information Technology Association of America, and the Professional Services Council. He is a member of the Selective Service Board for the State of Maryland and a member of the State of Maryland Child Care Business Partnership Team, and is a standing member of the New York City Internet Task Force. From 1999 through 2001, he served as a member of the Judith P. Hoyer Blue Ribbon Commission on the funding of early child care and education for the governor of Maryland.

Mr. Harris received a Juris Doctor in 1978 from the University of Connecticut and a B.A. from Tufts University in 1975.

Wendell C. Lawther is an Associate Professor of Public Administration at the University of Central Florida (UCF). He teaches courses on privatization, program evaluation, and human resource management.

Dr. Lawther has held numerous academic positions while at UCF, including director, Ph.D. Program in Public Affairs; chair, Department of Public Administration; and associate dean, College of Health and Public Affairs. He has also served as council member on several local chapters of the American Society for Public Administration.

His recent research interests include public-private partnerships, especially those that evolve in the deployment of intelligent transportation systems in metropolitan areas. He is the co-author of a forthcoming advanced text entitled *Capital Purchases*. He has also studied the impact of privatization on public employees. He is the author of *Privatizing Toll Roads* (Praeger, 2000). He has published articles in journals such as *Review of Public Personnel Administration, Public Works Management and Policy,* and *Public Personnel Management.*

Dr. Lawther received a bachelor's and master's degree from the University of Delaware. His doctorate is from Indiana University.

Lawrence L. (Larry) Martin is an Associate Professor at the Columbia University School of Social Work, where he also serves as Director of the Social Administration Program. He earned his B.S., M.S.W. and Ph.D. from Arizona State University and his M.B.A. from the American Graduate School of International Management (Thunderbird). From 1988 to 1994, he was on the faculty of Florida Atlantic University's School of Public Administration.

Dr. Martin has served in a variety of state and local government positions including director of Aging Programs for the Arizona Department of Economic Security (1976–78), assistant and deputy director of the Maricopa County (Phoenix, Arizona) Human Resources Department (1980–1982), and director of the Maricopa County (Phoenix, Arizona) Office of Management Analysis (1984–1988).

Dr. Martin is the author of *Financial Management for Human Service Administrators* (2001), *Contracting for Service Delivery: Local Government Choices* (1999), and *Total Quality Management in Human Service Organizations* (1993). He is the co-author of *Designing & Managing Programs* (1999), *Measuring the Performance of Human Service Programs* (1996), and *Purchase of Service Contracting* (1987); and co-editor of *Handbook of Comparative Public Budgeting & Financial Management* (1993). He is also the author of a previous IBM Endowment grant report, "Determining a Level Playing Field for Public-Private Competition" (1999). In addition, he has published over 70 articles, book chapters, and monographs dealing with performance-based contracting, service contracting, public-private competition, performance measurement, financial management, and human service administration.

Dr. Martin has taught courses in social administration, financial management, program evaluation and performance measurement, public management, and state and local government. He has provided consultation and training for state and local governments and nonprofit organizations nationally and has lectured and delivered invited presentations to governments and non-governmental organizations in Canada, France, Germany, and Sweden. He is currently working with the National Institute of Governmental Purchasing to revise and update its training and certification materials dealing with contracting for public sector services.

M. Jae Moon is Assistant Professor at the George Bush School of Government Affairs and Public Service in Texas A&M University. Before joining the Bush School, he was at the Graduate School of Public Affairs at the University of Colorado at Denver (1998–2002), where he was named Teacher of the Year in 1999 and 2001. He also taught several summer classes (in organization and management) to MPA and JD students at the Maxwell School of Citizenship and Public Affairs at Syracuse University. He has taught master's and doctoral courses in public management, organizational change and management, globalization and public policy, technology and environmental program management, and research methodology.

His research interests include public management, information technology, and comparative public administration. His research has recently appeared in major public administration and policy journals, including *Technology Forecasting and Social Change, Governance, Public Administration Review, Journal of Public Administration Research and Theory, Public Performance and Management Review, International Review of Public Administration,* and *Administration and Society.*

Dr. Moon earned a B.A. in political science from Yonsei University, Korea (1988), an M.A. in international politics from Kyunghee University, Korea, and a Ph.D. in public administration from Syracuse University.

James L. Perry is Associate Dean and Chancellor's Professor in the School of Public and Environmental Affairs (SPEA) at Indiana University-Purdue University, Indianapolis. He has also held faculty appointments at the University of California, Irvine, the Chinese University of Hong Kong, and the University of Wisconsin, Madison. In 1992, he served as special assistant to the assistant secretary for personnel administration, U.S. Department of Health and Human Services. In 1999–2000, he was senior evaluator at the Corporation for National Service. He received an undergraduate degree from the University of Chicago and M.P.A. and Ph.D. degrees from the Maxwell School of Citizenship and Public Affairs at Syracuse University.

Dr. Perry directs the Institute for the Study of Government and the Nonprofit Sector, which is jointly sponsored by SPEA, the Indiana University Center on Philanthropy, and the Indiana University Center on Urban Policy and the Environment. His recent research focuses on public service motivation, community and national service, and government reform. His research appears in such journals as *Academy of Management Journal, Administrative Science Quarterly, Nonprofit Management and Leadership, Nonprofit and Voluntary Sector Quarterly,* and *Public Administration Review.* He is author and editor of several books, including the *Handbook of Public Administration,* second edition (Jossey-Bass, 1996).

Dr. Perry has received several national awards, including the Yodel-Honeymoon Award for innovative personnel research from the Society for Human Resource Management. He received two awards, the Charles H. Levine Memorial Award for Excellence in Public Administration and the Distinguished Research Award, given jointly by the American Society for Public Administration (ASPA) and the National Association of Schools of Public Affairs and Administration (NASPAA). He serves on the Executive Council of NASPAA, as a fellow of the National Academy of Public Administration, and as a commissioner for the Indiana commission on Community Service and Volunteerism.

Trefor P. Williams is an Associate Professor of Civil Engineering at Rutgers University. He teaches courses on construction management and engineering, and is a member of the Department of Civil Engineering's Center for Advanced Infrastructure and Transportation.

His recent research interests include competitive bidding on construction projects, factors affecting construction costs, and the implementation of information technology in the construction industry. He also has conducted aviation safety and intelligent transportation system (ITS) research. He is a member of the Construction Research Council of the American Society of Civil Engineers and the Construction Management Committee of the Transportation Research Board.

Williams' industrial experience includes work as a traffic engineer involved in the design and implementation of ITS projects. He is a registered professional engineer in New York and New Jersey. Dr. Williams holds a B.S. in civil engineering from Syracuse University and an M.S. and Ph.D. in civil engineering from the Georgia Institute of Technology.

David C. Wyld currently serves as an Associate Professor of Management at Southeastern Louisiana University in Hammond, Louisiana, where he teaches courses in business strategy and methods for dealing with contemporary workplace issues. He earned his doctorate in management from the University of Memphis in 1993.

Dr. Wyld has written over 60 journal articles on a wide variety of subjects dealing with contemporary management issues. These have appeared in many leading business, health care, and education journals, including *American Business Review, Business and Public Affairs, Futures Research Quarterly, International Journal of Management, Journal of Business Ethics, Journal of Business Research, Journal of Contemporary Business Issues, Journal of Services Marketing, Management Research News, Managerial Law,* and *Public Personnel Management.*

He has also presented over 80 papers at professional conferences, garnering four best paper awards for these efforts. In the area of grant writing, Dr. Wyld has served as principal investigator on four grants, securing over $300,000 in funding to upgrade both the classroom presentation technology and computer labs of the College of Business and Technology at Southeastern Louisiana University. In recognition of these accomplishments, Dr. Wyld was awarded the campus-wide "President's Award for Excellence in Research" in 1998 at Southeastern Louisiana University.

In addition to his traditional teaching duties and research efforts, Dr. Wyld has served as a consultant to major corporations on a myriad of topics. He has participated extensively in delivering college classes to non-traditional students in divergent settings, teaching in executive MBA programs, and working with emerging online universities.

About the IBM Endowment for
The Business of Government

Through grants for research, the IBM Endowment for The Business of Government stimulates research and facilitates discussion of new approaches to improving the effectiveness of government at the federal, state, local, and international levels.

Research grants of $15,000 are awarded competitively to outstanding scholars in academic and nonprofit institutions across the United States. Each grantee is expected to produce a 30- to 40-page research report in one of the areas presented on pages 470-472. Grant reports will be published and disseminated by the Endowment. All the chapters presented in this book were originally prepared as grant reports to the Endowment.

Founded in 1998, the Endowment is one of the ways that IBM seeks to advance knowledge on how to improve public sector effectiveness. The IBM Endowment focuses on the future of the operations and management of the public sector.

Who is Eligible?
Individuals working in:
- Universities
- Nonprofit organizations
- Journalism

Description of Grant

Individuals receiving grants will be responsible for producing a 30- to 40-page research report in one of the areas presented on pages 470-472. The research paper should be completed within a six-month period from the start of the project. Grantees select the start and end dates of the research project.

Size of Grant

$15,000 for each research paper

Who Receives the Grant

Individuals will receive the grant, unless otherwise requested.

Application Process

Interested individuals should submit:
- A three-page description of the proposed research
- A résumé, including list of publications

Application Deadlines

There are two funding cycles annually, with deadlines of:
- The 15th of April
- The 15th of November

Applications must be postmarked or received online by the above dates.

Submitting Applications

Hard copy:

> Mark A. Abramson
> Executive Director
> IBM Endowment for The Business of Government
> 1616 North Fort Myer Drive
> Arlington, VA 22209

Online:

> www.businessofgovernment.org/apply

Program Areas

E-Government

Specific areas of interest:
- Government to Business (G2B)
- Government to Citizen (G2C)
- Government to Employees (G2E)
- Government to Government (G2G)
- Capital investment strategies for e-government
- Enterprise architecture

Examples of previous grants in this area:

State Web Portals: Delivering and Financing E-Service by Diana Burley Gant, Jon P. Gant, and Craig L. Johnson (January 2002)

Leveraging Technology in the Service of Diplomacy: Innovation in the Department of State by Barry Fulton (March 2002)

Federal Intranet Work Sites: An Interim Assessment by Julianne G. Mahler and Priscilla M. Regan (June 2002)

Financial Management

Specific areas of interest:
- Cost accounting and management
- Financial and resource analysis
- Financial risk management and modeling
- Internal controls
- Financial auditing
- Contract management
- Reconciliation
- Erroneous payment recovery
- Asset management
- Systems modernization

Examples of previous grants in this area:

Credit Scoring and Loan Scoring: Tools for Improved Management of Federal Credit Programs by Thomas H. Stanton (July 1999)

Using Activity-Based Costing to Manage More Effectively by Michael H. Granof, David E. Platt, and Igor Vaysman (January 2000)

Audited Financial Statements: Getting and Sustaining "Clean" Opinions by Douglas A. Brook (July 2001)

Human Capital

Specific areas of interest:
- The components of human capital management required to accomplish an organization's mission (such as knowledge, skills, abilities, attitudes, and experience)
- Employee recruitment and retention
- Workforce planning and analysis
- Pay for performance

Examples of previous grants in this area:
Organizations Growing Leaders: Best Practices and Principles in the Public Service by Ray Blunt (December 2001)

A Weapon in the War for Talent: Using Special Authorities to Recruit Crucial Personnel by Hal G. Rainey (December 2001)

A Changing Workforce: Understanding Diversity Programs in the Federal Government by Katherine C. Naff and J. Edward Kellough (December 2001)

Managing for Results

Specific areas of interest:
- Policy, management, and resource allocation decisions that make use of performance and results information
- Balanced scorecards and measurement of customer service
- Collaboration between organizations to achieve common outcomes
- Performance-based budgeting

Examples of previous grants in this area:
Using Evaluation to Support Performance Management: A Guide for Federal Executives by Kathryn Newcomer and Mary Ann Scheirer (January 2001)

Managing for Outcomes: Milestone Contracting in Oklahoma by Peter Frumkin (January 2001)

Using Performance Data for Accountability: The New York City Police Department's CompStat Model of Police Management by Paul E. O'Connell (August 2001)

New Ways to Manage

Specific areas of interest:
- Contracting out
- Competition
- Outsourcing
- Privatization
- Public-private partnerships
- Innovations in management of public organizations

Examples of previous grants in this area:
Understanding Innovation: What Inspires It? What Makes It Successful? by Jonathan Walters (December 2001)

Making Performance-Based Contracting Perform: What the Federal Government Can Learn from State and Local Governments by Lawrence L. Martin (June 2002)

21st-Century Government and the Challenge of Homeland Defense by Elaine C. Kamarck (June 2002)

Transforming Organizations

Specific areas of interest:
- New organizational values in the public sector
- Changed public sector cultures
- Enhanced public sector performance
- Studies of outstanding public sector leaders

Examples of previous grants in this area:
Creating a Culture of Innovation: 10 Lessons from America's Best Run City by Janet Vinzant Denhardt and Robert B. Denhardt (January 2001)

Transforming Government: Dan Goldin and the Remaking of NASA by W. Henry Lambright (March 2001)

Managing Across Boundaries: A Case Study of Dr. Helene Gayle and the AIDS Epidemic by Norma M. Riccucci (January 2002)

For more information about the Endowment
Visit our website at: www.businessofgovernment.org
Send an e-mail to: endowment@businessofgovernment.org
Call: (703) 741-1077